LYMAN TRUMBULL

Conservative Radical

Senator Lyman Trumbull in Washington.

LYMAN TRUMBULL

Conservative Radical

Mark M. Krug

New York: A. S. Barnes and Company, Inc.
London: Thomas Yoseloff Ltd

A. S. Barnes and Company, Inc.
8 East 36th Street
New York 16, N.Y. 10016

Thomas Yoseloff Ltd
18 Charing Cross Road
London W.C.2, England

To Francis S. Chase

6168

Printed in the United States of America

Contents

Illustrations

Acknowledgments

THE AUTHOR IS INDEBTED FOR EXCELLENT COOPERATION TO DR.
C. P. Powell and the staff of the manuscript division of the
Library of Congress where the major collection of the Trumbull
Papers is housed.

In June, 1963, the Illinois State Historical Library acquired,
through the efforts of Miss Margaret Flint, the Lyman Trumbull
Family Papers. This rich collection of 2,970 items containing
402 letters written by Trumbull to his first and second wife, to
the members of his family and friends was bought from the
heirs of Mary Ingraham Trumbull. The Family Papers also include two small volumes of a diary kept by Trumbull. This new
and unexplored collection of Trumbull papers proved to be invaluable for a better understanding of Lyman Trumbull as a
husband and father.

In addition to the Trumbull Family Papers, the Illinois State
Historical Library made available the Trumbull Collection and
the rich collection of papers of Dr. William Jayne, Horace
White, Gustave Koerner, John Palmer and Richard Yates. The
author acknowledges with gratitude the generous cooperation
and the many kindnesses he received from Miss Margaret Flint,
Assistant State Historian of the State of Illinois.

I wish to express my appreciation to the staff of the Chicago
Historical Society for the cooperation extended to me in the
use of the Trumbull Collection, the David Davis Papers, and
the excellent files of Chicago newspapers. The author was also
greatly helped by the kind cooperation of the staff of the New-

berry Library in Chicago, the New York Public Library, the Grosvenor Library in Buffalo, and the Cincinnati Public Library.

A great deal of the research was done in the Harper Library of the University of Chicago and special appreciation is due to Mr. Robert Rosenthal of the Special Collections and to Mr. S. Kingsley Miner, head of the Stacks Division.

I am deeply obligated to Mr. Paul Angle, director of the Chicago Historical Society, to Mr. Willard L. King, and to my colleagues in the History Department, Professors Walter Johnson, William Hutchinson, Bernard Weisberger, and to Dean Francis S. Chase of the Graduate School of Education who read many of the chapters and offered valuable advice and criticism.

The book could not have been written without extended periods of research at libraries in many places. The trips were made possible by two generous grants from the Social Science Research Committee of the University of Chicago, headed by Dean D. Gale Johnson.

Introduction

IN SPITE OF THE FLOOD OF BOOKS ON THE CIVIL WAR, LYMAN
Trumbull remains a relatively obscure figure. His name is seldom
found in college or high school history textbooks, and while
scholars have used the Trumbull Papers extensively, Trumbull's
role in Congress during the Civil War and reconstruction has not
received the attention it deserves. For twenty years after his
death in 1896, no historian was attracted to the writing of Trumbull's biography. The one biography in existence was written in
1917 by Horace White, a journalist and a friend of Trumbull.
In contrast, there are ten biographies of Charles Sumner and
nine of Thaddeus Stevens.

No visitor to the gallery of the Senate in the late fifties, or
through the war and the period of reconstruction, could have
left the Senate chamber without being impressed by the stature
and influence exerted by Lyman Trumbull. Since he wore spectacles and had an aloof manner, Trumbull was not physically
impressive. But his frequent speeches were logical and persuasive. In a time when political oratory was aimed at passions and
emotions, he appealed to reason and logic.

As chairman of the powerful Senate Judiciary Committee,
Trumbull was the author of many of the legislative acts passed
by Congress during the crucial decade between 1861 and 1871.
He wrote and introduced the First and the Second Confiscation
Acts, the Freedmen's Bureau Bill, and the first Civil Rights Act
ever adopted in this country. Trumbull, as he often recalled
with pride, was the father of the Thirteenth Amendment to
the Constitution and the sponsor of the first Civil Service Re-

form Law to be adopted by Congress. In fact, most of the reconstruction legislation was prepared and piloted through the Senate by him.

Trumbull's contemporaries in the Senate had a great deal of respect for their colleague, whose speeches were, as a rule, dry and unemotional but erudite, logical, and persuasive. Senator Roscoe Conkling observed that "whenever the Senator from Illinois makes up his mind to do anything we all know that he is able to give reasons plausible at least for the action he prepared to take." [1] James Dixon, the able Connecticut senator who was battling Trumbull on the Freedmen's Bureau Bill, conceded that "the Senator from Illinois exceeds many members in this body in legal knowledge. He exceeds them all in that particular solemnity of manner in which he can point out the enormities of those who differ from him on this floor." [2] Even at the close of his senatorial career, when Trumbull found himself a man without a party, Senator Oliver P. Morton acknowledged his high standing in the Senate. "I want him," he said, "to be on our side. I know his strength and I know his power. . . ." [3]

Trumbull was for many years Lincoln's close political associate. In 1858 Lincoln paid this handsome tribute to Lyman Trumbull: "Neither in that thing, nor in any other, in all the years I have known Lyman Trumbull, have I known him to fail of his word or tell a falsehood, large or small." [4] Jesse W. Weik, after a careful examination of the correspondence between Lincoln and Trumbull, observed that "both the Lincoln and Herndon letters to Trumbull convince me that the latter was held in higher esteem than history represents." [5]

---

[1] *Cong. Globe*, 40 Cong., 1st Sess. (March 27, 1867), p. 382.

[2] *Cong. Globe*, 39 Cong., 2nd Sess. (February 27, 1866), p. 1651.

[3] *Cong. Globe*, 42 Cong., 2nd Sess. (February 23, 1872), p. 1182.

[4] *The Lincoln-Douglas Debates*, ed. Edwin Erle Sparks, Collections of the Illinois State Historical Library, Vol. VIII (Springfield. Ill., 1908), p. 306. "That thing" refers to a charge Trumbull made against Douglas in the 1858 senatorial campaign in Illinois. (See Chapter VII of the present work.)

[5] Jesse W. Weik to Horace White, November 29, 1908, Horace White Papers, Illinois State Historical Library, Springfield, Ill.

It might well be that historians have shied away from writing about Lyman Trumbull because they encountered some difficulty in putting him into a specific category in a period when men in public life were usually classified as either radicals or conservatives. Writers often refer to Trumbull as a radical and sometimes as a conservative, with little justification for the use of either term. The ambiguity in the use of the term "radicals" for men who differed greatly in their political, economic, and social views and whose approach to the problem of the reconstruction of the South ranged from the "conquered territory" theory to a limited determination to guarantee the personal security of the freedmen and the unionists, constitute one of the most serious pitfalls in reconstruction historiography. When applied to Lyman Trumbull the term radical is a misnomer.

And yet, one historian puts Trumbull in the same category with Zachary Chandler, and another lists Wade, Chandler, and Trumbull as "the three musketeers of radicalism." [6] Still another writer of a popular book described the Republican side of the Senate in 1861 where "sat men who . . . denied State sovereignty, hated slavery and loved power." She then listed these men as including Ben Wade, Zachary Chandler, Charles Sumner, John Hale, William Pitt Fessenden, and Lyman Trumbull. [7] In fact, Fessenden and Trumbull hated slavery, but they never denied state sovereignty, and they did not excessively love power. Sumner and Chandler had no illusions about Trumbull's and Fessenden's "radicalism." Sumner often denounced Trumbull as a foe of radical reconstruction, and Chandler on several occasions sneeringly referred to Fessenden as the "conservative Senator from Maine." [8] A dedicated radical, Senator Charles D. Drake of Missouri, when angered by Trumbull's opposition to

[6] William B. Hesseltine, *Lincoln and the War Governors* (New York, 1955), p. 120; and T. Harry Williams, *Lincoln and the Radicals* (Madison, Wis., 1960), p. 44.

[7] Margaret Leech, *Reveille in Washington, 1860–1865* (New York, 1941), p. 22.

[8] *Cong. Globe*, 40 Cong., 1st Sess. (July 20, 1867), p. 752.

his extreme amendment to the Second Reconstruction Act, turned to the Illinois senator and said: "I regret very much indeed, Mr. President, to have discovered . . . in the brief time I have been here, . . . there is such a thing on the floor of this Senate as conservative radicalism." [9] This was indeed an acute observation by a freshman senator, because Lyman Trumbull was, throughout his long political career, just that—a conservative radical. The term is ambiguous and seemingly paradoxical, but it does describe Trumbull's peculiar ability to be basically a conservative who at times advocated radical political and economic ideas and measures. He was, as Allan Nevins perceptively put it, "an able, calm, statesmanlike man, destined to prove in a dramatic impeachment trial his power to resist the fanatics in his party, and in a period of social turmoil his ability to accept radical, new politico-social ideas." [10] The *Chicago Tribune*, which always faithfully supported Trumbull, editorialized, in 1872, that a close scrutiny of Trumbull's political record would have disclosed that "no American statesman has ever stood *so nearly midway* between the violence of fanaticism on both sides." [11]

Trumbull's role during the Civil War and during Reconstruction was that of a middle-of-the-road, moderate Republican, dedicated to the crushing of the rebellion and the reconstructing of the South, always within the Constitution, as he understood and interpreted it. To treat Trumbull's advocacy of tough measures for the prosecution of the war and for Congressional reconstruction as a temporary aberration of an otherwise sane and wise man constitutes a misreading and misunderstanding of Trumbull's life and record.

The myth that the "Jacobin Chieftains," the wild-eyed group of radicals led by Sumner and Stevens, dominated Congress during and after the Civil War, is still repeated with almost tedious

[9] *Ibid.* (March 14, 1867), p. 100.
[10] Allan Nevins, *Ordeal of the Union: A House Dividing, 1852–1857* (New York, 1947), p. 413.
[11] *Chicago Tribune*, April 26, 1872. (Italics mine.)

regularity. Sumner did not dominate the Senate but, on the contrary, he usually found himself in the defeated minority. The fact was that the 37th, 38th, 39th, and 40th Congresses were dominated and ruled not by Sumner, Wade, Chandler, Wilson, but by a coalition of moderate and conservative Republicans and the Democratic minority. This coalition, operating similarly to the present coalition of conservative Southern Democrats and the Republicans, was led by Lyman Trumbull and Senator William Pitt Fessenden of Maine. During the years 1867 to 1869 these two men, often joined by Senators Grimes of Iowa and Sherman of Ohio, were usually successful in beating down many extreme measures proposed by the radicals and in pushing through a more reasonable and moderate legislation.

While Stevens, because of the rules of the House of Representatives and the large number of radical members, was able to dominate the House, Sumner's position in the Senate was not at all comparable. As a matter of fact Sumner, supported by Chandler, Wade, Howard, Drake, and several other radicals, suffered repeated defeats at the hands of the moderate Republican-Democratic coalition led by Trumbull and Fessenden. Sumner and his radical friends wanted a simple bill abolishing slavery, instead of the Thirteenth Amendment; they fought for a positive affirmation of franchise for Negroes in the Fourteenth Amendment; they wanted the First Reconstruction Bill to pass the Senate as it came from the House, leaving out any steps by which the Southern states could be readmitted. In all these cases—and many similar ones—they were beaten by the moderate-conservative coalition. Even more important was the refusal of Trumbull and Fessenden to permit the radical group to keep Congress in continuous session or to give the power of reconvening to the Speaker of the House and the president pro tem of the Senate. They would have no part of this scheme, which would have subverted the principle of the separation of powers and given executive power to Congress. It is often overlooked that reconstruction measures, however undesirable they might seem to be, were *compromises* hammered out, usually in face of bitter opposition of the radicals. The operation of the moderate Republican-Democratic coalition has not been adequately explored. Trumbull's role in this ruling coalition is important not only for a better understanding of his place and contribution to history, but also for a clearer and more judicious understanding of the period of Reconstruction—a turbulent and critical period in our nation's history.

In 1872 Trumbull was one of the strongest contenders for the nomination for President on the Liberal Republican ticket. He might have won the nomination if he had had some quality of warmth and only some of Salmon P. Chase's ambition to occupy the White House. He did little to further his candidacy in spite of the fact that he considered himself to be better qualified for the Presidency than the other candidates. The story of Trumbull's candidacy for the nomination at the Cincinnati convention throws an important light on the short history of the Liberal Republican movement.

Finally, there is evidence that Lyman Trumbull, when in his eighties, had made a contribution to the emerging ideology of Populism. The picture of Lyman Trumbull, a very old man, bringing three thousand massed Populists, gathered in Chicago's Music Hall, to a pitch of enthusiasm by his castigation of rapacious capitalists and monopolists, provided a fitting climax to the long, meritorious, and honorable career of this important American statesman.

LYMAN TRUMBULL

Conservative Radical

1

The First Steps

LYMAN TRUMBULL, BORN ON OCTOBER 12, 1813, WAS A SEVENTH-generation Connecticut Yankee. He was born in Colchester, New London County, to a family long distinguished in the history of the state. The history of the American Trumbulls began when John Trumble, a cooper by trade, and his wife Ellenor Chandler, of New Castle, in Cumberland County, England, came to the United States in 1639 and settled in Rowley, Essex County, Massachusetts. They had with them a son, John, who later became a clergyman in Suffield, Connecticut, and had four sons: John, a well-known poet and tutor at Yale College; Joseph, a merchant; and Benoni Ammi and Benjamin, who were farmers.[1] The Trumble family was hard-working and God-fearing. The choice of names of their children indicates the strong attachment to the Old Testament common to many Puritan families. They struggled hard to make a decent living in a new country and did all they could to provide educational opportunities for their children. Lyman Trumbull's paternal grandfather, Benjamin Trumble, who lived in Hebron, was graduated from Yale College in 1759 and was a minister in North Haven, Connecticut, where he held a pulpit for sixty years. He fought

[1] Mary Trumbull to Horace White, September 18, 1912, Horace White Papers, Illinois State Historical Library, Springfield, Ill.

and was a chaplain in the Connecticut militia during the Revolutionary War and wrote the first history of Connecticut. In 1766 the family changed its name from Trumble to Trumbull, although many of their friends continued to use the old name for a long time. Lyman Trumbull's New England acquaintances who settled in Illinois used to address him as Trumble as late as the Civil War. [2]

The most distinguished member of the Trumbull family was Jonathan Trumbull, who graduated from Harvard in 1727 and was successively a Connecticut assemblyman, county judge, chief justice, and governor of the state from 1769 until 1784. During the War of Independence, Governor Trumbull was a friend, supporter and counselor of George Washington. His nickname "Brother Jonathan" was for a long time, and is still, used occasionally as a sobriquet for the United States. Jonathan's son John Trumbull, was a well-known artist whose paintings "Battle at Bunker Hill" and "Death of Montgomery" are now exhibited in the Yale School of Fine Arts.

Benjamin Trumbull, the son of the historian who lived in North Haven, married on March 15, 1800, Elizabeth Mather, a descendant of the Reverend Richard Mather. Reverend Mather came to this country from England in 1635 and was the father of Increase Mather and grandfather of Cotton Mather, the celebrated Puritan clergyman and writer.

Trumbull was proud of his distinguished family background and his aspirations and mode of life reflected his determination to carry on the traditions of the Trumbull and Mather families. His moderation and abhorrence of excessive drinking, his austere and outwardly cold demeanor, his deep religious beliefs and his life-long devotion to honesty and integrity in public life were part of his Puritan heritage. He loved and was devoted to his adopted state of Illinois, but his roots in the New England soil

[2] John S. Martin, Samuel Harvey, Leander Munsel, and Daniel C. Lockwood to Lyman Trumble, February 22, February 26, March 5 and March 20, 1861, Trumbull Collection, Illinois State Historical Library, Springfield, Ill.

and society were deep and lasting. Many years after the death of his first wife, Trumbull went, in 1877, like Isaac the son of Abraham of old, to the land of his fathers, to find a wife in Saybrook, Connecticut.

Lyman Trumbull was the seventh son of eleven children born to Benjamin and Elizabeth Trumbull. Eight children survived: five brothers, David, George, John, Erastus, Benjamin and Lyman; and two sisters, Julia and Sarah. His father was a graduate of Yale college, a farmer, a lawyer, and a judge. For several years he served in the Connecticut legislature. The family home in Colchester, adjacent to a medium-sized farm, was known as "Judge Trumbull's House." [3]

The Trumbulls were a large and close family and the children grew up in an atmosphere of love and affection. Many years later, Trumbull wrote to his wife that perusing old family papers he "felt almost transported back to the old homestead when we were children together. If ever a family of children grew up loving each other most tenderly surely ours was one." [4] Tragedy struck the happy household in 1828 when his mother, Elizabeth, died after a brief illness. Lyman, who was fifteen at the time, often recalled "the bleak day" when his mother, "the best and kindest of mothers," passed away.[5] The scene of his father and brothers and sisters standing around the bed of his dying mother remained vividly engraved in Trumbull's memory.

The entire responsibility for bringing up the children fell on the shoulders of the father. The elder Trumbull, who never remarried, accepted the responsibility and carried it out with utter devotion. Lyman and his brothers and sisters always remembered the debt of gratitude they owed their father. They gave

---

[3] The house was still in good repair in 1870. See Asa Bigelow, Jr. to Lyman Trumbull, June 1, 1870, L. T. Papers.

[4] Lyman Trumbull to Julia Jayne Trumbull, September 24, 1857, L. T. Family Papers.

[5] Lyman Trumbull to Julia Jayne Trumbull, October 20, 1858, L. T. Family Papers.

him throughout his long life (he died at eighty) their love and devotion.

The financial situation of the family was precarious and the father was often "cramped for means to clothe and feed" the children.[6] The salary of a judge was small and farming demanded hard labor of many hands. The sons, including Lyman, had to help with chores on the farm. Judge Trumbull, in spite of the hardships, insisted that his children get a good education. Lyman attended the Bacon Academy in Colchester where he was an eager and hard-working student. He read widely and was particularly fond of Latin and Greek, and read Virgil, Cicero, and Homer in the original. There was no money for Trumbull to go to Yale, so at eighteen he became a teacher at Portland, Connecticut. His salary was ten dollars per month, and every Saturday he walked home thirteen miles only to return, again on foot, on Monday mornings. Years later, one of his former students at the Portland school acknowledged that he had learned a great deal from his eighteen-year-old teacher.[7] To earn more money, which he saved very carefully, Trumbull gave up the job in Portland and took a teaching position in New Jersey. He taught there for several months.

In 1833, at the age of twenty, Trumbull decided to leave his home state and seek his fortunes elsewhere. His father gave him one hundred dollars, and with his own savings he had enough to undertake the long journey south. Traveling by schooner, he arrived in Charleston, South Carolina, where as he records he had his first experience with the issue of slavery. On the evening of his arrival he attended a meeting in a large warehouse in Charleston where he heard Governor Hayne and Senator Calhoun extol slavery and threaten nullification.[8] From Charleston,

6 *Ibid.*

7 E. Sage (from Portland, Connecticut) to Lyman Trumbull, January 26, 1856, L. T. Papers.

8 Autobiographical sketch, Horace White Papers, Illinois State Historical Society, Springfield, Ill.

Trumbull went, mostly by foot, to Greenville in Meriweather County, where he found employment as a teacher and principal of the Greenville Academy. His salary was two hundred dollars per year plus part of the tuition paid by the students. Shortly after assuming this position, Trumbull repaid the one hundred dollars that he had borrowed from his father. He was an effective and dedicated teacher and greatly enjoyed his work. Thirty years later, a student wrote to him that she considered it her good fortune "to enjoy in Greenville, for nearly three years, the advantage of your profound teachings." [9] Trumbull, in his answer, expressed his gratitude that he had not been forgotten after so many years and said that he remembered many of his former students and cherished the memory of his short teaching career.[10]

But Trumbull did not wish to become a professional teacher—he realized that he lacked the educational background and the inclination for it. He decided to prepare himself for a career, as a lawyer, and, in the fashion of those days, read law in the office of Hiram Walker, judge of the Superior Court of Georgia and later, Supreme Court judge of that state. Under Judge Walker's guidance, Trumbull read law books, observed courtroom procedure and was admitted to the bar. The studious and personable young man from Connecticut made many friends in Georgia, but he did not consider settling in the South. We have no record of his impressions of slavery, but it is easy to surmise that the Connecticut Yankee didn't like it and that he was eager to return to the North. Practicing great thrift, he was able to accumulate one thousand dollars in savings, quite a substantial capital for a modestly paid teacher. After three years of living in Greenville, Trumbull set out north, mostly on horseback, and arrived in Illinois at Shawneetown, on the Ohio River. From there he went to Belleville where he presented letters of introduction given to him by his Georgia friends to two lawyers,

[9] Mrs. F. C. Gary (from Morgan, Georgia) to Lyman Trumbull, May 17, 1866, L. T. Papers.
[10] Trumbull to Mrs. F. C. Gary, June 17, 1866, L. T. Papers.

Adam W. Snyder and Alfred Cowles. He liked the people and the town and decided to settle and practice law. Characteristically, he made this decision after a long and arduous journey to visit his three brothers in Henrietta, Michigan, and his family in Colchester.

Upon his return to Belleville, he became associated in law practice with former Governor John Reynolds. Reynolds was the most distinguished citizen of Belleville and of Illinois. He was a former Illinois Supreme Court judge, assemblyman, governor, and a member of the U.S. House of Representatives. Reynolds, a Pennsylvanian by birth, remained a pro-slavery man until his death in 1865. Since Reynolds was a member of the House in 1837 and was spending a great deal of time in Washington, the practice in his busy law office was left to Trumbull. Only recognition of the young man's unusual ability could have caused the "Old Ranger," as Reynolds was affectionately known, to entrust his law business to an unknown twenty-four-year-old lawyer. His trust was well rewarded, because Reynolds formed with Trumbull not only a prospering law partnership but an even more important political association that lasted for a number of years.[11]

We have an excellent description of Trumbull's appearance and an insightful evaluation of his personality in the early years of his residence in Belleville. It was written by a shrewd observer of men, Gustave Koerner, a lawyer and leader of the German community in Belleville. Of Trumbull, Koerner wrote: "He was tall, well-proportioned, with a slight stoop, probably owing to his great shortsightedness and had rather light hair and blue eyes. His features were regular and handsome." Koerner, who often rode the court circuit with Trumbull, considered him a very able lawyer whose arguments to the judge and jury were logical and impressive. He was serious in court although occasionally "his smile was sneeringly sardonic." Trumbull, Koerner

[11] See sketch of Reynolds' life in *The Bench and Bar of Illinois*, ed. by John M. Palmer (Chicago, 1899), pp. 15, 18, 161.

continued, was not an orator but was an excellent and logical debater and prepared his cases with extreme care. He was not interested in literature, sciences, music, or the fine arts, and he did not find much pleasure in social intercourse. His manner with people was reserved, almost cold. Trumbull's principal power, Koerner found, was "in his ability to concentrate his mind on a few subjects. His aim was to become a great lawyer and to play a conspicuous part in politics. To everything else he seemed indifferent." [12]

Belleville around 1840 was "a firm city of brick," [13] located across the Mississippi, a short distance from St. Louis. It had a population of about five thousand. Like most of the people of southern Illinois, its people were, in a large part, Kentuckians and Tennesseans who had migrated north. German immigrants also came and settled in Belleville in ever increasing numbers during this period. The peak of this immigration came in 1849 and 1850 after the collapse of the 1848 revolution in Germany. The city was the county seat of St. Clair County and sold "large quantities of dry goods, hardware, and groceries to towns and villages in Southern and central Illinois and Missouri." [14] The main export was excellent lager beer from a number of big breweries established by German immigrants. Since the city had a busy courthouse where circuit judges sat for several months a year, Belleville had twelve lawyers.[15] Among the Belleville lawyers who were to play important roles in Illinois politics, in addition to Trumbull, were Gustave Koerner, Sidney Breese, William H. Underwood, Edward Omelveny, and Philip B. Fouke. All of them became, in time, high state officials, judges, or U.S. congressmen. The city was located in the valley of the Richland Creek and was surrounded by swamps. The water of the creek was constantly polluted by the refuse from the breweries and

[12] *Memoirs of Gustave Koerner* (Cedar Rapids, Iowa, 1909), I, 425.
[13] *Belleville Advocate,* September 24, 1841.
[14] *Ibid.*
[15] Advertisements of local law firms in *Belleville Advocate,* September 24, 1841.

distilleries. Consequently, Belleville was not a healthy place in which to live. The local newspaper carried advertisements of many doctors who promised cures and medicines for a variety of diseases including "Bilious fevers," "Liver complaints," "Acute and Chronic Rheumatism," "Corrupt tumors," "Dyspepsia," and of course the most common "Fever and Ague." [16] But the growing and prospering city, surrounded by rich farm lands, had a busy social life, centered in the two city hotels, and Trumbull wrote home that he had attended many balls and cotillions.[17] He soon had close ties with the German immigrants, whose level of education was high and who had established under the leadership of Gustave Koerner a fine public library, a literary society and a German newspaper, the *Belleviller Zeitung*.[18] Politically, Lyman Trumbull, who was a Democrat like his father, was happy to find that the people of Belleville overwhelmingly shared his political beliefs.

Not everybody, however, was favorably impressed with Belleville. Charles Dickens, who visited Belleville in 1842, found it to be "a small collection of wooden houses, huddled together in the very heart of the bush and swamp." [19] He made fun of the Mansion House, Belleville's main hotel, which he described as "an odd, shambling, low-roofed outhouse." Dickens described a trial of a horse thief that he witnessed in the courthouse as "farcical, vulgar and an unruly affair." Governor William A. Kinney was so annoyed by what he considered to be Dickens' slander of a fair city in his state that he issued a pamphlet attacking Dickens and Great Britain.[20]

Although Trumbull had a fairly busy law office in Belleville, his main trial work was done "on the circuit." For three months in the fall and in the spring, circuit judges traveled in their

---

16 *Ibid.*
17 Horace White, *The Life of Lyman Trumbull* (Boston, 1913), p. 8.
18 Koerner, *Memoirs,* I, 291.
19 Charles Dickens, *American Notes,* 2 vols. (London, 1922), p. 128.
20 Koerner, *Memoirs,* I, 474.

respective judicial circuits and held court in the county seats.[21] Lawyers like Trumbull, Koerner, Abraham Lincoln, and John M. Palmer traveled with the judges and usually picked up clients as they went along. They traveled by buggy or horseback over rutted roads which had no gravel and no fences. When rains would come, the mud would be knee-deep. Since the taverns and inns on the roads were often miserable hovels, there was little rest for the weary travelers. However, there were compensations for the circuit riders. When the weather was good, in the spring and in the fall, the wide-open Illinois prairies bloomed with luxuriant grass and flowers, and the comradeship of intelligent men was rewarding and exhilarating. Most attractive to the ambitious lawyers, who were all determined to seek political office, was the political aspect of the life on the circuit. As one circuit rider put it, "in a new country, as Illinois was then, lawyers from their relations to the people, were more or less necessarily politicians and office seekers." [22] Illinoisans, bored with the long and cold winter or the hot and enervating summer, used to come by the hundreds to the county seats where the circuit judge and his retinue of lawyers were to hold court. Usually, after the court adjournment at noon or in the evening, the lawyers or even judges would address the crowds on the political issues of the day. During Presidential or Congressional elections, these meetings were a part of the election canvass and provided the young aspiring lawyers, Whigs and Democrats, with an opportunity to become known and to show off their oratorical and debating talents.

Trumbull probably did not enjoy circuit riding as much as did Lincoln,[23] because he lacked Lincoln's sociability, his popular touch, and the gift of story telling, but the court sessions and

[21] For a background on the life on the circuit see Henry Clay Whitney, *Life on the Circuit with Lincoln* (Caldwell, Idaho, 1940).

[22] *Personal Recollections of John M. Palmer* (Cincinnati, Ohio, 1901), p. 40.

[23] Judge David Davis wrote, "Lincoln was happy, as happy as he could be, when on this circuit—and happy no other place." A statement from Davis to William Herndon, dated September 19, 1866, Herndon-Weik Papers, Library of Congress.

the political meetings gave him a reputation as a good lawyer and a sharp political debater. After three years of circuit riding he was ready to try for a political office. Later he left the law office of John Reynolds, although they remained close political allies, and began a law practice with his brother George. In 1840 Trumbull, with Reynolds' powerful support, announced his candidacy, as a Democrat, for the Illinois House of Representatives from St. Clair County. The Presidential election campaign of that year started early and lasted for many months. The Whigs nominated the Indian fighter General William Henry Harrison of Ohio for President, while the Jacksonian Democrats nominated President Van Buren. The canvass in Illinois was unusually bitter. "No political contest in the history of the country," reminisced John Palmer, "was characterized by more bitterness than that of 1840." [24] Palmer might have exaggerated a bit, but the contest was indeed a hard one.[25] Lincoln and Douglas followed each other around the state battling for their respective candidates and engaging in bitter debates.[26] Trumbull, who was making his political debut, limited his campaign to St. Clair County. The Whigs triumphed by electing Harrison, but they lost Illinois, which gave Van Buren 47,433 votes to 45,576 for Harrison. Lyman Trumbull won the election to the Illinois Legislature and stood on the threshold of his political career. The victory was won by hard campaigning. "Trumbull and I," wrote Koerner, "made speeches in every precinct and organized clubs in every little town." [27] German voters, who were suspicious of the anti-alien, Know-Nothing influences in the Whig Party, gave Trumbull strong support. [28]

[24] Palmer, *Personal Recollections*, p. 37. See also Robert G. Gunderson, *The Log Cabin Campaign* (Lexington, Ky., 1957).

[25] Whig leaders charged the Democrats with fraud in the elections, especially in manipulating the votes of the Irish immigrants. "If the Irish did not vote more than three times we could easily carry the State." David Davis to William P. Walker, November 6, 1840, Davis Papers, Chicago Historical Society, Chicago, Ill.

[26] *Sangamo Journal*, July 17, August 2, 1840; *Chicago Democrat*, April 29, May 20, 1840.

[27] Koerner, *Memoirs*, I, 446.

[28] *Ibid.*

In November, 1840, when Governor Thomas Carlin called a special session of the legislature, Trumbull went to the state capital for the first time as an elected state official. Springfield was, in 1840, a small town with a population of about 3,000 including a large number of Irish, Dutch, and Norwegian immigrants. The city had two newspapers, eight churches, and a little railroad.[29] There were a few large homes; the outstanding among these was the mansion of Ninian W. Edwards, who married Elizabeth Todd of Kentucky. After Elizabeth's sister, Mary Todd, came to Springfield in 1839, the Edwardses did a great deal of entertaining in her honor. The winter of 1840–41 was bitterly cold, but the evenings at the Edwards' house were warm and gay. Trumbull was a frequent visitor, and there are some indications that he courted the vivacious young lady from Kentucky. In 1865 Mary Todd Lincoln recalled: "In our little coterie in Springfield, in the days of my girlhood, we had a society of gentlemen, who have since been distinguished. . . . My great and glorious husband comes first . . . Douglas, Trumbull, Baker, Hardin, Shields, such choice spirits were habitués of our drawing room." [30]

Even with those social distractions, Trumbull devoted himself primarily to gaining a position of prominence in the state House of Representatives. This was not an easy task for a twenty-seven-year-old assemblyman who had to compete with many men who were destined to become politicians of state and national stature. This group included Abraham Lincoln, John A. McClernand, William H. Bissell, William A. Richardson, John A. Logan, Edward D. Baker, Ebenezer Peck, and Orville H. Browning. But even in this distinguished body of men, Trumbull more than held his own. He became the leading member and spokesman for the Judiciary Committee and showed himself to be a persuasive speaker and an able parliamentarian and politician. While

[20] A Copy of the *Independent Democrat*, Number 1, Volume 1, in the Horace *Lived: A History of Lincoln's Springfield, 1821–1865* (Springfield, Ill., 1935).

[30] Mary Lincoln to Mrs. Gideon Welles, Gideon Welles Papers, Library of Congress, quoted in Ruth P. Randall, *Mary Lincoln* (New York, 1953).

many legislators, including Trumbull, were men dedicated to public welfare, they were compelled in order to assure their re-election to haggle and bargain and barter for legislative advantages and appropriations for their own districts. The result was a large number of private bills dealing with local appointments, improvements, and contracts that were dealt with on the ancient political principle of reciprocity or logrolling. At times, the spectacle presented was not very attractive. One observer wrote, "Legislation in our Western States is generally based upon barter, trade and intrigue—'You vote for my measure and I will vote for yours.' " [31]

The legislature was called into the special session in November, 1840, because, with the state's treasury empty, the governor wanted the legislature to raise funds to pay the interest on the state debts. This huge debt was the result of the Internal Improvement Bill, which had been adopted in February, 1837, by large majorities composed of Democrats and Whigs. The bill, which had been passed amid great optimism over the prospects of economic growth and large-scale immigration, provided for the expenditure of $9,350,000 for the construction of railroads, $400,000 for river improvements, and $200,000 for roads and bridges. [32] When the bill was adopted the rejoicing, especially in southern Illinois, which was favored by many of the bill's provisions, was almost unbounded. The *Alton Telegraph* wrote: "Illinois yesterday gave birth . . . to the splendid system of Internal Improvement by which Illinois is to be more benefited than by probably any other bill which has ever passed by any Illinois Legislature." [33] The projected construction of the railroad connecting Alton and Terre Haute, Indiana, it was generally assumed, would soon transform Alton, Belleville, and Cairo

31 David Davis to William P. Walker, March 18, 1839, Davis Papers, Chicago Historical Society.

32 George W. Smith, *History of Illinois and Her People* (Chicago, 1927), p. 227. Also *Journal of the House of Representatives of the State of Illinois,* 1836–37 (Springfield, 1837), 1st Session, pp. 363, 366, 443, 680; *Journal of the Senate of the State of Illinois* (Springfield, 1837), 1st Session, pp. 445, 452, 466, 474–75, 487.

33 *Alton Telegraph,* March 8, 1837.

into large industrial and commercial centers. The citizenry of Belleville had held an enthusiastic torchlight parade and a mass meeting at which Governor William A. Kinney and ex-Governor Reynolds extolled the bill.[34]

The financial difficulties, however, had grown steadily as the state borrowed large sums of money from domestic and foreign sources and from the sale of bonds at high interest rates. In 1839 Governor Carlin had sent ex-Governor Reynolds and R. M. Young as special commissioners to London and Europe to negotiate a $4,500,000 loan for the Illinois and Michigan Canal and for the internal improvements. They had "made some ill-advised and bungling loans, attended with heavy losses to the State." [35] Reynolds used the journey for an expensive, private junket throughout Europe at the expense of the state. By 1840 the annual revenue of Illinois was only $117,821, barely enough for meeting the regular expenditures with no money to pay the substantial interest on the huge state debt. In addition, the State Banks, facing bankruptcy, had suspended the specie payments, thus lowering the confidence of the people in the value of the circulating currency. Since the State Banks of Illinois had $8,000,000 of state money deposited in them, the suspension was a severe blow to the state.[36]

In his message to the special session of the legislature, Governor Carlin bemoaned the state's precarious financial straits, which had resulted directly "out of our system of internal improvements, adopted by improvident legislation." [37] He listed the state debt as amounting to about $14,000,000 and stressed the inability of the state to pay the huge interest on this debt. The special legislative session lasted only two weeks and it accomplished little to alleviate the financial crisis.

During the two-week session the young Representative of St.

[34] *Alton Telegraph,* May 17, 1837.

[35] Alexander Davidson and Bernard Stuve, *A Complete History of Illinois From 1673–1873* (Springfield, Ill. 1876), p. 444.

[36] *Alton Telegraph,* June 14, 1837.

[37] *Journal of the House of Representatives of the State of Illinois, 1840–41* (Springfield, 1841), p. 18.

Clair County gave a clear indication of the direction of his legislative efforts. It became obvious that he would fight for a clean and honest government. Trumbull, unlike many of his Democratic colleagues, supported a resolution to investigate the Whig charges of frauds in the November election.[38] He also repeatedly took the floor to propose bills and resolutions to force the Fund Commissioners of the canal and the clerks and agents involved in the internal improvement projects to produce their records for public inspection. He was beaten, but his resolution demanding an inquiry into the operations of the Board of Commissioners of the Illinois and Michigan Canal was approved.[39]

The pattern of Trumbull's views on government and on the issues confronting the state emerged with greater clarity during the regular session which opened on December 7. He was entrusted with the responsibility for piloting on the floor of the House an "Act to provide for the payment of interest upon the public debt," which was prepared by the Judiciary Committee. Many years later, Trumbull's critics, and especially Stephen A. Douglas, charged that Trumbull favored repudiation of state debts and thus was willing to sacrifice the honor and the good faith of Illinois. His support of the bill providing for the payment of interest on the state debt, which he reported on behalf of the Judiciary Committee, refutes the accusation. However, Trumbull was determined that the state should bear the responsibility only for debts legally contracted. He proposed that no interest be paid "on any State bonds *which have been parted without the authority of law.*" [40] After a bitter debate, Trumbull's amendment was accepted by a vote of 41 to 40, with Lincoln and his Whigs and some Democrats voting in the negative.[41]

In his vigorous fight for a new charter regulating the relation-

---

[38] *Ibid.*, p. 35.
[39] *Ibid.*, p. 39.
[40] *Ibid.*, p. 90. (Italics mine.)
[41] *Ibid.*, p. 102.

ship between the State Banks and the state, Trumbull indicated a concern for the interests of the common people, an interest that was to remain with him until the end of his life. When the legislature considered a bill to renew the banks' charter, Lyman Trumbull and John A. McClernand fought for a provision that would have forbidden the banks to suspend specie payments and would have forced them to post a large bond to guarantee the continuous operation of the banks. When their amendments were rejected and the bill was passed, Trumbull and McClernand and nine other legislators published, on February 26, 1841, an *Open Protest* in which they denounced the bill for allowing the banks to suspend payments and thus "set vicious example" in "violation of all good faith, opposed to good morals." [42] The people, the protesters said, opposed these willful suspensions that "depreciate the value of the circulating medium." [43] "This suspension," the open letter stated, "will give the foundation to the belief that the State does not intend, or desire, to do justice to the creditors of the State." [44] The signers declared that the suspension of specie payments did not aid the people, as the authors of the bill had claimed, but that it was intended to benefit only the wealthy stockholders.

Judicial reform occupied a great deal of Trumbull's attention. There were several reasons for the need to reorganize the judiciary system. The growth of population brought about a need for more judges, and some circuit judges proved to be lacking in legal knowledge and temperament. The Democrats had an additional reason to press for judiciary reforms. The Whigs had a majority on the Supreme Court of the state, and Democrats feared that the court might decide to bar aliens from voting in elections. Since these alien immigrants, primarily the Irish and the Germans, voted overwhelmingly Democratic, such a ruling would have been a heavy blow to the Illinois Democracy. The

[42] *Ibid.*, p. 538.
[43] *Ibid.*
[44] *Ibid.*

new plan provided for the abolition of the circuit judgeships, and for the addition to the Supreme Court of five Democratic judges who, together with the four judges already on the court, were to hold court in the several judicial circuits. The bill passed in February, 1841, over the governor's veto.[45] Trumbull, who was in charge of the bill, exerted strong pressure on his Democratic colleagues to vote for the bill.[46]

When, at the end of the session, Stephen A. Douglas resigned from his post as Secretary of State, Governor Carlin appointed Trumbull to take his place.

[45] *Ibid.*, p. 432; *Illinois State Register*, February 12, 1841.
[46] Theodore C. Pease, *The Frontier State, 1818–1848* in the *Centennial History of Illinois* (Chicago, 1922), p. 281.

2

The Rising Young Politician

TRUMBULL'S APPOINTMENT, AT THE AGE OF TWENTY-EIGHT, AS Secretary of State came unexpectedly. He was only slightly acquainted with Governor Carlin, who did not consult him before he made the appointment. "How he [Governor Carlin] came to make the appointment," Trumbull wrote to his brother, "the Lord only knows." [1] He ascribed the appointment to "good fortune and not to any deserts of mine." [2]

The annual salary was $1,500, plus extra allowances, every other year during the sessions of the General Assembly and special fees for preparing copies of official papers and for affixing of the state seal. The duties of the office of Secretary of State were not arduous, especially after Trumbull invited his younger brother Benjamin to come to Springfield from Colchester to become a clerk in his office. Banjamin accepted and brought his family to the Illinois capital. His salary was $400 per year plus about $200 in fees, and he performed the routine work of the office of Secretary of State. Trumbull made no bones about the fact that his job was a political sinecure. He wrote to his sister Julia who lived with his father in Colchester: "My situation here is very pleasant. The business of the office is very trifling and

[1] Lyman Trumbull to David Trumbull, October 12, 1841, L. T. Family Papers.
[2] *Ibid.*

35

Benjamin does it all. It probably does not occupy him an hour a day upon an average." [3]

Trumbull devoted most of his time to his law practice in Belleville where, with his brother George, he built an office building at the cost of $500.[4] In addition to his law business in St. Clair County, Trumbull rode the circuit in his horse and buggy. There was a lot of traveling to do. Courts moved on the circuit of many towns in March, April, May, August, September, and October. The Illinois Supreme Court sat, usually in Springfield, in July and December. In addition, Trumbull had some business before the District U.S. Court which handled bankruptcy cases.

During the biannual sessions of the Illinois Legislature, the duties of the Secretary of State were greatly increased. When asked by the House of Representatives, in 1842, why he had failed to prepare a digest of the laws of the state as he was requested to do, Trumbull complained of the heavy load of work. There was not enough time, he said, to work on the digest because, in addition to the ordinary duties, "the undersigned was required by the last legislature, in conjunction with the Treasurer, to superintend the appropriations made towards the further completion of the State House." [5] Trumbull further pointed out that he served on three other boards, one to examine claims on accounts of public buildings, one to scrutinize and settle accounts of contractors, and still another to investigate the procedures and acts of the State House Commissioners. There is evidence to suggest that Trumbull was cautious in the spending of public funds. During the building of the $200,000 Illinois State House, he insisted on a careful scrutiny of the bills submitted by the contractors.[6]

[3] Lyman Trumbull to Julia Trumbull, March 20, 1842, L. T. Family Papers
[4] Lyman Trumbull to David Trumbull, October 15, 1841, L. T. Family Papers.
[5] *Reports made to the Senate and House of Representatives of the State of Illinois*, 13th Assembly, 1st Session (Springfield, Ill., 1842), p. 267.
[6] Lyman Trumbull to W. B. Archer, March 8, 1841, L. T. Family Papers.

The young Secretary of State was a serious, hard-working young man. He lived in one of the committee rooms in the State House and was "the only lodger in the building." [7] He usually spent his free evenings in his room or in the new State Library which was kept in the office of the Clerk of the Supreme Court. Trumbull took his meals in a private boarding house or at the home of his brother Benjamin. He was not a recluse, however, and in a short time, he made the acquaintance of many of the eligible young ladies of Springfield society. The best place to meet young girls was at the evening receptions held by the sewing societies of the local churches. At one such reception at the First Presbyterian Church, Trumbull met Julia Jayne, a daughter of a prominent Springfield physician Dr. Gershom Jayne. Trumbull attempted to explain his attraction for Julia in a letter to his sister. He wrote: "She cooks a little like you and she bears your name." [8] He added that his sister "need not be alarmed about my getting married," because he had to leave Springfield to attend court on the circuit and would be gone for more than two months.

While he enjoyed his good fortune, Trumbull had no illusions about the durability of his state job. "How long I may be continued in office," he wrote to his brother, "is, of course, quite uncertain. A change of politics in the state would very soon bring about a change of officers." [9]

Trumbull's tenure of office was placed in jeopardy soon after the inauguration in December, 1842, of Thomas Ford as Governor of Illinois. Ford was much better equipped than his predecessor to deal with the grave financial situation of the state. He was a well-educated lawyer who had been, successively, a prosecuting attorney, a circuit judge and a judge of the Illinois Supreme Court. He was a man of good judgment and was popular with the people. [10] Elected to office in the midst of a

[7] Lyman Trumbull to Julia Trumbull, March 20, 1842, L. T. Family Papers.
[8] Ibid.
[9] Lyman Trumbull to David Trumbull, October 12, 1841, L. T. Family Papers.
[10] The Bench and Bar of Illinois, p. 33.

deep financial crisis, he asserted his leadership by a vigorous, well-thought-out message to the legislature. He blamed the low state of affairs in the state on "ill-conceived legislation and on worse execution of laws bad in themselves." [11] The governor rejected repudiation of the state debt in any form and announced that his administration was determined to honor all of its obligations. Repudiation, he stated, would fatally injure the prestige and the reputation of the state and cut down the flow of immigration, without which the state could not continue to grow. Ford proposed a gradual liquidation of the State Banks. Under the plan the banks would be ordered to resume the specie payments, and if unable to do so, would be given a short period of time to withdraw their notes from circulation, deliver the bonds to the state, and then liquidate their operations. The message also proposed the completion of the Illinois and Michigan Canal and the selling, at reasonable prices, of most of the state lands.[12]

Lyman Trumbull vigorously opposed Governor Ford's proposals. He was a rising, ambitious politician from a southern county, and the general opposition of Little Egypt to the canal influenced his position. However, Trumbull's opposition to Ford's plan for the gradual liquidation of the State Banks was not a matter of political expediency but of principle. He was, as he showed in his *Open Protest* in November, 1842, strongly opposed to the continued operation of the State Banks. The banks, in his opinion, had betrayed the trust of the state, caused economic suffering for the people and served primarily to enrich their wealthy stockholders.[13] He therefore favored revoking the banks' charters and proposed placing them under receiverships.

Lyman Trumbull, the Secretary of State, decided to break with the governor and "put himself at the head of the op-

[11] *Reports Made to the Senate and House,* 1842, p. 267.

[12] *Ibid.,* p. 27.

[13] Thomas Ford, *A History of Illinois,* 2 vols., ed. Milo Milton Quaife (Chicago, 1946), Vol. II. Ford later admitted that "the banks were odious to the people for long-continued and repeated delinquencies" (p. 118).

position to the bank bill." [14] Some historians have charged that Trumbull's opposition to the measure, in which he was joined by Ebenezer Peck of Chicago, then Clerk of the State Supreme Court, was motivated by "the hope of receiverships if the banks were smashed." [15] This, in view of Trumbull's high standards of integrity, was an unwarranted insinuation. Even Ford suggested that "In taking this ground Mr. Trumbull was probably less influenced by a hope of pecuniary advantage to himself than by a desire to serve his friends, to be considered a thoroughgoing party man and by hatred of McClernand and Shields." [16] The main reason for Trumbull's opposition was his conviction that the interests of the common people would be served best by closing the banks. Defying his superior, Trumbull addressed a meeting of representatives and senators in the State House and directed the southern assemblymen in their opposition to McClernand's bill. "From this moment," Ford related later, "I determined to remove Trumbull from office." [17]

In spite of Trumbull's opposition, the Illinois Assembly passed the compromise bank act by overwhelming majorities. The process of liquidation of the banks was slow but effective. On February 8, 1843, Governor Ford reported to the State Assembly that the State Banks had delivered to the state $2,073,501.01 in bonds. He added: "The occasion is fit and proper for congratulation, that we have thus fortunately and happily made commencement in the great work of extinguishing the State debt and that we have succeeded in dissolving, without loss to the State, the odious connection between bank and State. . . ." [18] The bonds delivered by the banks were burned, in the presence of the governor, in front of the State House, on Thursday, February 9, at a public ceremony, to the great rejoicing of the public. [19] Governor Ford and those who supported his policies had good

[14] *Ibid.*, p. 129.
[15] Pease, *op. cit.*, p. 314.
[16] Ford, *op. cit.*, p. 129.
[17] *Ibid.*, pp. 132–36.
[18] *Reports Made to the Senate and House*, 1843, p. 207.
[19] *Illinois State Register*, February 12, 1843.

reasons to rejoice, because the governor had succeeded in diminishing the state debt, in liquidating the State Banks without applying arbitrary and confiscatory measures, and in pushing the work on the canal through a new company and a new scheme of financing. Most important, he had succeeded through bold and wise measures and strong leadership in overcoming the crisis of confidence which brought Illinois to the brink of disaster.

Governor Ford decided not to tolerate Trumbull's opposition to his policies any longer. On March 4, 1843, in a brief and polite note, he asked for the resignation of his Secretary of State. The governor said that he acted in consonance with the wishes of the Democratic party in the state. Trumbull, apparently agreeing that his position had become untenable, acknowledged in a letter dated on the same day the right of the governor to remove him from office and submitted his resignation. While the parting was amicable, it soon became clear that Trumbull had many influential friends who were ready to fight the governor. Thirty-two leading Democrats, including Ebenezer Peck, Samuel H. Treat, and Mason Brayman, decided to give Trumbull a testimonial dinner to express to him their esteem and appreciation for his services as a public servant. When the *Illinois State Register*, undoubtedly at Governor Ford's instigation, refused to print the announcement of the dinner, the group published the invitation and a long statement of support for Trumbull's views and record in a special newspaper entitled *Independent Democrat*, whose history of publication was confined to Number 1, Volume 1.[20] The paper also contained an exchange of correspondence between the group and Trumbull. Trumbull, in his reply to the invitation, expressed his regret that his early departure from Springfield would not make it possible for him to attend the dinner. He further stated that he was a "humble and obscure" representative who had not solicited the office

20 A Copy of the *Independent Democrat*, Number 1, Volume 1, in the Horace White Papers, Illinois State Historical Library, Springfield, Ill.

of Secretary of State, but did all in his power to discharge the duties of his office with devotion and fidelity. He explained his opposition to the bank bill by his conviction that the State Banks had "defrauded the people" and had caused a great many citizens to suffer financial losses. Trumbull acknowledged that the governor had the right to remove him, but he denied that there was any demand for his dismissal in the Democratic party.

Trumbull chose not to ascerbate his relations with the Democratic leaders and returned to Belleville to resume his private practice of law. His political career, which had begun so auspiciously in November, 1840, ended in his almost complete isolation in the Democratic party. When, on March 21, 1843, the leaders of Illinois Democracy issued "An address to the Democratic Party," which called for party loyalty in the forthcoming elections, it was signed by Governors Ford and Carlin, McClernand, Shields, and others.[21] Trumbull's name was conspicuously absent.

However, Trumbull was not allowed to leave his office in Springfield quietly, because his successor, Thomas Campbell, immediately upon taking office, instituted a suit against Trumbull to recover four hundred dollars, which he claimed Trumbull received illegally from the state. The background of the suit presented a rather complicated legal situation. The Illinois Legislature, on March 3, 1843, appropriated six hundred dollars for the Secretary of State to make an index of state laws with marginal notes. Trumbull was removed from office on March 4, but he had worked on the index for about three months before his dismissal and had two-thirds of the job completed. In his last week of office he sent a voucher to the State Auditor ordering a compensation of four hundred dollars for the work done on the index, and the voucher was immediately honored.

The Sangamon Circuit Court issued, on December 12, 1846, a pro forma, tentative decision ordering Trumbull to return to Campbell two hundred dollars. It decided that Trumbull was

21 *Chicago Democrat,* March 21, 1843.

overpaid, but in the same decision the lower court asked the Supreme Court to rule on the legal issue involved. Trumbull engaged Abraham Lincoln to represent him before the Supreme Court. Lincoln prepared a legal brief on behalf of his client,[22] and the Supreme Court, in a decision rendered by Judge Samuel Treat, ruled on February 19, 1847, that Campbell could not sue Trumbull and that his suit could only have been directed against the state of Illinois.[23]

What was the image of Lyman Trumbull that began to emerge from his first period of service as a legislator and a state official? There was general agreement that he was a promising young politician who would play an important role in Illinois politics. He was well-informed, hard-working, ambitious, and an excellent debater. In these qualities he was not unique. There were a number of young politicians who held great promise, the most prominent among them Abraham Lincoln and Stephen A. Douglas, who were equally ambitious and effective in the political give and take. Trumbull was different in the Puritan characteristics of his nature that made him a zealous fighter for frugal government. In his relations with others he seemed cold and unemotional. Few people realized that under the forbidding cold mask, there was a man who had a warm sympathy for the welfare of the people, a man who craved friendship, but whose friendships, while not easily or frequently given, were lasting and abiding. While he had a deep concern for the common man, he was aloof in his personal contacts, even with his close neighbors in his home town. Most of his colleagues in politics agreed with Ford who wrote: "So far from possessing that appearance of generosity and magnanimity which often recommends a man to the people, his manners were precise and his appearance would be called by many puritanical." [24]

[22] Copy of the legal brief entitled "Thomas Campbell v. Lyman Trumbull" in the Lincoln Collection, Illinois State Historical Society Library, Springfield, Ill.

[23] Text of the Court's opinion in the Horace White Papers, Illinois State Historical Society Library, Springfield, Ill.

[24] Ford, *op. cit.*, II, 267–68.

There was no agreement among Trumbull's contemporaries who worked with him in Springfield as to whether he was a radical, a liberal, or a conservative. Ford thought that Trumbull was "not remarkable for his liberal views," [25] but Koerner concluded that Trumbull was a radical Democrat.[26] Historians, it seems, are still puzzled by this question.

While the outsiders might have been at times repelled by Trumbull's cold demeanor, his family knew him as a warm and affectionate son and brother. He kept up a steady and lively correspondence with his father, sisters, and brothers. When, as it happened on occasions, the correspondence lagged, Trumbull hastened to assure his family that it was not "from any indifference felt by either of us for the welfare and happiness of the other." [27] Lyman did all he could to make his brother Benjamin and his family comfortable in Springfield. When Trumbull was dismissed from his post as Secretary of State, Benjamin, of course, lost his job with him. Trumbull helped his brother purchase a farm near the state capital and regularly reported to his father on Benjamin's fortunes as a farmer.[28]

In June, 1843, Trumbull married Julia Jayne in the First Presbyterian Church in Springfield. The Jayne family was prosperous and belonged to the local aristocracy. The father, Dr. Gershom Jayne, was a veteran of the 1812 War and a respected physician and political leader. The family came to Illinois from Massachusetts where many of their relatives still lived.

Julia was a young girl, well-educated and with deep religious convictions. The wedding of Lyman Trumbull and Julia Jayne was a great social occasion in Springfield. Norman P. Judd of Chicago was best man and Mrs. Abraham Lincoln, the former Mary Todd and a close friend of Julia, was the bride's attend-

[25] *Ibid.*, p. 267.
[26] Koerner, *Memoirs*, II, 426.
[27] Lyman Trumbull to David Trumbull, October 12, 1841, L. T. Family Papers.
[28] Lyman Trumbull to Benjamin Trumbull, December 23, 1843, L. T. Family Papers.

Julia Jayne Trumbull.

ant.[29] The newly married couple took two honeymoon trips, one to Trumbull's family in Connecticut and another to Massachusetts to visit Mrs. Trumbull's relatives there. The Trumbulls in Colchester accepted Julia with love and affection. Three years later Julia recalled that visit in a letter to her father-in-law. "Soon did you teach me to feel that I had only left one Parent to meet another . . . those were happy days." She hoped to see him soon, but added: "as our lives are all uncertain, we must not indulge too much in such happy anticipations. God grant that we may at least meet around His throne when the frail thread of life is broken." [30]

Trumbull's ties to the Jayne family also became close and affectionate. Dr. Gershom Jayne spared no efforts to keep the Trumbull family in good health and Lyman developed life-long friendships with Julia's brother William and her sister Ellen. Both William and Ellen were frequent visitors in the Trumbull home in Belleville and then in Alton.

For the time being, however, Julia and Lyman stayed in the Jayne home in Springfield. This seemed to be a sensible arrangement, with Julia pregnant and Trumbull traveling on the circuit. When their first child, Lyman Jr., was born in May, 1844, Trumbull was away on law business in Belleville.[31] The young couple were deeply affected by this forced separation. "You know not how I long to see you," wrote Trumbull, "it is but eight days since we parted and it seems almost an age." [32]

Finally, in July, 1844, Lyman Trumbull took his wife and son and two servant girls to Belleville. They rented a house, which Trumbull furnished with household goods bought in St. Louis.[33] Neither Trumbull nor Julia wanted to buy a home in Belleville,

[29] Lyman Trumbull to Benjamin Trumbull, August 20, 1843, L. T. Family Papers.

[30] Julia Jayne Trumbull to Benjamin Trumbull, December 23, 1843, November 19, 1846, L. T. Family Papers.

[31] Julia Jayne Trumbull to Lyman Trumbull, May 13, May 15, May 20, 1844, L. T. Family Papers.

[32] Lyman Trumbull to Julia Jayne Trumbull, July 7, 1844, L. T. Family Papers.

[33] Lyman Trumbull to Julia Jayne Trumbull, July 4, 1844, L. T. Family Papers.

because they had no intention of settling there permanently. Julia spent many months each year at her parents' home in Springfield. It was in Springfield that young Lyman, only a few months old, died. Early in 1846 Julia gave birth to another son, Walter.

Soon after his settling in Belleville, Trumbull helped his father and his two unmarried sisters, Julia and Sarah, to move from Colchester to Henrietta in Jackson County, Michigan. A few years before, his brothers John and Erastus bought farms in Henrietta. His brother David had a farm in nearby Barry. By hard work and by pooling their resources, the Trumbulls soon prospered in Michigan.[34] Lyman and Julia were frequent visitors in Henrietta and Benjamin Trumbull and his daughters often stayed with the Trumbulls in Belleville.

In Belleville Trumbull devoted his time to law and to politics. He was much more successful in the former than in the latter. The Democratic party in St. Clair and Madison counties was split into two hostile factions. One faction was led by John Reynolds and Lyman Trumbull, and the other, which was allied with Governor Ford, had James Shields, Gustave Koerner, and William Bissell among its leaders.

The feuding did not involve serious differences on political issues but was primarily a quarrel between two sets of politicians, aggravated by Governor Ford's bitterness toward Trumbull and the personal ambitions of former Governor Reynolds. Reynolds, like his friend Trumbull, had an aversion to party regularity.

The 1843 Congressional election started early, with a Democratic mass meeting in Belleville. The meeting became the scene of a vindictive debate between Trumbull and Shields that lasted the entire day. Shields read a letter from Governor Ford explaining why he had removed Trumbull from office and Trumbull, in turn, denounced the governor and his supporters. The

---

34 Julia Jayne Trumbull to Benjamin Trumbull, November 19, 1846, L. T. Family Papers; and John Trumbull to Lyman Trumbull, December 7, 1846, L. T. Family Papers.

audience was on Trumbull's side. Newspaper reports concluded that "The Trumbull and Reynolds party carried the day." [35]

The contest for the Congressional nomination in the first district, which included Belleville, was a bitter one. Governor Ford, aided by Koerner and Bissell, supported James Shields, a handsome Irish lawyer who was former State Auditor and then Illinois State Supreme Court Judge. Trumbull, whose antagonism to Shields turned into hate during their service in Ford's administration, kept up a constant barrage of attacks on him.[36] To assure Shield's defeat at the district convention, Reynolds and Trumbull, both of whom wanted the nomination, decided to withdraw from the race and to throw their support to Robert Smith, a successful businessman who had little experience in public affairs and was clearly less qualified than Shields for service in Congress. After an acrimonious debate in the convention and a great deal of maneuvering, Smith defeated Shields by a vote of 14 to 11.[37] In August Smith was elected, and while his election was a triumph, of sorts, for Trumbull and Reynolds, it deepened the rift in the party and increased Ford's determination to prevent Trumbull from attaining public office.

The feud between the two factions continued with unabated fury. The *Belleville Advocate*, owned by ex-Governor Reynolds and edited by his son, and the *Springfield Times*, which became Lyman Trumbull's organ in the state's capital,[38] kept up a constant barrage of attacks on the *Alton Telegraph*, the *Sangamo Journal*, and the *Illinois State Register*, the papers supporting Ford and his Springfield clique.[39] Finally, both sides succeeded in finding some issue to cover up the intense personal rivalries.

[35] *Alton Telegraph and Democratic Review*, April 22, 1843.

[36] *Belleville Advocate*, March 30, June 8, 29, 1843. The *Alton Telegraph and Democratic Review* wrote that Trumbull hated Judge Shields "with the bitterest hatred." February 17, 1844.

[37] *Alton Telegraph and Democratic Review*, July 8, 15, 1843.

[38] "Trumbull is the chief cornerstone of the Times—its very life and soul," wrote the *Alton Telegraph and Democratic Review*, February 17, 1844.

[39] *Belleville Advocate*, January 1, 18, February 1, March 6, April 25, May 2, 1843.

The Reynolds-Trumbull-Peck group was charged by its opponents with being Democratic "radicals" because they advocated "the free trade doctrine, an exclusive metallic currency and the destruction of all Banks."[40] The "Old Ranger," the wealthy, eccentric John Reynolds, suddenly found himself referred to as the head of the "Radical Clique." [41] The supposedly ideological split was obviously just window dressing.

Reynolds decided, with the help of Trumbull, to get the nomination for the House of Representatives. He insisted that Smith, in 1843, in exchange for his and Trumbull's support, had agreed to serve only one year and not to be a candidate for re-election in 1844.[42] Smith, who liked his job in Washington, denied that he had ever made such a bargain, and the convention without much trouble, beat down the opposition and Smith was nominated for re-election. Reynolds decided to defy the party and ran as an independent, and Trumbull faithfully campaigned for him. At one outdoor meeting, he warmed up so to his subject that "he took off his coat and his spectacles" and harangued the crowd in support of the "Old Ranger."[43] Reynolds declared himself for Van Buren as the nominee at the Baltimore Convention of the Democratic party, for free trade, and for exclusive hard money currency, and he declared all banks a menace to the country.[44] The regular state convention, which met in June, adopted a platform that opposed a National Bank and a high protective tariff.

In spite of all the efforts of Trumbull and the *Belleville Advocate*, Reynolds lost the election to Smith by about three thousand votes. He carried only the county of Pulaski, losing his own St. Clair by a large majority.[45] The rout of the Reynolds clique was complete, and it marked a serious setback in Reynolds' active political career. Trumbull's political fortunes were also

[40] *Alton Telegraph and Democratic Review*, February 10, 1844.
[41] *Alton Telegraph and Democratic Review*, January 20, February 17, 1844.
[42] *Belleville Advocate*, January 25, 1843.
[43] *Alton Telegraph and Democratic Review*, April 13, 1844.
[44] *Ibid.*, April 6, 1844.
[45] *Belleville Advocate*, August 8, 1844.

at a new low. Since Reynolds was a strong pro-slavery man, Trumbull's political association with him was based not on political affinity, but on their mutual opposition to Ford. This alliance of expediency brought him little glory and distinction. To add to his woes, the prestige and power of Governor Ford were growing because his policies on the state debt and the banks were gradually bringing Illinois out of the depths of economic depression. While the state still had its troubles, there were firm signs of economic recovery. In his message to the Illinois Assembly, of December 2, 1844, Ford, who was re-elected Governor, stated that as compared with the situation in December, 1842, there was "individual and general prosperity." The state debt, he continued had been greatly reduced and worthless "paper [money] circulation has been liquidated" and "gold and silver and paper of solvent banks substituted." The governor stressed that the flow of immigration into the state had resumed at an increased rate.[46]

With Governor Ford in control of the Democratic party in the state and with Reynolds a political has-been, Trumbull set out to repair his political fences. He made peace with the regular Democratic party leaders by campaigning for Polk in the fall of 1844. Trumbull's reconciliation with the party was made easier when his political foe William Walters, the influential owner and editor of the *Illinois State Register*, gave up the editorship, which was assumed, in June, 1846, by Charles H. Lanphier.[47] As a peace offering, Trumbull also broke his political association with John Reynolds, whose *Belleville Advocate* began attacking Trumbull at regular intervals, charging him with secret dealings and bargains with Ford and the Springfield clique.[48] The Trumbull-Reynolds alliance, which, in view of their sharp disagreement on the increasingly crucial issue of slavery, was largely the result of political opportunism, was at an end.

However, neither Trumbull nor Ford took any steps toward

[46] *Reports Made to the Senate and House*, 1845, pp. 3–4.
[47] Pease, *op. cit.*, p. 299.
[48] *Belleville Advocate*, June 25, 1845.

reconciliation. On the contrary, Ford was convinced that Trumbull led the opposition to him in the Illinois Legislature that convened in January, 1845. He charged that Trumbull, "who had his private griefs to assuage," organized the opposition to measures proposed by the governor to complete the Illinois and Michigan Canal. In this undertaking, he was aided "by an ambitious aspirant for the United States Senate [Stephen A. Douglas]." [49] Trumbull's collaboration with Douglas ended in early 1846, when Douglas was elected to the United States Senate. The specific measure vigorously opposed by Trumbull was a permanent mill tax (in 1846 one mill and a half) for the payment of the interest on the state debt and for the completion of the canal. While it is understandable that Ford assumed that Trumbull's opposition was motivated by his animosity to him, it would be more reasonable to assume that Trumbull, on the issue of the canal, faithfully represented the views of his southern Illinois constituents. There was bitter disappointment in Little Egypt at the slow realization of their high hopes for the growth of Cairo and Alton as great commercial ports and railroad hubs and a general conviction that the Illinois and Michigan Canal would benefit only the northern part of the state. It was quite obvious even in 1845 that Chicago was destined to become a large city and a magnet for thousands of immigrants. The fear of Yankee domination was an important factor in the attitude of southern Illinois to the canal. Whether or not Trumbull personally shared the fears and apprehensions of his section, he had no choice but to pay heed to them. The southerners attacked the tax bill "as a local measure intended only for the benefit of the North." [50] When the measure passed, Trumbull and several legislators from southern Illinois threatened to make speeches throughout the southern part of the state against the

[49] Ford, *op. cit.*, II, 266.
[50] *Ibid.*, p. 276.

bill.[51] Nothing came out of the threat, because the reaction of the people to the bill was overwhelmingly favorable. Northern Illinois actually went wild with joy. A Chicago newspaper headlined the news of the passage of the tax bill and of the new canal bill with this headline: "Joyful News!! Get Out Your Spades and Go on Digging!" Even two county conventions in the south came out for the canal and for the new tax.[52]

When in February of 1846 Trumbull declared himself a candidate for governor, he advocated the completion of the canal. He had strong support for the nomination at the State Democratic Convention and received, on the first ballot, 56 votes to 47 for Augustus C. French and 44 for John Calhoun. He was beaten and French was nominated when Governor Ford induced the Calhoun supporters to switch to French.[53] An able historian observed that "the choice, in accordance with a line of precedents which seemed almost to indicate a settled policy, fell upon him who had achieved least prominence as a party leader and whose record had been least conspicuous." [54] Nevertheless, Augustus C. French went on to become a frugal, effective and respected governor of Illinois. On April 24, 1848, French was the unanimous choice for re-election at the Democratic State Convention.[55] Trumbull himself ascribed his defeat to the influence of Governor Ford.[56]

[51] *Ibid.,* p. 278. Trumbull angered Ford by influencing the legislature to pass a resolution to cut the salary of the governor by twenty-five per cent. Ford, in a letter to the legislators rejected the resolution on the basis of the principle of separation of powers and asserted that it was his duty "to sustain the independence of the Office of Governor." *Reports to the Senate of the State of Illinois,* 14th Assembly (Springfield, Ill., 1845), p. 174.

[52] *Chicago Daily Journal,* March 3, 1845; and Ford, *op. cit.,* p. 275.

[53] *Illinois State Register,* August 22, 28, October 3, 1845; *Belleville Advocate,* March 14, 1846. See also, Lyman Trumbull to Julia Jayne Trumbull, April 4, 1846, L. T. Family Papers.

[54] John Moses, *Illinois: Historical and Statistical* (Chicago, 1895), I, 505.

[55] *Ibid.,* II, 560. See also a very favorable appraisal of Governor Ford's administrations in Palmer (ed.), *The Bench and Bar of Illinois,* I, 127–28.

[56] White, *op. cit.,* p. 18. See further details on the convention in John F. Snyder, M.D., "Forgotten Statesmen of Illinois, Hon. Richard M. Young," *Transactions of the Illinois State Historical Society for the Year, 1906* (Springfield, Ill., 1906), pp. 321–26.

Trumbull was to suffer one more humiliating defeat before his political fortunes began to improve. His alliance with Reynolds and his defiance of the party leaders proved to be costly indeed. After complicated maneuverings and pressure, the Democratic district convention that met in April in Kaskaskia nominated Trumbull as its candidate for Congress from the First Congressional District in Illinois. The convention was a stormy one, and Trumbull's victory did not come until the supporters of the incumbent Representative Robert Smith, representing mostly Madison County, bolted the convention, charging unfair tactics of the Trumbull supporters.[57] With Ford's encouragement, Smith decided to run as an independent candidate and defeated Trumbull by a thumping majority of two thousand.[58] The defeat, suffered in spite of the support of the regular party organization, was indeed humiliating. Governor Ford noted with glee that "when Trumbull was defeated for Congress by so large a majority, thus disappointing the popular belief in his destiny, his power and consequence vanished in a moment." [59]

Trumbull took his defeat very hard. This was his first experience with political intrigues and scheming politicians and he did not like what he saw. Writing from Kaskaskia during the convention, he observed that "a few intriguing politicians can succeed over the people." [60] He added that he wished he had not sought the nomination. During the election campaign, Trumbull became chagrined over "calumnies and misrepresentations" spread by his opponents, who charged him with fraud and bribery of convention delegates. Disgusted, Trumbull wrote his wife: "I now must devote myself to correcting these slanders . . . Oh, the bother of politics!" [61]

[57] *Alton Telegraph and Democratic Review,* May 2, 1846.
[58] *Illinois State Register,* August 17, 1846; *Alton Telegraph and Democratic Review,* August 14, 1846.
[59] Ford, *op. cit.,* II, 269.
[60] Lyman Trumbull to Julia Jayne Trumbull, April 28, 1846, L. T. Family Papers.
[61] Lyman Trumbull to Julia Jayne Trumbull, May 3, 1846, L. T. Family Papers.

After his defeat, Trumbull considered moving out of Belleville and out of Illinois and settling in St. Louis. He was convinced that his political career was over and that St. Louis offered better prospects for his law practice. He did not believe that Belleville would grow and he foresaw that he and George would just be able to make a modest living in Belleville.[62]

It is doubtful that Trumbull was really serious about his moving to Missouri. While he suffered a crushing defeat in Madison County, his own St. Clair County gave him an overwhelming vote of confidence.[63] His prospects for a political comeback were far from dim. Furthermore, his law practice was growing and his family life was a source of pleasure and satisfaction. We have a glimpse of it in a letter written by Mrs. Trumbull to her father-in-law in Michigan. "I wish," Julia Trumbull wrote, "you could look in on us tonight and see what a happy little family we are. Lyman and myself have just been teaching Sarah [Lyman's sister] chess; now while I write, they sit before the fire reading." [64]

[62] Lyman Trumbull to Benjamin Trumbull, November 20, 1846, L. T. Family Papers.

[63] *Alton Telegraph and Democratic Review*, August 7, 1846. In St Clair County, Trumbull received 1,713 votes to Smith's 671.

[64] Julia Jayne Trumbull to Benjamin Trumbull, November 19, 1846, L. T. Family Papers.

3

Anti-Slavery Lawyer

WHILE HIS ATTEMPTS TO WIN AN ELECTIVE OFFICE WERE UNSUC-
cessful, Trumbull's law practice was prospering. A frequent
advertisement or "card" in the local newspaper read, "L. and G.
Trumbull, Attorneys and counselors at Law will practice law
as partners in St. Clair and the adjoining counties. Their office
is in Belleville, where one of the partners may at all times be
found." [1] George Trumbull dealt with local cases, tried before
the circuit court judge, Gustave Koerner, while Lyman rode
the circuit and tried cases in Springfield before the Illinois State
Supreme Court. He was usually successful and the firm prospered. The earnings of the law firm in 1847 were $2,300, a
substantial sum for those days. [2]

When the Mexican War came in 1846, most Illinois politicians were happy to turn their attention to the national scene,
away from the rather dreary state of local politics. The war
proved to be very popular in southern Illinois, and Henry Clay's
speeches condemning the United States for aggression against
Mexico were widely denounced. [3] The war and the demand for

[1] *Belleville Advocate*, September 24, 1846.
[2] Lyman Trumbull to Benjamin Trumbull, August 1, 1847, L. T. Family Papers.
[3] The *Belleville Advocate* stated that "The Mexican government, in her course
towards the United States has been insulting. . . . The mass of the American people
are in favor of it [the war]." November 12, 1846. On December 31, 1846, another

54

the annexation of Texas were especially popular in southern Illinois, because Illinoisans in that part of the state, mostly immigrants from the South, were in the main a hardy and bellicose folk, always ready for a good fight. Little Egypt was for fighting the Mexicans. It had little sympathy for Lincoln's "spot resolution" and his speech in the House of Representatives in which he blamed the United States for aggression against Mexico. The Germans in St. Clair and Madison counties, who had left Germany in search of freedom, were also enthusiastic supporters of the war. They were heartily in favor of expanding American freedom and liberty to neighboring territories ruled by a despotic government, even by the force of arms. Gradually, in spite of some ineffectual Whig opposition, the war received the support of the people throughout the state. The patriotic fervor, the sense of pride in the success of American arms were welcomed by a people beset, for a number of years, by economic panics, depressions and domestic troubles.[4] Governor Ford's call for volunteers was answered quickly and enthusiastically, and within a short period of time six Illinois regiments of infantry and four companies of cavalry went to the front amidst scenes of general enthusiasm. Illinois troops performed gallantly on the fields of battle, and the state rejoiced in their successes and hailed two of its sons, General James Shields and Colonel William H. Bissell, as genuine heroes of the war. Shields fought with great distinction in the battle of Cerro Gordo, in which he was almost fatally wounded, and Bissell performed valiantly in the battle of Buena Vista.[5] The companies of German volunteers also received warm commendations from their officers.[6]

Trumbull gave his full support to the war and addressed

---

editorial denounced the Whig opposition to the war and said, "We say, and every patriot will say the same, push on the war, until an honorable and permanent peace shall span the political heavens." See also a bitter editorial attacking Henry Clay, December 9, 1847.

[4] Koerner, Memoirs, I, 495–96; and Pease, op. cit., p. 400.

[5] Alton Telegraph and Democratic Review, July 4, 1846.

[6] Koerner, Memoirs, I, 496.

several patriotic mass meetings held in Belleville. When the news of the Buena Vista victory reached Belleville, Judge Koerner promptly adjourned his court and several hundred people gathered in front of the Court House to hear speeches by John Reynolds, Koerner, Joseph Gillespie, and Trumbull. Reporting on the meeting in the local paper, the reporter noted, with understandable surprise, that Trumbull, whose speeches usually were calm and rather dry, spoke "with enthusiasm, eloquence and feeling." [7] However, when General Shields, who was previously reported killed in action, "mortally wounded by grape shot while storming the enemy's works," [8] survived his wound, Trumbull did not attend a meeting called by the citizens of Belleville to celebrate his miraculous recovery.[9] When in April, 1848, General Shields, whose bravery brought him a promotion to the rank of major general and a commendation from Congress, returned to Belleville, Lyman Trumbull again refused to go to the reception to pay honor to his political foe.[10]

Trumbull demanded that Mexico be forced to give up Texas and other territories adjacent to the United States. On Saturday, November 27, 1847, Trumbull, together with Bissell, Koerner, and ex-Governor Kinney, addressed a mass rally of Democrats of St. Clair County assembled on the lawn of the Belleville Court House. The resolutions, drafted by a committee of which Trumbull was a member, declared that the war was actually commenced by Mexico herself and that Mexico must relinquish "her imaginary rights to the State of Texas." The resolutions further stated that the war could be ended only by Mexico indemnifying America for its (Mexico's) unprovoked aggression by giving up the territories unjustly held by her.[11]

When the news of the 1848 revolutions in Europe and especially in Germany reached Belleville, Trumbull joined his friend

[7] *Belleville Advocate*, April 1, 1847.
[8] *Ibid.*, May 13, 1847.
[9] *Ibid.*, September 23, 1847.
[10] *Ibid.*, April 29, 1848.
[11] *Ibid.*, December 2, 1847.

Judge Koerner in addressing a large rally of Germans called to express solidarity with the European revolutionary movements. The meeting assured the freedom-fighters of the "feelings of joy and hope on the great prospects of civil and religious liberty in Europe." It went on to tell "the nations of Europe, rising upon their oppressors and establishing republican institutions of our cordial sympathies with their noble spirits." [12] Among the speakers who addressed the rally was the pro-slavery leader John Reynolds, who apparently saw no contradiction between his support of freedom in Europe and his avowed support for Negro bondage at home. Another cause in which Trumbull showed a keen interest was the temperance movement. He often addressed temperance rallies, condemning the evils of excessive drinking, and on one occasion received, at a public meeting, a Bible "in behalf of the ladies of Belleville." [13]

Trumbull was rapidly gaining a reputation as a learned and effective trial lawyer. In 1847 he was retained to appear in the widely celebrated murder case of James Duncan. The long trial took place before Judge Koerner, and Philip B. Fouke, later a member of Congress, was the prosecuting attorney. Trumbull was joined in the defense by Colonel William Bissell and Joseph Gillespie. The local paper commented that "there is an array of legal knowledge brought to bear on this case, seldom, if ever brought to bear on any case in Illinois." [14]

However, Trumbull found himself devoting increasingly more of his time and legal talents to cases that brought him no money and whose political benefit in his home town and county

12 *Ibid.*, April 13, 1848.

13 *Ibid.*, November 2, 1848. Trumbull remained an advocate of temperance all his life but opposed extreme temperance measures. When in 1867 the Senate debated a bill introduced by Senator Wilson of Massachusetts, which would have prohibited the sale of liquor in the Capitol Building, Trumbull said, "I myself am as much in favor of temperance as the Senator from Massachusetts, I think I have not been in the habit, as most Senators know, of drinking." But he opposed the bill because he feared it would give the public the impression that a lot of drinking went on in the Capitol. *Cong. Globe*, 40 Cong., 2nd Sess., p. 30.

14 *Belleville Advocate*, September 9, 1847.

Lyman Trumbull, Attorney at Law.

was at best doubtful. These cases involved Negroes who were held in virtual slavery by the system of indenture. Trumbull considered the system immoral and illegal and was determined to rid the state of it. The cases stemmed from the rather complicated legal history of slavery in the state.

The Northwest Ordinance for the government of the territories northwest of the Ohio River, which were ceded to the United States by Virginia and other states and which included the area later to become the state of Illinois, was passed by Congress in 1787. The sixth article of the ordinance stated that "there shall be neither slavery nor involuntary servitude in the said territory, otherwise than in the punishment of crimes, whereof the party shall have been duly convicted: Provided always, that any person escaping into the same, from whom labor or service is lawfully claimed in any one of the original states, such fugitive may be lawfully reclaimed, and conveyed to the person claiming his or her labor or service as aforesaid." [15] Thus while slavery was prohibited in the territory, fugitive slaves were to be forcibly returned to their owners. The governors of the states later carved out of the territory, including Illinois, Ohio, Indiana, Wisconsin, and Michigan, took the position that the ordinance did not pertain to slaves who were in the territory prior to 1787. This position was never challenged by the courts and thereby gained a de facto validity.[16] The Territorial Legislature passed, in 1812, a law which allowed owners of slaves, fifteen years of age and older, to take them before a clerk of the court to be declared indentured servants. Slaves under fifteen were held in servitude, even against their will, in cases of males till the age of thirty-five and females till the age of thirty-two. Children of indentured "servants" were held in

[15] *Illinois Constitutions,* ed. Emil Joseph Verlie, Collections of the Illlinois State Historical Library (Springfield, Ill., 1919), XII, 8.
[16] John P. Hand, "Negro Slavery in Illinois," *Transactions of the Illinois State Historical Society for the Year 1910,* Illinois State Journal Printers (Springfield, Ill., 1912), p. 42.

virtual slavery till the age of thirty for males and twenty-eight for females.[17]

When the State of Illinois was formed, the first constitution adopted in 1818 provided that "Neither slavery nor involuntary servitude shall *hereafter* be introduced into this state otherwise than for punishment of crimes whereof the party shall have been duly convicted." [18] However, the constitution recognized the existence of the system of voluntary servitude. Negroes had no choice but to accept "voluntary" servitude, because even if in rare cases they understood the legal procedure and had refused servitude, they were usually sold by slave traders in the adjoining states. The practice of kidnapping of free Negroes in Illinois was widespread and was carried out without much interference of the local or state authorities.[19]

The lot of Negroes was made even harder by the passage of the "Black Laws" during the session of the first Illinois Legislature. These laws were copied from the slave codes of Kentucky and Virginia, and under them "a Negro, free or slave, was practically without protection." [20] The new laws provided that any slave coming into Illinois who refused indenture within thirty days could be reclaimed by his former master and was to be delivered to him. If not claimed, he was to be arrested by the sheriff and sold into service for one year.

But even the "Black Laws" did not satisfy the pro-slavery people of southern Illinois. They were convinced that if Illinois were to become a full-fledged slave state, many Kentucky and Missouri slave owners would migrate into the state. From 1820 till 1824, Illinois was in the throes of a bitter campaign aimed at the calling of a constitutional convention that would repeal the constitutional prohibition of slavery. When finally after long debates a two-thirds majority in the Illinois Legislature

---

[17] Hand, *op. cit.*, p. 43.
[18] *Illinois Constitutions*, p. 3. (Italics mine.)
[19] Pease, *ap. cit.*, p. 363.
[20] Hand, *op. cit.*, p. 43.

recommended the calling of the convention, the people of Illinois killed the move, on August 2, 1824, by rejecting the proposal by a small majority of 1,668 votes.[21] John Reynolds, who supported the call for the convention and who wanted Illinois to become a slave state, recollected that "The convention question gave rise to two years of the most furious and boisterous excitement that ever was visited on Illinois. Men, women, and children entered the area of party warfare and strife, and families and neighborhoods were so divided and furious and bitter against one another that it seemed that a regular civil war might be the result." [22]

From 1824 the struggle of the anti-slavery people centered on attempts to abolish the illegal institution of "voluntary servitude" and to better the lot of the free Negroes. They considered the so-called voluntary servitude a shameful stigma on a free state and deplored the sale of free Negroes by the sheriffs and the frequent kidnapping of Negroes and their sale in the slave states. The only way leading to the abolition of the remnants of slavery and of the servitude system was to have the courts declare the 1812 Territorial Indenture Law and the "Black Laws" of 1818 illegal and in violation of the 1787 Northwest Ordinance. Lyman Trumbull was one of the most dedicated leaders of this movement.

Trumbull, true to his New England heritage, detested slavery. It outraged his moral and religious sensibilities, but he was opposed to abolitionism and to interference with slavery in the slave states. He was deeply shocked by the murder of Elijah P. Lovejoy in neighboring Alton in November of 1837. In a letter to his father, Trumbull gave a detailed account of the riot and deplored the action of the mob as an "awful catastrophe." Lovejoy's murder, he wrote, will make more adherents for the abolitionists than his newspaper could if it were published for a

---

[21] *Ibid.*, p. 44.
[22] John Reynolds, *My Own Times, Embracing Also the History of My Life* (Belleville, Ill., 1855), p. 79.

hundred years. The twenty-four-year-old Trumbull concluded the letter by saying: "As much as I am opposed to the immediate emancipation of the slaves and to the doctrine of abolitionism, yet I am more opposed to mob violence and outrage and had I been in Alton, I would have cheerfully marched to the rescue of Mr. Lovejoy and his property." [23]

Trumbull took an active part in anti-slavery agitation and late in 1837 traveled from place to place in southern Illinois to deliver talks against slavery. He gathered signatures on a petition to Congress demanding legislation that would prohibit slave trade between states and abolish slavery in the District of Columbia. John Palmer relates that during a trip to Griggsville, Illinois, he saw on the street in front of his hotel "a number of persons kicking a man by the name of Trumbull." He learned later that Trumbull had given an anti-slavery talk the evening before and circulated his petition among the audience.[24] A few years later, he joined a group of lawyers that included Abraham Lincoln, Gustave Koerner, and John Palmer in advising the Negroes held in bondage in Illinois that they were not legally held as slaves and that they were entitled to their freedom. "In many instances," wrote a historian of slavery in Illinois, "these men fearlessly stood by their opinions and defended successfully in the courts, without money and without price, Negroes who were thought to be deprived of their freedom." [25] The anti-slavery lawyers brought to the courts a succession of cases involving indentured servants in the hope that the Illinois Supreme Court would declare the entire system of involuntary servitude unconstitutional. In 1839 in the case of Nathan Cromwell versus David Bailey, Cromwell sued for the possession of a Negro girl named Nance, for whom he had a promissory note from Bailey. The judgment of the

[23] Lyman Trumbull to Benjamin Trumbull, November 12, 1837, L. T. Family Papers.

[24] Palmer, *Personal Recollections*, p. 23.

[25] Newton D. Harris, *History of Negro Slavery in Illinois and of the Slavery Agitation in that State* (Chicago, 1906), p. 82.

circuit court in Tazewell County, which was for the plaintiff, was appealed to the Illinois Supreme Court by Abraham Lincoln. The opinion written by Judge Sidney Breese found for the defendant and established that in Illinois the presumption was that a Negro was free and not subject to sale. This was an important decision because it established a legal precedent that a claim upon a Negro had to be substantiated by the evidence supplied by the claimant.[25] In view of the pro-slavery feeling of the representatives from southern Illinois, the struggle for the rights of Negroes was difficult.

In 1843 a Negro woman, Sarah Borders, who had three children and was held in servitude by Andrew Borders in Randolph County, escaped north to Peoria County. She and her children were arrested and held in jail to be returned to their master, but when brought before a justice of the peace, they were ordered freed. Andrew Borders appealed to the county circuit court, which reversed the decision and ordered the mother and her children returned as fugitive slaves. Lyman Trumbull and Gustave Koerner advised the woman to appeal to the Illinois Supreme Court and undertook to carry the appeal without fee. Their brief on behalf of Sarah Borders argued that the 1787 ordinance was still legally valid and that all indenture laws were null and void. Justice Walter B. Scates, writing on behalf of the court, rejected the argument and defended the constitutionality of the indentures.[27]

Trumbull was more successful in 1845, in the celebrated case of Jarrot versus Jarrot. The case involved a suit of Joseph Jarrot, whose grandmother was a French Negro slave before the passage of the 1787 Ordinance, who sued his mistress, Julia Jarrot, for wages. The legal issue involved was of unusual importance because it called for a legal opinion on the long-established assumption that the ordinance did not cover the French Negro slaves who were in the Northwest Territory before the passage of the

26 *Ibid.*, p. 45.
27 Pease, *op. cit.*, p. 378.

law. The case was first tried in 1843 in the St. Clair County Court before Judge Shields, and the jury brought in a verdict for the defendant, Mrs. Jarrot. Lyman Trumbull then advised Joseph Jarrot to appeal the case to the State Supreme Court and undertook to carry the appeal without compensation.[28] In a brilliantly reasoned brief, Trumbull argued that no person born in the area covered by the 1787 Ordinance could be held as slave and that any slave brought into Illinois, with or without his master's consent, was automatically free. The majority opinion of the Illinois Supreme Court, written by Justice Richard M. Young, sustained Trumbull's arguments and declared that Article VI of the ordinance forbidding slavery was retroactive and applied to all Negroes found in the Northwest Territory at the time of its passage. The decision was a signal victory for the anti-slavery forces and for Lyman Trumbull. While Professor Pease was correct in pointing out that the ruling of the court did not end the indenture system and did not, as Horace White and others have asserted, sweep away the whole basis of slavery in Illinois, it did bring freedom to all the French Negro slaves and their descendants.[29] In addition, the decision to allow some forms of slavery to continue was now left exclusively to the sanction of the state legislature in actual defiance of the decision of the State Supreme Court.

The Jarrot verdict was an important victory, but the indenture system, the kidnapping of free Negroes and the hunting of runaway slaves continued. Furthermore, southern members in the Illinois Assembly pressed vigorously for the passage of measures to prohibit the immigration of free Negroes into Illinois. In 1842 Gustave Koerner almost singlehandedly succeeded in bottling up in the Judiciary Committee of the Illinois Senate a bill passed in the House which provided that any Negro found in the state

[28] John F. Snyder, "Forgotten Statesmen of Illinois, Hon. Richard M. Young," *Transactions of the Illinois State Historical Society for the Year 1906* (Springfield, Ill., 1906), p. 320.

[29] Pease, *op. cit.*, pp. 378–79. White, *op. cit.*, p. 29.

who could not prove his freedom on the basis of legal papers was to be brought before a justice of the peace to be sentenced to 'one year in jail and expelled from the state.[30] In 1845 the Illinois Legislature adopted a revised criminal statute, of which Section Five read: "Every black or mulatto person who shall be found in this state, and not having such a certificate [of freedom] as required by this chapter, shall be deemed a runaway slave or servant." Such a Negro was to be brought before the sheriff whose duty it was "to have him sold for the best price he can get." [31] The *Belleville Advocate* often carried advertisements about the sale of runaway slaves. One of them read, "Runaway Slave. The jailer announces that he has a slave named John Johnson who says he lives in Cincinnati. Owner should come and claim him and pay all the charge, otherwise he shall be dealt with as the law provides." [32] Slaves were sold at public auctions to the highest bidder and then "hired out" as indentured servants.

Considering the pro-slavery sentiments of the great majority of the inhabitants of Belleville and the county where Trumbull practiced law and on whose votes he depended for election to office, his fight for the abolition of the remnants of slavery and the indenture system and for the betterment of the lot of free Negroes was an act of great personal and political courage. Even during his close political association with ex-Governor John Reynolds, his erstwhile patron and mentor and a leader of the pro-slavery forces in Little Egypt, Trumbull did not compromise his opposition to slavery. After paying tribute to several Illinois lawyers who fought against slavery, Dwight Harris, the author of the only comprehensive history of slavery in Illinois, stated, "Chief among them [the anti-slavery lawyers] was Lyman Trumbull, whose name should be written large in anti-slavery annals.

---

[30] Koerner, *Memoirs*, I, 487.
[31] D. W. Lusk, *Politics and Politicians: A Succinct History of the Politics of Illinois from 1856–1884* (Springfield, Ill., 1884), p. 345.
[32] *Belleville Advocate*, March 14, 1845.

He was a lawyer of rare intellectual endowments, and of great ability. He had few equals before the bar in his day. In politics he was an old-time Democrat, with no leanings toward abolitionism, but possessing an honest desire to see justice done to the Negro in Illinois. It was a thankless task, in those days of prejudice and bitter partisan feelings, to assume the role of defender of indentured slaves. It was not often unattended with great risk to one's person, as well to one's reputation and business. But Trumbull did not hesitate to undertake the task, thankless, discouraging and unremunerative as it was, and to his zeal, courage, and perseverance, as well as to his ability, is to be ascribed the ultimate success of the appeal to the supreme court." [33]

The unpopularity of Trumbull's anti-slavery struggle did not seem to affect his growing prestige and esteem. Even his pro-slavery neighbors in Belleville and in the adjoining counties were impressed with the high standards of integrity, personal austerity, and courage of this Yankee lawyer. They knew that he was not a wild-eyed abolitionist but a law-abiding citizen who considered slavery a moral and a social evil and who as a Christian considered it his duty to better the lot of the long-suffering Negro. On the other hand, Trumbull's fight against slavery made him the hero of slavery-hating Germans and Yankees in St. Clair and in Madison counties. His efforts on behalf of the Negroes also gained for Trumbull wide support and acclaim in Springfield and in northern Illinois.

Illinois politicians had long been convinced that the 1818 Illinois Constitution was outdated, but they were postponing the calling of a constitutional convention for fear of reviving the pro-slavery agitation. By 1846 it became clear, however, that the pro-slavery elements could not and would not attempt again to make Illinois a slave state, and in August of that year Illinois voters overwhelmingly voted to convene a constitutional con-

[33] Harris, *op. cit.*, p. 53.

vention to amend the state constitution. The election of delegates to the convention took place in April, 1847, and the convention assembled on June 7 of that year. The convention was large and unwieldy and was dominated by the Democrats, who had 92 out of 162 members.[34] The new constitution provided for the choosing of judges of the State Supreme Court and of all state officers by a popular election of the people.

The convention recommended the reduction of the salaries of the governor to $1,500 and of the Supreme Court judges to $1,200. After a bitter fight, the convention instructed the legislature to pass a law that would prohibit the immigration into the state of free Negroes and to prevent owners of slaves from bringing slaves into Illinois. The new constitution was ratified in a general election held on March 6, 1848. The article pertaining to Negro immigration was voted on separately and was approved by a vote of 49,060 to 20,883.[35] The vote in St. Clair County on the constitution was 1,593 for and 948 against and on the article concerning the Negroes, 2,056 for and 102 against.[36]

The judicial convention of the Illinois Democrats in the Southern Division requested Lyman Trumbull to become a candidate for Judge of the State Supreme Court in the popular election for the Supreme Court judges which was scheduled for September 4. There seems to have been general agreement that Trumbull was the logical candidate because of his legal knowledge and widespread reputation for honesty and integrity. He had no serious opposition. On May 4 the *Belleville Advocate* without comment reprinted on its editorial page the following editorial from the *St. Louis Union:* "The Delegates to the Democratic State Convention of Illinois, from the Southern Division, have requested the Hon. Lyman Trumbull to become a candidate for Judge of that Division of the Supreme Court. . . . We

[34] Moses, *op. cit.,* II, 555.
[35] *Ibid.*
[36] *Belleville Advocate,* March 16, 1848.

presume that no serious opposition will be made to him if he
consents to serve, as all admit him to be an accomplished lawyer
and a gentleman of incorruptible integrity." [37] The election was
an overwhelming victory for Trumbull, who won by large majorities in eleven out of seventeen counties. In St. Clair County
Trumbull got 1,776 votes to 165 votes for two of his opponents. [38]
One judge was to serve nine years, another six years, and the
third three years. Trumbull drew the lot for the three-year
term.[39]

Trumbull's election by large majorities in the southern counties of Little Egypt and especially his easy victory in St. Clair
County constituted a remarkable achievement. Southern Illinois
was strongly pro-South and pro-slavery as indicated by its
overwhelming vote for the convention in 1824 and for the
prohibition of Negro immigration in 1848. Belleville and St.
Clair Democrats were in large numbers opposed to the Wilmot
Proviso, which would have barred slavery or involuntary servitude
from any territory acquired from Mexico, and the *Belleville
Advocate* stated that the Democratic party "avows nor intimates
no power in Congress to legislate upon the irritable question
of Slavery." [40] Lyman Trumbull, on the other hand, was a declared opponent of slavery. And yet, there was near unanimity
on the question whether Trumbull should sit on the Supreme
Court, whose decisions were often in the past, and would be in
the future, decisive to the issue of slavery and the indenture system in Illinois. The answer to this seeming paradox can be
found in Trumbull's prestige as a lawyer and as a man of un-

37 *Ibid.*, May 4, 1848.
38 *Ibid.*, September 7, 1848.
39 Lyman Trumbull to John Moses, Esq., December 5, 1890, Trumbull Letters,
Chicago Historical Society. In a letter to his wife, Trumbull said that he was happy
that he drew the short term because "If I should want to leave the bench it is
fortunate that I have drawn the short term," Lyman Trumbull ot Julia Jayne
Trumbull, December 5, 1848, L. T. Family Papers.
40 *Belleville Advocate*, December 2, 1848. The   Illinois Assembly, however,
adopted a resolution (passed in the Senate, 14 to 11, and in the House, 38 to 34),
instructing the Illinois Senators and Congressmen to use all honorable means to
procure a declaration that there shall be no slavery or involuntary servitude in
all the territories acquired from Mexico. Moses, *op. cit.*, pp. 564–65.

impeachable character. Southern Illinoisans were impressed by this newcomer in politics who had the courage of his convictions and was personally incorruptible.

Shortly after his election to the Supreme Court, Lyman Trumbull decided to leave Belleville and settle in Alton. There were many reasons that prompted him to make this move. Belleville had a large incidence of malaria and other diseases, and Trumbull's wife and children were often sick. In his letters to his family Trumbull often reported on the frequent illnesses. In one of these he said, "We have all been sick this fall and this whole region of country has been more sickly than ever before known. George and myself both had attacks of bilious fever early in September which lasted about ten days. Since then Julia has had two attacks which lasted about ten days." [41] The openings of the breweries and distilleries by the German immigrants greatly contributed to the deteriorating health situation, because the refuse from the breweries polluted the creek, which was the town's only water source. The *Belleville Advocate*, while acknowledging the fact that the distilleries were "affording a fine market for grain, and giving employment to a great many hands," stated that they were causing a "vast amount of still-slop to be emptied at this low stage of water, producing fevers." It concluded that it was "a great pity that their creation should prove prejudicial to the health of the town and vicinity." [42] The cholera epidemic of the summer of 1849, which raged in southern Illinois, hit Belleville with particular severity. In spite of belated efforts to clean up garbage and refuse from the streets and the alleys, and the valiant work of the city's doctors, the small community had 212 victims.[43]

In addition, while the townspeople of Belleville supported

[41] Lyman Trumbull to Benjamin Trumbull, October 26, 1845, L. T. Family Papers.

[42] *Belleville Advocate*, September 24, 1846.

[43] *Ibid.*, January 25, 1848, February 15, June 21, July 4, 1849. Koerner later recalled that during the epidemic, "business ceased, stores were closed . . . hardly anyone was on the streets. . . . On the public square and other places, large piles of wood were lighted, for the purpose of purifying the air." Koerner, *Memoirs*, I, 543.

Trumbull in the election, he felt isolated and unhappy in the city composed largely of immigrants from the South. This sense of unease increased as the issue of slavery became more and more acute. In a letter to his father, Trumbull wrote that he decided to move to Alton because that city had more Yankee immigrants.[44] Since there was a college in Upper Alton, only three miles away, Trumbull felt that the city offered greater cultural opportunities.

In spite of its tarnished reputation because of the Lovejoy murder, Alton was generally considered to be a city with a great potential for growth. It was situated on the east bank of the Mississippi, just two miles from the mouth of the Missouri, and it engaged in busy commercial traffic of packets and barges from and to New Orleans, Louisville, and Cincinnati. Although the town, by the admission of its own newspaper, was "far from prepossessing" in appearance, it was healthy because the houses were located on a hilly site away from the river and the swamps.[45]

A Boston traveler in 1847 reported that Alton was "a rather rowdy city," still haunted by the murder of Elijah Lovejoy. The city's population was about 3,000, and "the principal portion of the inhabitants are New England people, and many originally from Boston." The city had a fine port, and "boats of the largest class come up to its levee and load at all seasons of the year; it is the head of navigation for freighting vessels and the completion of this railroad [the Springfield and Alton railroad] will be the means of increasing its trade to an almost incalculable amount." [46] The city had four large flour mills and the state penitentiary. The pride of Upper Alton was Shurtleff College, founded in 1835 through the generosity of Dr. Benjamin Shurtleff of Boston.[47] The authorization for the building of the railroad line between Springfield and Alton was given in 1847, and

44 White, *op. cit.*, p. 21.

45 *Alton Telegraph*, February 22, 1837.

46 J. H. Buckingham, "Illinois as Lincoln Knew It," ed. Harry E. Pratt, *Papers in Illinois History and Transactions for the Year 1937*, Illinois State Historical Society (Springfield, Ill., 1938), 152–58.

47 *Ibid.*, p. 157.

the line was completed in 1850. Since the Alton city fathers were already pressing the legislature to approve the extension of the railroad to Terre Haute, Indiana, there was a general expectation that Alton would become a great railroad hub and an important commercial center. In fact, there were many who believed that Alton would eventually supersede St. Louis as a western metropolis and would dominate the economy of central and southern Illinois.[48] Trumbull, happy with his election to the Supreme Court and eager to live in a friendlier and more promising community, decided to settle in Alton. The Trumbull family settled in a comfortable brick house that had an adjoining orchard.[49] The new Alton home, the first that Trumbull bought, was large enough to accommodate not only the family but also frequent visitors, especially William and Ellen Jayne, and Julia and Sarah Trumbull. Trumbull estimated that it would have taken $5,000 to build the house he had purchased.[50] It was a great joy for Julia to own a home of her own in a town in which they really felt settled. In 1856 Julia wrote to her husband from Alton where she was visiting: "I saw the pleasant home where you and I have passed so many happy hours—did we not have a delightful home?" [51]

The Trumbulls had their share of sickness in Alton. Julia, especially, was frequently ill with "fever and chills" and often spent the winter months in Springfield under the care of her father. In the fall of 1849 Trumbull's father, Benjamin, and his sister, Sarah, came for a long visit to Alton from Michigan. Benjamin Trumbull, Sr. was seventy-nine years old but still enjoyed remarkably good health.[52]

Trumbull's happy life was interrupted in June, 1850, when

[48] Arthur Charles Cole, *The Era of the Civil War, 1848–1870, The Centennial History of Illinois*, Illinois Centennial Commission (Springfield, Ill., 1919), III, p. 51.

[49] Lyman Trumbull to Julia Trumbull, February 8, 1849, L. T. Family Papers.

[50] *Ibid.*

[51] Julia Jayne Trumbull to Lyman Trumbull, April 30, 1856, L. T. Family Papers.

[52] Lyman Trumbull to John Trumbull, October 9, 1849, L. T. Family Papers.

news reached him in Ottawa, Illinois, where he sat with the State Supreme Court, that his father was desperately ill. The news came in a telegram from Dr. Gershom Jayne who went from Springfield to Henrietta, Michigan, to attend the elder Trumbull. Lyman set out immediately for his father's bedside. He wrote to Julia that while his father at eighty was an old man, he "cannot hear of his illness without feeling deeply." [53] Trumbull vividly described to his wife the last hours before his father's death when the four brothers and two sisters stood around the father's bed. Trumbull wrote with quiet resignation: "Everything was done for him which the most affectionate of children could do for the best of parents." [54] While the father's will, which left his property to the two daughters, was invalid because it was signed without witnesses, all six brothers released their rights to the inheritance in favor of the sisters.[55]

A month after his father's death, Trumbull's two-year-old son, Lyman [this was the second son named Lyman], died in his mother's arms. "His death," wrote Trumbull to his sister, "is deeply felt by his mother and myself." [56] Julia was sustained in her grief by her deep religious faith. "I thank God," she wrote to her husband after visiting the graves of both little Lymans, "that I do believe in a present Heaven of happy souls, and the final resurrection of the body, or I should go crazy, thinking of my buried ones." [57]

[53] Lyman Trumbull to Julia Jayne Trumbull, June 11, 1850, L. T. Family Papers
[54] Lyman Trumbull to Julia Jayne Trumbull, June 14, 1850, L. T. Family Papers.
[55] Lyman Trumbull to Julia and Sarah Trumbull, June 21, 1850, L. T. Family Papers.
[56] Lyman Trumbull to Julia Trumbull, July 21, 1850, L. T. Family Papers.
[57] Julia Jayne Trumbull to Lyman Trumbull, April 27, 1856, L. T. Family Papers.

4

The Emergence of the
Anti-Nebraska Leader

THE PEOPLE OF ILLINOIS WATCHED THE DEVELOPING CON-
troversy in Congress regarding slavery in the territories of Oregon,
New Mexico, Utah, and in California with deep interest and
anxiety. The sentiment to admit these territories as free states
was growing stronger. The settlement of a large number of
Illinoisans in California contributed to the close ties that developed between the far Western territories and Illinois, and to
the general conviction that the divisive issue of slavery should
not be introduced to plague the new lands. Illinois representatives in Congress, particuarly Senators Douglas and Shields,
and William H. Bissell of Belleville and John Wentworth of
Chicago, two anti-slavery representatives, voted to admit Oregon
under the Wilmot Proviso. In March, 1849, they helped to defeat a move to admit California without the prohibition of
slavery as provided in the constitution drawn up by the people
of that territory.[1] Even the pro-slavery leaders of southern Illinois
were indignant and dismayed when in reaction to President
Taylor's message to Congress, spokesmen of the South in Con-

[1] *Chicago Daily Democrat*, June 21, 1849. *Weekly Chicago Democrat*, April
3, 1849.

gress began warning of secession.[2] John A. McClernand, Senator Douglas' spokesman in the House of Representatives and an influential leader of Democracy in Little Egypt, wrote from Washington to the Illinois governor, Augustus French, to take immediate steps to increase and improve the fighting readiness of the state militia to fight any attempt made by the South to secede. "This," he concluded, "as a citizen of Illinois and a lover of the Union, I call upon you to do."[3] Senator Shields, who also was in anti-slavery man, and Representative Bissell wrote to Gustave Koerner "alarming letters" from Washington describing the arrogance and intransigence of the Southerners in Congress who talked openly of leaving the Union. Shields reported that after his strong speech in the Senate, advocating the admission of California as a free state, he was warmly congratulated by Clay and Webster.[4]

In order to break the impasse and to bring some lasting settlement in the North-South controversy, Henry Clay presented on January 29, 1850, a series of compromise resolutions that provided for the admission of California as a free state while New Mexico and Utah were to be left to decide by a popular vote whether to admit slavery. Slave trade in the District of Columbia was to be abolished. In order to gain the support of the South for his compromise settlement, Clay recommended the passage of a stringent Fugitive Slave Law and compensation to the state of Texas. The Illinois Congressional delegation threw its support to Clay's effort. This support was crucial because the senior senator from Illinois, Stephen A. Douglas, was the chairman of the Senate Committee on the Territories, while Representative John A. McClernand chaired the same committee of the House. Douglas was generally in favor of Clay's measures, although he doubted the wisdom of presenting them in a package deal.[5] The

[2] Bessie Louise Pierce, *A History of Chicago* (New York, 1940), II, 192–93.
[3] Cole, *op. cit.*, p. 66.
[4] Koerner, *Memoirs*, I, 553.
[5] *Cong. Globe*, 31 Cong. 1st Sess., p. 364.

Illinois press generally supported the compromise. The *Chicago Daily Journal* castigated John C. Calhoun for his willingness to "ignobly immolate the Union," and praised the Kentucky statesman for "pleading in tones of thrilling eloquence, with a voice sounding like a prophet's word . . . that the Union may be preserved." [6] Douglas and Shields voted for all the measures of the compromise, but were absent from the Senate when the vote on the law for the return of fugitive slaves was taken.[7] Douglas' opponents charged that his excuse that he had to be absent from the capital on business was a pretext and that he and his colleague were too cowardly to take a stand on a measure that was widely opposed in their home state.[8] The Chicago Common Council denounced the senators and congressmen who voted for the Fugitive Slave Law and ironically referred to those who "sneaked away from their seats" when the vote was taken.[9]

The growing opposition in Illinois to the extension of slavery into the free territories and to the threats of secession was clearly and forcefully expressed by Colonel William H. Bissell, a close friend of Trumbull from Belleville, in a speech he delivered in the House on February 21, 1850. Speaking directly to his colleagues from the South, Bissell observed that slavery had become the curse of the nation because it was the main source of strife and trouble for the last three decades. He continued, "I know the people of my state. I know the people of the great west and northwest; I know their devotion to the American Union. And I feel warranted in saying in my place here that when you talk to them of destroying this Union, there is not a man throughout that vast region who will not raise his hand and swear by the Eternal God, as I now do, it shall never be done, if our arms can save it. Illinois proffered to the country

---

[6] *Chicago Daily Journal,* March 6, 1850.

[7] *Cong. Globe,* 32 Cong., 1st Sess., Appendix 65.

[8] The *Ottawa Free Trader* wrote, "The law will be a dead letter. It cannot be enforced." See also the *Alton Telegraph,* October 22, 1850; *Chicago Daily Journal,* October 26, 1850; *Aurora Beacon,* October 24, 1850.

[9] *Chicago Daily Journal,* October 22, 1850.

nine regiments to aid in the vindication of her rights in the war with Mexico. And should danger threaten the Union from any source, or any quarter, in the South, she will be ready to furnish twice, thrice, yes, four times that number, to march where that danger may be, to return when it is passed or return no more." [10] The Southerners did not often hear in the halls of Congress such an eloquent and firm warning against an attempt to break up the Union.

Reflecting Bissell's sentiments, the Illinois Legislature, in January, 1851, passed a joint resolution that deprecated the slavery controversy and expressed strong support for the Clay compromise. The Illinois Congressional delegation was instructed to resist any attempt to undermine the Clay settlement.[11] Illinois wanted an end to the slavery agitation and was determined to sanction the Compromise of 1850, however imperfect, as the basis for peace between the North and the South. Trumbull, in deference to the high judicial post he was occupying, refrained from expressing his views on political questions, but as he told the Senate in 1859, he was strongly in favor of the compromise. He was happy when President Pierce in his inaugural address, early in 1853, expressed his support for the Clay measures as a basis of policies on the slavery issue.[12]

In the 1852 elections Trumbull was re-elected to the Supreme Court for a full nine-year term, virtually without opposition, but he was not happy on the bench. He was a politician who enjoyed the excitement of Illinois politics, and he chafed under the customary restriction on political activities by judges. The restraint became increasingly unbearable as the conflict over the extension of slavery was intensified. He was strongly opposed to any inroads of slavery into the free territories and deeply

[10] *Illinois State Register*, March 19, 1850; the Whig paper, the *Illinois State Journal*, endorsed Bissell's views with a call, "Rally! Friends of the Union, Rally!" May 2, 1850.

[11] *Laws of the State of Illinois, 1849–1869* (Springfield, Ill., 1849–1869), pp. 205–207.

[12] *Cong. Globe*, 36 Cong., 1st Sess., p. 39.

resented, as a strong Union man, threats of secession uttered from time to time by the Southern representatives in and out of Congress. In addition, the salary of $1,500 per year was insufficient to support his family. After considerable soul-searching he decided in 1853 to resign from the bench and to resume the private practice of law.[13]

The introduction by Senator Douglas of the Nebraska bill on January 4, 1854, brought Trumbull, as it did Abraham Lincoln, from political retirement. Indignation in Illinois ran high. The abolitionist agitation, which was subdued for a long time, was revived. Both the Whig and Democratic papers in Alton devoted little space to the slavery question in the years 1851–53. The Compromise of 1850 was *the* settlement and Illinois was content to accept the fact that both the Whigs and the Democrats in their respective national conventions in 1852 officially affirmed that they would "adhere to a faithful execution of the acts known as the compromise measure settled by the last Congress." [14] Both papers contained, in December of 1854, no warnings of the impending crisis.

Douglas' bill, which called for the creation of the "Territory of Nebraska" and was accompanied by a report from the Senate Committee on the Territories, which gave the people of the territory the right to vote slavery up or down, shattered the relative calm on the slavery question that settled after 1850.[15] The bill itself contained a clause that read, "And when admitted as a State or States, the said Territory, or any portion of the same, shall be received into the Union, with or without slavery,

[13] Moses had suggested that the resignation was caused by "failing health." This does not seem to be a plausible explanation because although it was true that Trumbull was occasionally ill, he had a remarkably sturdy constitution, and on the whole enjoyed good health. Moses, *op. cit.*, p. 594.

[14] The quote is from the 1852 Democratic platform as cited in Allan Nevins, *Ordeal of the Union: A House Dividing* (New York, 1947), p. 22. See also Charles A. Church, *History of the Republican Party in Illinois, 1854–1912* (Rockford, Ill., 1912).

[15] Nevins, *op. cit.*, p. 94. Also George Fort Milton, *The Eve of Conflict: Stephen A. Douglas and the Needless War* (Boston, 1934), p. 113.

as their constitution may prescribe at the time of their admission." [16] The Southerners would not accept this ambiguous wording and Douglas, presented with a virtual ultimatum served on him by Senators Atchison of Missouri, Butler of South Carolina, and Mason and Hunter of Virginia, capitulated; and on January 10, the *Washington Sentinel* printed the measure with an added section, which, as Douglas explained, had been left out from the original bill by a "clerical error." [17] The new section explicitly took away from Congress the power to legislate on slavery in the new territory and left the decision for or against slavery exclusively to the people residing in it. It also affirmed that the Fugitive Slave Law was binding on the territories as well as on the states. The added section dealt a death blow to the 1820 Missouri Compromise, which was considered sacred by the people of the North for more than three decades. They had looked upon it as the only effective barrier to the spread of slavery over the entire country. But the bill as it stood did not specifically repeal the compromise. Even the addition of the crucial section did not satisfy the representatives of the South, and Senator Archibald Dixon of Kentucky introduced an amendment repealing the Missouri Compromise. [18] The Southern Senators gave the amendment their vigorous support and Douglas promptly accepted it although he foresaw that his decision would "raise the hell of a storm." [19]

However patriotic were the reasons that caused him to capitulate to the demands of the Southern extremists, the results of his action were disastrous for the nation and eventually for Douglas himself. He delivered a death blow to the Whig party and inflicted a nearly fatal blow to the Democratic party, from which it was not to recover for many decades. The uneasy truce

[16] Nevins, *loc. cit.*

[17] *Washington Sentinel*, January 10, 1854.

[18] See H. B. Learned, "Relation of Phillip Phillips to the Repeal of the Missouri Compromise," *Mississippi Valley Historical Review*, VIII, 303–17.

[19] Susan B. Dixon, *True History of the Missouri Compromise and Its Repeal, by Mrs. Archibald Dixon* (Cincinnati, 1899), 442–44.

between the North and the South that was established by the joint efforts of Henry Clay and Daniel Webster was ended, and the moderates on the slavery question, both Whigs and Democrats, were forcibly pushed into the arms of free-soilism and abolitionism. Douglas was legally correct in asserting that his original bill did, de facto, repeal the Missouri Compromise, but he apparently failed to realize that the formal repeal would arouse bitter opposition. His bill caused the North to feel threatened by the removal of the firm line of demarcation between the free and the slave states. Douglas had no reason to be surprised at the storm that his bill raised, because he had himself affirmed the sacredness of the Missouri Compromise in a speech he made in Springfield on October 23, 1849. He stated, "The Missouri Compromise is tantamount to the compromises of the Constitution as our fathers made them. It has been canonized in the hearts of the American people, which no ruthless hand ought to disturb." [20]

Nevins, after considering the theories advanced to explain Douglas' action, including his interest in the building of the Pacific railroad, his Presidential ambitions, and his desire to assure the re-election to the Senate of his friend, Atchison, stated that the most mystifying aspect of this baffling question was Douglas' "curiously blind and callous" attitude to the free-soil opinion.[21] What was even more surprising was the degree to which this able and experienced politician, who had been a grass roots politician in Illinois and who had held several state and judicial posts, misjudged and underestimated the opposition that his action would arouse in his home state. This failure to correctly judge the mood of his own constituents was probably caused by his indifference to the issue of slavery and his belief in the inferiority of the Negro race. He refused to believe that

----

[20] *Illinois State Register*, November 8, 1849. Koerner recalling this speech charged that in introducing the Kansas-Nebraska Act, "Douglas had his eye fixed on the Presidency." Koerner, *Memoirs*, I, 616.

[21] Nevins, *op. cit.*, p. 107.

people could really become concerned about the fate of the miserable blacks. But Douglas' blunder may also have been caused by his vanity. His speeches in the Senate and his speeches delivered in the 1858 debates with Lincoln indicate that Douglas often underestimated his opposition.[22] Carl Schurz, who visited Washington in 1854 and listened for many hours to the debates on the Nebraska bill, recalled that "there was something in his [Douglas'] manners which very strongly smacked of the barroom. . . . And when then I saw him on the floor of the Senate plead his cause with the most daring sophistries and in a tone of most overbearing and almost ruffianly aggressiveness, and yet, undeniably with very great force and consummate cunning, I thought I recognized in him the very embodiment of that unscrupulous, reckless demagogy which, in my study of history has told me, is so dangerous to republics." [23]

The reaction in Illinois to the passage of the Kansas-Nebraska Act, which was signed by President Pierce on May 30, was swift and bitter. The Missouri Compromise had in Illinois an added sanctity because the bill incorporating the compromise measure was introduced in the Senate by Senator Jesse B. Thomas of Illinois. Thus it was particularly important to the people of Illinois, who took natural pride in a measure which was generally credited with saving and preserving the internal peace and tranquillity of the nation. In a revealing comment, Gustave Koerner pointed out that the Missouri Compromise, when it was adopted, was considered a generous concession by the North to the South and not vice versa. He wrote, "The Missouri Compromise . . . was a Southern measure, voted for at the time by the entire Southern delegation in Congress, *considered a great concession to the South, as Missouri was admitted as a slave state only on condition that the other territory west of it*

---

[22] Douglas told his brother-in-law a few years later, "I passed the Kansas-Nebraska Act myself. I had the authority and the power of a dictator throughout the whole controversy in both houses. The speeches were nothing. It was a marshalling and directing of men and guarding from attacks and with a ceaseless vigilance preventing surprises." Nevins, *op. cit.*, p. 113.

[23] *The Autobiography of Carl Schurz* (New York, 1961), 116–17.

should be forever free." [24] Many Illinoisans, particularly the free-soilers of Chicago, generally supported the Compromise of 1850 but considered the Fugitive Slave Law too high a price to pay for it. Now they were being asked to throw the Missouri Compromise into the bargain.

Douglas' opponents, anti-Nebraska Democrats and Whigs alike, had shrewdly decided to concentrate their entire campaign on the repeal of the Missouri Compromise almost to the total exclusion of other issues. Reporting on a mass protest meeting held in Alton, the *Telegraph* stated, "The meeting was composed of all classes, and Democrats, Whigs and Free Soilers, Germans, Irish and Americans met together with one common impulse; and forgetting all other consideration, seemed to be moved only by a strong and deep indignation against the authors of the repeal of the Missouri Compromise." [25] When an anti-Nebraska meeting at Ottawa passed a resolution asking for repeal of the Fugitive Slave Law, it was promptly rebuked by the anti-Nebraska press as distracting the people from the central issue. [26]

The *Illinois State Journal* blamed the Kansas-Nebraska bill on Douglas' ambition to become President and said, "We had hoped to gain a short respite from the old din of 'slavery agitation' and 'slavery extension' that has been warring in our country so often for the last twenty years but it seems that it is about to be let in upon us again, more repulsive and disgusting than ever." The influential paper warned that should the Douglas measure pass it would "rouse every sleeping energy of abolition fanaticism in the country." [27] The *Chicago Tribune* wrote that the "Nebraska Bill opens a great highway for the onward march of slavery. . . . Between slavery and liberty we cannot hesitate. If we must choose, we choose where humanity stands upright and free. We will give no quarter to traitors, but follow to his political grave every man who betrays freedom." [28] The largest group of Democratic voters that deserted Douglas were the Germans of Chicago

[24] Koerner, *Memoirs,* II, 25. (Italics mine.)
[25] *Daily Alton Telegraph,* June 5, 1854.
[26] *Ibid.,* August 11, 1854.
[27] *Illinois State Journal,* January 19, 22, 1854.
[28] *Chicago Tribune,* March 12, 1854.

and Belleville. Under the leadership of Lieutenant Governor Koerner of Belleville and George Schneider, the editor of the *Illinois Staats Zeitung*, the Germans denounced the repeal of the Missouri Compromise and presented a petition, through Koerner, to the Illinois Legislature urging it to repudiate the Nebraska Act. In Chicago, in March of 1854, the German population staged a mass protest rally. The speakers bitterly attacked Douglas as a "blemish on the honor of the State of Illinois." [29] The Germans, disregarding the prevailing caution of Douglas' opponents, stated in a solemn resolution that it was "high time to make war not only against the Nebraska bill, but in general stand upon the offensive . . . in reducing the slaveholding interest from its present position of a leading power to what it really is, a local institution existing by sufferance." The resolution was indicative of the feeling shared by many anti-slavery men in Illinois that the Nebraska bill was the result of the appeasement policies pursued in dealing with an aggressive and arrogant South. In reading the verbatim reports on the speeches made by the anti-Nebraska leaders at countless protest meetings held throughout the state, one constantly comes across the slogan "Slavery is Sectional, Liberty is National." The Missouri Compromise and extension of slavery were the issues on which no compromise was possible.

If Douglas counted on loyal support from the Democratic press in Illinois, he was disappointed. Only two newspapers of some influence in the state, the *Illinois State Register* and the *Quincy Herald*, supported the Democratic leader and his policies on Kansas.[30] Even Douglas' close friend, Charles Lanphier, the editor of the *Register*, did not have his heart in the fight but was merely putting up a brave front. The paper was clearly on

[29] *Daily Alton Telegraph*, March 23, 1854. See also Milton, *op. cit.*, p. 207; Koerner, *Memoirs*, Vol. I.

[30] Report on the reaction to Douglas' policy in the Democratic Press in Illinois published in the *Daily Alton Telegraph*, February 4, 1854. The *Belleville Advocate*, a Democratic paper, attacked Douglas for his support of the repeal of the Missouri Compromise, March 8, 22, 1854.

the defensive and its defense of the Nebraska bill centered on its support for the democratic principle of the right of the people to govern themselves. "The people of the territories," it wrote, "should be permitted to establish such domestic institutions and police regulations as may best be adapted to their wants. . . ." [31] Exasperated by the attacks on Douglas, the *Register* began to refer to his opponents as "Black Abolitionists." [32] In the midst of the storm, the *Register* consoled its readers with: "It has been an explosion, it is true, for it has been both brief and loud, but it began and ended in nothing." [33]

In spite of the growing swell of public protest, Douglas was successful in having the Illinois legislature pass a resolution endorsing the Nebraska bill. But it was a pyrrhic victory because it revealed within the Democratic party the emergence of a strong anti-Nebraska faction that adamantly rejected Douglas' leadership on the Kansas issue and that did not hesitate to bolt the party ranks and vote with the Whigs.[34]

The resolution to endorse the Kansas-Nebraska Act was introduced by Senator E. Omelvany, a lawyer from Belleville. Senator John M. Palmer, a Democrat from Carlinville, rose and offered a counter-resolution which stated that "the Missouri Compromise and the compromise measures of 1850 provide for a satisfactory and final settlement of the subject of slavery. . . ." [35] Among the Democrats who voted in the Senate against Douglas' policies were, in addition to John Palmer, two other influential Democratic leaders, Norman B. Judd of Chicago and Burton C. Cook of Ottawa, LaSalle County.[36] All three of these men later

---

[31] *Illinois State Register,* January 10, 1861.
[32] *Ibid.,* April 11, May 24, June 30, 1854.
[33] *Ibid.,* May 3, 1854.
[34] The *Alton Weekly Journal* urged that the legislature take no stand on the Nebraska bill because it was under consideration by Congress, March 2, 1854; and the *Telegraph* denounced, "Time serving politicians and ambitious demagogues [who] . . . have decided in favor of slavery in Kansas and Nebraska but the people themselves will yet speak. . . ." February 28, 1854.
[35] *Palmer, Personal Recollections,* p. 60.
[36] *Illinois State Register,* February 24, 1854.

became Trumbull's close political associates in the anti-Nebraska movement. Gradually, the bitterness of Douglas and his supporters made the position of the anti-Nebraska-ites within the Democratic party untenable. A few months after the vote in the Senate endorsing Douglas by vote of 14 to 8, Palmer addressed a Fourth of July patriotic rally at Virden, Sangamon County. His remarks about the true meaning of the first paragraph of the Declaration of Independence aroused a storm of protest from the pro-slavery listeners. "Before I left the ground," he related, "I was convinced that the Democratic Party was hopelessly divided and that the repeal of the Missouri Compromise had stirred up passions that could not be allayed. . . ." [37] Palmer's conviction that a new party was needed to fight for a free Kansas was shared by many anti-slavery Democrats. In May, Wentworth's *Chicago Democrat* denounced Douglas and his course on Kansas.[38] Meetings of anti-Nebraska Democrats were held in many parts of the state. A meeting at Freeport adopted a resolution to organize a new political party. It read, "Resolved, that the free states should now blot out all former political distinctions by uniting themselves into one great Northern Party and pledge their property and lives that there shall be no further extension of slavery, either by the abrogation of the Missouri Compromise or annexation from Mexico or Spain.[39]

Deeply concerned with the rise of the anti-Nebraska sentiment in Illinois, Douglas came to the state to address a number of "Vindication meetings." The first such meeting was to be held in Chicago on September 1. It was rumored for several weeks before Douglas' arrival that the anti-Nebraska and Whig elements were preparing hostile demonstrations for his reception. The *Illinois State Register* charged that the Whig and anti-Nebraska papers, and especially the *Tribune*, were stirring

[37] Palmer, *op. cit.*, p. 63.
[38] *Weekly Chicago Democrat*, May 27, 1854.
[39] *Illinois State Register*, April 4, 1854. On April 5, the *Illinois State Journal* endorsed the Freeport resolution and on September 10, the *Illinois Staats Zeitung* called for the establishment of a new "Freedom Party."

up the mob to make Douglas' stay in the city very uncomfortable.[40] The charge was at least partly true, because the *Tribune* did resort to a campaign of personal vilification against Douglas, coupled with attacks on Douglas' Irish supporters and his Catholic wife. One editorial said that Douglas, once loved and respected in Chicago, was now "almost universally despised, hated and condemned." [41] On the morning of the day of the meeting, the *Tribune* warned that "if he attempts to get up what he calls a vindication of his crimes; if he collects around him a crowd of Irish rowdies and groghouse politicians, and attempts to send forth their approbation as the 'voice of the people of Chicago' it will not be our fault if he arouses a lion which he cannot tame." [42] On the day of the meeting flags in the harbors were lowered at half mast and the church bells were tolling in protest, but in the evening eight thousand people came to hear Douglas. The meeting was a stormy one, because Douglas was heckled continuously by a hostile group in the audience. As the heckling, the groans and the hisses grew, the speaker became very much annoyed. The derogatory references to his opponents made the heckling and the interruptions even more frequent.[43] Doggedly, Douglas continued to defend his position on Kansas and bitterly attacked the anti-Nebraska-ites and the Know-Nothings.[44] From Chicago, Douglas proceeded to other cities, often followed by Lincoln and Trumbull, who denounced him for the repeal of the Missouri Compromise and for his indifference to the question of whether Kansas was to

[40] *Illinois State Register*, August 22, 1854.

[41] *Chicago Tribune*, August 29, 1854.

[42] Philip Kinsley, *The Chicago Tribune, Its First Hundred Years* (New York, 1943), p. 27.

[43] *Ibid*. See also Pierce, *op. cit.*, p. 209; Milton, *op. cit.*, p. 176; and Nevins, *op. cit.*, pp. 335–37.

[44] *Illinois State Journal*, October 17, 1854; *Alton Weekly Courier*, October 26, 1854. The *Daily Alton Telegraph* reported that at a mass anti-Nebraska meeting, held in Belleville, former Governor Reynolds "denounced the bill of Mr. Douglas as wrong, uncalled for, and contrary to the wishes of the American people. This frank avowal drew down the applause of the house." March 24, 1854.

be slave or free. Even such conservative Democratic leaders as ex-Governor John Reynolds and former State Supreme Court Judge Sidney Breese came out in opposition to Douglas.[45]

Opposition to the Nebraska Act proved to be a powerful force for unity. Anti-slavery men, including free-soilers, abolitionists, anti-slavery Whigs, and anti-Nebraska Democrats met at several conventions throughout the state in the summer of 1854. At the Ottawa meeting, the name "Republican" was suggested for the new anti-slavery party. The largest regional convention was held on August 30 at Rockford. It represented eight counties of northern Illinois and was called to "prevent the still further extension of slavery, and to protect the interests of free labor and free men." [46] The Rockford Convention adopted a set of strong anti-slavery resolutions, including the demand for a free Kansas, for Congressional legislation prohibiting slavery in the territories, for the abolition of slavery in the District of Columbia, and for the repeal of the Fugitive Slave Law.[47]

On September 7, 1854, a group of anti-slavery men issued, in Springfield, a call for a "mass convention" to be held at the State Capitol on October 5, the second day of the Illinois State Agricultural Fair. The call declared that the convention was called "for the organization of a party which shall put the government upon a Republican tack and to secure to non–slave holders throughout the Union their just and constitutional weight and influence in the councils of the nation." [48] The call did not spell out any abolitionist objectives; on the contrary it was a rather moderate appeal to anti-slavery men to meet and take counsel in an hour of peril to their common cause. Historians have generally referred to this Springfield convention as an abolitionist meeting attended by "anti-slavery radicals" [49] or by a "militantly

[45] Cole, op. cit., p. 128.
[46] Charles A. Church, History of the Republican Party in Illinois, 1854–1912 (Rockford, Ill., 1912), pp. 20–21.
[47] The Lincoln-Douglas Debates, p. 89.
[48] Church, op. cit., p. 23.
[49] Benjamin P. Thomas, Abraham Lincoln (New York, 1952), p. 152.

abolitionist group." [50] The source of these accounts is Herndon, who related that after Lincoln's speech Owen Lovejoy announced that a meeting of "all the friends of Freedom" would be held that evening. Herndon later wrote that to him that meant "of course the Abolitionists," and he advised Lincoln to leave town to avoid being branded an abolitionist by his opponents.[51] Lincoln indeed left Springfield under the pretext of having to attend court at Tazewell County. Herndon's account is generally used to prove Lincoln's moderation on the issue of slavery and his rejection of abolitionism. Whatever the merit of that contention, the Springfield anti-slavery convention can hardly be used as an argument for it.

Lincoln's speech on October 4, which included unequivocal condemnation of slavery, was cheered by the abolitionist leaders present. The *Illinois State Register* reported that "Ichabod [Codding] raved and Lovejoy swelled and all endorsed the sentiments of that speech." [52] Owen Lovejoy, who at that time was a United States Representative, is usually referred to as an abolitionist and a leader of the Springfield "Abolitionist Convention." The fact is, however, that Lovejoy, while an enemy of slavery and an opponent of the Fugitive Slave Law, had never, by his own testimony, advocated the abolition of slavery in the states where it existed. He said in a speech delivered at a mass meeting in Washington on December 23, 1861, "During my Congressional career, I have never voted for the abolition of

[50] Richard H. Luthin, *The Real Abraham Lincoln* (Englewood Cliffs, N. J., 1960), p. 177. However Nevins cautiously refers to the Springfield meeting as "a Republican Convention." *Op. cit.*, p. 339.

[51] *Herndon's Life of Lincoln,* ed. Paul M. Angle (New York, 1961), p. 300. It is of interest to note that only four years later, even those who were in Springfield in 1854 had difficulty in reconciling their recollections. Douglas, who as he had stated was in the hall, recalled that it was Codding, and not Lovejoy as Herndon stated, who announced the meeting of the Republican Convention. He asked all present not to stay in the Hall of the House to hear Douglas but to adjourn to the Senate Chamber. Douglas said he vividly recalled this scene. *The Lincoln-Douglas Debates,* pp. 117–18.

[52] *Illinois State Register,* October 12, 1854.

slavery in the States, as I did not conceive the Constitution gave me that power." [53]

An account of the Springfield convention written by Paul Selby, the editor of the *Jacksonville Morgan Journal*, who participated in the convention, has been largely overlooked. Selby disputed the idea that the convention was dominated by abolitionists and denied Herndon's assertion that it was attended by only twenty-six people. He maintained that the convention was well attended and that a great majority of its participants were as moderate in the actions they wanted taken to stop the extension of slavery as was Lincoln. He recalled that "some one raised the question whether Lincoln was in harmony with the views of the convention, and I remember it was Owen Lovejoy who responded with an earnest endorsement of Lincoln's position on the slavery question." [54] The resolutions adopted by this so-called "Abolitionist" convention were moderate, if not downright conservative. The platform condemned the Kansas-Nebraska Act and the repeal of the Missouri Compromise. It expressed opposition to the extension of slavery, but it did not demand the repeal of the Fugitive Slave Law, and it did not propose interference with slavery in the states where it existed. [55] "At this late date," Selby concluded, "after the name of Lincoln had been immortalized through the ages by his preservation of the union and the destruction of slavery, it is a poor tribute to his memory to picture him as resenting the act of a body of men who while honoring him with their confidence simply anticipated him in recognition of the necessity for that party organization in which he joined with patriotic zeal and enthusiasm two years later, and which finally resulted in his election to the Presidency." [56]

[53] Text of his speech in the *Bureau County Republican*, December 26, 1861. Abraham Lincoln testified that Lovejoy, who died in March, 1864, gave him unflinching support throughout his service in Congress during the Civil War. *The Living Lincoln*, ed. Paul M. Angle and Earl Schenck Miers (New Brunswick, N. J., 1955), p. 606.

[54] Paul Selby, "Genesis of the Republican Party in Illinois," *Transactions of the Illinois State Historical Society for the Year 1906* (Springfield, Ill., 1906), p. 277.

[55] *Ibid.*, p. 278.

[56] Selby, *op. cit.*, p. 288.

Lyman Trumbull was slated to answer Douglas' speech at the fair, which was to be delivered on October 3, but when Trumbull failed to arrive, Lincoln took his place and delivered a well-prepared speech. There is no indication as to the reason that caused Trumbull to fail to appear in the state capital on the appointed day, but he probably needed more time to determine his course in a confused political situation. Trumbull did come to the fair on Thursday, October 5, and it was announced that he would deliver a speech in answer to Douglas on that evening. In his speech, which, as even the reporter of the *Illinois State Register* was forced to admit, had a large audience, Trumbull attacked the Nebraska Act and decried the repeal of the Missouri Compromise. He ridiculed Douglas' theory of "popular sovereignty" and charged that it was designed to make Kansas a slave state. The *Register* stated that "he closed his speech in an argument against slavery in the usual abolition style and was greatly cheered by the members of the fusion convention, all of whom are present." [57] Another report said that the speech of "Judge Trumbull of Alton, the most prominent anti-Nebraska Democrat in the southern part of the state," lasted three and one-half hours and "was widely copied in the press of the state as a representative anti-Nebraska doctrine. Lincoln, through the influence of his friend Herndon, was given extravagant praise in the *Journal* of Springfield, but his speech created no widespread comment throughout the state such as Herndon would have us believe." [58]

By the time the fair was held, Trumbull had already decided to become a candidate for the House seat from the Eighth District. Since the Congressional elections were coming soon, his speech to the throngs that gathered at Springfield was important to his future political career. He had to prove to his fellow anti-Nebraska-ites and to the Whigs that he was a militant and effective speaker who, if elected, would be able to match Douglas' admitted power to sway his listeners. Trumbull was also called

[57] *Illinois State Register,* October 12, 1854.
[58] *Chicago Democratic Press,* October 6, 1854.

upon to prove that he was a speaker with a mass appeal who could please a partisan crowd by an aggressive and rousing speech. All contemporary accounts indicate that he passed the test. "The crowd during the whole time was very large," wrote the Springfield correspondent of the *Telegraph,* "and during the delivery of Judge Trumbull's speech, more compact and solid even than when Douglas spoke. . . . Judge Trumbull was argumentative throughout and made the clearest and most convincing speech against the Nebraska bill and the repeal of the Missouri Compromise. . . . Trumbull, by his effort, won golden opinions from all the parties, and has proved himself one of the most powerful breasted [sic] in the country." [59]

Why did Trumbull, who vowed after his defeat in the Congressional election in 1846 not to enter politics, change his mind and decide to run again? During most of 1853 and 1854, Trumbull was dangerously ill and Dr. Jayne and other doctors were unable to diagnose or to treat his illness. Trumbull and his family did not believe that he would recover. Coincidentally, Trumbull's recovery began when the news of the passage of Douglas' Anti-Nebraska Act reached Alton. Julia Trumbull believed that her husband's recovery was an act of God to allow Lyman to lead the battle against the spread of slavery. Two years later, in an emotion charged letter, she wrote to her husband: "I regard your long illness as but a preparation for your present position. In Alton, when life seemed to be receding from you, you felt how unsatisfying were all those aims which had their accomplishment in this world, and resolved that you would seek something beyond. God heard the solemn promise, the recording Angel marked it down and health and strength began to return." [60]

Trumbull himself had a more prosaic explanation for his return to political life. He wrote to his brother John: "You were perhaps surprised to learn that I had gone into politics again—I

[59] *Daily Alton Telegraph,* October 7, 1854.
[60] Julia Jayne Trumbull to Lyman Trumbull, April 10, 1856, L. T. Family Papers.

am surprised at myself and but for the slavery question . . . I should not have taken any active part in recent elections." [61]

Upon his return to Belleville, Trumbull turned his attention to the forthcoming Congressional elections. When Colonel Bissell announced in July, 1854, that because of illness he would not be a candidate for re-election to Congress from the Eighth District, which centered around Alton and Belleville, the Democrats were faced with an almost impossible task to nominate a successor acceptable to all factions of the party.[62] The anti-Nebraska Democrats, led by Trumbull, Koerner, and Judge William H. Underwood, served notice that they would not support any pro-Nebraska nominee, and when the Democratic Convention of the Eighth Congressional District met on September 5, 1854, at Carlyle, it was split so deeply on the Nebraska issue that it adjourned without naming a candidate.[63] It was obvious that the old party lines were becoming blurred and that there would be two candidates in the election, a Douglas Nebraska-ite and an anti-Nebraska-ite supported by many Democrats and Whigs. The Whig leaders in the district, realizing that they had no chance to elect their own man, announced that they would support an anti-Nebraska Democrat and urged Trumbull or Underwood to run.

On September 9, Philip B. Fouke, a Belleville lawyer and former Prosecuting Attorney of St. Clair County, announced his candidacy and stated his support for the Kansas-Nebraska Act and for the repeal of the Missouri Compromise. The Whig *Telegraph* commented, "Whoever has the stomach to swallow these two measures, will find no difficulty in swallowing Mr. Fouke." [64] Since Fouke was a formidable speaker and a man of courage and conviction, it was generally realized by the leaders of the anti-Nebraska camp that they could win only by uniting

[61] Lyman Trumbull to John Trumbull, December 4, 1854, L. T. Family Papers.
[62] *Daily Alton Telegraph,* July 25, 1854.
[63] *Ibid.,* September 8, 1854.
[64] *Daily Alton Telegraph,* September 9, 1854.

in support of a formidable candidate. When indications multi-
plied that Trumbull was ready to take the plunge, Gustave
Koerner and Judge Underwood publicly declined to enter the
contest, and the Whig leader, Joseph Gillespie, who was widely
mentioned as willing to make the race, removed himself from
consideration and announced that he would run for re-election
as a state senator.[65]

On October 10, a month after Fouke had been in the field
conducting a furious campaign, Trumbull announced his candidacy. He was promptly endorsed by the Democratic and the
Whig newspapers in Alton. The *Courier* praised Trumbull
as a man of unimpeachable character and excellent judicial
temperament and as a conservative upholder of the Constitution. The paper based its endorsement primarily on Trumbull's
opposition to the extension of slavery and the repeal of the
Missouri Compromise.[66] The *Telegraph* praised Trumbull, "an
unquestioned Democrat," for his opposition to the Nebraska
bill. "All we care to know," the editorial said, "is that he is opposed to the principle contained in the Kansas-Nebraska bill and
that he regards the repeal of the Missouri Compromise as a violation of national honor and good faith. In accepting this *single
issue*, we make no war upon the South, nor attack the institution
of slavery where it exists." [67] The editorial quoted Trumbull as
having said that he regarded the Missouri Compromise as "a
compact whose origin was akin to that of the Constitution" and
that its repeal was a "villainous breach of faith." [68]

Trumbull conducted an aggressive campaign.[69] He often addressed several meetings in a single day and proved himself to
be effective on the stump. His lack of oratorical talents and emotional appeal seemed to have been offset by his excellent abilities

[65] *Ibid.*, September 26, 1854.
[66] *Alton Courier*, October 14, 1854.
[67] *Daily Alton Telegraph*, October 10, 1854. (Italics mine.)
[68] *Ibid.*
[69] Koerner, *Memoirs*, I, 617.

as a debater.[70] The campaign was bitter and it attracted state-wide attention. The *Chicago Times* called for the people in the district to vote for Fouke and announced that the support of the Nebraska bill was the test for any "real" Democrat. The *Illinois State Register* charged Trumbull with having made promises of rewards to his Whig supporters.[71] On the other hand, Trumbull was greatly helped by the solid endorsement he received from the thousands of Germans who had settled in St. Clair County. The eighteen thousand German immigrants in the county deserted the Democratic party in mass because of their opposition to the extension of slavery.

In spite of the efforts of Trumbull's Democratic and Whig supporters, his election victory came only "by the greatest efforts." The effort needed was so great that there was considerable resentment in Belleville and in Alton when in February of the next year Trumbull resigned his seat in the House to run for the Senate and thus made it possible for the Democrats to capture the district. Trumbull won by a majority of about 2,700 votes, seemingly a decisive victory However, an analysis of the voting results shows that the victory was made possible only by an overwhelming plurality that Trumbull received in his home county of Madison. The vote in Madison County was 2,232 for Trumbull and 364 for Fouke. His townspeople in Alton gave Trumbull 386 votes to 33 for his opponent.[72] Never before did Trumbull's political future look brighter.

[70] *Daily Alton Telegraph,* October 26, 1854.
[71] *Chicago Times,* October 31, 1854. *Illinois State Register,* October 12, 1854.
[72] *Daily Alton Telegraph,* November 7, 1854. See also Church, *op. cit.,* p. 25.

5

The Anti-Nebraska
Junior Senator from Illinois

LESS THAN TWO WEEKS AFTER HIS ELECTION TO CONGRESS, TRUM-
bull was already deeply concerned with the forthcoming election
of a United States senator from Illinois, which was scheduled to
take place early in February. He was determined, if he could, to
prevent the re-election of James Shields whom he cordially disliked from the days of his feud with Governor Ford. He also
did not want to see any other Nebraska Democrat sent to the
Senate as Douglas' colleague.

The election, and the bitterness it engendered between Trumbull and his followers and the Nebraska pro-Douglas men,
forced Trumbull to give serious consideration to his position
in the Democratic party. The hard-fought campaign in the
Eighth Congressional District underscored the split in the
Democratic party. Trumbull, who was repeatedly attacked as a
renegade and traitor, wrote to Palmer that he was surprised to
find, on his tour of southern Illinois, a great deal of bitterness
manifested by the pro-Douglas men. "If the feeling of the
Nebraskaites . . . is to prevail, we are to have war to the knife,

and every anti-Nebraska Democrat is to be crushed, if they have the power to do it." [1] In the same letter Trumbull adroitly probed Palmer, who was re-elected to the Illinois Senate, about his views on the forthcoming election of a United States Senator. It was quite clear from the letter that Trumbull would have liked very much to replace James Shields in the Senate in order to have an opportunity to cross swords with Douglas on the Nebraska issue. But keeping in mind that he had just been elected to Congress after a bitter struggle and by a narrow margin, he told his friend that while "there are many reasons why I wish Shields defeated and I would be for almost any man as against him . . . it would be exceedingly impolitic for me to think of being a candidate." [2] Nevertheless, Palmer must have understood that Trumbull was a candidate from the suggestions or polite instructions he gave to the small anti-Nebraska group in the Illinois Assembly. He told them to be mindful of the fact that while small, they constituted the balance of power and could well decide the election, and suggested that they work for a united stand of the anti-Nebraska men in the General Assembly. He instructed them not to attend the Democratic caucus in order not to be bound by party discipline on the decisions taken. Shrewdly analyzing the political situation, Trumbull added, "Yourself, Judd, and Cook could control this matter in the Senate and in the House." He affirmed his desire to do all that was possible to "attain the end we all have in view, the triumph of Freedom over Slavery." [3] Trumbull's would-be rival for the Senate election, Abraham Lincoln, foresaw the probability of Trumbull wanting a Senate seat. In a letter to his Whig friend, Joseph Gillespie, he asked him to ascertain "whether Trumbull

[1] Lyman Trumbull to John M. Palmer, November 23, 1854, "A Collection of Letters from Lyman Trumbull to John M. Palmer, 1854–1858," ed. George T. Palmer, *Journal of the Illinois State Historical Society*, Springfield, Ill., April-July, 1923, p. 21.
[2] *Ibid.*, p. 22.
[3] *Ibid.*, p. 23.

intends to make a push. If he does, I suppose the two men in St. Clair and one or both in Madison will be for him." [4]

There is no reason to believe that the contemplated break with the Democratic party was particularly painful to Trumbull. He was not, by the testimony of his contemporaries, and the evidence of his political career, a party man. Many years later, Trumbull said, "I was never a party man to the extent of being willing to serve the party against my country. . . ." [5] and Clarence Darrow said of him that he "has been too consistent to bind himself irretrievably to any party." [6] Dedicated as he was to the fight against Douglas' policies, he was ready to incur the wrath of some of his Belleville and Alton friends and make a bid for the Senate election.

When the legislature met in Springfield, the situation was uncertain and confused. The Nebraska group was ready to dump Shields, who became a liability because of his ambivalent attitude to the Kansas-Nebraska bill, and elect Governor Joel Matteson. Shields, a known anti-slavery man long opposed to the extension of slavery, had voted for the Nebraska bill. When pressed for an explanation, the popular Irishman, whose many friends included anti-Nebraska-ites (among them his former law partner Lieutenant Governor Gustave Koerner), at first explained his vote by pointing to the instructions of the Illinois Legislature and stressed his personal loyalty to Douglas. However, these excuses apparently proved too galling to a proud and gallant man, and on October 11, 1854, speaking in Paris, Illinois, he threw caution to the winds and denied that his stand resulted from the vote of the Illinois Legislature and stated that he "voted conscientiously for the bill." [7] This statement made it impossible for any anti-Nebraska Democrats or Whigs to support him. The Nebraska camp was split, with the men closest

[4] Lincoln to Joseph Gillespie, December 1, 1854, *The Living Lincoln*, p. 181.
[5] White, *op. cit.*, p. 398.
[6] *Chicago Tribune*, October 7, 1894.
[7] *Wabash Valley Republican*, clipped in the *Daily Alton Telegraph*, October 26, 1854.

to Douglas favoring Shields, while others supported Governor Matteson.

The Douglas men were in a quandary because the House of Representatives showed its anti-Nebraska sentiments by voting 41 to 32 for Owen Lovejoy's resolution to restore the Missouri Compromise.[8] Since the situation in the Senate was also uncertain, the Nebraska group decided not to act on the resolution calling for the convening of the General Assembly for the purpose of electing a senator. Lincoln foresaw that the Nebraska-ites would attempt to "stave off the election if they can," [9] and the *Alton Telegraph* was sure on Wednesday morning, February 7, that the election would be postponed to a special session of the legislature sometime in October. The paper reported that the anti-Nebraska group of three senators and two representatives "fluctuated between Messrs. Underwood and Trumbull."

Abraham Lincoln, with the aid of David Davis and Leonard Swett, was campaigning furiously for his election.[10] He was, in the words of Herndon, like "a little engine that knows no rest." Lincoln had resigned his seat in the Illinois House of Representatives to which he was elected in November.[11] Trumbull's chances depended upon his ability to hold the votes of the five anti-Nebraska-ites who held the balance of power in the General Assembly.

Apparently convinced that their candidate had a chance, the Nebraska men in the Senate gave up their opposition and moved, on Wednesday, February 7, for the adoption of the House resolution to convene both houses for the election of a senator. The motion, which was adopted by an overwhelming majority, fixed the election for the next day. The political fever and tension,

[8] *Daily Alton Telegraph,* February 9, 1855.

[9] *Ibid.*

[10] Willard L. King, *Lincoln's Manager, David Davis* (Cambridge, Mass., 1960), pp. 104–06. Also *Herndon's Life of Lincoln,* pp. 302–03.

[11] J. McCan Davis, "The Senator from Illinois—Some Famous Political Combats," *Transactions of the Illinois State Historical Society for the Year 1909* (Springfield, Ill., 1910), p. 88.

which were high during the entire session, climbed even higher. "The Capitol was a beehive of activity," wrote one eyewitness, ". . . Caucuses, whisperings in the dark corners, earnest conversations and general unquiet everywhere." [12] The outcome of the contest was in doubt. "Even not to the shrewdest of them," wrote a correspondent from Springfield, "was it known what would be the result of the next day's work." [13] The three major groups held caucuses which lasted until late into the night. The Nebraska-ites, prodded by Douglas, who relayed his instructions from Washington, voted to stand by Shields as long as possible. It was understood that in case the going for Shields got rough they would switch to Matteson.[14] The Whig caucus decided to make Lincoln their first choice, then allowed its members to vote as they wished. The anti-Nebraska Democrats, conscious of their key role as the balance of power, "made a mutual agreement to stand by Judge Trumbull in every emergency; to vote for him as long as there was even a faint hope of securing his election. . . ." [15] The anti-Nebraska group of five was small, but it consisted of determined and able men, including John M. Palmer, Norman B. Judd, and Burton C. Cook.

On Thursday, long before the appointed hour of three o'clock in the afternoon, the lobby and galleries of the Hall of the House of Representatives began to fill with senators, representatives, and their guests. Among the well-dressed and excited ladies in the gallery were Mrs. Lincoln and her friend Julia Jayne Trumbull. Lincoln and Trumbull circulated in the lobby talking to their friends. At three o'clock sharp, the senators, preceded by Lieutenant Governor Koerner, filed into the Hall of the House, and after the members of the assembly were sworn in, the balloting began. There were one hundred mem-

[12] The Springfield correspondent in the *Daily Alton Telegraph*, February 12, 1854.

[13] *Ibid.*

[14] Milton, *op. cit.*, pp. 201–02.

[15] *Daily Alton Telegraph*, Febrauary 12, 1855. (Italics mine.) See also *Chicago Weekly Democrat*, February 15, 1854, and *Belleville Advocate*, February 14, 1854.

bers, and the successful candidate needed fifty-one votes to be elected. On the first ballot Lincoln received 45 votes, Shields 41, Trumbull 5, and Matteson 1. The second and third ballots were inconclusive, with the five anti-Nebraska-ites voting for Trumbull. On the fourth ballot, Trumbull increased his vote to 11 and Lincoln's total dropped to 33, while the Nebraska group gave its 41 votes to Shields. The situation did not change on the fifth and sixth ballots. On the seventh ballot the Nebraska group switched to Matteson and picked up three votes to a total of 44. On the ninth ballot, Governor Matteson increased his lead to 47, and most Whigs and Know-Nothings switched from Lincoln to Trumbull, who received 35 votes.[16] Lincoln got 15 votes. It was clear that unless the Trumbull and Lincoln forces united, Matteson would be elected. Lincoln, who was in the lobby, sent his manager, John T. Stuart, who was Mrs. Lincoln's cousin and his former law partner, to confer with the anti-Nebraska men to ascertain whether they would consider voting for him. Stuart was informed by Palmer, Judd, and others that they could not vote for Lincoln, because they were pledged by the decision of their caucus to stick to Trumbull and considered themselves to be instructed by their constituents to vote only for an anti-Nebraska Democrat. In addition, they felt that since the majority of the legislature was Democratic, a Democrat should be elected.[17] After hearing Stuart's report, Lincoln instructed his friends to vote for Trumbull, who was elected on the tenth ballot after receiving no more than the minimum of 51 votes. The announcement of Trumbull's election was received with "prolonged cheers throughout the Hall." [18]

Mrs. Lincoln did not appreciate her husband's gesture and openly expressed her resentment. The election marked an end

[16] George T. Allen of Madison, one of the five anti-Nebraska insurgents, several years later boasted to Trumbull that he "managed to give him the entire Know-Nothing vote." George T. Allen to Trumbull, June 14, 1866, L. T. Papers.

[17] Lusk, *op. cit.*, p. 52. *Daily Alton Telegraph*, February 8, 1857.

[18] *Daily Alton Telegraph*, February 12, 1857. See also *Illinois State Journal*, February 9, 1854.

to her friendship with Julia Jayne Trumbull. Mrs. Trumbull wrote to her husband three months after the election from Springfield that Mary Lincoln publicly snubbed her. "Coming out of church," Julia wrote, "I took some pains to meet Mary, but she turned her head the other way and though I looked her full in the face, she pretended not to see me." [19]

Some years later, Mary Lincoln accused Trumbull of "cold, selfish treachery" in the 1855 election.[20] In contrast, Abraham Lincoln, when he met Julia Trumbull on the train from Chicago to Springfield, greeted her with great cordiality, took a seat near her, and regaled her with his stories.[21] Mary Lincoln also never forgave Norman Judd for his role in Trumbull's election and did all she could to thwart his political career.

The election was the cause of a life-long animosity between Trumbull and Judge David Davis, who in 1860 was Lincoln's manager in the Chicago Convention. Davis was absent from Springfield on the day of the election and felt that "Mr. Lincoln ought to have been elected . . . 46 men should not yield their preference to 5. [22] He explained to his brother-in-law that Trumbull's election made him unhappy because "he has been a Democrat all his life—dyed in the wool—as ultra as he could be. His antecedents don't suit me although I hope it will be all right." [23] Lincoln himself was deeply disappointed, but, being a forgiving man and a disciplined politician, he quickly reconciled himself to the turn to events. He admitted in a letter to Elihu B. Washburne that while the ordeal of the election lasted, he suffered an "agony," but that he felt satisfied with his decision to withdraw from the race in order to prevent the election of Matteson. He cautiously added: "On the whole, it is perhaps as well for our general cause that Trumbull is elected." [24]

[19] Julia Jayne Trumbull to Lyman Trumbull, April 14, 1856, L. T. Family Papers.
[20] Mary Lincoln to David Davis, September 12, 1865, Davis Papers, Chicago Historical Society.
[21] Julia Jayne Trumbull to Lyman Trumbull, April 6, 1856, L. T. Family Papers.
[22] King, op. cit., p. 108.
[23] Ibid., p. 108.
[24] Abraham Lincoln to Elihu B. Washburne, February 9, 1854, The Lincoln Reader (New York, 1954), pp. 225, 227. Horace White related, without giving

How did it happen that Trumbull, who had only five votes pledged to him with no party organization behind him, was elected to the Senate defeating Abraham Lincoln and Governor Matteson? Many factors contributed to this generally unexpected result. Douglas' preference for Shields prevented Governor Matteson from getting the needed majority on the eighth and ninth ballots. One can only imagine how the "Little Giant" reproached himself in later years for this miscalculation.

A friend wrote to Douglas from Illinois that "the severest blow we have received has been given us. . . . Trumbull is your personal enemy. His ambition will lead to such position as they [the anti-Nebraska Democrats] wish him to take—your enemy and their protector." [25] Two years later, during his debates with Lincoln in 1858, when the coalition of Lincoln and Trumbull threatened his dominant position in Illinois, Douglas made a desperate attempt to cause a split between his adversaries by charging that in 1855 Trumbull betrayed an agreement entered into with Lincoln to support the latter for the Senate in 1855, in exchange for Lincoln's support of Trumbull in the Senate election of 1858.[26]

Herndon's statement that "the student of history in after years will be taught to revere the name of Lincoln for his exceeding magnanimity in inducing his friends to abandon him . . . and save Trumbull, while he himself disappeared beneath the waves of defeat," [27] is touching and poetic but quite inaccurate. The fact was that Lincoln, unless he was prepared to send Matteson to the Senate, had no choice but to direct his remaining supporters to vote for Trumbull. It was not magnanimity but a sound assessment of the political situation and of the prospects for his own future career that made Lincoln do what he did.

---

a source for it, that at a reception given at the mansion of Ninian Edwards, in the evening after the election, Lincoln shook Trumbull's hand, saying, "Not too disappointed to congratulate my friend Trumbull." White, *op. cit.*, p. 45.

[25] James W. Sheahan to Stephen A. Douglas, February 8, 1855, Douglas Papers, University of Chicago.

[26] *The Lincoln-Douglas Debates*, pp. 296–97.

[27] *Herndon's Life of Lincoln*, p. 305. (Italics mine.)

John Moses, the Illinois historian, has pointed to a generally overlooked fact that of the senators who voted for Trumbull only three came from southern Illinois and out of the representatives only six resided south of Springfield. The election of Trumbull was a manifestation of the growth in the population, economy, and political influence of central and northern Illinois, which were for a long time dominated by the southern part of the state.[28]

The reaction to the election in the Whig and the anti-Nebraska newspapers indicated that in February of 1855 many people in Illinois considered Trumbull a greater man and a more effective politician than Abraham Lincoln. There was a widespread feeling that Trumbull, as a Democrat, would be able to fight it out with Douglas in the Senate more effectively than would the Whig Lincoln. There is evidence that the Whigs and the anti-Nebraska Democrats were impressed with Trumbull's ability as a debater and a stump speaker, an ability he had demonstrated during his campaign for Congress and at the Springfield tour. Gustave Koerner, who presided over the legislature that elected Trumbull, wrote that "No Democrat, I knew very well from my intimate knowledge of Trumbull's peculiar ability, could cope with Douglas better than he. He was as untiring and indefatigable in argument as Douglas; indeed, no one could wear him out . . . he was a master in discovering every weak point in the aims of his antagonist and never failed to hit it." [29]

Finally, there was a widespread conviction that only the election of Trumbull, an anti-Nebraska Democrat, could have induced thousands of like-minded Democrats to join the Whigs in a new anti-slavery party.[30] Taking into account the long-stand-

[28] Moses, *op. cit.*, p. 593.
[29] Koerner, *Memoirs*, I, 625.
[30] Lincoln's own organ, the *Illinois State Register*, wrote, "Mr. Lincoln's friends can well say that, while with his advice they ultimately cast their votes for, and assisted in the election of Mr. Trumbull, it was not 'because they loved Caesar less, but because they loved Rome more.'" February 9, 1855.

ing partisan animosities, the election of Lincoln could not have had a similar result. The many letters that Trumbull received in his first months in Washington from old-line Democrats attest to the correctness of this analysis. Horace White wrote later, "Lincoln's defeat was my first great disappointment in politics, and I was slow in forgiving Palmer, Judd and Cook for their share in bringing it about. But before the campaign of 1858 came on I was able to see that they had acted wisely and well. They had not only satisfied their own constituents, and led many of them into the new Republican organization, but they had given a powerful reinforcement to the party of freedom to the nation at large, in the person of Lyman Trumbull, whose high abilities and noble career in the Senate paved the way for thousands of recruits from the ranks of the Democratic Party." [31]

Trumbull's election was accepted with enthusiasm by Whig and anti-Nebraska papers alike. Significantly, the Whig papers expressed no regret at Lincoln's defeat. The Whig *Alton Telegraph* greeted the election with a "Thank God!" It said that Trumbull was "extensively known, throughout the length and breadth of Illinois, as a most eminent jurist, an accomplished statesman, and an excellent citizen." The editorial continued that Trumbull's opponents were fine men but that Trumbull "will probably prove more acceptable to the people of the State than any one of them would have been." [32]

The *Chicago Tribune* praised Trumbull as a gentleman, a scholar, a jurist, and a fine statesman. Comparing Trumbull and Lincoln, the paper had this to say: "*He is a man of more real talent and power than Abram [sic!] Lincoln.*" [33] John Wentworth's *Chicago Democrat* stated that it was not surprised by the result, because it knew that only an anti-Nebraska Democrat could get behind him a majority in the legislature that was

[31] Quoted in the *Journal of the Illinois State Historical Society*, April-June, 1923.

[32] *Daily Alton Telegraph*, February 10, 1855.

[33] *Chicago Tribune*, February 9, 1855. (Italics mine.)

composed of so many diverse elements. Of Trumbull, Wentworth said, "He met Mr. Douglas on the stump in the discussion of the Nebraska question and hence his election as Senator is a withering rebuke to the latter. *He is an able man and will make his mark in the Senate, and will not play second to any man from the West.*" [34] Horace Greeley added his powerful voice to the chorus of approval by stating that "this glorious result is a fitting finale to the Repeal of the Missouri Compromise by Douglas and Co., . . ." [35]

Not all of the comments about the new senator were laudatory, however. There were complaints about Trumbull's lack of popular appeal and his coldness, aloofness, and absence of emotional involvement. Gustave Koerner felt that Trumbull, in spite of his large following, "never could be said to have been popular." [36] Charles A. Church, who wrote a comprehensive history of the Republican party in Illinois, related that a contemporary of Trumbull told him that "he was regarded as the most cold-blooded man who had ever appeared in public life in Illinois." [37] Governor Thomas Ford, who disliked Trumbull, thought that he was a good lawyer but "was rather unfitted to be popular by any natural means with the people amongst whom he resided." [38] Trumbull, according to Ford, thought that the best way to succeed as a politician was to be a demagogue and he "was unfitted by nature to be a demagogue." [39] Paul Selby recalled that Trumbull was always "deliberate, cool and calculating," and John Moses said that "Trumbull's "manners were naturally reserved, his habits abstemious, and he lacked the geniality of temperament generally characteristic of, and looked for, in the public men of his day." [40]

---

[34] *Weekly Chicago Democrat*, February 8, 1855. (Italics mine.)
[35] *New York Tribune*, February 9, 1855.
[36] Koerner, *Memoirs*, I, 426.
[37] Church, *op. cit.*, p. 28.
[38] Ford, *op. cit.*, p. 267.
[39] *Ibid.*
[40] Selby, *op. cit.*, p. 234; Moses, *op. cit.*, p. 594.

This important testimony must be contrasted, however, with the fact that Trumbull maintained many lifetime intimate friendships. He was a loyal and warm friend of Governor John M. Palmer, Governor Richard Yates, Judge James R. Doolittle of Wisconsin, and of a number of lesser Illinois officials. Through all the vicissitudes of stormy Illinois politics, he was loyal to them, and they reciprocated his friendship and loyalty. "We met first in December, 1839," Palmer wrote in his autobiography, ". . . Mr. Trumbull and I became intimate friends, and agreed upon all questions of principle and policy." [41]

Trumbull loved his children dearly and was an affectionate father. It would be difficult to recognize the "cold and unemotional" man from his letters to his small son Perry, born in 1851, who spent the winter of 1857 with his grandparents in Springfield. At that time he wrote: "We do not have as many letters from you this year as last. I hope you have not forgotten your Father and Mother. . . . I expect you hung up your stocking Christmas eve, and if you did, should not wonder if old Santa Clous [sic] put something in it. . . . In about two months Congress will adjourn and then I shall come to see my little boy. . . . You must write me a letter. I want to hear from you very much. . . . Just returned from Church. The President was there. He is an old Gentleman and his hair is white. . . . Mama wants very much to see you and so do I. . . . Now you are six years old, I shall expect you to be a very good boy. I gave Mama the kiss you sent her, right on her lips, was that right?" [42]

There is evidence to suggest that Trumbull mellowed during his service in the Senate and was able to soften his forbidding demeanor, which had made people think of him as a cold, calculating person. Gustave Koerner recalled that he noticed a gradual change during his periodical visits to Washington. Trumbull still was preoccupied exclusively by law and politics,

[41] Palmer, *Personal Recollections*, Introduction, v.
[42] Lyman Trumbull to Perry Trumbull, January 2, 1857, February 1, 1857, Jayne Papers.

Koerner wrote, and while previously "ancient or modern literature, the sciences, music, and the fine arts had no charm for
him, in time his views had become broader. . . . He lost a great
deal of his coldness and I found that for friends he could feel
very warmly." [43]

The newly elected senator was a tall, good-looking man. He
was 5 feet 10½ inches tall and kept his weight at 165. He had
bright sandy hair and piercing blue eyes. Since he was very short-
sighted, he wore gold-rimmed spectacles. His complexion was
pale and his "features were very regular and handsome." [44]
Trumbull went to church regularly and usually attended the
New Book (Presbyterian) Avenue Church in Washington. He
went to church even during inclement weather.[45] Everything
that we know about him combines into a picture of a very
hard-working (the seventy-two volumes of the Trumbull Papers
indicate that his correspondence with his constituents and political associates was enormous), devout, serious, and clean-liv-
ing man.

The new senator and his wife came to Washington in January,
1856. They left their two sons Walter and Perry with the grandparents in Springfield. This was their first trip to the nation's
capital and they both felt as "entire strangers." They took rooms
at the Willard Hotel where many of the members of Congress
stayed. Life in the hotel was a rather exciting experience for the
sedate and modest couple from a small Illinois town.

Breakfast for the men was at 7:00 A.M., but the ladies did
not eat until nine. Dinner was at 2:30 P.M. and 4:30 P.M. The
latter was considered to be the "principal dinner" because "the
ladies appear in their best bib and tucker." After dinner most
of the ladies went to the parlor where they played cards and
danced with invited gentlemen. Virtually every evening there

[43] Koerner, *Memoirs,* I, 426.
[44] Mrs. Mary I. Trumbull to Horace White, July 26, 1907, Horace White Papers,
Illinois State Historical Society, Springfield, Ill.; Koerner, *Memoirs,* I, 426.
[45] Lyman Trumbull to Dr. William Jayne, January 8, 1871, Jayne Papers.

was a party. Tea was served at 7:00 P.M. until 9:00 P.M. when supper commenced. It lasted until 11:00 P.M. or later.

There were receptions somewhere in Washington every night. The Trumbulls attended only a few, although they received many invitations. Trumbull gave an excellent description of a party given by President Buchanan, which he and Julia attended, in a letter to his brothers in Michigan. He wrote: "The President gives a reception every Friday evening. They commence at 8:00 o'clock and last until ten. . . . Everybody goes who chooses, no special invitations are given. . . . There were probably five or six hundred present the night we were there . . . all were dressed and well-behaved persons . . . though some of them stole my overcoat. . . . No refreshments of any kind are provided by the President. The Marine band is in attendance and gives music most of the evening." [46]

Trumbull thought that the White House and the Capitol were not as impressive as he had imagined them to be. Neither was he impressed with some of the leading political figures in Washington. "None of them," he wrote, "are so vastly superior to men whom I have met before and a great many of those whose names are heralded abroad as great are really small men." [47] The new senator was surprised and disturbed by the deep cleavage between the Northern and Southern senators. "There is no good feeling," he reported to his brothers, "between northern and Southern members of Congress who differ in their views on the extension of slavery. . . . Every person opposed to slavery extension is regarded by the South and their northern allies as an abolitionist. . . . I am treated civilly by the Nebraska members and that is all. *The government is completely in the hands and under control of the South.*" [48] Trumbull considered the cleavage wrong, because, in his opinion, national legislation

[46] Lyman Trumbull to John and Erastus Trumbull, January 22, 1857, L. T. Family Papers.
[47] *Ibid.*
[48] *Ibid.* (Italics mine.)

should be concerned with the good of the entire country and not represent sectional interests.

A few years later the Trumbulls bought a large home in a nice section of Washington and found the change very gratifying. "The new quarters," Trumbull told his brother-in-law, "are in some respects the pleasantest we have ever occupied. We have good servants, are keeping house and getting along nicely." [49] To defray part of the expenses for the upkeep of the house, the Trumbulls took in their friend Representative Burton C. Cook of Chicago as a boarder.[50] Mrs. Trumbull's mother and sister Ellen and Trumbull's nephews and nieces were staying with them frequently and for long periods.[51]

Financially, Trumbull, while comfortable, was not a wealthy man. He owned a home and some other property in Alton and a home in Washington, and his wife, Julia, had several parcels of land in Springfield.[52] As years went by, Trumbull, through frugal living, through his income from a large legal practice before the Supreme Court, and through some wise and cautious stock investments, was able to improve his economic condition, although in comparison to other Illinois politicians like Douglas, Fell, Palmer, Davis, and others, who engaged in very profitable land and railroad speculation, he remained a man of modest financial means. He owned Illinois Canal and Jersey Company bonds, and his stock portfolio included stocks of Union Pacific and the Illinois Central. Trumbull dabbled for a time in gold speculation, but without success.[53]

With his family comfortably settled, Trumbull approached his Senate career with some trepidation. He had a big job before him and he found himself under immediate attack from his

[49] Lyman Trumbull to Dr. William Jayne, December 24, 1865, Jayne Papers.
[50] Ibid.
[51] Lyman Trumbull to Dr. William Jayne, December 15, 1867, Jayne Papers.
[52] Trumbull to Dr. William Jayne, December 24, 1865, Jayne Papers.
[53] Statements from Gilman & Co., July 21, 1862, February 4, 1865, May 22, 1866, June 1, 1869, October 23, 1869. Trumbull Collection, Illinois State Historical Society, Springfield, Ill.

enemies. Jolted by Trumbull's election, the Douglas Democrats began a move to prevent him from taking his Senate seat on the ground that the Illinois Constitution made the judges of the State Supreme Court ineligible for any state or federal position during the term of office for which they were elected and for one year thereafter. Since Trumbull was re-elected in June, 1852, for a nine-year term, it was contended that the law applied to him. The Nebraska Democrats—who considered Trumbull, in the words of Charles Lanphier, the editor of the *Illinois State Register*, "a traitor who plotted to overthrow the Democratic party" [54]—were hopeful that Douglas with the help of his Southern friends would sustain the protest and deny him the seat. Trumbull was informed of the plot by John Palmer and expected that "every obstacle [will be] thrown in the way of my taking a seat which malice and spleen can invent." He was confident, however, that the effort would fail.[55] He lost no time in informing Lincoln of the threat and in a cordial letter, which belies any suggestion of "betrayal" or ill-feeling between them, told him: "I shall be happy to hear from you frequently and particularly to know your views as to the best means of meeting and overwhelming the Slavery extensionists in Illinois." [56] Trumbull's offer of an alliance between the Whigs and the anti-Nebraska Democrats was accepted. Trumbull and Lincoln closely co-ordinated their policies, aimed at a cautious and step-by-step formation of a moderate Republican party in Illinois. In August of 1855 both Trumbull and Lincoln refused Owen Lovejoy's invitation to join him in calling a "Springfield Convention" to organize a new party. Trumbull wrote Lovejoy that he was determined to go slow in defining his future course. "I should feel disinclined at this time," he wrote, "to go into a political convention of any kind." He did not think that the anti-Nebraska

54 *Illinois State Register*, February 8, 1855.
55 Trumbull to John M. Palmer, "A Collection of Letters from Lyman Trumbull to John M. Palmer, 1854–1858," *op. cit.*, p. 24.
56 Lyman Trumbull to Abraham Lincoln, R. T. L. Collection.

Democrats, particularly around Alton and the southern part of the state were, as yet, ready to join a new party, and there was little sentiment for a fusion with the Whigs. The only issue that might possibly unite the diverse elements was opposition to the extension of slavery. He felt that the invasion of the Missouri "ruffians" into Kansas would do a great deal to unite the anti-slavery elements. Writing with rather startling frankness, Trumbull revealed his conviction that an eventual conflict with the South was inevitable. He wrote: "The South never will, I trust consent to ban slavery taken to and established in Kansas by force of arms." [57]

Lincoln answered Lovejoy a few days earlier and also declared himself not ready to join a new party. "The political atmosphere is such just now," he wrote, "that I fear to do anything." He was convinced that it was essential to secure the support of the Know-Nothings, provided that they were willing to give up their nativist theories which he found abhorrent. "I have no objections to 'fuse' with anybody," he stated, "provided I can fuse on ground which I think is right." [58] By the time Trumbull was ready to leave Alton for Washington in late November, 1855, he was still a Democrat and Lincoln was still a Whig,[59] but both were united in their determination to stop the extension of slavery, which they both detested. They were ready, sometime soon, to organize a new fusion party on a platform of the restoration of the Missouri Compromise, free Kansas, and opposition to further extension of slavery. It was a moderate platform, not because Trumbull and Lincoln opposed the abrogation of the Fugitive Slave Law, and the abolition of slavery in the District of Columbia. Rather, the platform was moderate because Trumbull and Lincoln were astute and shrewd politicians and 1856

[57] Lyman Trumbull to Owen Lovejoy, August 20, 1855, Jayne Papers.

[58] Abraham Lincoln to Owen Lovejoy, August 11, 1854, *The Living Lincoln*, p. 186.

[59] Abraham Lincoln to Joshua Speed, August 24, 1855, *The Living Lincoln*, p. 191. In the same letter Lincoln denounced the Kansas-Nebraska bill as an "enactment not as a law, but as violence from the beginning. It was conceived in violence, passed in violence, and is being executed in violence."

was a Presidential election year. They knew that only on such a limited platform could they hope to elect a Republican governor, get a majority in the legislature and carry the state for the Republican nominee.

The anti-slavery people of Illinois, and Trumbull himself, felt that his primary objective in the Senate was to give battle to Douglas and to prevent Kansas from becoming a slave state. Trumbull soon realized that this was a formidable task. Congress was in the midst of a tense struggle over Kansas, and the coalition of Southerners and Nebraska Democrats was riding roughshod over the minority of anti-slavery Whigs and free-soilers. The lot of an anti-slavery newcomer, like Trumbull, who was generally considered a renegade and a traitor to his own party, did not promise to be an easy one. On a later occasion Trumbull described the Senate as it convened at the first session of the Thirty-fourth Congress on December 3, 1855: "At that time it [the Senate] consisted," he said, "of sixty-two members, of whom fifteen were Republicans. It was a time of high party excitement. The majority were domineering and often offensive to members of the minority. They controlled the business of the Senate and could take their own time to assail minority Senators. . . . It was not uncommon for the members of the dominant party to go out of their way to seek controversies with and assail certain Senators in the minority. . . ." [60] The chief among those who used their power and experience to dominate the debates was the senior senator from Illinois, Stephen A. Douglas. The odds in the contest between Trumbull and Douglas were all in the latter's favor. He was a veteran of nine years in the Senate and under the seniority system had acquired a position of power that was greatly enhanced by his oratorical skills and organizational abilities. He was chairman of the powerful Senate Committee on the Territories and a strong contender for the Democratic nomination for President in 1856.

Trumbull had his work cut out for him, but first he had to

[60] *Cong. Globe*, 41 Cong., 2nd Sess. (December 14, 1869), p. 113.

get the Senate to reject the protest from Illinois and confirm
his election. There was no trouble about Trumbull's taking his
seat. His credentials, which were signed by George T. Brown,
Secretary of the State of Illinois, were presented to the Senate
by the venerable Senator John J. Critttenden of Kentucky. An
oath was administered to Trumbull and he was seated. However,
Senator Lewis Cass of Michigan informed the Senate that a
protest against the legality of Trumbull's election had been
received and that it was signed by thirteen Illinois senators and
twenty-nine representatives. The protest was referred for action
and recommendation to the Judiciary Committee. Senator Douglas refrained from commenting on the elegibility question, but
instead of welcoming his junior colleague to the Senate as is the
custom, he took strong exception to Trumbull's claim that he
was a Democrat. The claim, Douglas said, "will be news to the
Democracy of Illinois. Such a statement is a libel upon the
Democracy of that State. . . . So far as I am advised and believe,
he received no vote except from persons allied to Abolitionism
and Know-Nothingism." [61] Trumbull, completely confident, considered his seating a clear victory and asserted that Governor
Matteson, who engineered the protest, "gained nothing by his
meanness." [62]

The consideration of Trumbull's eligibility was long and protracted. During the several months of the controversy, Trumbull
did all he could to make a good impression on the Senate, and
he assiduously cultivated many influential Southern senators,
including Senator Butler of South Carolina, the chairman of
the Senate Judiciary Committee. The Southerners were, on the
whole, well impressed with the erudite, cautious junior senator

[61] Milton, op. cit., p. 204.

[62] Trumbull to John Palmer, December 3, 1855, "A Collection of Letters from
Lyman Trumbull to John M. Palmer, 1854–1858," op. cit., p. 26. Governor Joel
Matteson was thought to have been the chief instigator of the move to deny Trum-
bull his Senate seat, D. L. Phillips to Trumbull, December 26, 1855, L. T. Family
Papers.

from Illinois. He was surely no rabble-rousing trouble-maker. In his few speeches, delivered between December, 1855, and March, 1856, Trumbull was careful to stress that he considered himself to be a good Democrat, that he was not an abolitionist, that he had advocated the enforcement of the Fugitive Slave Law, and that he was opposed to any interference with slavery in the states where it existed. He did tell the Senate that he opposed the extension of slavery and believed in the right of Congress to prohibit slavery in the territories.[63] On the whole, then, his was a thoroughly moderate and respectable position. Trumbull obviously was determined not to antagonize the Southerners, whose votes he needed for the confirmation of his seating, which was forthcoming. Answering the protest of the Illinois legislators, Trumbull in a forthright speech said that he believed the clause in the Illinois Constitution to be inoperative because he had resigned from the Illinois Supreme Court more than a year and a half ago. He added, that "the spirit of the Constitution of the State of Illinois does not apply to my case, though it is possible that its letter may." [64] Trumbull's supporters, among them Senator William Seward, maintained that according to the Constitution the Senate was the sole judge of the qualifications of its members and was not bound by any restrictions to be found in the state constitutions.[65] Senator Butler recommended, on behalf of his committee, the seating of Trumbull, and his report was supported by Senator James Mason of Virginia and others.[66] The final vote came on March 6, and Trumbull's right to sit in the Senate was confirmed by a vote of 35 to 8. Only two Southerners, Jones of Arkansas and Slidell of Louisiana, voted

[63] *Cong. Globe*, 34 Cong., 1st Sess. (February 20, 1856), p. 467. It was Senator Judah P. Benjamin of Louisiana who sponsored Trumbull's admission to practice before the Supreme Court, Certificate of Admission, dated, December 22, 1859, in the L. T. Family Papers.

[64] *Ibid*. (February 2, 1856), p. 466. Also Lyman Trumbull to A. P. Butler, April 9, 1855. L. T. Family Papers.

[65] *Ibid.*, p. 343.

[66] *Ibid*. (February 24, 1856), p. 579.

in the negative.[67] Douglas, who did not participate in the effort to bar Trumbull, did not vote.

Four days before the decisive vote, Trumbull wrote to his brother John that he and Julia did not particularly enjoy their stay in Washington. "We keep well," he wrote, "but I cannot say it is particularly pleasant here. In fact, I would enjoy myself much better at home in Illinois. I am a sort of outsider here. The Old Whigs did not like me particularly, the so-called democracy here is completely in the hands of pro-slavery men with whom I will not co-operate—so you see I am pretty much a gang by myself." [68]

[67] *Ibid.* (March 6, 1856), p. 584.
[68] Lyman Trumbull to John Trumbull, March 2, 1856, L. T. Family Papers.

6

Taking on the "Little Giant"

THE INVASION OF KANSAS BY ARMED BANDS OF MISSOURI "BORDER
Ruffians" to force the outcome of the election for the Territorial
Legislature, which was scheduled for March 30, 1855, was a
body blow to Douglas' theory of "popular sovereignty." The fact
that one of the bands was led by Senator David R. Atchison, a
personal friend of Douglas, was not lost on the people of Illinois.
Governor Reeder, unable to resist the pressure of the pro-slavery
forces in Kansas and in Missouri, ignored the evidence of fraud
and intimidation and confirmed two-thirds of the elected legislators. At the same time he decided to go to Washington to
report to President Pierce on the unbearable conditions in the
territory.

"Had a resolute and impartial man sat in the White House,"
Nevins wrote, "his [Reeder's] errand might have accomplished
something, but as it was it proved futile." [1] Pierce was sympathetic when Reeder described the violence and the intimidation
used by the pro-slavery forces but refrained from taking any
action. Upon Reeder's return, the fraudulently elected legislature promptly made Kansas a slave state and passed laws that
made it a criminal offense for anyone to deny the existence of
slavery in Kansas. No one was allowed to hold office who would

[1] Nevins, *op. cit.*, p. 386.

115

nɔt acknowledge the institution of slavery. An election law was adopted that made sure that the free-soil elements would have no chance for a victory. Resisting the onslaught, the free-soilers organized a "Free State Convention" in Topeka, which adopted a new state constitution that made Kansas a free state. This constitution was submitted to a popular vote and was adopted, although only a small number of votes were cast. The Topeka Constitution was then forwarded to Congress for approval. Forced to take a stand, President Pierce sent, on January 24, 1856, a special message to Congress dealing with the Kansas situation. He upheld the legality of the pro-slavery legislature and endorsed its laws as based on a legally adopted Constitution of the Territory.

Trumbull, in Washington, did not have long to wait for the reaction of his constituents to the events in Kansas and to Pierce's message. It was swift and violent. The threat of seeing another free territory swallowed by slavery and virtually sealed off to immigration of white settlers gave a strong impetus to the anti-slavery forces in Illinois. From Alton a correspondent wrote Trumbull that "every respectable man with whom I converse is anti-Nebraska. I have traversed over the County [St. Clair] . . . and feel, from all I hear and see, that the Kansas-Nebraska bill is daily becoming more and more unpopular. . . ."[2] Pierce's message was generally and vehemently denounced as a sell-out to the South and the forces of slavery. A prominent political leader asserted that the message exhibited "a total subserviency to the South, and an entire abandonment of the principle . . . that Slavery is Sectional—freedom National," and a widely respected and learned lawyer who earned the nickname of "Lord Coke of Illinois," indignantly asked, "What is the matter with your President—Franklin Pierce? He seems to be "a fugitive" from freedom.[3] John Palmer was sure that Pierce's

[2] George T. Allen to Trumbull, January 19, 1856, L. T. Papers.
[3] D. L. Phillips to Trumbull, January 18, 1856; David J. Baker to Trumbull, February 9, 1856. See also General Usher F. Linder, *Reminiscences of the Early Bench and Bar of Illinois* (Chicago, 1879), p. 124.

message would stir the North to resistance. He was sure that the people of the North would not "submit to be kicked . . . by this miniature Negro driver, this small sample of a miniature Carolina overseer, who speeks to us as if we were slaves." [4]

The fight for a free Kansas, which brought to fore once again the aggressive spirit of the slave states and the intransigence of the Southern leaders in Congress, hardened the opposition to the extension of slavery of the great majority of Illinoisans. The Chicago Tribune suggested that the slaveholders be told: "This far shall you accursed system go but no farther, dissolve the Union if you dare." [5] Trumbull received daily scores of letters from cities, towns, villages, and hamlets of Illinois urging him to stand firm to fight for a free Kansas. The letters came from well-educated people who wrote well and from plain folk who could hardly write; all of them felt frustrated and betrayed by weak-kneed leaders who for years had appeased the slave states only to be confronted by new demands which, if given in to, could in their opinion end only in the spread of slavery throughout the entire nation. It makes little sense to argue, as some have done, that this fear was groundless because slavery could not have endured in Kansas or in Utah or in Oregon. The fact is that many sincere people in the North believed that the evil and depraving institution of slavery would, unless checked, spread to the North.[6] There was a growing conviction that the old party lines were meaningless and that the time had come for all anti-slavery elements to unite and to form a new party. "It strikes me," wrote a prominent Democrat and lawyer from Alton, "that daily the breach between North and the South is becoming wider and the distinctive features that have marked great political parties are becoming less and less visible. . . . Whigs and Democrats of strong

[4] John M. Palmer to Trumbull, January 11, 1856, L. T. Papers.

[5] Chicago Tribune, February 15, 1856.

[6] Professor B. Turner of the Illinois College wrote to Trumbull, "Go on my dear sir, and still hold high over the defenseless and the oppressed." B. Turner to Trumbull, February 18, 1856, L. T. Papers. Also E. A. Paine to Trumbull, December 31, 1855, L. T. Papers.

Southern prejudices and proclivities are identifying themselves
with Atchison and Douglas while those who believe that the Revolutionary Fathers fought . . . to have this a free nation . . . are
becoming more firm and more determined to stand by the great
principle that Slavery is sectional and Liberty is national." [7] A
Democratic leader, from Edwardsville, found it "mortifying to
the mass of real democracy to see their old leaders and associates
insulting the intelligence of the country, and degrading the very
name Democrat by throwing themselves into the arms of Slavocracy and prostituting the whole power of the government for
the advancement of an *Institution which is a disgrace to the
Nation.*" [8] Trumbull's mail in the early months of 1856 provides
evidence that the people of Illinois opposed the extension of
slavery mainly because they thought slavery evil, and contrary
to the basic principles of American freedom. Even the pro-
slavery ex-Governor Reynolds deplored the situation in Kansas
and came up with the ingenious suggestion to give the whole
territory back to the Indians. [9]

While there was general agreement that a new Republican
party should be organized, there remained the question, especially acute in an election year, as to what *minimum* platform
the new party should adopt. Trumbull and his Democratic
friends were determined not to support Pierce, Douglas, or
Buchanan, who were the leading candidates for the nomination
at the forthcoming Democratic National Convention in Cincinnati. [10] Trumbull wanted the new party to concentrate on the
opposition to the extension of slavery and on the advocacy of
the restoration of the Missouri Compromise. Shrewdly assessing
the political situation in Illinois, he was convinced that only
such a minimum program could induce the thousands of Democrats to desert their party and vote for the Republican candidates

[7] John Trible to Trumbull, January 25, 1856, L. T. Papers.
[8] J. Rutherford to Trumbull, January 15, 1856, L. T. Papers.
[9] John Reynolds to Trumbull, February 15, 1856, L. T. Papers.
[10] John M. Palmer to Trumbull, January 11, February 28, 1856, L. T. Papers.

in the state and national elections. "When I speak of the Republicans," he wrote to Palmer, "I do not mean such as have assumed that name in Illinois and who oppose the fugitive slave law, the admission of any more slave states under any circumstances, but I mean all these who on the slavery question simply make this issue, opposition to its spread into free territory." [11] Trumbull wrote many letters to his Democratic friends in Illinois, urging them to concentrate on the "single issue" of slavery extension.[12] One correspondent suggested that the anti-Nebraska Democrats should join the Republican party to "hold them in check and respectable." [13]

Many Whigs, too, wrote to Trumbull asking him to lead in the organization of the new party and asking his advice about the selection of candidates for state offices.[14] Trumbull and Lincoln, in full agreement on the program of the Republican party to be organized, used Herndon as their intermediary. Herndon assured Trumbull that he (and Lincoln) would not join any party which would "not regard the Constitution." [15]

Assured as to the direction that events were taking, Trumbull decided to give his support to the call that was issued in Springfield in May, 1856, for a Republican convention to gather in Bloomington on May 26. It was understood that the anti-slavery elements had agreed in advance to the nomination of an anti-Nebraska Democrat, former Congressman William H. Bissell, for governor. In a letter to Joseph Gillespie, a state senator from Edwardsville, Trumbull told him that he considered his main task in Washington to "stand up to the 'Little Giant' because Pierce has gone body and soul to the South" and that there was an imperative need for strong anti-slavery men in Congress. "If

[11] Trumbull to John M. Palmer, January 24, 1856, "A Collection of Letters from Lyman Trumbull to John M. Palmer, 1854–1858," *op cit.*, p. 28, April-June, 1923. Also T. Tuck to Trumbull, January 24, 1856, L. T. Papers.
[12] H. Barber to Trumbull, January 30, 1856, L. T. Papers.
[13] J. Dugger to Trumbull, February 26, 1856, L. T. Papers.
[14] George T. Brown to Trumbull, January 28, 1856, L. T. Papers.
[15] William H. Herndon to Trumbull, February 15, 1856, L. T. Papers.

the North will submit," he wrote, "to what is now going on, and continue in power an administration which is using all its influence and power to put down free state men in Kansas, and to enforce laws enacted by armed men from another state, *I do not know what they would not submit to.*" [16] Bissell, who was very popular in the state and was a staunch anti-slavery leader, was highly acceptable to Trumbull.[17] He urged John M. Palmer to attend the Bloomington convention. "That convention," he told his fellow Democrat, "is evidently going to be a very respectable one. It will nominate Bissell for Governor and I presume take conservative measures avoiding all truisms." [18] Orville H. Browning, a close friend of Lincoln and a Whig leader from Quincy, wrote Trumbull: "We wish, if possible, to keep the party in this State under the control of Moderate men and conservative influences and if we do so, the future destiny of the State is in our hands—victory will inevitably crown our exertions." [19] The moderation of the Whig and of the anti-Nebraska leaders was not dictated by a lukewarm attitude to slavery but by a conviction that Republican victory in the election depended upon a moderate platform, centered on the opposition to the extension of slavery.

Anti-Nebraska Democrats, generally, believed that since their votes constituted the balance of power that could bring the new party a victory at the polls, they should take over the control and direction of the Bloomington convention, which was called

[16] Lyman Trumbull to Joseph Gillespie, February 25, 1856, Joseph Gillespie Papers, Illinois State Historical Society, Springfield, Ill.

[17] William H. Bissell to Trumbull, January 19, 1856, Joseph Gillespie Papers, Illinois State Historical Society, Springfield, Ill. Bissell wrote to Gillespie on February 17, 1856, "The time has come when every man, every American—who has patriotism enough to wish his country well *must take his position on the slavery question;* not with a view to disturb it where it already exists by virtue of state laws but to prevent its extension to Territories now free." William H. Bissell to Joseph Gillespie, February 17, 1856, Joseph Gillespie Papers, Illinois State Historical Society, Springfield, Ill.

[18] Trumbull to John M. Palmer, May 21, 1856, "A Collection of Letters from Lyman Trumbull to John M. Palmer, 1854–1858," *op. cit.,* P. 30.

[19] Orville H. Browning to Trumbull, May 19, 1856, L. T. Papers.

by a special committee of citizens.[20] The Bloomington convention had widespread support of Illinois newspapers, including the *Chicago Tribune*, the *Illinois State Journal*, the *Alton Telegraph*, the *Alton Courier*, and the *Belleville Advocate*. In addition to Palmer, Trumbull wrote to many of his friends urging them to go to Bloomington.[21] Norman B. Judd, who became Trumbull's lieutenant and deputy in Illinois, reported to his chief that "our leading anti-Nebraska Democrats are for the Bloomington Convention" and assured him that Burton C. Cook and John Lock Scripps, co-owner of the *Democratic Press*, would be in Bloomington.

The Bloomington convention, which Trumbull attended, was presided over by John M. Palmer and nominated William H. Bissell for governor. A leader of Germans, Francis A. Hoffman, was nominated for lieutenant governor. Trumbull's friends Jesse K. Dubois and Oziah M. Hatch were nominated for State Auditor and Secretary of State, respectively. The resolutions, as framed under the direction of Lincoln, Trumbull and Browning, reaffirmed the right of Congress to outlaw slavery in the territories and urged a free Kansas under a restored Missouri Compromise. The convention stated its unshakable resolve to stand by and defend the Union against any attempts of "disunionists" to break it up.[22]

The main arena of the struggle for a free Kansas shifted to the Senate of the United States. On March, 1856, Stephen Douglas presented, on behalf of his committee, a report on the Kansas situation in which he upheld the legality of the Kansas pro-

[20] William H. Bissell to Trumbull, May 5, 1856, L. T. Papers. C. H. Ray to Trumbull, March 21, 1856, L. T. Papers.

[21] W. Kitchell to Trumbull, May 25, 1856; J. C. Sloo to Trumbull, May 16, 1856; T. F. Houts to Trumbull, May 19, 1856; and Charles Ray to Trumbull, May 4, 1856, L. T. Papers.

[22] Text in D. W. Lusk, *op. cit.*, p. 28. See also the excellent account on the Bloomington Convention in Mildred C. Stoller, "The Democratic Element in the New Republican Party in Illinois, 1856–1860," *Papers in Illinois Hisotry, and Transactions for the Year 1942*, Illinois State Historical Society, Springfield, Ill., 1944, pp. 45–47. Also *The Diary of Orville Hickman Browning* (Illinois Historical Collections, XX, Springfield, 1925), 1:237–39.

slavery legislature and all of its acts. He denounced the Topeka Constitution as illegal and castigated the activities of the Emigrant Aid Societies as provocative, but carefully refrained from even rebuking the Missouri border ruffians.[23] Douglas then introduced a bill that called for the admission of Kansas when her population would reach the figure of 93,420. Since Kansas had at the time about thirty thousand white settlers, the required figure would not be reached for several years. In the meantime, the disputed state was to remain a slave territory, controlled by a pro-slavery legislature, chosen at least partially by fraud and intimidation, and be governed by a pro-slavery governor. To prevent this development, Senator William Seward introduced a Republican-sponsored bill on Kansas.

Seward's bill called for the admission of Kansas under the Topeka Constitution. The debate in the Senate on the two bills raged with an unprecedented intensity through the months of March, April, May, June, and July. Some writers have taken the position that both Douglas' and Seward's bills were partisan and illegal. However, it must not be overlooked that the issue of the expansion of slavery had become a deep emotional involvment for many thousands of people in the North and in the South. Granted that Seward's bill was legally weak, the question remains as to what other plan could have been calmly proposed to assure that Kansas would enter the Union as a free state. Granted that there were other issues in the Kansas struggle and that some modus vivendi could have been reached between the Southern pioneers in the region and the free-state settlers, it is a fact that for the thirty thousand white settlers in Kansas there was only one issue, namely slavery or freedom. They did not recognize the existence of any other issues and did not see any possibility of a compromise between the pro- and anti-slavery groups. Under these circumstances, the Kansas issue was indeed an "irrepressible conflict."

[23] Cong. Globe, 34 Cong., 1st Sess. (March 12, 1856), p. 639.

The debate on the Douglas bill produced some dramatic and effective speeches by Seward and Sumner. These were great oratorical efforts, but the contribution of Lyman Trumbull to the struggle for a free Kansas should not be minimized. Seward and Sumner had seniority and status in the Senate and in the country, and the risks that they had to take in attacking Douglas were rather limited. On the other hand, Trumbull, a freshman senator who had just been confirmed in his seat and who was considered a renegade by most of his Democratic colleagues, risked his political future by attacking his powerful senior colleagues, especially since the latter had the solid support of the powerful and aggressive bloc of the Southern senators. But Trumbull was neither daunted nor awed when he took the floor of the Senate on March 14, 1856, for his maiden speech.

After a brief wrangle during which some senators objected to Trumbull's right to make the speech attacking the Douglas report on Kansas because Douglas was not given the customary notice and was absent, Trumbull, supported by Sumner and Seward, was allowed to proceed. He attacked the majority report presented by Douglas and defended the minority report submitted by Senator Jacob Collamer of Vermont, which defended the Topeka Constitution and asked Congress to restore the Missouri Compromise. In a three-hour speech, Trumbull asserted that the developments in Kansas had proven the sham of Douglas' theory of popular sovereignty. Launching into a personal attack on his colleague, he told the Senate that Douglas had to be held responsible for the acts of violence and fraud perpetrated by the pro-slavery elements in Kansas. Trumbull rejected Douglas' contention that the free-soil settlers were being sent into Kansas to "abolitionize" the territory. "What! Abolitionize Kansas!" he said. "It was said on all sides of the Senate Chamber, that it was never meant to have slavery go into Kansas. What is meant, then, by abolitionizing Kansas?" Trumbull disputed the claim made in the report that because Governor Reeder had recognized the pro-slavery legislature, Congress had no right to inquire into its validity. He defended the objectives and actions of the Emigrant Aid Societies and called upon Congress to rescind the Kansas-Nebraska Act and to restore the Missouri Compromise.[24]

Senator Douglas, who entered the Chamber in the middle of Trumbull's speech, asked for the floor and was recognized. Flushed and angry, he accused Trumbull of discourtesy in delivering the speech in his absence. He played on the sympathy of his audience by describing "the feeble state" of his health and then accused Trumbull of making "the most vulgar and coarse of all partisan assaults ever made on the Democratic side of the House by a Senator." The senior Senator from Illinois told the Senate that Trumbull was elected by the combined vote of Know-Nothings and abolitionists and that he was "the head and front of Black Republicanism in Illinois." Conceding the fact that Trumbull was becoming a thorn in his side, Douglas suggested that both he and Trumbull should resign their seats in the Senate and submit to an election to see which one duly represented the people of Illinois.[25]

Trumbull took the floor for a rebuttal. He said that he did not know that Douglas would be absent and ridiculed Douglas' assertions about his supporters. "I am not driven," he said, "into the defense of either Abolitionism or Know-Nothingism. I have nothing to do with them. I never was affiliated with them." He rejected Douglas' offer of a joint resignation on the ground that such a step would only give Governor Matteson an opportunity to appoint a Nebraska-ite to the Senate. Trumbull coldly concluded, "The gentleman has made an unprovoked assault on me personally, and I have thought it to be my duty to meet him as I shall always meet him." [26]

The Illinois constituents were elated by Trumbull's first encounter with Douglas in Congress. They had been waiting for

[24] *Cong. Globe*, 34 *Cong.*, 1st Sess. (March 14, 1856), p. 653.
[25] *Ibid.*, pp. 655–56.
[26] *Ibid.*, p. 657.

a long time for someone to give battle to the all-powerful "Little Giant," and Trumbull was flooded with letters of congratulation and high praise for his performance in the debate. There was a general opinion that Trumbull came off a victor in the exchange.

The Alton editor George T. Brown wrote to Trumbull: "You have no idea what a deep feeling pervades the entire people of the section, at your thorough and fearless identification with sound principles, and at your herding and subduing the Nebraska Lion in his peculiar theatre." Brown also told him that even those who doubted the wisdom of Trumbull's election were now convinced that it happened for the best.[27] Herndon assured Trumbull that his speech was considered in Springfield an "excellent hit" and that "the very best people in this city," commended him very highly.[28] "The roar of your Senatorial battle has reached Illinois," wrote Palmer, "and your friends here feel that you have acquitted yourself well and nobly." Palmer added that the people of Illinois were convinced that Douglas now had in the Senate an opponent who was "his equal in intellect and superior in manners."[29]

The expressions of warm approval of Trumbull's speech were not limited to Illinois. Charles Sumner wrote to a friend that "Trumbull is a hero and more than a match for Douglas. . . . You will read the main speech which is able; but you can hardly appreciate the ready courage and power with which he grappled with his colleague and throttled him. We are proud of his work."[30] Coming from Sumner, who rarely praised someone else's speeches, the letter provides a clue to the impression that

[27] George T. Brown to Trumbull, March 29, 1856, L. T. Papers. Charles H. Ray wrote: "For God's sake, and your own, do not yield an inch to his [Douglas'] insolence," C. H. Ray to Lyman Trumbull, March 18, 1856, L. T. Family Papers.
[28] William H. Herndon to Trumbull, March 28, 1856, L. T. Papers.
[29] John M. Palmer to Trumbull, March 24, 1856, L. T. Papers. See also letters from H. N. Hibbard to Trumbull, March 28, 1856; John Russell to Trumbull, March 27, 1858; A. T. Norton to Trumbull, March 29, 1856; Anson Miller to Trumbull, March 27, 1856; Grant Goodrich to Trumbull, March 28, 1856, L. T. Papers.
[30] White, op. cit., p. 66.

Trumbull made on the Senate. The *New York Tribune* reported that Trumbull's long speech commanded the full attention of the Senate and of the packed galleries and that Douglas made his undignified reply in "bad temper." [31] Governor Salmon P. Chase of Ohio sent Trumbull his warm compliments for an able speech whose "logic" was irresistible." [32]

Trumbull, however, must have been pleased most by a letter from his wife Julia who reported that the home folks in Springfield were very pleased with their junior senator. "I feel," she wrote, "that in hearing your speech so well spoken as I do, I am in great danger of being 'puffed up' and need to pray for the grace of humility. . . . Why should not a wife be proud of her husband when he contends for the right, not forgetting that the gifts of mind come directly from God. Oh how much we two owe Him, the devotion to his service of all our powers can not repay him." [33]

Trumbull's reaction to the attack of Congressman Brooks on Sumner was restrained. He made no speech attacking Brooks and the South but merely expressed his satisfaction when Brooks sent in a meaningless letter of "apology." [34] Trumbull's restraint was undoubtedly motivated by the extremely provocative nature of Sumner's "Rape of Kansas" speech and even more by the fact that he entertained warm feelings of regard and gratitude to Senator Butler of South Carolina, a particular object of Sumner's assault. Butler befriended Trumbull when he entered the Senate and recommended his seating on behalf of the Senate Judiciary Committee.

Trumbull continued his struggle for a free Kansas and on June 9 introduced his own substitute bill which provided for the annexation of Kansas to Nebraska, the extension of the Nebraska laws prohibiting slavery in Kansas and the abolition

[31] *New York Tribune*, March 15, 1856.
[32] Samon P. Chase to Trumbull, April 14, 1856, L. T. Papers.
[33] Julia Jayne Trumbull to Lyman Trumbull, April 10, 1856, L. T. Family Papers.
[34] *Cong. Globe*, 34 Cong., 1st Sess. (June 2, 1856), p. 1348.

of all offices and the repealing of all laws in the Territory of Kansas. This bill would have put to naught over two years of work by Congressional committees and the Executive, and it had no chance to be adopted. However, Trumbull's speech in support of his bill was important because of the question that he posed to his chief adversary. Trumbull asked Douglas whether or not he believed that the people of a territory could lawfully exclude slavery prior to the formation of a state constitution, and whether or not a slaveholder had a right to take and hold slaves in a territory in the absence of municipal law on the subject.[35] Douglas in reply dodged a direct answer and asserted that only the Supreme Court could decide the question.[36] If Douglas' answer did harm to his Presidential ambitions in the South, the damage was done in the Senate in 1856.[37] As his bitter exchange with Trumbull continued, the "Little Giant" had to admit that the going was rough. "I know," he said, "that this is not the proper time or occasion to get up a debate in this irregular way, and I regret having been forced into it, but I was compelled to do so by the remarks of my colleague who has put me on the defensive all the time." [38] Trumbull relentlessly and with great skill exploited Douglas' discomfiture and pressed him even further. He was particularly intent to force Douglas either to identify himself with the views of the Southern senators or openly break with them. The central issue, he said, was "whether Slaveholders can take their Slaves into a Territory . . . all of them in the South say they have a right to take their slaves into a Territory, and to hold them there, while all in the North deny it." [39] Trumbull demanded to know where Douglas stood on these crucial questions. While he received no reply, this was undoubt-

[35] *Ibid.* (June 9, 1856), p. 1369.
[36] *Ibid.*
[37] See an excellent discussion in D. E. Fehrenbacher, "Lincoln, Douglas, and the 'Freeport Question,' " *The American Historical Review,* LXVI, No. 3 (April, 1961), pp. 599–617.
[38] *Cong. Globe,* 34 Cong., 1st Sess. (June 9, 1856), p. 1374.
[39] *Ibid.,* p. 1375.

edly one of the most difficult moments that the senior senator from Illinois had experienced during his long and distinguished career in Congress.

When his bill died an abortive death in Douglas' committee, Trumbull set out to amend the Kansas Enabling Act, which was reported from the Senate Committee on the Territories. The amendment, if adopted, would have eliminated the bill's worst feature, because it provided that slavery was to be permitted or excluded in Kansas by a free vote of the people, but that until such an election could be held, no slaveowner would have the right to bring slaves into the territory.[40] In speaking on the amendment, Trumbull pointed to a flaw in the bill that later became a point of contention in the Lecompton controversy. He charged that Douglas' bill did not specifically provide that the constitution, as framed by the Territorial constitutional convention, was to be submitted to ratification by a vote of the people.[41] "In my judgment," he said, "this bill, if it pass, will not satisfy the country, . . . two things are necessary to be done. In the first place, slavery should be excluded from Kansas while a Territory. Next, abolish all the acts of the so-called Territorial Legislature and dismiss all persons pretending to hold office under it." [42] Only if these two conditions were fulfilled was an election for a new constitutional convention to be held. Trumbull, to whom legal considerations were paramount, did not agree with Seward and Sumner, who demanded the unconditional admission of Kansas under the so-called Topeka Constitution.

The new Republican party, still a rather loose federation of old-line Whigs, anti-Nebraska Democrats, Know-Nothings and free-soilers, was getting ready to nominate its first national ticket at the convention scheduled to meet June 17 in Philadelphia. Since the Democrats, meeting in Cincinnati, had endorsed the Kansas-Nebraska Act, the issue in the forthcoming election was

[40] Ibid. (July 2, 1856), Appendix, p. 798.
[41] Ibid., p. 779.
[42] Ibid., p. 781.

clearly defined. Trumbull did not intend to go to Philadelphia, but he changed his mind after an urgent appeal from Abraham Lincoln. In a friendly and frank letter, Lincoln told Trumbull that he was "in" (the Republican party) and considered himself bound to support any nominee of the new party, but suggested that a Whig should become the new party's standard bearer. His own choice was the seventy-one-year-old Judge John McLean, Associate Justice of the United States Supreme Court. "I address this to you," Lincoln added, "because your influence in the Anti-Nebraska nomination will be greater than that of any other Illinoisan." [43] In a subsequent letter, Lincoln specifically asked Trumbull to go to Philadelphia to keep the convention on a moderate, conservative keel. Trumbull responded that he had hesitated about going "but your letter just received decides the question. I will go . . . and do what I can to have a conservative man nominated and conservative measures adopted." [44] If there ever had been any ill-feeling between Lincoln and Trumbull as a result of the 1855 election, it was quickly replaced by a firm political alliance between the two men.

In Philadelphia, Trumbull was informed that the *Chicago Tribune*, after praising his record in Congress and his encounter with Douglas, suggested his name as a possible nominee for the Presidency.[45] The Chicago delegation was dominated by former Democrats, including Trumbull, Palmer, Koerner, and Judd. It seemed to Koerner that the "Democrats ruled the Convention" and that Trumbull, who knew many leaders from all over the country, exerted a great amount of influence.[46] The convention nominated John C. Frémont for President. Lincoln received one hundred and ten votes in the contest for the vice-presidential nomination.[47] The platform adopted in Philadelphia bore the

[43] Abraham Lincoln to Trumbull, June 7, 1856.
[44] Trumbull to Abraham Lincoln, June 15, 1856, Jayne Papers.
[45] Kinsley, *op. cit.*, p. 53.
[46] Koerner, *Memoirs*, II, 14–15.
[47] There is an unresolved dispute on who placed Lincoln's name in nomination. Horace White, without giving his source, wrote that Lincoln was nominated by

mark of Trumbull's and Lincoln's moderating influences. It affirmed the sanctity of the Union and declared that Congress had the right to prohibit slavery in the territories. The platform also denounced the Kansas pro-slavery legislature and demanded the admission of a free Kansas.

The 1856 campaign in Illinois was long and bitter. Many Whigs from the southern counties, attracted by Buchanan's reputation as a moderate statesman, refused to support Frémont. Trumbull, Lincoln, Palmer, Yates, Koerner, and Judd campaigned furiously for Bissell and Frémont. They made many speeches throughout the state and were occasionally joined by Republican leaders from outside of the state. These included John P. Hale of New Hampshire, Nathaniel P. Banks of Massachusetts, and Francis P. Blair of Missouri. Stephen Douglas, who also conducted a vigorous campaign, received assistance from Horatio Seymour of New York and Lewis Cass of Michigan. During the summer months, Trumbull sent many letters to his friends in Illinois urging them to campaign vigorously for the Republican ticket.[48] On July 5 Trumbull told Lincoln that he estimated Frémont's chances as improving provided that he "gets the mass of Whigs, as I trust he will." He suggested that Lincoln tour "Little Egypt" where he expected trouble from the Democrats.[49] He wrote in a similar vein to Palmer, whom he assured that he would come to Illinois in early September and would "attend meetings whenever I can be of service." [50]

Judd urgently requested that Trumbull come to Illinois, writing, "What we want just now is just such a person as you to give form and organization to the contest." Koerner echoed

Wiliam B. Archer, an Illinois congressman, while John Palmer recalled that he has nominated Lincoln. White, *op. cit.*, p. 69; Palmer, *Personal Recollections*, p. 74.

[48] W. H. Herndon to Trumbull, June 16, July 12, 1856; Parmenias Bond to Trumbull, June 28, 1856; James C. Conkling to Trumbull, August 8, 1856, L. T. Papers.

[49] Trumbull to Abraham Lincoln, July 5, 1856, Jayne Papers.

[50] Trumbull to John M. Palmer, July 31, 1856. "A Collection of Letters from John M. Palmer to Lyman Trumbull, 1854–1858," *op. cit.*, p. 31.

Judd's sentiments.[51] Responding to the appeals, Trumbull went home in September and campaigned vigorously until election day.

The results of the election in Illinois, which gave Buchanan a small plurality over Frémont, were nevertheless a humiliating defeat for the Democrats, because the Republicans elected the entire slate of state officials, headed by Bissell, and won four out of nine seats in Congress. For a new, loosely organized party, this was a signal victory. Among the Republican Congressmen who were elected were such strong anti-slavery men as Owen Lovejoy and John F. Farnsworth.[52]

Lyman Trumbull had reason to be satisfied with the election results and to feel rewarded for the efforts he had made on behalf of his new party. There was, however, little time for rejoicing, because the Kansas controversy was reaching a new height of intensity. Buchanan's newly appointed governor of the Kansas Territory, Robert J. Walker of Mississippi, took steps to carry out the provisions of the Kansas Enabling Act, but he assured the free-soilers that the new constitution would be submitted to a popular vote. The constitutional convention met at Lecompton and adopted a constitution that was likely to make Kansas a slave state. The convention had also decided that the people of Kansas would not have an opportunity either to accept or to reject the constitution, but would be allowed only to vote on the slavery clause deciding either "for the constitution, with slavery," or "for the constitution without slavery." The vote on this issue was set for January 4, 1858.

Stephen Douglas, realizing that he had underestimated Northern opposition to the extension of slavery, was now determined to recoup his political losses. Knowing the strong sentiment in Illinois for a free Kansas, he also had no intention of endanger-

---

[51] Norman B. Judd to Trumbull, August 3, 1856; Gustave Koerner to Trumbull, July 29, 1856, L. T. Papers.

[52] Lusk, op. cit., p. 32; and Pease, op. cit., pp. 150–52. See also Illinois State Journal, November 19, 1856.

ing the chances for his re-election to the Senate in 1858.[53] In addition, Douglas felt that the pro-slavery forces in Kansas had violated his principle of "popular sovereignty." He therefore broke with President Buchanan over the Lecompton Constitution. Somewhat dazed by Douglas' move, Trumbull was nevertheless not ready to forget and forgive by welcoming Douglas back to the fold. He was convinced that "our little man will keep within the ring. . . . He will be permitted to oppose the admission of Kansas under the Lecompton Constitution . . . but I do not believe he will do anything which will cut him off the South and the administration." [54]

In Congress, Trumbull attacked Buchanan's message, which denounced the Topeka movement and constitution as a "revolutionary organization" and which endorsed the legality of the Lecompton convention. Trumbull protested the President's stand and said, "Now sir, I deny in toto that convention possessed any authority whatever." [55] The Kansas Legislature, he said, that convened the Lecompton convention was an illegal body born in fraud and intimidation and therefore had no right to convene a constitutional convention. He stated that "the free people of Kansas have no right, under the Lecompton constitution, to determine on the organic law under which they shall live." [56] Douglas, too, spoke against Buchanan's message and demanded that the people of Kansas be given an opportunity to ratify or to reject the entire Lecompton Constitution. His speech was received by thunderous applause. But in spite of the fact that Douglas for the first time agreed with his views, Trumbull did not join in the applause. Neither he nor Lincoln had any intention of welcoming Douglas into the Republican party, be-

---

[53] There were few illusions in Illinois as to Douglas' motives. The Illinois governor wrote to Trumbull, "His course is believed to be dictated solely by his fears connected with the next senatorial election." William H. Bissell to Trumbull, December 12, 1857, L. T. Papers. The publishers of the *Springfield State Journal* wrote that "Douglas is making a bold stroke to regain his lost ground in Illinois." Bailhache and Baker to Trumbull, December 16, 1857, L. T. Papers.

[54] Trumbull to Abraham Lincoln, December 5, 1857, Jayne Papers.

[55] *Cong. Globe*, 35 Cong., 1st Sess. (December 8, 1857), p. 7.

[56] *Ibid.*, p. 8.

cause they did not believe that Douglas was interested in stopping the extension of slavery. The Dred Scott decision, which was handed down on March 6, 1857, provided Lincoln and Trumbull with proof that Douglas would not and could not join their anti-slavery alliance. Douglas endorsed the Dred Scott decision as the law of the land,[57] while Lincoln and Trumbull denounced it.

The complete harmony of views between Lincoln and Trumbull on political questions of the time continued to be evident in their reaction to the Dred Scott decision. Both considered the decision written by Chief Justice Taney as illegal, because it dealt with a broad *political* question on which, in their opinion, the Supreme Court was not entitled to rule. They maintained that the Court could only rule on whether Scott was a citizen. Taney was wrong, Lincoln told a mass meeting in Springfield on June 12, 1857, when he stated that Negroes were not included in the Declaration of Independence. "It is not resistance," he said, "it is not factious, it is not even disrespectful, to treat it [the Dred Scott decision] as not having yet quite established a settled doctrine for the country." [58] Trumbull told the Senate that "The Supreme Court has no power to lay down political doctrines in the country. . . . The Court did decide that Dred Scott had no right to bring a suit in the United States Courts, and *that is all it decided.*" The judges of the Supreme Court, Trumbull stated, "traveled out of the record" when they attempted to "lay down political principles for this Government." [59]

Lincoln, in time, moderated his views on the powers of the Supreme Court, but Trumbull stubbornly clung to his position. A strong believer in the principle of the balance of powers and jealous of the prerogatives of the Congress and of the President, he was quite willing to limit the authority of the Supreme Court.

[57] *Illinois State Journal,* July 1, 1857.
[58] *The Living Lincoln,* p. 201.
[59] *Cong. Globe,* 36 Cong., 1st Sess. (December 8, 1859), p. 58. (Italics mine.)

7

Lyman Trumbull and the
Lincoln-Douglas Debates

IN THE EARLY SUMMER OF 1858, ILLINOIS HAD THREE OUTSTAND-
ing political leaders, Stephen A. Douglas, Lyman Trumbull, and
Abraham Lincoln. Both Douglas and Trumbull enjoyed a much
wider national reputation and had more influence in Illinois
than did Lincoln.

Douglas was a powerful and respected senator, chairman of
the important Committee on Territories, and an acknowledged
strong contender for the Presidential nomination of the Democratic party. He narrowly missed getting the nomination in 1856
when the Democratic party made Buchanan its standard bearer.
By the sheer force of his personality and his abilities, Stephen
Douglas rose rapidly to prominence in Illinois politics by filling
in relatively rapid succession the offices of State's Attorney,
member of the legislature, Secretary of State, Judge of the
Supreme Court of Illinois, Representative in Congress and finally Senator of the United States. He was a born leader of
men, a powerful orator and sharp debater, who earned his nickname of "Little Giant" even before he entered Congress. Horace
White was probably right in stating that "He [Douglas] was the

only man then living who could have carried through Congress a bill to repeal the Missouri Compromise." [1]

Abraham Lincoln in 1858 had behind him a respectable, if not a distinguished, career as a three-term member of the Illinois Legislature and as the man who was largely responsible for making Springfield the state capital. He was widely known as an able and successful lawyer. In national politics, Lincoln was an old-time Whig and a devoted follower of Henry Clay. Elected to the House of Representatives in 1846, he served only one term.

Lincoln's opposition to the Mexican War proved to be very damaging to his political standing in his home state, where the Mexican War was popular. Herndon wrote that Lincoln's speech in the House denouncing the war "sealed Lincoln's doom as a Congressman." [2] On the other hand, Lincoln's forthright opposition to the extension of slavery into Oregon, California, and New Mexico, his consistent support of the Wilmot Proviso, [3] and his effort to have slavery abolished in the District of Columbia gained him important support in Illinois, which made it possible for him, after 1856, to become one of the leaders of the Republican party.

However, there can be little doubt that in July, 1858, when Lincoln proposed to Douglas a series of debates, Lyman Trumbull had greater stature and prestige than his Republican colleague. Trumbull was completing over two years in the Senate, where he had been sent for the express purpose of standing up to the "Little Giant" and where he had become a thorn in Douglas' flesh.

Trumbull's entrance into the Senate, as we have seen, was not a very auspicious one, but he soon gained a reputation as a man of integrity, an erudite and effective speaker, and an ex-

[1] Horace White, "Abraham Lincoln in 1854," *Transactions of the Illinois State Historical Society for the Year 1908*, Illinois State Historical Library (Springfield, Ill., 1909), p. 29.

[2] *Herndon's Life of Lincoln*, p. 234.

[3] Thomas, *op. cit.*, pp. 125–28.

cellent parliamentarian. His encounters with Douglas on the Kansas question raised his stature and influence in the Senate.

Senator Douglas' break with Buchanan over the Lecompton Constitution greatly complicated the Illinois political situation. Many Illinois Republicans were impressed with Douglas' insistence on the right of the people of Kansas to a popular vote on slavery and were ready to endorse him as their leader.[4] In December, 1857, Douglas visited Chicago and huddled in his hotel room with a number of Republican leaders, assuring them that he intended to do all he could to have Kansas free. They were impressed. Norman B. Judd, a Cook County Republican leader, wrote Trumbull that Douglas "made some of their eyes stick out at his zeal."[5] Dr. Charles Ray, the editor of the *Chicago Tribune*, desperately wrote Trumbull for guidance, "We are almost confounded here by his anomalous position," he wrote, "and know not how to treat him and his overtures to the Republican party. Personally I am inclined to give him the lash; but I want to do nothing that will damage our cause or hinder the Emancipation of Kansas."

Thousands of Illinois Republicans who were faithful readers of the *New York Tribune* were astonished and confused by Greeley's suggestion that they allow Douglas to win the election by default and increase the breach between Douglas and Buchanan. This breach, Greeley calculated, would allow the Republicans to carry Illinois in 1860.[6] Lincoln was deeply perturbed by Greeley's stand, and he too, significantly, wrote to Trumbull and asked, "what does the 'New York Tribune' mean by its constant eulogizing and admiring and magnifying Douglas? Does it in this, speak the sentiments of the Republicans in Washington? Have they concluded that the Republican

[4] Charles Wilson, editor of the *Chicago Daily Journal,* to Trumbull, November 26, 1857, L. T. Papers.

[5] Norman B. Judd to Trumbull, December 1, 1857, L. T. Papers.

[6] *The Lincoln-Douglas Debates of 1858,* III, 21.

cause, generally, can be best promoted by sacrificing us here in Illinois?" [7]

Trumbull was calmly weighing the situation. He had no intention of allowing Douglas, who had called him a renegade Democrat and a Black Republican in bitter Senate debates, to take over the leadership of the Republican party of Illinois, which Trumbull had earned by hard work and great courage. He advised caution to see first how deep the breach between Douglas and Buchanan really was, but his rejection of Douglas was definitive. Trumbull advised Lincoln and the state party leaders who had written him for guidance, to begin a broad enlightenment campaign to convince the Illinois Republicans that Douglas could not be embraced as long as he supported the Dred Scott decision, as long as he denied the right of Congress to exclude slavery from the territories and as long as he supported the repeal of the Missouri Compromise.[8] While the Illinois Republicans endorsed Trumbull's position,[9] Horace Greeley continued his campaign to convince the rank and file of Illinois Republicans to ditch Lincoln and jump on Douglas' bandwagon. Greeley minced no words as to his conviction that Lincoln would be no match for Douglas. "As he [Lincoln] served only one term in the Lower House of Congress . . . there must be many who would like to know how he will be likely to

[7] A. Lincoln to Trumbull, December 28, 1857, "A Lincoln Correspondence," *Century Magazine* (February, 1909), p. 620.

[8] Trumbull to Lincoln, December 25, 1857, Trumbull Collection, Illinois State Historical Library, Springfield, Ill. Trumbull wrote to John M. Palmer, "Trust you are not dumbfounded by the course Douglas and Co. have taken as to have lost your reckoning." May 20, 1858, "A Collection of Letters from Lyman Trumbull to John M. Palmer, 1854–1858," *op. cit.*, p. 36.

In a letter to William B. Archer of Marshall, Illinois, Trumbull wrote, "he [Douglas] seems to be looking out for a safe place for himself but he must take several more steps yet before he can be fellowshipped by Republicans no man who endorses the dicta put forth in the Dred Scott decision deserves the confidence of Republicans or can get it." Trumbull to Archer, July 8, 1858, Trumbull Papers, Chicago Historical Society.

[9] George T. Brown to Trumbull, April 25, 1858; D. L. Phillips to Trumbull, March 2, 1858; and John M. Palmer to Trumbull, May 25, 1858, L. T. Papers.

fill the place of the now so notorious—I might say distinguished Douglas. Is he a match for his 'illustrious predecessor'?" [10] The *Cincinnati Commercial* stated editorially that "in dignity, intellect and majesty of mind, it is not pretended that he [Lincoln] is Douglas' equal." [11]

But Trumbull and the entire leadership of the Illinois Republican party firmly rejected Greeley's advice. They had no intention of committing political suicide, even if it would serve some real or fancied purpose on the party's national scene. The Republican State Convention, which met at Springfield on June 16, 1858, declared in a succinct and telling resolution that "Abraham Lincoln is the first and the only choice of the Republicans of Illinois for the United States Senate." [12] However, it has been generally overlooked that the convention had previously adopted another and equally significant resolution offered by Burton C. Cook, which read: "Resolved: That the Hon. Lyman Trumbull in the Senate of the United States has illustrated and defined the principles of the Republican party with distinguished ability and fidelity, and we hereby express our emphatic approval of his course." [13] The convention resolution made it clear to Douglas that in the 1858 campaign he would have to battle both Lincoln and Trumbull—a formidable combination. In order to destroy, or at least weaken this alliance, the Democrats made strenuous efforts to neutralize Trumbull's role in the campaign by sowing distrust between Trumbull and Lincoln and their respective supporters. The main tactic was to resurrect the 1855 senatorial election and to accuse Trumbull of cheating Lincoln out of the Senate seat in 1855. Trumbull's enemies, both Democrats and Republicans, persisted in alleging that Lincoln was promised the Senate seat in 1855 but that Trumbull with the help of Judd, Palmer, and Cook broke the

[10] *New York Tribune*, June 26, 1858.
[11] *Cincinnati Commercial*, July 13, 1858.
[12] *Illinois State Journal*, June 16, 1858.
[13] *Ibid.*

agreement.[14] The *Missouri* Republican (a Democratic organ) wrote, "Mr. A. Lincoln is the special object of admiration among the Black Republicans of Illinois. . . . Two years ago he occupied much the same position but he was diddled out of the place of Senator by the friends of Trumbull, and the same thing may happen to him again." [15]

Trumbull and his friends always indignantly denied this accusation, and Lincoln repeatedly exonerated Trumbull of any blame. Nevertheless, it could well be assumed that the charge was one of the factors that prompted Illinois Republican leaders to urge Trumbull to campaign for Lincoln in the state. Primarily, however, they wanted to make use of Trumbull's experience in debating with Douglas in the Senate, his talents as a speaker, his appeal to the voters in southern Illinois, especially in St. Clair and Madison Counties, and his acknowledged organizing abilities. By 1858, Trumbull, through well-placed federal appointments, through voluminous correspondence with local political leaders, through constant attention to the requests and interests of his constituents, and through a remarkably effective method of distribution of his Senate speeches throughout the state, had succeeded in organizing a strong personal political following.

Republican organizations in a number of cities and towns extended invitations to Trumbull to address large meetings.[16] Judd, chairman of the Illinois State Central Republican Committee, officially urged Trumbull to join in the canvass.[17] Dr. Ray wrote to Trumbull, "We must press you into the work on hand and that pretty soon. The pot begins to boil and you must help to keep up the fire. We have been looking for you

[14] "Long John" Wentworth repeated the accusation in 1859. See Trumbull to Lincoln, January 28, 1859, "A Lincoln Correspondence," *op. cit.,* p. 621.

[15] *Missouri Republican,* July 11, 1858.

[16] Mildred C. Stoller, "The Democratic Element in the New Republican Party in Illinois, 1856–1860," *Papers in Illinois History and Transactions for the Year 1842,"* the Illinois State Historical Society (Springfield, Ill., 1944), p. 59.

[17] Judd to Trumbull, July 16, 1858, L. T. Papers.

before now, and shall continue to look and hope until you come. I think you can do a great good in Madison, St. Clair and Randolph where we want aid badly; and of course your labors would be thankfully accepted elsewhere." [18] John M. Palmer, who nominated Trumbull for the Senate in 1855, strongly hinted in a letter to Trumbull that both of them must support Lincoln, "to whom we are under great obligation." [19] Old-line Whigs were equally insistent on Trumbull's coming to campaign for Lincoln. Many of them were still convinced that an ex-Democrat could be more effective in fighting a Democrat than a Whig.[20]

There is some evidence that Trumbull entered the canvass reluctantly and that he came to Illinois at the end of July primarily because he could not resist the pressure of his friends and of his party. On July 26 he wrote from Springfield to his friend Judge James R. Doolittle in Wisconsin that he came to Illinois because he was urged to do so by his friends. He added: "*Suppose I must do so*, for it will never do to let him be reelected, if we can help it." [21] The wording of the letter does suggest that Trumbull had no great desire to campaign and that he was more interested in beating Douglas than in electing Lincoln. It is difficult to tell how much of this reluctance to campaign was ascribable to his lack of enthusiasm for Lincoln, and how much to his tiredness from the strenuous battles with Douglas in the Senate or to his great dislike for addressing preelection mass meetings. We have it on the authority of a man who often shared the meeting platforms with Trumbull that the latter had a strong dislike for political campaigns. "He

[18] Ray to Trumbull, July 17, 1858, L. T. Papers.

[19] Palmer to Trumbull, May 25, 1858, L. T. Papers. Trumbull agreed with Palmer's contention, Trumbull to Palmer, June 19, 1858, "A collection of Letters from Lyman Trumbull to John M. Palmer, 1854–1858," *op. cit.*, p. 40.

[20] In a letter to Trumbull, Jesse K. Dubois wrote, "My observation is that we old line whigs belon[g]ing to the Republican ranks are not worth a curse to carry on a campaign. . . ." July 17, 1858, L. T. Papers.

[21] Trumbull to James R. Doolittle, Trumbull Collection, Illinois State Historical Society, Springfield, Ill. (Italics mine.)

[Trumbull] was no ranter," wrote Gustave Koerner, "was in fact an excellent and impressive and often sarcastic debater, not disposed and not able, indeed, to stir up a promiscuous crowd on the eve of an important election." [22] It is significant that Lincoln himself did not request Trumbull to come to his aid. He apparently was convinced that he could handle Douglas without Trumbull's assistance.

Trumbull opened his campaign in Chicago on August 7. He told an enthusiastic crowd that the Buchanan administration was spending money, power, and patronage to encourage the spread of slavery. On the question of the extension of slavery Trumbull declared: "I acknowledge a power higher than presidents, higher than Congresses, higher than supreme courts, and to that power, whose name is the people, I will appeal." He charged that in 1856 Douglas had purposely caused the omission of an amendment to the Nebraska Enabling Act, which called for submitting to the people any constitution that might be framed. "I will force the truth [of the charge] down any honest man's throat until he cannot deny it and to the man who does deny it, I will cram the lie down his throat until he shall cry enough." Douglas' deed, he added, was "the most damnable effrontery that man ever put on, to concoct a scheme to defraud and cheat a people out of their right and then claim credit for it." [23]

Trumbull's accusation was packed with political dynamite. If he could make it stick, it would expose Douglas' opposition to the Lecompton Constitution as a sham and deceit. In addition, it would tag Douglas with the charge of disloyalty by proving that he had first agreed with President Buchanan's position on the final legality of the Lecompton Constitution and then had turned and betrayed his chief. On August 9 Trumbull pressed his attack by stating, "I charge tonight that the very men who traverse the country under the banner

[22] Koerner, *Memoirs*, II, 435.
[23] *Chicago Press and Tribune*, August 8, 1858.

proclaiming Popular Sovereignty by design, concocted a bill on purpose to force a Constitution upon that people." [24]

Trumbull's attack infuriated Douglas. He lost his usual composure and in an answer to Trumbull at Beardstown he called his colleague a liar and a coward. He said, ". . . the miserable, cravenhearted wretch, he would rather have both ears cut off than use that language in my presence, where I could call him to account." Counterattacking, Douglas resurrected the old charge that Trumbull broke faith with Lincoln in the 1855 election. Trumbull, Douglas stated, welched on a deal that gave the 1855 Senate seat to Lincoln in exchange for Lincoln's and Whig support for Trumbull in 1858.[25]

George F. Milton pointed out that Trumbull, in his opening speeches in Chicago, said "hardly a word . . . about Lincoln or on his behalf."[26] Douglas complained that instead of fighting only Lincoln for the nomination he was forced, unfairly, to take on both Lincoln and Trumbull.[27] On August 13, Lincoln, in a speech at Havana, Illinois, took note of Douglas' attempt to gain sympathy by charging that Trumbull and Lincoln were ganging up on him. He said, "It is true that Judge Trumbull has made a speech in Chicago, and I believe he intends to co-operate with the Republican Central Committee in their arrangements for the campaign to the extent of making other speeches in different parts of the state. Judge Trumbull is a Republican, like myself, and he naturally feels a lively interest in the succcess of his party. Is there anything wrong about that?" [28]

Lincoln was pleased with Trumbull's effective encounters with Douglas, but he decided to challenge Douglas in a direct debate. Furthermore, Douglas was winning some sympathy for

[24] *Chicago Press and Tribune,* August 10, 1858.

[25] *Chicago Press and Tribune, August* 11 and 12, 1858.

[26] Milton, *op. cit.,* p. 335.

[27] The *Boston Daily Traveler,* August 23, 1958, carried a report on the Illinois Senatorial campaign under this banner: "Illinois, Trumbull and Douglas." *The Lincoln-Douglas Debates,* p. 58.

[28] *Chicago Press and Tribune,* August 15, 1858.

having to stand up against both Lincoln and Trumbull.[29] The best course was to force Douglas to debate with Lincoln, and not with Trumbull. Professor Edwin Erle Sparks has reasoned that "Lincoln saw that he was likely to be ignored if Trumbull were permitted to monopolize the attention of Douglas and in that case his political chances would be jeopardized. Manifestly his only course was to challenge Douglas to a series of set debates in which the political issues of the day would replace personal matters at stake between Douglas and Trumbull." [30]

In addition, Lincoln had to convince Illinois Republicans, and if possible the nation, that he too was a match for Douglas. Consequently, on July 24, Lincoln, through Judd, proposed a series of debates, a challenge that was promptly accepted by Douglas.

If Lincoln had hoped that the issues raised by Trumbull would not enter the debates, these hopes were only partially realized. Douglas was too deeply stung by Trumbull's charge to let go of the issue. In the first debate, on August 21 at Ottawa, Douglas elaborated on his accusation of a "deal" between Lincoln and Trumbull allegedly made in 1854. The agreement, said Douglas, called for Lincoln to "Abolitionize the old Whig Party," and for Trumbull to do the same with the old Democratic party and then to "connect the members of both into an Abolition party, under the name and disguise of a Republican party." [31] Here Douglas blundered by reading a set of "racial" anti-slavery resolutions and stating that these had been adopted with Lincoln's approval at a Republican state convention in Springfield in 1854. As Douglas had to acknowledge later, the resolutions he read had been adopted at Rockford, at a county convention, not at Springfield, where a moderate platform was adopted that did not call for the repeal of the Fugitive Slave

[29] *Philadelphia North American* wrote, "Alone and unaided he [Douglas] faced in the lists Trumbull and Lincoln, the best debaters afforded by the Republicans in the West, and probably equalled only by Seward in the East." July 25, 1858.
[30] *The Lincoln-Douglas Debates,* p. 58.
[31] *Ibid.,* p. 88.

Law and the abolition of slavery in the District of Columbia. These two provisions were, in Douglas' eyes, damnable demands of "Black Republicans."

Douglas denounced Lincoln for his opposition to the war with Mexico. Overlooking the patriotic motives that animated Lincoln to take an anti-war and an anti-expansionist stand, Douglas charged Lincoln with "taking the side of the common enemy against his own country." [32] Douglas also mistakenly charged Trumbull with advocating the repudiation of a large portion of the state debt in 1843–44.[33] In his Ottawa speech and in Freeport, Jonesboro, and Charleston debates, Douglas attacked Trumbull for reneging on a deal made with Lincoln, first to "abolitionize" the Whig and the Democratic parties, and second to give Lincoln the Senate seat in 1855. The purpose of these accusations was to split the powerful Lincoln-Trumbull coalition. At the Freeport debate, Douglas devoted a great deal of time to speculating as to whether or not Trumbull would vote in the Senate to admit Kansas before she had the requisite population. He recalled that Trumbull voted not to admit Oregon because of its small population. Douglas wanted to know what Lincoln's position would be should Trumbull vote negatively on the admission of Kansas. "I would like Mr. Lincoln to answer this question," stated Douglas. ". . . *If he differs with Mr. Trumbull, let him answer his argument* against the admission of Oregon, instead of poking questions at me. . . . *As Mr. Trumbull is in the field, fighting for Mr. Lincoln, I would like to have Mr. Lincoln answer his own question, and tell me whether he is fighting Trumbull on this issue or not.*" [34]

At Jonesboro, Douglas made an attempt to substantiate the accusation of Trumbull's breach of faith with Lincoln by citing

[32] *Ibid.*, p. 91.

[33] Ford, *op. cit.*, p. 137. Ford wrote, "The bill passed by a large majority, and was approved by the council of revision. Judge Douglas *notwithstanding he had advised the measure before the finance committee, voted against it in the council.*" (Italics mine.)

[34] *The Lincoln-Douglas Debates,* pp. 160–61. (Italics mine.)

a speech made in 1856 by Colonel James H. Matheny, a friend of Lincoln's, in which he charged that "Trumbull succeeded by pledging all that was required by any party, in thrusting Lincoln aside, and foisting himself, an excrescence from the rotten bowels of the Democracy, into the United States Senate." [35] As he had done previously, Lincoln denied the charge. He said: "I wish simply to say what I have said to him before, that he cannot know whether it is true or not, and I do know that there is not a word of truth in it. . . ." He added that Colonel Matheny did an "immoral thing" by making his charges.[36]

Lincoln replied to the often-repeated charge of Douglas that Republicans spoke on slavery differently in northern, central, and southern Illinois. In a speech in Freeport, he stated that there were three factions in Illinois on the question of slavery, but that they had compromised their views and united in their opposition to the Nebraska Act and to the extension of slavery. Lincoln made it clear to Douglas that his efforts to split him from Trumbull and to divide northern and southern Illinois Republicans would not succeed. "He is afraid," said Lincoln, "we'll all pull together." [37]

The Charleston debate of September 18, 1858, concerned basically, the original charge made by Trumbull at the opening of the campaign in Chicago that Douglas himself was responsible for dropping the amendment demanding the submission of the framed constitution to the popular vote in Kansas. In his opening speech, Lincoln said that when Trumbull first made the accusation, he, Lincoln, said nothing about it but, knowing Trumbull as a man of truth, was sure that proof would be forthcoming. Subsequently, Lincoln related, Trumbull did, in a speech at Alton, produce a copy of the 1856 Kansas Enabling Act, called the Toombs bill, which originally had the following words: ". . . which [the Constitution] if accepted by the Con-

[35] Ibid., pp. 160–61.
[36] Ibid., p. 232
[37] Ibid., p. 183.

vention and ratified by the people at the election for the adoption of the constitution, shall be obligatory upon the United States and the said State of Kansas." [38] These words, Trumbull said, were omitted from the bill when it was reported to the Senate by Douglas as chairman of the Committee on Territories. Since Douglas said in Jacksonville that he intended to hold Lincoln responsible for Trumbull's "slanders," Lincoln told the Charleston audience that he had studied the evidence and was convinced that Trumbull's accusation was true. He concluded that Douglas' statement that Trumbull's evidence "was forged from beginning to end," had no basis in fact.[39] Douglas in his reply told the audience that in his speech reporting the Toombs bill he did say that a vote should be held in Kansas on the constitution. Furthermore, he asked, why did Trumbull not arraign him on this charge in 1856 in the Senate instead of waiting until the campaign? [40] Showing continued discomfort at his having to fight both Trumbull and Lincoln, Douglas asked the audience: "Are you going to elect Mr. Trumbull's colleague upon an issue between Mr. Trumbull and me? I thought I was running against Abraham Lincoln, that he claimed to be my opponent, had challenged me to a discussion of the public questions of the day with him . . . but it turns out that his only hope is to ride into office on Trumbull's back. . . ." [41] In his rejoinder, Lincoln gave a wholehearted testimonial to Trumbull's veracity and integrity. "Neither in that thing, nor any other," he said, "in all the years that I have known Lyman Trumbull, have I known him to fail of his word or tell a falsehood, large or small." [42]

Historians generally have not appraised the debates highly. They have, as a rule, overlooked the role played by Trumbull in the debates and have belittled the importance of the issues

38 *Ibid.*, p. 272.
39 *Ibid.*, p. 279.
40 *Ibid.*, p. 282.
41 *Ibid.*, p. 286. (Italics mine.)
42 *Ibid.*, p. 306.

debated. Albert Beveridge, Lincoln's biographer, said: "Solely on their merits, the debates themselves deserve little notice. For the most part, each speaker merely repeated what he had said before. Few and unimportant were the points made. . . . But the debates served to advertise Lincoln to the country." [43] George Fort Milton wrote as follows: "Judged as debates, they do not measure up to their reputation." [44] James G. Randall saw very little of substance in the debates. He wondered why the debates were devoted completely to one issue—slavery—and excluded other national issues including tariff, railroads, education, land grants, etc. Randall asserted that only a limited and comparatively unimportant aspect of the subject of slavery was discussed in the debates. Furthermore, Randall stated, "on the broad problems of racial relations they [Lincoln and Douglas] did not fundamentally differ. . . . As to slavery in Kansas, Lincoln wanted Kansas free by congressional prohibition; Douglas favored a program that would inevitably have made Kansas free. . . ." [45] A different interpretation of the debates seems to be indicated.

In accordance with his doctrine of popular sovereignty, Douglas wanted to assure the people of Kansas of the right to decide whether they wanted slavery or not. He did not care, as he said, whether they voted slavery "up or down." Lincoln cared—he cared very much. Lincoln and Trumbull fought repeatedly in the Illinois Supreme Court to have voluntary servitude outlawed in Illinois.[46] On July 9, 1858, Lincoln said, in a speech in Chicago, "I have always hated slavery; I think as much as any Abolitionist—I have been an Old-Line Whig—I have always

---

[43] Albert J. Beveridge, *Abraham Lincoln 1809–1858* (Boston, 1928), II, 635.

[44] Quoted in J. G. Randall, *Lincoln the President* (New York, 1945), p. 127. Herbert Agar asserted: ". . . the debates are disappointing. They show the ability of both speakers to set traps and to avoid them. And they show that there was little difference between the candidates in regard to slavery." *The Prince of Union* (Boston, 1950), p. 388.

[45] J. G. Randall, *op. cit.,* pp. 122, 125, 127.

[46] Hand, *op. cit.,* p. 44.

hated it, but I have always been quiet about it until this new era of the introduction of the Nebraska bill began." [47]

Lincoln saw clearly the fundamental difference between himself and Douglas. It was, that he considered slavery an evil that must be fought, while Douglas did not. In the Ottawa debate Lincoln said, "When he [Douglas] invites any people, willing to have slavery, to establish it, he is blowing out the moral lights around us. When he says he 'cares not whether slavery is voted down or voted up' . . . he is, in my judgement, penetrating the human soul and eradicating the light of reason and the love of liberty in this American people." [48]

Lincoln did not want to abolitionize (using Douglas' favorite word) slavery. He wanted to stop its spread but he also looked hopefully to its end in all the Southern states. He said at the Galesburg debate on October 7, "*Now, I confess myself as belonging to that class in the country who contemplate slavery as a moral, social, and political evil . . . [I] desire a policy that looks to the prevention of it as a wrong, and looks hopefully to the time when, as a wrong, it may come to an end.*" [49]

In Quincy, on October 13, Lincoln defined "the true issue of this controversy" as being this: "I suggest that the difference of opinion, reduced to its lowest terms, is no other than the difference between the men who think slavery a wrong and those who do not think it wrong." [50] Disputing Douglas' assertions, Lincoln stated that the Founding Fathers did not make the nation half free and half slave. They found it so and left it "because they knew of no way to get rid of it at the time, but they looked to its speedy extinction." [51] On October 15, in the last

[47] Henry J. Raymond, *The Life and Public Services of Abraham Lincoln, Together with His State Papers* (New York, 1865), p. 60.

[48] *Ibid.*, p. 64. On a later occasion Lincoln wrote: "I am naturally anti-slavery. If slavery is not wrong, nothing is wrong. I cannot remember when I did not so think, and feel." Lincoln to A. G. Hodges, August 4, 1864, R. T. L. Collection.

[49] *Ibid.*, p. 69. (Italics mine.)

[50] *Ibid.*, p. 70.

[51] *Ibid.*, p. 71.

debate at Alton, deep in southern Illinois, Lincoln reiterated his conviction that "the real issue in this controversy is the sentiment on the part of one class that looks upon the institution of slavery as a wrong, and of another class that does not look upon it as wrong." [52]

Benjamin P. Thomas was right when he wrote, "the fundamental difference was ethical. Slavery being what it was, Lincoln knew that men of moral sensitivities would inevitably take their stand against it. Douglas thought these sensitivities could and should be suppressed." [53]

The debates also brought to light another important difference between Douglas and Lincoln. Douglas advocated the principle of white supremacy, and the view that the United States Government was a government created by the white people for the white people. He said at Jonesboro: "I hold that this Government was made on the white basis, by white men, for the benefit of white men and their posterity forever, and should be administered by white men and none others. I do not believe that the Almighty made the Negro capable of self-government." [54]

Lincoln believed not only that the Declaration of Independence applied to Negroes, but also that the United States must strive to perfect itself to assure full happiness for all of its citizens. He said at Alton: "They [the Founding Fathers] meant to set up a standard maxim for a free society . . . constantly looked to, constantly labored for, and even though never perfectly attained, constantly approximated . . . and augmenting

---

[52] *The Lincoln-Douglas Debates,* p. 482.

[53] Thomas, *op. cit.,* p. 192. Paul Angle, commenting on the complaints of historians that the speakers in the debates were concerned only with slavery in the territories wrote: "Such positions ignore basic reality, namely, that any issue, no matter how hollow, which stirs large numbers of people is a historical fact of first importance." *Created Equal? The Complete Lincoln-Douglas Debates of 1858* (Chicago, 1958), p. 29. See also discussion on the essence of the debates in Harry V. Jaffa, *Crisis of the House Divided* (Garden City, N.Y., 1957).

[54] *The Lincoln-Douglas Debates,* ed. Sparks, p. 225.

the happiness and value of life of all people of all colors, everywhere." [55]

Randall wrote that "any attempt to add luster to Lincoln's fame by belittling Douglas or by exaggerating the seriousness of differences between the two men, would be a perversion of history." [56] One could say, with more justice, that any attempt to detract from Lincoln's luster by inflating the image of Douglas or by minimizing the seriousness of their differences would be a perversion of history.

It is not surprising that Lincoln, Trumbull, and Douglas limited their speeches in the 1858 campaign to the issue of slavery. From 1854 this was *the* issue in the country. Trumbull's correspondence between 1855 and 1858 reveals how deeply not only the leaders but also the plain people were stirred and disturbed by the issue of slavery.

It is now agreed that the importance of the "Freeport doctrine," as it emerged from the debates, has been greatly exaggerated. Neither Lincoln's question nor Douglas' answer was new, either to them or to the nation, including the South. Lincoln reminded Douglas at the Jonesboro debate that "In the Senate of the United States, in 1856, Judge Trumbull, in a speech substantially, if not directly, put the same interrogatory to Judge Douglas, as to whether the people of a territory had the lawful power to exclude slavery prior to the formation of a constitution." [57] Douglas in the Senate, in the presence of the Southern senators, had given Trumbull substantially the same answer he gave Lincoln in Freeport. He expressed his willingness to see the Supreme Court decide the question and pointed to the need of cooperation from the local authorities in the establishment of slavery.[58] There is general agreement among

[55] *Ibid.*, p. 469.

[56] J. G. Randall, *op. cit.*, p. 127.

[57] *The Lincoln-Douglas Debates,* ed. Sparks, p. 243. See also *Cong. Globe,* 34 Cong., 1st Sess., pp. 1369–75.

[58] See D. E. Fehrenbacher, "Lincoln, Douglas, and the Freeport Question," *The American Historical Review,* LXVI, No. 3 (April, 1961), pp. 599–617.

historians that the "debates so advertised Lincoln that he became, a figure of national importance." [59] But what was even more important for Lincoln's future career was that the debates proved to the people of Illinois that Lincoln was a match for Douglas. He had also shown that while he had the powers of intellect and the erudition to deal with political and constitutional questions equal to those of Trumbull, he had far greater popular appeal than did his Republican colleague. He, unlike Trumbull, had the ability to stir men's souls to moral indignation. It was this revelation that caused the *Chicago Tribune*, Judge Davis, Norman Judd, and others to work with wholehearted devotion for Lincoln's nomination in 1860.[60]

What remains to be discussed is the question raised by "Long John" Wentworth as to whether or not Trumbull gave his wholehearted support to Lincoln in the 1858 canvass. Lincoln did not entertain such doubts. He wrote to Trumbull, "I do not for a moment doubt that you, Judd, Cook, Palmer, and the Republicans generally, coming from the old Democratic ranks, were as sincerely anxious for my succcess in the late contest as I myself. . . . I cannot conceive it possible for me to be a rival of yours [in 1860, when Trumbull's term was to expire] or to take sides against you in favor of any rival." [61] The evidence is overwhelming that Lyman Trumbull, with his customary integrity, acted with complete devotion to discharge his deeply felt obligation to help elect Lincoln.[62]

[59] J. G. Randall, *loc. cit.*

[60] The *Chicago Tribune*, which before the debates thought of Trumbull as superior to Lincoln, changed its editorial mind after the election: "If it should turn out that . . . Mr. Lincoln shall fail in the election to the Senate, his fame is already secure." *Chicago Press and Tribune*, November 15, 1858.

[61] *Ibid.*, p. 621

[62] Trumbull wrote to Palmer on June 19, 1958, "I fully appreciate the considerations you suggest in regard to Mr. Lincoln and feel more deeply than anyone else the obligations we are under to him." "A Collection of Letters from Lyman Trumbull to John M. Palmer, 1854–1858," *op. cit.*, p. 40.

8

Trumbull and Lincoln's
Nomination and Election

EARLY IN JANUARY, 1859, TRUMBULL THOUGHT THAT THE DEMO-
cratic party was "very much demoralized," and he set out to
clarify the principles of the Republican party.[1] He had already
told the Senate and the country, during the debate on the admission of Oregon, that he believed that "negro slavery was an
evil," but that he had "never contended for giving the negro
equal privileges with the white man." [2] Speaking a few months
later, Trumbull foresaw the day when Negroes would be free
and expressed his hope that they would be colonized in "some
region of country, not far distant to which our free negro population may be taken. . . ." "The free Negroes should be sent,"
Trumbull continued, "to a place where they would not be dominated and where they could develop their powers." [3]

On January 7, 1859, Trumbull clarified, in a Senate speech,
his position on the sectional conflict. He believed that his position represented the stand of the Republican party. He reiterated
his opposition to any interference with slavery in the states

[1] Lyman Trumbull to Burton C. Cook, January 20, 1859, L. T. Papers.
[2] *Cong. Globe*, 35 Cong., 1st Sess. (May 5, 1858), p. 165.
[3] *Cong. Globe*, 36 Cong., 1st Sess. p. 60.

where it existed, but expressed his determination to oppose any further extension of slavery. Trumbull, addressing himself directly to the Southern senators, put them on notice that the laws of the Union would be enforced in the South regardless of cost and consequences. "When the Republican party attains power, it will not, as the senator from Georgia [Senator Iverson] supposes, make any encroachments on the rights of the South, but it will, I trust, be equally ready to enforce the law of both North and South, and its army and navy will be called into requisition alike in all parts of the Republic whenever needed for the enforcement of the law. . . ." [4] This was a harsh declaration, put in words seldom addressed to the South by a spokesman of the North. It gave a strong hint of the uncompromising position Trumbull was to take a year later on the issue of secession. Lincoln, who read the speech in a pamphlet form, called it a "capital one" and gave it his full endorsement.[5]

On domestic issues Trumbull gave his full support to the Pacific Railroad bill and especially to the Homestead Act, bitterly castigating those senators who voted to put this bill aside in favor of a bill calling for the acquisition of Cuba for thirty million dollars. He considered the Homestead Act to be "of more benefit to the country than any other prospect that has been introduced." [6] He felt it was wrong for the Senate to go around debating about the "acquisition of a country that does not belong to us, instead of providing for the settlement of the country which we own." [7] Trumbull confirmed his opposition to foreign adventures, his devotion to economy in government, and his basic opposition to a large military establishment when he proposed a drastic fifty-percent cut in the Army and Navy

---

[4] Cong. Globe, 35 Cong., 2nd Sess. (February 25, 1859), p. 1352.

[5] Abraham Lincoln to Trumbull, January 29, 1859, "A Lincoln Correspondence," op. cit., p. 620.

[6] Cong. Globe, 35 Cong., 2nd Sess. (February 25, 1859), p. 1352.

[7] Ibid. See also Trumbull's expressed opposition to the acquisition of Cuba in a letter to Burton C. Cook, January 20, 1859, L. T. Papers. Lincoln wrote to Trumbull that there was no popular clamor for Cuba in Illinois and that he should vote as his conscience dictated. "A Lincoln Correspondence," op. cit., p. 621.

of the United States. In view of the impending crisis, this was an unwise move, but it revealed Trumbull's deep distrust of the military, which was to remain with him throughout his life. He thoroughly disliked the standing army and the West Point and Annapolis academies and wanted to rely, in time of war or insurrection, on a people's volunteer army. "Why, Sir, we want no navy," he stated, "except a few revenue vessels to protect our commerce against smuggling and against pirates, if there are any. A great portion of the Army is worse than useless to the country." [8]

The raid of John Brown on Harper's Ferry, which came a few weeks after Trumbull's unsuccessful attempt to cut the size of the armed forces of the United States in half, proved how unwise was his proposal. The raid was a source of deep embarrassment to Illinois Republican leaders and particularly to Trumbull, who made every effort on the floor of the Senate to disassociate himself from any tinge of abolitionism. As a matter of fact, he invited his fellow senators to attack the abolitionists to their heart's desire.[9] He wrote to Koerner and others anxious letters urging them to condemn the raid as an act of a madman.[10] In the first stages of the John Brown drama the Republican press and leaders in Chicago vigorously condemned the raid. The *Chicago Press and Tribune* wrote: "We desire to see all parties engaged in that bloody *émeute* brought to punishment. . . . If hanging is the penalty—hang; if imprisonment—imprison." [11] But as time progressed, Brown's impressive conduct in prison and at the trial and the courage he exhibited at the

[8] *Cong. Globe,* 35 Cong., 2nd Sess. (February 12, 1859), p. 992.

[9] *Cong. Globe,* 34 Cong., 3rd Sess. (December 2, 1856), p. 15.

[10] Koerner, *Memoirs,* II, 78.

[11] *Chicago Press and Tribune,* October 21, 1859. The owners of the *Tribune* did not know that their star reporter, Horace White, was Brown's supporter. White testified later before the Senate Select Committee of Inquiry on John Brown's Raid that he was one of the founders of the National Free Kansas Committee and that he saw Brown several times in New York and voted to give Brown some money and two rifles. Text of the testimony in Horace White Papers, Illinois State Historical Library, Springfield, Ill.

execution brought a wave of sympathy in the North, and John Brown became the symbol of anti-slavery martyrdom.

The motion for a thorough inquiry into the raid came immediately after the Thirty-sixth Congress convened, on December 5, 1859. Lyman Trumbull rose to offer an amendment, proposing that the inquiry include also the bloody raid of Missouri pro-slavers on the United States arsenal in Liberty, Missouri, on December 5, 1855. Trumbull condemned Brown's act and the motives behind it. "No man," he said, "who is not prepared to subvert the Constitution, destroy the Government, and resolve society to its original elements, can justify such an act. No matter what evils either real or imaginary, may exist in the body politic, if each individual, or every set of twenty individuals, out of more than twenty millions of people, is to be permitted, in his own way and in defiance of the laws of the land, to undertake to correct those evils, there is not a government on the face of the earth that could last a day." Summarizing, Trumbull conceded that "no man can justify the deeds done at Harper's Ferry," but he contended that the Liberty, Missouri, raid was equally reprehensible because it was intended to obtain arms to force slavery upon Kansas.[12]

Senator Mason of Virginia, the proponent of the motion for an inquiry, bitterly assailed Trumbull's amendment to investigate an obscure, five-years-old event, as aimed to obstruct the Harper's Ferry investigation. Mason objected also to Trumbull's sarcastic reference to the "shrieks of outrage," that came from Virginia at the news of Brown's raid and asked Trumbull to withdraw his amendment.[13] Trumbull refused, and taking the floor again, asserted, amidst a storm of protests and interruptions from Southern senators, that the Liberty raid was more serious than John Brown's attack because while the former cost hundreds of lives, only one life was lost at Harper's Ferry.[14]

[12] *Cong. Globe*, 36 Cong., 1st Sess. (December 5, 1859), p. 5.
[13] *Ibid.*, p. 7.
[14] *Ibid.*, p. 38.

Lincoln informed Trumbull that he had read the speech and found that it "really is an excellent one, many of the points being admirably made." [15]

As a result of his stand on Brown's raid, Trumbull's relations with his colleagues from the South, which had been cordial from the time of his coming to Washington, were rapidly deteriorating. The Southerners began to realize that in Trumbull they had a determined and an irreconcilable foe. Trumbull, on the other hand, with a great deal of insight and wisdom, foresaw the probability of an armed clash with the South.[16]

Before turning his attention to the national scene and the approaching national conventions, Trumbull was busy with his own back yard in Illinois. His first concern was to win the special elections in the fall of 1859 for Republican candidates. He was especially eager to elect his friend John M. Palmer to Congress. Trumbull was also aware of the fact that any diminution of Republican strength in the state would have endangered the chances of his re-election to the Senate. He campaigned furiously throughout Illinois and addressed many large and enthusiastic meetings.[17] Trumbull established his campaign headquarters in Springfield and showed himself to be a skillful organizer and a resourceful politician who knew that elections are won or lost at the grassroot level. From the state capital he sent out streams of letters and messages to his political friends throughout the state, urging them to conduct a door-to-door campaign for the members of the legislature. In one such letter he wrote to Richard Yates: "Let every Republican voter in your county be sure and urged, not only to vote himself, but to bring a friend to the Polls. . . . It is important that tickets [ballots]

[15] Lincoln to Trumbull, December 25, 1859, "A Lincoln Correspondence," *op. cit.*, p. 622.

[16] Lyman Trumbull to Richard Yates, January 2, 1860, Uriah L. Reavis Collection, Chicago Historical Society.

[17] Lyman Trumbull to Julia Jayne Trumbull, October 12, October 16, October 22, 1859, L. T. Family Papers.

be placed in the hands of reliable men in each precinct who will go for the absent voters who do not appear by 2 o'clock." [18]

Trumbull was constantly badgered by the feud- and faction-ridden Republican party in Illinois. There was little unity or solidarity among the cliques and factions. Basically, there were two large factions. One centered around the able, colorful, and eccentric "Long John" Wentworth, the editor of the *Chicago Democrat*, and included Judge David Davis and Leonard Swett. The *Tribune* clique included Joseph Medill, Norman B. Judd, Ebenezer Peck, and, with some degree of aloofness, Lyman Trumbull. In the spring of 1860 the two factions put up rival candidates for governor: Leonard Swett and Norman Judd. Since Judd had been instrumental in Trumbull's election to the Senate in 1855 and was a former anti-Nebraska Democrat, Trumbull was duty-bound to support him. But there is reason to believe that he was not unhappy when the state convention, which met in Decatur on May 9, nominated his good friend, an ex-Whig, Richard Yates of Jacksonville, as a compromise candidate.[19] Trumbull and Judd and their faction, while unable to elect Judd, did succeed in eliminating John Wentworth from any position of leadership in the state party organization. He was excluded from the State Central Committee and was not named a delegate to the Chicago convention.[20] Judge Davis put strong pressure on Lincoln to name Wentworth as a delegate-at-large, but Lincoln refused and named Davis, Judd, Koerner, and Browning.[21]

Trumbull loyally supported the endorsement by the state convention of Abraham Lincoln for the Presidential nomination

[18] Lyman Trumbull to Richard Yates, October 21, 1859, Uriah L. Reavis Collection, Chicago Historical Society.

[19] *Chicago Press and Tribune*, May 11, 1860; *Illinois State Journal*, May 16, 1860. Some of Trumbull's friends feared that Judd's election might alienate the Whigs and cause Trumbull's defeat for the Senate. William Jayne to Trumbull, May 13, 1860, L. T. Papers.

[20] William Jayne to Trumbull, May 13, 1860; Horace White to Trumbull, May 14, 1860, L. T. Papers.

[21] David Davis to Trumbull, May 8, 1860, L. T. Papers.

at the forthcoming Republican convention at Chicago. He had, however, little enthusiasm for Lincoln's candidacy. As a matter of fact, with the exception of Davis, Swett, and possibly Medill, few Republican leaders in Lincoln's home state believed him suited for the White House. They were too near to him and had known him for too long in the rough and tumble of Illinois politics to be able to appreciate his qualities of wisdom and leadership. Even Orville H. Browning, Lincoln's Whig friend from Quincy, was not interested in the movement to nominate Lincoln for the Presidency. He openly supported an Old-Line Missouri Whig, Edward Bates,[22] and did not come around to supporting Lincoln until the middle of May.[23] Even then, he still considered Bates superior to Lincoln.[24]

Lyman Trumbull was not convinced that Lincoln should be the nominee, although he was willing to support his candidacy. While he respected Lincoln, he did not consider himself inferior to him in intellect and in leadership qualities. In an almost brutally frank letter, Trumbull told Lincoln that in a contest with Seward for the nomination, the latter would win. He told Lincoln that he was "urging [his] claims" in Washington, but that people there preferred Seward. Trumbull did not believe that Seward could win the election and suggested that Judge McLean, of Ohio, could, but he loyally assured Lincoln: "Now I wish you to understand that I am for you first and foremost, want our state to send only delegates instructed in your favor. . . ." He wondered, however, whether such personal considerations should be decisive. "From what I have written," he concluded, "you will readily see, that I am inclined to favor this McLean movement." [25] Almost simultaneously with the receipt of this letter, Lincoln was warned by Judge Davis that the *Tribune* clique was really interested in nominating Trumbull.

[22] Browning, *Diary,* I, 381–82.
[23] Koerner, *Memoirs,* II, 87–89.
[24] Browning, *Diary,* I, 407–08.
[25] Trumbull to Lincoln, April 24, 1860, "A Lincoln Correspondence," *op cit.,* pp. 623–24.

He wrote Lincoln that Wentworth "believes that the *Tribune* Clique, as he calls them, are devoted to the elevation of Trumbull and that their going for you is a mere blind. . . . *I must confess to sharing his opinion a good deal.*" [26]

Lincoln decided to act quickly. He made it clear to Trumbull that he wanted the nomination and politely but firmly warned his friend not to support publicly or privately any other candidate. The letter is a perfect example of the inner strength and deep knowledge of human nature that so few people, including Trumbull, recognized in Lincoln. Choosing his words carefully Lincoln wrote: "A word now for your own special benefit—You better write no letters which can possibly be distorted into opposition, or quasi-opposition to me. There are men on the constant watch for such things out of which to prejudice my peculiar friends [an obvious reference to Davis and Wentworth] against you. While I have no more suspicions of you than I have of my best friend living, I am kept in constant struggle against suggestions of this sort—I have hesitated some to write this paragraph, lest you should suspect I do it for my own benefit, and not for yours; but on reflection I concluded you will not suspect me." [27] Trumbull took the hint and stopped promoting the McLean candidacy, and even Judge Davis gave him a clean bill of health and assured Lincoln: "I don't think Trumbull is playing you false." [28]

Republican opinion in Illinois gradually solidified for Lincoln, not because the Republican leaders found him increasingly attractive but because they found his opponents increasingly unattractive. McLean was seventy-six years old; Bates was a conservative Whig from a slave state, was opposed by the Germans, and had little following on the Eastern seaboard. Seward, the strongest competitor of Lincoln, in spite of his great prestige as

[26] David Davis to Lincoln, April 23, 1860, R. T. L. Collection. (Italics mine.)
[27] Lincoln to Trumbull, April 29, 1860, *Collected Works of Abraham Lincoln*, ed. Ray Basler (New Brunswick, N. J., 1953), IV, 45–46.
[28] David Davis to Lincoln, May 5, 1860, R. T. L. Collection.

a former governor and as a senator, was disliked by Illinois Republicans, who blamed him and Greeley for Lincoln's defeat in 1858.[29] In addition, Seward was handicapped by his old anti-Masonry connections, his support, as Governor of New York, of Catholic parochial schools, and his alleged radicalism on the slavery question.[30] Trumbull was sure that Seward could not carry Illinois and that he, Trumbull, would lose the election to the Senate in the case of Seward's nomination.[31] Seward's opposition in New York to the Know-Nothings antagonized some elements in Illinois, although it brought him the solid support of the Germans.[32]

While none of his opponents had overwhelming support, few believed that Lincoln could be nominated.[33] Lincoln got the nomination because of the frantic, and partially successful, efforts of Horace Greeley to block Seward's nomination, and because of the determined efforts of the Illinois delegation led by Davis, Judd, Palmer and Browning. All feuds and factional hatreds were submerged—a real tribute to Lincoln's peculiar ability to be in the thick of politics and slightly above them. The Wentworth-Davis clique and the *Tribune* spoke for the first time with one voice.[34]

Much has been made of the pro-Lincoln parades, the packing of the Wigwam with Lincoln's supporters and the usual backroom deals and bargains of Davis, Swett, and Judd to secure the votes of Indiana, Pennsylvania, New Jersey, and other delegations. All these efforts were important and contributed to

[29] Ebenezer Peck to Trumbull, November 22, 1858, L. T. Papers. See also Koerner, *Memoirs*, II, 79.

[30] *Chicago Press and Tribune*, February 27, 1860.

[31] Trumbull to Lincoln, April 24, 1860, "A Lincoln Correspondence," *op. cit.*, p. 623.

[32] *Chicago Democrat*, May 18, 1860. Gustave Koerner to Trumbull, December 23, 1859; April 16, 1860, L. T. Papers.

[33] William Jayne to Trumbull, May 20, 1860, L. T. Papers; William H. Bissell to Salmon P. Chase, February 4, 1860, Chase Papers, Library of Congress.

[34] John M. Palmer wrote, "Undoubtedly Judge Davis and Norman B. Judd contributed most to the nomination of Mr. Lincoln, they were indefatigable in their efforts to secure his nomination." Palmer, *Personal Recollections*, p. 81.

Lincoln's victory, but Carl Schurz might have been correct when he sensibly remarked in his autobiography: "Much has been said about the superior volume and fierceness of the shouting for Lincoln in the packed galleries and its effect upon the minds of the delegates. But that is mere reporters' talk. The historic fact is that, as the convention would not take the risks involved in the nomination of Seward, it had no other alternative than to select Lincoln as the man who satisfied the demands of the earnest anti-slavery men without subjecting the party to the risks thought to be inseparable from the nomination of Seward." [35]

Trumbull did not attend the convention, but asked some of his political associates to throw their support to Lincoln. Gustave Koerner received a letter from Trumbull, urging him to support Lincoln.[36] Trumbull received scores of letters from Illinois, expressing confidence that Lincoln would carry the state and win the Presidency.[37] Immediately after the convention, Trumbull sent his congratulations to Lincoln and pledged his wholehearted cooperation in the campaign. Lincoln in reply thanked him for his support and requested that Trumbull give his regards to Senators Hamlin, Seward, Cameron, and Wade.[38]

The relative peace between the Trumbull-Judd and Davis-Wentworth factions which prevailed during the convention did not last. Shortly after the convention, feuding flared up anew, but this time the stakes were higher. They battled for influence over the future President and the all-important control of patronage. The rivalry continued with great ferocity until Lincoln's inauguration. Both sides vied for Lincoln's favor and occasionally used intrigue and devious maneuvers to get it. Judge Davis and his faithful lieutenant, Leonard Swett, made a determined effort to restore "Long John" Wentworth to a position of influ-

[35] *The Autobiography of Carl Schurz*, p. 160.
[36] Koerner, *Memoirs*, II, 93.
[37] William Jayne, J. A. Mills, William H. Herndon, H. G. McPike to Trumbull, May 20, June 4, June 14, June 29, 1860, L. T. Papers.
[38] Abraham Lincoln to Trumbull, May 26, 1860, L. T. Papers.

ence and insisted that Lincoln invite the popular Chicago mayor to participate in the campaign.[39] Trumbull and Judd, who in March, 1860, in a show of Republican unity and under Lincoln's pressure had supported Wentworth in his mayoralty campaign, now wanted Wentworth kept on the sidelines.[40] Trumbull had not forgotten that Wentworth had accused him of bad faith in the 1858 campaign and that he had warned Lincoln that Judd was conspiring to make Trumbull the Republican nominee for President.[41] Lincoln, who was a master in exploiting rivalries of hostile factions in order to assure for himself complete freedom of action, made a gesture of peace toward Wentworth and invited him to participate in the campaign.[42] "Long John" ignored Lincoln's kind gesture and launched an editorial campaign in the *Chicago Democrat* that proved to be embarrassing and potentially dangerous to the Republican nominee. Wentworth in his editorials praised the doctrine of "irrepressible conflict," demanded the immediate repeal of the Illinois "Black Laws" of 1853, and predicted that Lincoln, once in the White House, would free the four million slaves.[43] Joseph Medill, whose *Tribune* gave Lincoln its wholehearted support, was so alarmed that he warned Lincoln that "If he [Wentworth] can make people in the North believe that you are a radical ultra fanatic, he expects that it will drive the conservative moderate voters away from you." [44]

Medill was wrong in assuming that Wentworth's aim was to defeat Lincoln. The biographer of Wentworth was closer to the truth when he suggested that Wentworth's "main target was

[39] David Davis to Lincoln, May 28, 1860, R. T. L. Collection.

[40] Norman B. Judd to Lincoln, May 2, 1860, R. T. L. Collection. On Trumbull's participation in the Wentworth campaign, see *Chicago Press and Tribune,* March 5, 1860. See also the excellent account in Don E. Fehrenbacher, *Chicago Giant: A Biography of "Long John" Wentworth* (Madison, Wis., 1957), pp. 172–75.

[41] John Wentworth to Lincoln, April 21 and 30, 1858. R. T. L. Collection. (Letter misdated May 30.)

[42] Lincoln to David Davis, July 27, 1860, Rockwell Papers, quoted by King, *op. cit.,* p. 149.

[43] *Chicago Daily Democrat,* July 2, July 31, 1860.

[44] Joseph Medill to Lincoln, August 9, 1860, R. T. L. Collection. See *Chicago Tribune,* May 19, 1860, a most effective editorial entitled "Honest Old Abe."

probably Trumbull rather than Lincoln." [45] "Long John" knew that his editorials would frighten the voters in southern Illinois and would result in a Democratic majority in the Illinois Legislature. Judge David Davis assured Lincoln that Wentworth's editorials were not aimed at him, but were written to "assure Trumbull's defeat." [46] This explanation did not reassure Lincoln, who knew that Trumbull's defeat would probably mean the loss of Illinois.

Trumbull, who was in Washington, attempted to prevent a coalition of Thurlow Weed, Seward's manager in Chicago, and the Davis-Swett-Wentworth faction. When Weed, at Judge Davis' instigation, visited Lincoln in Springfield, Trumbull warned the Republican nominee not to succumb to the wiles of that "shrewd, fascinating man." Trumbull related to Lincoln that he "remarked to the Gentlemen who spoke to me on the subject that you was [sic!] too prudent and cautious a man to get complicated by promises to anybody." [47]

At the end of July, Trumbull went to Illinois and began an intensive campaign on behalf of the Republican candidates. He spoke in all parts of the state but concentrated mainly on southern Illinois where his influence was most needed to overcome the strong Democratic allegiance of this section. He addressed large meetings in Chicago and Belleville and received a tremendous reception in Alton "with cannons and torches." Trumbull wrote to Julia from Alton that he made "for me, I think, a partly good speech for I caught the enthusiasm and felt well." [48]

On August 8, Trumbull, Senator James R. Doolittle of Wisconsin, Gustave Koerner, and Orville Browning addressed a Republican rally at the Springfield fairgrounds. It was an immense and enthusiastic meeting.[49] Exhausted but happy at the end of the arduous campaign, which culminated in another speech in

[45] Fehrenbacher, *Chicago Giant,* p. 182.
[46] David Davis to Lincoln, October 4, 1860, R. T. L. Collection.
[47] Trumbull to Lincoln, May 31, 1860, R. T. L. Collection.
[48] Lyman Trumbull to Julia Jayne Trumbull, July 13, 1860. Also July 14, August 19, October 23, 1860, L. T. Family Papers.
[49] George Trumbull to Lyman Trumbull, August 13, 1860, L. T. Family Papers.

Alton, Trumbull wrote to his wife: "I feel as if my task were really done." [50]

Trumbull's furious campaign was motivated both by his desire to assure the election of an Illinois Legislature with a Republican majority in order to assure his re-election to the Senate, and by his determination to see Lincoln elected to the Presidency. He was undoubtedly instrumental in rallying the former Democrats in Illinois for a vigorous campaign for Lincoln. "They [the Democrats] carried with them," Professor Cole wrote, "the old fighting spirit, far superior to anything that old Whiggery had been able to arouse in its ranks." [51] Koerner, who did an excellent job in getting the support of German voters for the Republican ticket, testified that "Trumbull, Judd, Palmer, I. N. Arnold, Cook . . . did magnificent work on the stump." [52] Trumbull was greatly encouraged with the way the campaign was proceeding. "Everything looks well," he wrote to a friend. "I think we will succeed in this State, Legislature and—of course, Old Abe is to be elected triumphantly." [53]

On election night, Springfield was an excited city. Crowds stood in front of the telegraph office, and the State House was packed with Republicans eager to get the latest election results. Lincoln and Trumbull were in the hall of the House of Representatives and from time to time received telegraphic messages "mostly addressed to Mr. Lincoln, but in some cases to Senator Trumbull." [54] An eye-witness described the scene as the messages were read to the crowd: "Men pushed each other, threw up their

[50] Lyman Trumbull to Julia Jayne Trumbull, November 1, 1860, L. T. Family Papers.

[51] Cole, "President Lincoln and the Illinois Republicans," op. cit., p. 17. See also Tracy E. Strevey, "Joseph Medill and the Chicago Tribune in the Nomination and Election of Lincoln," Papers in Illinois History, 1939, pp. 39–65.

[52] Koerner, Memoirs, II, 84.

[53] Trumbull to William B. Archer, October 19, 1860, Lyman Trumbull Collection, Illinois State Historical Society, Springfield, Ill. Trumbull exhibited the same confidence in his letter to Edwin D. Morgan, chairman of the Republican National Committee, September 21, 1860, L. T. Family Papers.

[54] William E. Baringer, A House Dividing: Lincoln as President Elect (Springfield, Ill., 1945), p. 318.

hats, hurrahed, cheered for Lincoln, cheered for Trumbull." [55]
The elation at the election results was well justified. Not only
was Lincoln elected President, but Republicans won a decisive
victory in Illinois. Lincoln carried the state by 172,171 votes to
160,205 for Douglas, Richard Yates became governor, and Republicans were assured of a safe majority in the legislature.[56]
When the legislature convened in January, 1861, Trumbull was
re-elected senator by a majority of 54 to 46.[57]

After returning to Washington, Trumbull spent a great deal
of his time on problems connected with the formation of Lincoln's Cabinet. He, like many others, was convinced that Lincoln
would lean heavily on members of his Cabinet and leave many
crucial decisions to them. In addition, Trumbull was determined
to maintain his influence with the administration and wanted to
have friends in Lincoln's closest official family. He had two
important objectives: first, to keep out of the Cabinet Simon
Cameron of Pennsylvania, to whom Davis and Swett had
allegedly promised a Cabinet job; second, to get a Cabinet job
for his ally and friend Norman B. Judd. With less enthusiasm,
Trumbull supported a Cabinet post for Seward, whom he praised
for giving loyal support to Lincoln after the Chicago convention.[58] Lincoln requested Trumbull and Hamlin to extend to
Seward an invitation to become Secretary of State, an assignment which Trumbull willingly fulfilled.[59]

Trumbull opposed Simon Cameron for several reasons. He

---

[55] *Illinois State Journal,* November 7, 1860.

[56] Church, *op. cit.,* p. 81.

[57] *Ibid.* Koerner wrote, ". . . there was no trouble in electing Trumbull United
States Senator. He had made himself a great name in the Senate, and had exerted
himself mightily in the last campaign; so that he was deservedly elected without
opposition for the next term." Koerner, *Memoirs,* II, 109.

[58] Trumbull to Lincoln, December 8, 1860. R. T. L. Collection. On January 20,
Trumbull to Lincoln: "Gov. Seward's appointment is acquiesced in by all our
friends," R. T. L. Collection.

[59] Charles Eugene Hamlin, *The Life and Times of Hannibal Hamlin* (Cambridge, Mass., 1899), p. 97. See also Gideon Welles, *Diary of Gideon Welles,* ed.
John T. Morse (Boston, 1911), II, 388–89; and Lincoln to Seward, December 8,
1860, R. T. L. Collection.

believed that Cameron was a "trading, unreliable politician," who would endanger the success of the new administration.[60] He was urged by Cameron's enemies in Congress and by his foes in Pennsylvania to oppose the appointment of Cameron as Secretary of War, a post for which Trumbull recommended Montgomery Blair, an ex-Democrat.[61] On the other hand, Cameron's appointment was strongly urged upon Lincoln by the ex-Whig faction in Illinois, headed by Judge Davis and Leonard Swett, with whom Trumbull had been feuding for many years. Trumbull was convinced that the inclusion of Cameron would have been a signal victory for the Davis group, and that it would diminish his influence with the new President.

Lincoln gave Trumbull's views careful consideration and at one point was ready to exclude Cameron from the Cabinet. He deliberated upon the decision for several weeks and sought the advice of many friends. One such consultation took place in Gustave Koerner's hotel room in Springfield. Lincoln came into Koerner's room early in the morning while the latter was still in bed. He awakened Koerner and brought in Norman Judd, who stayed in the same hotel, and asked them whether Cameron should be appointed. Both men told Lincoln that they opposed Cameron because he could not be trusted. "I know, I know," said Lincoln, "but can I get along if that state should oppose my administration?" Finally, Lincoln decided to appoint Cameron Secretary of War, but wisely softened the blow by appointing Salmon P. Chase, who was strongly supported by Trumbull and other anti-slavery senators, as Secretary of the Treasury.[62]

[60] Trumbull to Lincoln, December 31, January 20, 1861, R. T. L. Collection.

[61] Trumbull to Lincoln, December 18, 1860, R. T. L. Collection. There was apparently no personal animosity between Cameron and Trumbull because in October, 1860, Simon Cameron contributed $800 to be used in Trumbull's campaign for the Senate. Simon Cameron to David Davis, October 24, 1860, David Davis Papers, Chicago Historical Society.

[62] See excellent treatment of the subject in Reinhard H. Luthin, "Salmon P. Chase's Political Career before the Civil War," *The Mississippi Valley Historical Review*, VXXXIX, No. 4, March, 1943, 517–40. Also the *New York Herald*, February 28, 1861, and *Diary of Gideon Welles*, VI, 126.

Trumbull did not fare much better in his effort to get a Cabinet post for Norman B. Judd. His failure was rather surprising, because Lincoln had strong reasons to make the appointment, quite aside from Trumbull's pressure. The President thought highly of Judd's abilities as a political "fixer" and strategist, and Judd had given him loyal support in the 1858 campaign. It was Judd who had arranged the debates with Douglas which brought Lincoln national prominence, and it was Judd who, by suggesting that Illinois was a "neutral state," had influenced the National Republican Committee to select Chicago as the site of the 1860 convention. There was general agreement that Judd was one of the chief architects of Lincoln's victory at Chicago. Lincoln's personal relations with Judd were friendly and they had bought land together in Council Bluffs, Iowa, a venture which proved to be profitable to Lincoln.[63]

Trumbull opened his campaign for Judd's appointment with a polite letter in which he said that he trusted that Lincoln would not "overlook Mr. Judd, in whom I personally feel more interest than in any other person around." [64] A few days later, he wrote again on the subject and attached a memorandum urging Judd's appointment, which was signed by several prominent Republican senators.[65] In view of this impressive endorsement, the prospects for success looked good, and Ebenezer Peck reported to Trumbull from Springfield that while "Davis and his squad are moving against Judd," Lincoln was giving indications that he would make the selection.[66] Judd also received powerful support from Joseph Medill, who told Lincoln that Judd would prove to be invaluable to him "in a thousand ways" as a "confidential adviser" on whom he could rely.[67]

[63] *The Living Lincoln*, p. 375. Norman B. Judd to Judge Davis, July 19, 1860, David Davis Papers, Chicago Historical Society.

[64] Trumbull to Lincoln, December 27, 1860, R. T. L. Collection.

[65] Trumbull to Lincoln, January 7, 1861, R. T. L. Collection.

[66] Ebenezer Peck to Trumbull, January 10, 1861, L. T. Papers. See also Dr. William Jayne to Trumbull, January 10, 1860, L. T. Papers; and A. C. Fuller to Trumbull, L. T. Papers.

[67] Joseph Medill to Lincoln, December 18, 1860, R. T. L. Collection.

Things looked promising, but Davis and Swett redoubled their efforts to prevent Judd's appointment. Leonard Swett, who went to Washington to survey the situation, wrote that everything pointed to Judd's inclusion in the Cabinet. Frantically he wrote to his chief: "Now I think you ought to go to Lincoln immediately and talk to him fairly and fully and very plainly, but kindly. . . . Now don't fail, Judge. . . ." [68] Mrs. Lincoln, who apparently never forgave Judd for his role in the 1855 election of Trumbull, was determined to get her revenge. From New York, where she went shopping, the First Lady wrote to Judge Davis imploring him to press Lincoln not to make the appointment. She insinuated that her conversation with some Wall Street figures had convinced her that Judd's business dealings might prove to be embarrassing to the new administration. Mrs. Lincoln told the judge that she had "heard a report" discussed at a breakfast table by prominent New York Republicans who asserted that Judd's appointment "in these times when honesty in high places is so important," was not advisable.[69].

The most telling argument against Judd was advanced by the wise and shrewd Jesse W. Fell. Fell, an Illinois publisher and businessman (great-grandfather of Adlai Stevenson) was an important Republican leader in Illinois, and his influence was greatly enhanced by his steadfast and sincere disavowal of any ambition for an elective or appointive office. He was close to Judge Davis but maintained friendly relations with Trumbull. Jesse Fell told Lincoln that he liked Judd personally, but that he considered it inadvisable to give him a Cabinet post because the Whig faction in the Republican Party was bitterly hostile to him. "Should [Judd] . . . be appointed," Fell wrote, "to so important a position, I risk nothing in saying it will be a bitter pill for many of your old and truest friends." He concluded with

[68] Leonard Swett to David Davis, January 1, 1861, David Davis Papers, Chicago Historical Society.
[69] Mrs. Mary Lincoln to David Davis, January 17, 1861, David Davis Papers, Chicago Historical Society.

the sage advice to Lincoln that in order not to increase the feud between the two factions, no representative of either should be appointed to the Cabinet.[70] Lincoln took Fell's advice and offered Judd the post of Minister to Prussia, which the latter reluctantly accepted.

Trumbull was disappointed at the defeat he had suffered and made no effort to conceal his feelings. He wrote a friend that "Mr. Lincoln's making a grave mistake, by not taking Judd." [71]

Lincoln had strong reasons for refusing Judd a post in his official family, even if it meant antagonizing a strong and influential political ally. He did not want, nor did he need, a "confidential adviser," and Judd could have filled only such a post. Lincoln had his heart set on having in his Cabinet, in an hour of crisis to the nation, only men of stature and political prestige and influence, and Judd obviously, in spite of his acknowledged skills as an able operator in smoke-filled rooms, did not meet these standards. Jesse Fell's argument that Judd's appointment would only increase the feuding and bickering among the Republicans in his home state sounded convincing to Lincoln.[72] It might be that Lincoln had also not forgotten Judd's role in Lincoln's defeat in 1855. Finally, the refusal to include Judd in the Cabinet served notice on Trumbull and others that Lincoln was determined to be his own President and would exercise the powers of his office in the light of his own judgment.

The Judd affair, coupled with other snubs, brought about a considerable cooling off in the personal relations between Trumbull and Lincoln. Their ties had been cordial all through 1859 and especially during the nomination and the election campaign of 1860. Trumbull undoubtedly resented the fact that Lincoln, on the advice of Davis and Ward Hill Lamon, did not take the house in Washington that Trumbull and Elihu B. Washburne

---

[70] Jesse W. Fell to Lincoln, January 2, 1861, R. T. L. Collection.

[71] Trumbull to William Butler, January 9, 1861, William Butler Collection, Chicago Historical Society. See also Joseph Medill to Norman B. Judd, January 20, 1861, William Butler Collection, Chicago Historical Society.

[72] Koerner, *Memoirs*, II, 115.

had rented for him.[73] Lincoln, upon arrival in the capital, checked into the Willard Hotel in a suite of rooms reserved for him by Lamon. Judge Davis occupied two adjoining rooms. Once in Washington, Lincoln virtually ignored Trumbull; he dined on Saturday with Seward, went with Seward to church on Sunday, and then called on President Buchanan with his future Secretary of State. On February 25, 1861, Trumbull wrote to Lincoln a cold formal note informing him that a joint committee of Congress, of which he was a member, would like to call on him with an official notification of his election. The committee, he wrote, "will if agreeable to you, call at your room tomorrow evening at 8 o'clock to perform that duty." [74]

The relations between the two men remained cool after the inauguration, and Dr. William Jayne, Trumbull's brother-in-law, complained that "Mr. Trumbull has been in the White House but twice to see Lincoln. . . . Mr. Lincoln has not treated Mr. Trumbull as he should and Mr. T. said this morning, that he should not step inside the White House again during Mr. Lincoln's four years, unless he changed his course." [75] Dr. Jayne's letter, of course, exaggerated the rift, but there was a cooling off and a strain in the *personal* relations between Lincoln and Trumbull. The two men, however, in spite of occasional disagreements, established an effective working relationship. While the estrangement could be traced to the Judd affair and to Trumbull's difficulties, in the early days of the new administration, in providing jobs for the hungry hordes of Illinoisans who had descended on the capital, there were deeper causes for the rather sudden change in their relationship after Lincoln's inauguration.[76] Trumbull, along with most of his contemporaries, did

[73] Lincoln to Elihu B. Washburne, February 15, 1861; and Washburne to Lincoln, February 19, 1861, R. T. L. Collection.

[74] Trumbull to Lincoln, February 25, 1861, R. T. L. Collection.

[75] Dr. William Jayne to William Butler, William Butler Collection, Chicago Historical Society, March 3, 1961.

[76] A Quincy, Illinois, man wrote to a friend from Washington: "There are Hundreds here yet from the North West and a large majority of them mad. . . ." B. M. Prentiss to Henry Asbury, Benjamin M. Prentiss Collection, Chicago Historical Society.

not really understand Lincoln. The fact that he had known his compatriot intimately for many years, as a circuit riding lawyer, legislator, and aspiring politician, did not give him an insight into Lincoln's potential greatness. On the contrary, it made him believe that Lincoln was ambitious but indecisive, a compromiser who could be swayed by knowledgeable advisors of the type of William Seward. Many years after Lincoln's death, Trumbull still maintained that "Mr. Lincoln was a follower not a leader in public affairs." [77] Lincoln's greatness was of a type that needed the perspective of time to be fully appreciated. Trumbull never maintained that he was Lincoln's confidant. "I do not claim," he wrote, "to have been his confidant, and doubt if any man ever had his entire confidence." [78] That Lincoln kept his own counsel and purposely shunned close friendships while he was President, in order to insure for himself a complete freedom of action, was attested also by Judge David Davis. Davis, who after a great deal of pressure and grief finally received from Lincoln an appointment as Associate Justice of the United States Supreme Court, was soon to discover, as did his rival Trumbull, that Lincoln needed his counsel and advice very infrequently, if at all. The bitter disappointment that he suffered still showed in his letter to William Herndon, written after the Civil War. "Lincoln," Davis wrote, "was a peculiar man. He never asked my advice on any question. . . . He depended on himself always. . . . I knew that it was the general opinion in Washington that I knew all about Lincoln's thoughts, but I knew nothing. Lincoln never confided to me anything. . . . Lincoln had no spontaneity . . . no strong emotional feelings for any person . . . he was the most reticent secretive man I ever saw or expect to see." [79] Gustave Koerner, who knew Lincoln well for many years,

[77] Letter on Lincoln's character and career written at the request of his son Walter (no date) in L. T. Papers.

[78] *Ibid.* In 1865, Trumbull congratulated William Herndon on his lecture on Lincoln. "The wonderful events which transpired during his administration and the manner of his taking off were such as to blind most men to everything except the bright side of his character." L. Trumbull to William H. Herndon, December 27, 1865, L. T. Family Papers.

[79] King, *op. cit.*, p. 231.

maintained that he was not "really capable of what might be called warm-hearted friendships." [80] But unlike others, including Trumbull, who saw this trait as a defect in Lincoln's character, Koerner, with an unusual insight, saw in Lincoln's aloofness and enigmatic character a positive value. "It is doubtful to my mind," the shrewd German leader wrote, "whether anyone but Lincoln could have carried the Union through the raging war of rebellion. It required just such a complex and anomalous character." [81]

[80] Koerner, *Memoirs*, p. 112.
[81] *Ibid.*, p. 116.

9

No Compromise!

THE ELECTION OF LINCOLN BY A VOTE THAT WAS SMALLER THAN the combined total received by his three opponents increased the clamor for secession in the lower South. Southern leaders considered Lincoln a "sectional President, nominated by a sectional convention, elected by a sectional vote." [1] Without waiting to see what the new administration would do, six Southern states withdrew from the Union between December 20 and January 26, 1861. Commenting on the often advanced theory that hot-headed extremists were responsible for the secession of these states, Nevins wrote: "It would have been impossible for even a far larger and better organized body of conspirators to have carried the South into this sweeping movement for independence had it not been that a large body of people in the cotton states had lost their old attachment to the Union." [2]

Lincoln made one rather half-hearted attempt to quiet the spirit of rebellion in the South. He asked Trumbull to include in his speech for the victory celebration at Springfield, which took place on November 20, two paragraphs that Lincoln had

[1] Jefferson Davis, *The Rise and Fall of the Confederate Government* (New York, 1961), p. 620.

[2] Allan Nevins, *The Emergence of Lincoln: Prologue to Civil War, 1859–1861* (New York, 1950), p. 329.

written. Since Lincoln was present at the meeting, Trumbull became the official spokesman of the President-elect. In the statement that Trumbull incorporated in his speech, Lincoln reiterated his assurance that slavery in the South would not be interfered with. The President-elect also expressed his hope that Union men in the South would rise against the secessionists and "suppress any uprisings there." [3] Trumbull's speech went largely unnoticed. Lincoln, disappointed, complained that Democratic and Southern papers either ignored or misinterpreted Trumbull's (and Lincoln's) assurances.[4] This experience confirmed Lincoln's view that silence on his part would be the wisest course under the circumstances. He, however, had every intention of adhering to the pledge contained in the 1860 Chicago Republican platform, which called upon Congress to pass legislation to keep slavery out of the free territories. Neither Lincoln nor Trumbull were in a mood to engage in negotiations with or make concessions to the leaders of Southern rebellion, and for this attitude they have been severely reproached by some historians. For example, Nevins states: "Lincoln viewed the situation at first with excessive optimism, believing (as did many other Illinois Republicans, including Trumbull and the editors of the *Chicago Tribune* and the *Illinois State Journal*) that the secession was largely bluff." [5] This may well be so, but it is equally true that Lincoln, Trumbull, and other leaders of the Republican party knew that their uncompromising position might well bring about a war with the South and were ready for that eventuality. There is evidence to suggest that they welcomed a final and, if need be, an armed showdown. The suggestion that Lincoln's policy of silence and inaction between his election in November and the March inauguration was "a colossal mistake" [6] needs to be examined in order to ascertain whether it was caused by his and Trumbull's

---

[3] Baringer, *op. cit.*, p. 32; and White, *op. cit.*, p. 110.
[4] Thomas, *op. cit.*, p. 227.
[5] Nevins, *The Emergence of Lincoln*, p. 355.
[6] Luthin, *op. cit.*, p. 244.

underrating of the strength of the secessionist movement or from their conviction that a continued policy of conciliation and appeasement toward the South would merely strengthen Southern extremists, weaken and divide the North, and at best gain a temporary and not a very advantageous postponement of the day of reckoning.

Lincoln's and Trumbull's views on the deepening crisis were revealed by their attitude to the compromise proposals introduced by John J. Crittenden of Kentucky. The "Crittenden Compromise," in the form of amendments to the Constitution, would have revived the Missouri Compromise line and extended it to California, prohibiting slavery north of it but affirming its existence south of it. Another amendment would have forever forbidden Congress to abolish slavery in the slave states and still another made it impossible for Congress to abolish slavery in the District of Columbia as long as slavery existed in Virginia and Maryland. Other conditions provided for a vote of the inhabitants of the district and for compensation to the owners of the slaves. Crittenden's plan received wide popular support as the only plan that had a chance of averting a civil war. In Congress, Northern Democrats, headed by Senators Stephen A. Douglas and William M. Bigler of Pennsylvania, supported the proposals.

Abraham Lincoln, the President-elect, chose not to take a public stand on the Crittenden compromise but privately instructed his closest allies in Congress to oppose it. To Trumbull, Lincoln wrote: "Let there be no compromise on the question of extending slavery—if there be, all our labor is lost, and, ere long, must be done again—the dangerous ground—that into which some of our friends have a hankering to run—is Pop. Sov. —have none of it. Stand firm. *The tug has come and better now than any time hereafter.*" [7] Seven days later, Lincoln again exhorted Trumbull to oppose the compromise formula. "If any

[7] Lincoln to Trumbull, December 10, 1861, in "A Lincoln Correspondence," *op. cit.*, p. 626. (Italics mine.)

of our friends do prove false, and fix up a compromise on the territorial question, I am for fighting again—that is all. It is but repetition for me to say I am for an honest enforcement of the Constitution—fugitive slave clause included." [8] Similar letters from Lincoln were received by Congressmen William P. Kellogg and Elihu B. Washburne. [9]

Lincoln was determined to keep true to his opposition to the extension of slavery, which he had proclaimed repeatedly since 1854, and he considered himself bound to remain faithful to the Republican platform, which pledged the party to keep the territories free from slavery. He was convinced that the Crittenden proposals would lead to the expansion of slavery. Since he firmly believed in and desired the eventual extinction of slavery, he could not, in good conscience, support the Crittenden proposal for an amendment to the Constitution, which would have assured the existence of slavery in perpetuity. He was ready, and he confidentially requested Trumbull, to ask Seward to introduce a set of three resolutions that would have assured the enforcement of the Fugitive Slave Law but provided that the escaped slaves would be entitled to a jury trial. Another resolution would have declared that all state laws conflicting with the Fugitive Slave Law ought to be repealed. The third resolution affirmed the determination to preserve the Union. [10] The crucial words in Lincoln's letters are those that he repeated, almost verbatim, to Trumbull and to Kellogg, "the tug has come and better now than any time hereafter" (to Kellogg, "better now than later"). If war over secession of the Southern states was to come, Lincoln considered it better not to postpone the showdown by another conciliation or appeasement of the South. The fact that by the end of December South Carolina had already seceded and Mississippi, Florida, and Alabama had elected conventions with solid secessionist majorities, strengthened Lincoln's convic-

[8] *Ibid.*, p. 626.

[9] John G. Nicolay and John Hay, *Complete Works of Abraham Lincoln*, 2nd ed. (New York, 1905), VI, 77–78.

[10] White, *op. cit.*, p. 112.

tion that any concession to or compromise with the South would merely embolden the secessionists and weaken the determination of the North to stand firm and united.

He did not believe that his speaking out would change the situation or even alleviate the crisis. When Henry J. Raymond, the editor of the New York Times, asked him to make a statement on the situation, Lincoln answered that anything he might say would be misinterpreted by the "political friends [who] are not half sick enough yet." He pointed to Trumbull's speech and asked, "Has a single newspaper, heretofore against us, urged that speech upon its readers with a purpose to quiet public anxiety? Not one so far as I know." [11] To Alexander Stephens, the future Vice-President of the Confederacy, Lincoln defined the issue in two telling sentences. "You think slavery is right," he wrote, "and ought to be extended, while we think it is wrong and ought to be restricted. That I suppose is the rub." [12]

Lyman Trumbull was in full accord with Lincoln in his opposition to the Crittenden proposals and to any other compromise with the South.[13] He wanted the secessionist movement crushed, if need be, by force, and urged the newly elected Governor of Illinois, Richard Yates, to take "a strong Union ground" in his inaugural message to the Illinois Legislature and to declare secession a "revolution and rebellion." [14] The secession of South Carolina and its defiance of Federal authority and laws was to Trumbull not a question of controversy over slavery but a question of "whether we have a government capable of maintaining itself." "A people," he wrote, "who would not fight in such a cause do not deserve to be free." [15] There is convincing evidence

[11] The Living Lincoln, p. 363.
[12] Ibid., p. 369.
[13] Trumbull wrote to his wife that the Republicans in Congress were determined not to accept any compromises and stand firm for the preservation of the Union, Lyman Trumbull to Julia Jayne Trumbull, December 4, 1860, L. T. Family Papers.
[14] Trumbull to Richard Yates, December 19, 1860, Richard Yates Papers, Illinois State Historical Society, Springfield, Ill.
[15] Trumbull to David Davis, December 24, 1860, David Davis Papers, Chicago Historical Society.

that Trumbull did not underestimate the strength of the secessionists and did not consider the secession of the lower South a
bluff. He fully understood the seriousness of the situation and
the risks involved and requested Governor Yates to "get up volunteer companies so as to be ready to come to the support of
the Constitution and the laws if the occasion should require." [16]
Trumbull was convinced that "The people of most of the Southern States are mad and in no condition to listen to reasonable
propositions." [17] He felt that in view of the strength of the secessionist sentiment in the South "it [was] not advisable . . . for
Republicans to concede or talk of conceding anything." [18] On
January 10, Trumbull took the floor of the Senate to answer a
speech by Jefferson Davis of Mississippi and declared his opposition to the Crittenden proposals. Trumbull assailed Davis'
demand that the Federal Government withdraw its troops from
Charleston in order to assure peace. Davis, said Trumbull, was
proposing that the government abdicate. "They," he said, "are
making war and modestly ask us to have peace by submitting
to what they ask. . . . Why sir, any people can have peace at
the price of degradation." [19] Turning to the Crittenden proposals, Trumbull asserted that while he had no objection to
the restoration of the Missouri Compromise, which would assure
that Kansas and Nebraska would be free states, he was opposed
to the recognition and the perpetual establishment of slavery
south of the 36° 30′ line. He did not wish to lend a hand to
"sanctify slavery in the U. S." [20] He would support the enforcement of the Fugitive Slave Law but was opposed to its provision
that obliged private citizens to assist in its execution. "Now,
then, if the Senator from Missouri [Green] wants to know if I
will voluntarily make myself a catcher of runaway Negroes I tell

[16] Trumbull to Governor Richard Yates, January 2, 1861, Reavis Collection,
Chicago Historical Society.
[17] Trumbull to E. C. Larned, January 7, 1861, L. T. Papers.
[18] *Ibid.*
[19] *Cong. Globe*, 36 Cong., 2nd Sess. (January 10, 1961), p. 312.
[20] *Ibid.*, p. 313.

him, no." [21] In a later speech, Trumbull paid tribute to the high motives and patriotism of Crittenden, but stated that by the sanctification of slavery below the line fixed in the Missouri Compromise, the Crittenden proposals went far beyond the restoration of the 1820 compromise and would in reality bring about the extension of slavery, because, New Mexico, for example, could never vote slavery out. "The proposition known as the Crittenden proposals," said Trumbull, "is no more like the Missouri Compromise, than is the Government of Turkey like that of the United States." [22] The Constitution of the United States, Trumbull concluded, did not need to be improved by any of the amendments proposed by Crittenden. Furthermore, he did not believe that Congress had the power to pass an amendment that it would never interfere with slavery in the states. "No such power exists," he wrote to his brother-in-law, "and I do not believe in tinkering with the Constitution unnecessarily." [23] When the opportunity arose, Trumbull voted for a resolution that stated that the Constitution did not need amending and opposed the Crittenden proposals when they came to a final vote on March 2, 1861. [24]

Trumbull's position received the enthusiastic support of his constituents in Illinois. The opposition to any further compromises with the South was not limited to the two Republican fire-eating newspapers, the *Chicago Tribune* and the *Illinois State Journal*. These papers were almost hysterical in their rejection of the "Compromise." The *Tribune* wrote: "We greatly misjudge the temper of our people if the day of compromises, which means a demand by Slavery and a concession by Freedom, has not gone forever." [25] But the more moderate *Belleville Advocate* was also adamant in its opposition to compromises, and Wentworth's *Chicago Daily Democrat* called the Crittenden

[21] *Ibid.,* p. 315
[22] *Ibid.,* pp. 1380–81.
[23] Trumbull to Dr. William Jayne, February 17, 1861, Jayne Papers.
[24] *Cong. Globe,* 36 Cong., 2nd Sess., p. 409.
[25] *Chicago Tribune,* December 22, 1860.

proposals "sickening." [26] Trumbull's hometown newspaper, the *Alton Telegraph*, did not hesitate, in spite of Crittenden's great popularity in southern Illinois, to brand him a traitor and declared that "there may be a compromise with partisanship but none with treason . . . the only way to deal with this rebellion is to put it down. . . . Any talk of compromise is treason." [27]

Trumbull was virtually deluged by letters from cities, towns, villages, and hamlets in Illinois pleading with him to stand fast and oppose any more compromises with the South. This mail leaves no doubt that Republican leaders and many of the rank-and-file members of the party were ready to use all means, including force, to suppress the Southern rebellion. Horace White of the *Chicago Tribune* wrote: "We live in revolutionary times, and I say God bless the revolution." Gustave Koerner told Trumbull: "I am prepared for the application of force. *In fact, a collision is inevitable.*" William Herndon warned that if the Republican leaders should yield to the temptation to compromise, "I am their Enemy—now and forever . . . this thing Slavery must be met and finally squelched. . . ." H. G. McPike, an Alton friend, asserted that "if that compromise—so-called—was made part of the Constitution it would be the downfall of the Union at no distant day," and the President of Illinois College, J. M. Sturtevant, said: "We want the Constitution as it is, the Union as the fathers framed it, and the Chicago platform." Joseph Gillespie wanted "an energetic display of force in the direction of Charleston," and W. H. Hanna was in favor of a "20 year war rather than the loss of one inch of territory or the surrender of any principal [sic] that concedes the right of secession." [28]

[26] *Belleville Advocate,* December 14, 1860; *Chicago Daily Democrat,* January 5, 1861.

[27] *Alton Telegraph,* June 28, July 5, 1861.

[28] Horace White to Trumbull, December 30, 1860; Gustave Koerner to Trumbull, January 21, 1861 (italics mine); William H. Herndon to Trumbull, February 9, 1861; H. G. McPike to Trumbull, January 24, 1861; J. M. Sturtevant to Trumbull, January 30, 1861; W. H. Hanna to Trumbull, December 19, 1860, Trumbull Papers, Library of Congress; and Joseph Gillespie to Trumbull, February 12, 1861; L. T. Letters.

When the state of Virginia proposed the convening on February 4 of a "Peace Conference" in Washington, Lincoln, Trumbull, and Washburne took the position that Illinois should not send commissioners to the conference.[29] Lincoln told William Herndon that "he would rather be hung by the neck till he was dead on the steps of the Capitol before he would beg or buy a peaceful inauguration." [30] The *Illinois State Journal* advised Governor Yates not to trouble himself to appoint the commissioners.[31] Yates would have been glad to take this advice, but some Republican members in the legislature threatened to vote with the Democrats in approving the sending of the commissioners. Ebenezer Peck informed Trumbull that the election of the delegates became necessary because "some of your knock-kneed brethren, would have united with the democracy," and Dr. Jayne sarcastically reported to his brother-in-law: "Some of our friends are getting very anxious to save the Union." [32] Yates yielded and requested Lincoln to select the commissioners, which the latter did with great reluctance. The Illinois delegation was to include ex-Governor John Wood, Judge Stephen T. Logan, Congressman Burton C. Cook, Thomas Turner, and Gustave Koerner. When Koerner refused the assignment, John M. Palmer was appointed in his stead. Illinois delegates who came to Washington were received at the White House by Lincoln, who told them that he expected nothing from the convention, because he thought it impossible to restore the Union without a war. The Illinois delegation agreed with the President.[33]

The Peace Conference, after long deliberations, adopted, by

[29] William Jayne to Trumbull, January 18, 1861, L. T. Papers; Elihu Washburne to Lincoln, January 7, 1861, Elihu Washburne Papers, Library of Congress.

[30] William H. Herndon to Trumbull, January 27, 1861, L. T. Papers.

[31] *Illinois State Journal*, January 30, 1861. See also *Chicago Tribune*, February 8, 1861.

[32] Ebenezer Peck to Trumbull, February 2, and Dr. William Jayne to Trumbull, January 31, 1861, L. T. Papers. See also Norman B. Judd to Trumbull, January 17, 1861, L. T. Papers; and Koerner, *Memoirs*, II, 113.

[33] Palmer, *op. cit.*, p. 84.

a small majority, a proposed amendment to the Constitution which stated that Congress had no right to interfere with slavery in the states or in the territories. The amendment also forbade the abolition of slavery in the District of Columbia without the consent of Maryland. Another resolution called for the strict enforcement of the Fugitive Slave Law.[34] The Peace Conference report was presented to the Senate on January 27 and was referred to a Select Committee appointed by the Vice-President, which included Senators Crittenden, Seward, Trumbull, Bigler of Pennsylvania, and Thomson of New Jersey.[35] The committee endorsed the report by a vote of 3 to 2 with Trumbull and Seward voting in the negative. A short time before the adjournment of the session, despairing of the adoption of his own proposals, Crittenden submitted the Peace Conference amendment to the Constitution as a substitute for his own resolutions. Senators Mason of Virginia, Johnson of Arkansas, and Green of Missouri took the floor and opposed the substitute proposal, because, in the words of Senator Johnson, it was "a thousand fathoms beneath the propositions of the Senator from Kentucky." [36] The Peace Conference Amendment, when put to a vote, lost 28 to 7—with Trumbull, the Republicans, and the Southerners voting against it.[37] When Crittenden's "Compromise" was moved again, it lost by a vote of 20 to 19. Trumbull voted no, with Fessenden, Doolittle, Grimes, Dixon, Chandler, Sumner, Wade, Wilson, and others.[38] He knew that some period of peace, temporary at best, if judged by the experiences with other compromises on the slavery issue, could be bought, but he was not willing to pay the price asked by the slave states.

Trumbull's determination to crush the South was greatly strengthened by the belief of many Republican leaders in Illi-

[34] Text in Raymond, op. cit., p. 123.

[35] Good account of the sequence of events in Robert Gray Gunderson, Old Gentlemen's Convention (Madison, Wis., 1961), pp. 94–97.

[36] Gunderson, Old Gentlemen's Convention, p. 95.

[37] Ibid.

[38] Raymond, op. cit., p. 129.

nois that "Little Egypt" was ready to join the secession.[39] Trumbull never believed in such an eventuality, but he knew that any show of weakness in Washington would only strengthen the hand of the enemies of the Union in southern Illinois.

When the crisis over the holding and the re-enforcement of Fort Sumter developed, Trumbull advocated a policy of firmness and demanded the full assertion of Federal authority in the South. He bitterly opposed Seward's attempts to conciliate the South. On March 28, Trumbull introduced a resolution in the Senate that contained a strong condemnation of Seward's policy of conciliation. It said, in part, "Resolved that in the opinion of the Senate, the true way to preserve the Union is to enforce the laws of the Union; that resistance to their enforcement, whether under the name of anti-coercion or any other name, is encouragement to disunion; and that it is the duty of the President of the United States to use all means in his power to hold and protect the public property of the United States, and enforce the laws thereof. . . ." [40] As the hour of crisis was approaching, Trumbull's policy of firmness had the complete support of his constituents and of the Republican press in his home state. One correspondent suggested that Southern states be warned that if they went through with secession they would revert to "territorial pupillage." [41] In an almost hysterical letter, Herndon asserted that "Liberty and Slavery are absolute antagonisms and all human experience and all human philosophy says 'Clear the ring and let these natural foes—*these eternal enemies now fight it out.*' . . ." [42]

---

[39] Medill wrote to Trumbull: "I believe, upon my soul, that if the Union is divided on the line of the Ohio, we shall be compelled to struggle to maintain the territorial integrity of this State," quoted in Allan Nevins, *The War for the Union: The Improvised War, 1861–1862* (New York, 1959), p. 16.

[40] *Cong. Globe*, 36 Cong., 2nd Sess. (March 28, 1861), p. 1519.

[41] W. B. Slaughter to Trumbull, February 15, 1861; William Butler to Trumbull, March 14, 1861, L. T. Papers.

[42] William H. Herndon to Trumbull, December 21, 1860, L. T. Papers. (Italics mine.) See also an editorial calling for the active defense of the Union in the *Illinois State Journal*, March 30, 1861.

A few days after Lincoln issued his proclamation asking for seventy-five thousand volunteers to crush the rebellion, Trumbull left Washington to help Governor Yates to mobilize the state and to combat the threat of secession in southern Illinois. Trumbull received many letters warning him of a secessionist movement in southern Illinois. His former mentor and law partner, ex-Governor Reynolds, was quoted as having said that "the revolution in the South is the greatest demonstration of human greatness and grandeur that was ever performed on the globe." [43] The Chicago Tribune warned that "There are nests of rank traitors in Southern Illinois who need looking after." [44] Trumbull established his headquarters in the State House in Springfield and there worked night and day to help Yates to put Illinois on a war footing. Gustave Koerner, the lieutenant governor, also helped valiantly. He wrote in his Memoirs that "Trumbull and myself are the confidential advisors to Yates and have to direct him with everything." [45] Koerner related that when he arrived at Springfield, summoned by Yates, he was overwhelmed by the press of business. "Fortunately," he added, "I found Trumbull also there." [46] It was lucky for Yates to have the assistance of Trumbull and Koerner, but it was even more lucky for Illinois that Richard Yates was its governor in the hour of crisis. Yates, the son of a distinguished Illinois family, was a dedicated and patriotic Unionist, a splendid speaker and a born leader. His response to Lincoln's Proclamation was swift and decisive. The President issued his call on April 15, and Governor Yates responded on the same day with a proclamation calling the Illinois Legislature into a special session to call out special militia companies to help in the preservation of the Union. Without waiting for the legislature to convene on April 23, Yates called out the state militia and ordered the regiments to rendezvous in

[43] James C. Conkling to Trumbull, February 12, 1861; S. E. Flannigan to Trumbull, April 9, 1861, L. T. Papers. See also Palmer, Personal Recollections, p. 91.
[44] Chicago Tribune, April 22, 1861.
[45] Koerner, Memoirs, II, 123.
[46] Ibid., p. 120.

Springfield with the greatest possible dispatch.[47] The response to the call of the fighting governor was overwhelming. Yates soon found Springfield flooded with soldiers for whom he did not have enough rifles and field equipment. Trumbull wrote to his friend Judge Doolittle of Wisconsin that Yates was "embarrassed" by the number of volunteers and that "three regiments too many have already assembled and thirteen regiments are pressing to get into service." [48]

Democrats in the central and northern parts of Illinois were caught and engulfed by this surge of patriotic enthusiasm. "Union" and "flag" became the catchwords of unity. But the mass of Democrats in southern Illinois was sullen and seething with rebellion. A mass rally of citizens held in the Marion Court House enthusiastically adopted a resolution stating that the coercive policies toward the South would drive the border states from the Union. "In that event," the resolution continued, "the interests of the citizens of Southern Illinois imperatively demand a division of the State. We hereby pledge ourselves to use all means in our power to effect the same and to attach ourselves to the Southern Confederacy." [49] The city of Jonesboro in Union County was the scene of pro-Confederate meetings, where cheers for Jeff Davis were heard frequently. On April 20, the *Jonesboro Gazette*, which was to remain a Copperhead paper during the entire Civil War, reported, "The news of the surrender of Fort Sumter was received with becoming cheers and expressions of joy by almost everyone in Jonesboro. . . . The cannon was brought out and fifteen shots fired in honor of a United South." [50] The *Golconda Weekly Herald*, published in Golconda, across the Ohio River from Kentucky, appealed to the "yeomanry of Pope county to rub up their old rusty rifles and

[47] *Illinois State Register*, April 20; *Illinois State Journal*, April 25, May 1, 1861. See Cole, *op. cit.*, pp. 174–77.

[48] Trumbull to James R. Doolittle, April 27, 1861, James R. Doolittle Papers, State Historical Society of Wisconsin, Madison, Wis.

[49] *Marion Intelligencer*, April 18, 1861.

[50] *Jonesboro Gazette*, April 20, 1861.

flint locks, buy in plenty of ammunition . . . [and] do it with
a determination to resist the march of a Black Republican army
over the soil of Egypt." [51]

The most alarming news came from the strategically located
Cairo, which guarded the approaches to Illinois against the rebel
forces in Missouri and the South. The Cairo secessionists, egged
on by the pro-Confederate *Cairo Gazette*, openly talked of
seceding from the Union, and the *Memphis* [Tennessee] *Bulletin* wrote that "The feeling is universal that Tennesseeans and
Mississippians can thrash out three times their number of Yankees . . . the determination to invade Cairo grows with every
hour." [52] Believing that the danger to Cairo was real and immi-
nent, Governor Yates dispatched Illinois militia troops, which
occupied Cairo on April 24. On the next day, a steamboat of
Illinois militia crossed the Mississippi, went ashore and emptied
the St. Louis Arsenal of 21,000 muskets, 500 carbine artillery,
and cartridges. The arms and ammunition were taken to Alton
and from there to Springfield. Yates explained his action in a
special message to the legislature in which he stated that infor-
mation had reached him of the existence of "a conspiracy of
disaffected persons to seize upon Cairo and the southern portion
of Illinois Central Railroad and cut off communication with
the interior of the State." [53] After taking the emergency action,
the governor sent Trumbull to make an on-the-spot investigation
of the strength of the secessionists in Cairo and in St. Louis.
Trumbull visited Alton, Cairo, and St. Louis, where he conferred on the critical situation of the Union forces in Missouri
with Captain Lyon, General Harney, and Col. Frank P. Blair, Jr.
In a letter to Judge James R. Doolittle of Wisconsin, Trumbull
told his friend that he did not believe that Cairo would be
attacked and that the Unionists in St. Louis felt "very secure."
He praised the capture of Camp Jackson and wondered whether

[51] *Golconda Weekly Herald,* April 17, 1861.
[52] *Memphis Bulletin* clipped in *Chicago Tribune,* June 16, 1861.
[53] *Text* in the *Chicago Tribune,* April 26, 1861.

"the Government in Washington [will] be equally prompt." [54]
Trumbull's optimism was confirmed by the correspondent of
the *Alton Telegraph* who reported from Cairo that "the Union
sentiment is being rapidly developed in 'Egypt.' " [55]

Union forces received an infusion of strength when Stephen
Douglas patriotically pledged to Lincoln his support and then
hurried to Illinois to quell the secessionist sentiments among
the Democrats in "Little Egypt." At seven o'clock in the evening of April 23, the leader of the Democratic Party, weary and
ill, but with his great oratorical powers unimpaired, entered the
Illinois State House to address a joint session of the Illinois
Legislature. He was greeted by a long standing ovation. The
legislators leaped again to their feet when Speaker of the House
Shelby M. Collum introduced the "Little Giant." Douglas
denounced secession as "a mad attempt to overthrow the Republic. . . ." "Allow me to say," he continued, "to my former
political enemies, you will not be true to your country if you
seek to make political capital out of these disasters and to my
old friends, you will be false and unworthy of your principles,
if you allow political defeat to convert you into traitors to your
national land." [56] Douglas concluded his stirring address by an
appeal to all to protect the Union and the flag. A correspondent
of the *Illinois State Journal* described the scene that followed:
"Men wept and cheered in turn. Old Democrats who parted
with the Senator on the slavery question now cheered vehemently. O! the power of patriotism!" [57] Douglas' appeal swayed
thousands of Democrats to the support of the Union and when
finally, after a long hesitation, the influential Democratic Congressman from southern Illinois, John A. Logan, went to Fort

[54] Trumbull to James R. Doolittle, May 10, 16, 1861, James R. Doolittle Papers,
State Historical Society of Wisconsin, Madison, Wis. See also Koerner, *Memoirs*,
II, 143.
[55] *Alton Telegraph*, May 10, 1861. Also Koerner to Trumbull, May 31, 1861,
L. T. Papers.
[56] *Chicago Tribune*, April 26, 1861.
[57] *Illinois State Journal*, April 26, 1861.

Yates and volunteered his services to the Union army, the threat of secession in the southern part of the state was eliminated at least for the time being. Trumbull, reassured that his home state would loyally support the Union, returned to Washington to take part in the special session of Congress called by President Lincoln for July 4.

10

For a Tough War
Under the Constitution

SITTING AT HIS DESK IN THE SENATE AT NOON ON JULY 4, 1861, watching the proceedings attendant to the opening of the special session of Congress, Trumbull must have reflected how radically the situation in the Senate and his role in it had changed. The senators of the eleven states who comprised the delegations of the Southern slave states were gone. Only Andrew Johnson of Tennessee remained. Trumbull did not regret the absence of the Southern bloc in spite of the fact that the Senate chamber looked rather empty. He, no doubt, agreed with his friend Carl Schurz, who after several visits to the Senate complained that the Southerners were "overbearing, defiant, dictatorial, vehemently demanding a chance for unlimited expansion . . . threatening the Union, the National Republic itself!" [1] It was the threats to the Union that Trumbull resented most. While he hated slavery, he was not, in 1861, a zealous crusader for the political rights of the Negroes. He was a moderate on the Negro question and a strong believer in the preservation of the check and balance principle in the relations between the Executive and

[1] Schurz, *Autobiography*, p. 120.

189

the Congress, and he had a healthy respect for the powers and prerogatives of both. There was, however, one issue on which Trumbull was not a moderate, and this was the issue of secession. Trumbull was a radical and an extremist when confronted with the attempt of the South to destroy the Union. This scion of pioneering Connecticut Yankees considered secession and the firing of Confederate guns on the flag of the United States an outrage and a crime, which called for the use of overwhelming force to bring the rebels to their knees. Because of this dedicated resolution, Trumbull was uncompromising in his demands that Lincoln pursue a vigorous, all-out war on the Confederacy. If in order to crush the massive Southern rebellion it was necessary to arrest suspected spies, to suspend the writ of habeas corpus, to confiscate rebel property and to free some slaves, Trumbull was ready to suppress his deepest convictions about laws and the Constitution, provided that Congress was given an opportunity to approve of these acts. If, to defeat the rebellion, it was necessary for Trumbull to vote with radicals like Sumner, Wade, and Chandler, he was willing to do so, although the area of agreement on fundamental questions between them and him was very narrow indeed. But the power of the rebellion was so great, the threat to the Union so dire, that Trumbull was ready to vote with them, although often with great misgivings. That explains why he, "for all his general moderation often voted with his radical colleagues." [2] That is why he found himself, often to his surprise and chargin, "more often in alliance with the Radicals than the moderate nature of his mind would seem to suggest." [3]

Contemplating his own role in the Senate, Trumbull undoubtedly noted how much it had changed for the better. He was forty-eight and at the height of his physical and intellectual powers. Horace White, who visited the Trumbulls' home on G Street before the start of the session, described his host as "straight as an arrow, weighing one hundred and sixty-seven

[2] Nevins, *The War for the Union*, p. 182.
[3] J. G. Randall, *The Civil War and Reconstruction* (Boston, 1937), p. 363.

pounds, of faultless physique, in perfect health, and in manners a cultivated gentleman." [4] To his brother John, Trumbull wrote: "We are comfortably situated here and as I am in no business, intend remaining here for some time." [5] After Douglas' death in June, Trumbull was now the senior senator from Illinois, a veteran of six years in the Senate and chairman of the powerful Judiciary Committee.

For the forthcoming session, Trumbull had one central objective in mind—to do all he could to influence Lincoln to prosecute the war with utmost vigor, but with due regard to the legal framework of the Constitution. His personal relations with Lincoln were cool, but Trumbull was not as yet ready to accuse Lincoln of dragging his feet in the war. His conversations with Lincoln left him convinced that the President was for "efficient measures and for giving to Illinois the position she is entitled to." [6] He disregarded the many complaints against Lincoln that poured into his office from Illinois,[7] and he was inclined to place the blame for the apparent inefficiency and incompetency of the administration in mobilizing the nation for war on the Secretary of War, Simon Cameron, whose appointment he had so bitterly opposed. Trumbull sympathized with Governor Yates' impatience with Cameron's blunders in directing the recruiting and equipping of new state militia forces, but he refused to put the blame on Lincoln. He, no doubt, agreed with an editorial written by his friend and spokesman in Alton, George T. Brown, the editor of the Telegraph, in which Brown wrote that, "It is very cheering to see all this zeal for the Government, but more cheering still to know the Government has wisdom enough not to be any less cautious, and self-possessed by reason of it." [8]

Trumbull found nothing objectionable in Lincoln's message

[4] White, op. cit., p. 168.
[5] Lyman Trumbull to John Trumbull, June 20, 1859, L. T. Family Papers.
[6] Lyman Trumbull to Julia Jayne Trumbull, May 27, 1861, L. T. Family Papers.
[7] William Butler to Trumbull, February 7, 1861, W. B. Plato to Trumbull, March 29, 1861, L. T. Papers. See also Koerner, Memoirs, II, 114.
[8] Alton Telegraph, May 3, 1861.

to the new session of Congress. He believed, with the President, that the Republican victory in the election was not the cause of secession, which, in Lincoln's words, the South had planned for the last thirty years. While he had serious reservations about the constitutional right of the President to suspend the writ of habeas corpus and arrest persons suspected of treason, Trumbull was happy to note that Lincoln had no objection to Congress passing appropriate laws to legalize his actions. "Whether there shall be any legislation on the subject," Lincoln's message said, "and if any, what, is submitted entirely to the better judgement of Congress." [9] Confronted with the growing strength of the Confederacy and aware of the influence and the activity of the Copperheads in the North, Trumbull was in no mood to interfere with the Commander-in-Chief in the execution of his mandate in an hour of acute emergency and peril to the nation, but neither was he willing to abdicate the constitutional prerogatives of Congress. All he wanted was to give the President the legal sanction to do his job, as Lincoln saw fit.

On July 31, Trumbull introduced in the Senate a "Bill to Suppress Rebellion and Insurrection and for Other Purposes." The bill was carefully prepared, and, as Trumbull told the Senate, it was approved by the President and by General Scott. It gave the commanding general and the commanders of military departments the right to suspend the writ of habeas corpus and provided that "no military officer shall be compelled to return the body of any person or persons detained by him." All persons charged with sedition were made liable to be tried by military tribunals, and the commanding generals of the districts were given the right to force persons suspected of treason to take an oath of allegiance to the Union. Those who refused could be detained for indefinite periods.[10] In explaining the bill to the Senate, Trumbull stated that the object of the bill was to "provide for putting down rebellion in a constitutional and

---

[9] Raymond, *op. cit.*, pp. 193–94.
[10] *Cong. Globe*, 37 Cong., 1st Sess., p. 336.

legal manner." [11] Speaking later in the debate, and answering a Republican colleague who wanted to shelve the bill, Trumbull made a ringing declaration of principle, which was to become the often-repeated credo that clearly put him at variance with the views of the radicals. He said, "In my judgement this is of far more importance than any other bill before the Senate . . . I think that constitutional liberty and the maintenance of the Constitution of the Government are more important than any appropriation bill." [12] Trumbull's insistence in pressing his bill resulted in the first of his many clashes with the Senate's radical wing. Senator Wilson, chairman of the Senate Armed Services Committee, declared that the legislation proposed by Trumbull was unnecessary and introduced a simple resolution approving the President's acts. Trumbull opposed Wilson's move and prevented its passage by marshalling the support of moderate Republicans and of the Democrats. In refuting Wilson's arguments, Trumbull asked whether a declaration of the Senate could make the illegal acts of the President legal. "I am not disposed," he said, "to say that the Administration has unlimited power and can do what it pleases, after Congress meets." [13] But Trumbull's own bill was also shelved to the regular session and did not actually become law until February 23, 1863, when it passed the Senate by a vote of 24 to 13.[14] Fighting for the passage of the bill, Trumbull once again reiterated his firm belief that respect for law and for the Constitution was essential even in time of war. "I defend no measure," he said, "I vote for no bill which, in my opinion, is not constitutional . . . I am for exercise of constitutional power, not arbitrary power . . . the bill is not to legalize arbitrary arrests; it is to make just and proper arrests constitutionally and legally." [15] He also maintained that Congress, and not the President, had the right to suspend the

[11] *Ibid.,* p. 338.
[12] *Ibid.,* p. 342.
[13] *Ibid.,* p. 392.
[14] *Cong. Globe,* 37 Cong., 3rd Sess. (February 23, 1863), p. 1208.
[15] *Ibid.,* p. 1185.

writ of habeas corpus. He was willing to approve the acts of the government because the one overriding necessity was "that the work we are now engaged in should be prosecuted with all the power and all the expedition within the command of the Government." [16]

The failure of Congress to pass Trumbull's bill when it was proposed proved to have important consequences. Gustave Koerner, who came to Washington and helped Trumbull to work on the legislation, wrote later: "Had it passed, the numerous arbitrary arrests in the border States and even the loyal States, the armed collusions which took place even in Illinois between the loyalists and disloyalists would have been avoided. The government found it necessary in the course of the war to do without law what they could have done under law." [17]

Consistent with his firm belief that any concession to the South would only encourage the secessionists and divide the North, Trumbull opposed the resolution introduced by Congressman Crittenden, which stated that the purpose of the war was to preserve the Union and the Constitution and not to subjugate the Southern states or to interfere with slavery. When the resolution, which passed the House by a vote of 117 to 2, came to the floor of the Senate, Trumbull was one of five senators to vote in the negative.[18]

After the House passed a bill to "confiscate property used for insurrectionary purposes," the Senate referred it to the Judiciary Committee. Trumbull then reported it back with an amendment providing that whenever any slave should be required or permitted by his master to take up arms against the Union or be employed in any capacity to help the enemy's military effort he should be entitled to his freedom.[19] The Confiscation Bill

---

[16] *Ibid.,* p. 339.
[17] Koerner, *Memoirs,* II, 158.
[18] *Cong. Globe,* 37 Cong., 1st Sess. (July 25, 1861), pp. 222–23.
[19] Text in Raymond, *op. cit.,* p. 201.

was fought bitterly by the Democrats, led by Breckinridge in the Senate and Crittenden in the House, but it passed the House by a vote of 60 to 48. The vote in the Senate came on August 6 and stood 24 to 11. The bill was vague in that it provided for no procedure as to how the forfeiture of the rebel property was to take place. Because the bill was vague, and because Lincoln did not want to antagonize the border states, he did not enforce it. Trumbull felt that had his bill been enforced, a great many slaves could have been emancipated. He was always proud, however, to note that his Confiscation Bill was the first step toward the emancipation of slaves.[20]

The humiliating defeat of the Union forces in the Battle of Bull Run, which Trumbull witnessed with a group of other senators and congressmen, was a sobering experience for him. At the opening of the session he had tried, unsuccessfully, to obtain permission from the Republican caucus to introduce in the Senate a resolution requiring the Union army to move and occupy Richmond.[21] He wrote to his wife that he also went to see Lincoln and urged him to order the Union army to attack.[22] Trumbull must have regretted this pressure for an immediate attack on the Confederate army by Union troops that were not ready for an offensive. Ward Hill Lamon wrote to a friend that the "scheming contemptible politicians" forced General Scott to attack. He wrote: "They brought on this battle prematurely— then went there to witness it and they and a d—n fat abolitionist Lieutenant were first to run." [23] Trumbull, in an attempt to find a scapegoat for the defeat and for his own folly, put the blame on the regular officers. As a convinced anti-militarist, he had no use for West Point graduates. "Our disaster," Trumbull

---

[20] *Cong. Globe*, 38 Cong., 1st Sess., p. 1313.

[21] *Diary of Orville Browning*, I, 480–81. Trumbull made repeated attempts in the caucus of the Republican senators to have a resolution passed declaring that it was "the duty of the Gov't to march on Richmond and occupy it before the 21st [July]." Francis Fessenden, *Life and Public Services of William Pitt Fessenden*, 2 vols. (Boston, 1907), I, 189.

[22] Lyman Trumbull to Julia Jayne Trumbull, July 16, 1861, L. T. Family Papers.

[23] King, *op. cit.*, p. 185.

wrote to Koerner, "was in my judgement all owing to the want of proper officers . . . there was no order, no head." He was, however, well impressed with Major General George McClellan, who, in his opinion, "made a good start and may remedy the evil." [24]

After the adjournment of Congress, Trumbull, unhappy and depressed, went to find cooler weather and solace with his relatives in Connecticut. From there he wrote to James R. Doolittle: "What a sad condition the country is in. Worse and worse. . . . The war has now been raging for four months and we are still acting on the defensive. I fear the men at the head of affairs do not realize our condition. . . . We must mete out to secessionists the same measure they deal out for the Union and then we will have friends in the South. . . ." [25] He deplored the practice of some Union commanders who delivered runaway slaves back to their masters, and he complained, justifiably, that there was "no action or business talent in Cabinet." "Lincoln," he concluded, "though a most excellent and honest man lacks these talents." [26] After returning to Washington, Trumbull, Chandler, and Wade called on Lincoln and urged him to prod McClellan into an offensive. Some writers have dealt very harshly with Trumbull on this matter. It seems that from that point on he was branded as one of the radicals who allegedly became a thorn in Lincoln's flesh.[27] John Hay called the trio of senators who visited the White House the "Jacobin Club," an insinuating and completely misplaced title. Consequently, Trum-

[24] Letter quoted in Koerner, *Memoirs*, II, 162. See also Lyman Trumbull to Julia Jayne Trumbull, July 22, 1861, L. T. Family Papers.

[25] Trumbull to James R. Doolittle, August 31, 1861, James R. Doolittle Papers, State Historical Society of Wisconsin, Madison, Wis.

[26] *Ibid.*

[27] John Hay wrote: "The Jacobin Club, represented by Trumbull, Chandler, and Wade, came up to worry the administration into a battle. The wildest howl of the summer is to be renewed. The President stood up to McClellan's deliberateness." *Lincoln and the Civil War in the Diaries and Letters of John Hay,* ed. Tyler Dennett (New York, 1939), p. 31. Harry T. Williams wrote that the "Jacobin Chieftains, 'three musketeers of radicalism' went to the White House to demand a military offensive." Williams, *op. cit.,* pp. 42, 44. See also Luthin, *op cit.,* p. 305.

bull was referred to as a Jacobin in many histories of the Civil War and Reconstruction.

What were Trumbull's complaints against the conduct of the war by the President? He complained in his letter to Doolittle that the administration was inefficient and incompetent in organizing the war effort. It was. Lincoln was not an efficient administrator, Cameron was a poor Secretary of War, and McClellan was a procrastinating commanding general suffering from a persecution complex. It is doubtful whether Lincoln was really ruffled by the blunt intervention of the three senators, because he liked plain speaking and he seldom held a grudge. After the visit of Trumbull, Chandler, and Wade, he went with Hay to McClellan's headquarters and told the general of the public's impatience for a Union offensive and victory.[28] Some months later, an exasperated Lincoln wrote to McClellan, "And once more, let me tell you, it is indispensable to you that you strike a blow. I am powerless to help this. . . . The country will not fail to note, is now noting, that the present hesitation to move upon an entrenched enemy is but the story of Manassas repeated." [29]

Trumbull's complaint that the practice of returning slaves who crossed into the Union lines should be discontinued expressed the conviction of most Republicans in Congress. He resented McClellan's order of May 26, issued to the people in the district in his command, in which he assured them that the Union army "not only will abstain from all interference with your slaves, but we will on the contrary, with an iron hand, crush any attempt at insurrection on their part." [30] This order, at least as it pertained to slaves of masters who either actively took part in the rebellion or aided and abetted it, was a violation of Trumbull's Confiscation Bill.

In spite of the serious nature of these complaints, there is evidence that Lincoln did not usually resent the pressures put

[28] *Lincoln and the Civil War in the Diaries and Letters of John Hay,* p. 33.
[29] Raymond, *op. cit.,* p. 273.
[30] *Ibid.,* p. 205.

on him either by the radicals or the conservatives. This crossfire pressure, often served him well, because it protected his freedom of action. He was not averse to telling the radicals that he had to give consideration to the views of the conservatives and vice versa. He made this clear in a letter to the radical faction in Missouri headed by Charles Drake, to whom he wrote: "The Radicals and the Conservatives each agree with me in some things and disagree in others. I could wish both to agree with me in all things; for then they would agree with each other, and would be too strong for any foe from any quarter. They, however, choose to do otherwise, and I do not question their right. I, too, shall do what seems to be my duty." [31]

There is little doubt that at least as far as Trumbull was concerned, his remonstrances with Lincoln were motivated not by partisan, but by patriotic impulses. Trumbull's patriotism and pure motives were clearly demonstrated in his reaction to the revocation of the emancipation order of General Frémont of the Western Department and the general's forced resignation. On August 21, General Frémont issued a proclamation declaring martial law throughout the state of Missouri and emancipating the slaves of all persons who had taken up arms or aided the rebellion against the Union. Lincoln wrote to Frémont that his order exceeded the Confiscation Bill of August 6, and requested him to rescind it. When Frémont refused, the President revoked the order.[32] The revocation of Frémont's proclamation brought a wave of protest and indignation in Illinois. The *Chicago Tribune* refused even to believe that the action was taken and stated on September 5, "Frémont's proclamation is our platform henceforth to the end of the war. Attach no credit to the report from Kentucky that the President disapproves of the proclamation of Maj. Gen. Frémont." [33] The *Alton Telegraph*

[31] *Ibid.*, p. 436.

[32] Lincoln explained in a letter to General David Hunter that Frémont's action "was purely political, and not within the range of military law, or necessity." Lincoln to General David Hunter, *The Living Lincoln*, p. 435.

[33] *Chicago Tribune*, September 5, 1861.

wrote that the people hailed Frémont's proclamation and added: "Imagine the astonishment and indignation with which the announcement that the President has countermanded the proclamation is received." [34] Trumbull received many communications and letters from Illinois Republican leaders protesting the President's action.[35] Among the critics were two civilian aids of General Frémont and close friends of Trumbull, Congressman Owen Lovejoy and Gustave Koerner. Koerner, however, conceded that Frémont was "cold . . . reticent and did many acts entirely against the established rules of the services." [36] In spite of his misgivings about Frémont, Koerner wrote to Trumbull that the Germans were convinced that Lincoln's action was a major blunder. "Only from the democrats," he wrote, "did the President receive a warm indorsement of his course; from the rankest copperhead sheets, even, came the assertion that the president deserved the praise of every honest Union man." [37] Horace White fulminated that "the President has broken his own neck if he has not destroyed his country. . . . Accursed be the day that I ever voted for such cowards and black legs." [38] The Republican papers in Illinois were unanimous in their denunciations of Lincoln and even some Democratic papers supported Frémont.[39]

Amidst all the furor, Trumbull remained calm and refused to join in the chorus of protest and indignation. He knew and liked Frémont, who was a frequent guest in his home in Washington, and he had previously protested to Lincoln that Frémont was not getting enough support and supplies from the War Depart-

[34] *Alton Telegraph,* February 20, 1861.
[35] William H. Herndon to Trumbull, November 20, 1861, John Russell to Trumbull, December 17, 1861, D. Kitchell to Trumbull, December 10, 1861. L. T. Papers.
[36] Koerner, *Memoirs,* II, 168.
[37] Gustave Koerner to Trumbull, November 18, 1861, L. T. Papers.
[38] Horace White to David Davis, September 14, 1861, Davis Papers, Chicago Historical Society.
[39] *Illinois State Register,* October 7, 1861; *Rock River Democrat,* September 17, 1861, September 24, 1861.

ment.[40] But Trumbull, upon a careful examination of the legal issue involved, concluded that the President was fully within his rights in repudiating the action of a general who had exceeded his authority. Being a strong believer in the principle of civilian control over the military, Trumbull gave his full support to the President. "We are fighting," he wrote, "to sustain constitutional government and regulated liberty, and, of course, to set up any military leader in opposition to the constituted authorities would be utterly destructive of the very purpose for which the people of the loyal states are now so liberally contributing their blood and treasure. . . ." [41] The Chicago Tribune, always faithful to Lincoln and Trumbull, soon changed its position and attacked Frémont for his extravagant abuse of power and his propensity for surrounding himself with thieves and corrupters.[42] While Wade and Chandler publicly blasted Lincoln for his treatment of Frémont, Trumbull remained silent but privately exerted his influence to quiet the furor.[43]

Annoyed at the refusal of the administration and of the commanding Union generals to enforce his Confiscation Bill, Trumbull, immediately upon the opening of the regular session of Congress, introduced a tougher measure along the same lines. Trumbull's friend, Congressman Isaac N. Arnold of Chicago, introduced a similar measure in the House. It called for the forfeiture to the United States of every species of property, real and personal, of all persons participating in or abetting the rebellion, provided that these persons could not be reached by the ordinary civilian authority. The slaves of the rebels were to be declared free, and no runaway slaves were to be returned, unless their masters were able to prove that they were loyal to

[40] Koerner, Memoirs, II, 158; and Trumbull to James R. Doolittle, August 31, 1861, James R. Doolittle Papers, State Historical Society of Wisconsin, Madison, Wis.

[41] Lyman Trumbull to M. Carey Lea, November 5, 1861, L. T. Papers.

[42] Chicago Tribune, October 3, 1861.

[43] Benjamin Wade to Zachary Chandler, September 23, 1861, Zachary Chandler Papers, Library of Congress.

the United States. Unlike the First Confiscation Bill of August 6, 1861, the bill did not require court action before captured slaves could be freed. The bill also directed the President to provide for the voluntary colonization of freed Negroes in "some tropical country, where they may have the protection of the Government, and be secured in all the rights and privileges of freemen." [44]

In his speech in support of the bill, Trumbull was one of the first Republican leaders in Congress to declare that the freeing of the slaves was one of the aims of the Civil War. He said: "The right to free the slaves of rebels would be equally clear with that to confiscate their property generally, for it is as property that they profess to hold them; but as one of the most efficient means of attaining the end for which the armies of the Union have been called forth, the right to restore them the God-given liberty of which they have been unjustly deprived, is doubly clear." [45] The legislation he proposed did not acknowledge the superiority of the military over the civilian power, even in time of war. "So far from admitting," he said, 'the superiority of the military over the civil power in time of war, or that there is any necessity that it should be so, I hold that under our Constitution the military is as much subject to the control of the civil power in war and in peace. . . . As unpopular as the avowal may for the moment be among the thoughtless, I here declare that I am for suppressing this monstrous rebellion according to law, and in no other way." [46] His belief in the civilian control of the military, in the Constitution and in the civil rights of all citizens, was to become the cause of bitter conflicts between Trumbull and the Republican radicals in the Senate.

The Second Confiscation Act was debated for many months and was attacked by the radicals as too weak and by the conservative senators as too strong. During a prolonged debate on

---

[44] *Cong. Globe,* 37 Cong., 2nd Sess. (December 5, 1861), pp. 18–19.
[45] *Ibid.,* p. 20.
[46] *Ibid.*

the bill, on February 25, Senator Collamer attacked the bill as an unlawful and unconstitutional interference by Congress with the existence of slavery in the states.[47] On the other side, Charles Sumner maintained that the bill had too many loopholes for the slave owners. He denounced the "timid" senators who proposed "when the life of our Republic is struck at, to proceed as if by an indictment in a criminal court." [48] Trumbull paid no attention to the assaults of the radicals but, seeing his bill endangered, hastened to assure the conservatives that he was ready to compromise and that if he could not get a strong measure he would take a weaker one. "I have," he said, "no pride of opinion about this measure. I shall vote for the best confiscation bill I can get." [49]

In the debate on the bill, Trumbull was obliged to face an assault from another quarter. His conservative colleague from Illinois, Senator Orville H. Browning, who was close to Lincoln, advanced the theory that the President as Commander-in-Chief could order the confiscation of property, real or personal, at his pleasure and therefore there was no need for the Confiscation Bill. Browning's constitutional view found little support in the Senate, which on May 6 voted 24 to 14 to refer the bill with the amendments to a select committee of nine. The select committee inserted a clause that provided for judicial review in emancipation cases, but failed to provide, in accordance with the Constitution, that the forfeiture of property would pertain only during the lifetime of the offender. Lincoln made it known that he would veto the bill unless it was changed. After a conference between the President and Senator William Pitt Fessenden, the House and the Senate passed a joint resolution that provided that punishment or proceedings under the Confiscation Act would not involve a forfeiture of the real estate of the persons participating or aiding the rebellion beyond their natural

[47] Raymond, *op. cit.*, pp. 240–41.
[48] *Ibid.*, p. 242.
[49] *Cong. Globe,* 37 Cong., 2nd Sess., p. 1964.

life. The bill finally passed both Houses and was signed by Lincoln and became law on July 17, 1862. On the same day, Congress passed the Militia Act, which gave freedom to any slave who would render military service to the United States.

The fate of Trumbull's Second Confiscation Bill was like that of the first one. Lincoln, who did not believe that the bill was necessary, refused to enforce it.[50] And Trumbull, whose main motive in pressing for the bill was his conviction that if properly executed, it could free many slaves and hurt the rebel cause, was bitter over Lincoln's attitude.[51] Very little rebel property was confiscated and relatively few slaves were freed, but the Confiscation Bill marked the first step toward the emancipation of slaves.[52] The provision in the bill that gave the President the right to employ in the war effort as many persons of African descent as he deemed necessary allowed Lincoln eventually to employ about 150,000 Negroes as soldiers and laborers. Another provision that was to figure importantly during the early months of Reconstruction was the one that gave the President the right to grant pardon and amnesty to rebels at his discretion.

The long, arduous, eight-month battle for the passage of the Second Confiscation Bill revealed clearly the power structure of the Senate, which was to remain essentially unchanged during Civil War and Reconstruction. Sumner, Howard, Wade, Chandler, and other radicals pushed for extreme legislation pressing for the immediate emancipation of slaves without regard for constitutional restrictions, while the moderate group led by Trumbull, Fessenden, Sherman, and Grimes, aided by the War Democrats and even some Democrats, wanted a constitutional amendment abolishing slavery and favored granting of limited

[50] Text of Lincoln's message in Raymond, *op. cit.*, pp. 245–47.

[51] Speaking in the Senate several years later, Trumbull asserted that had his Second Confiscation Bill been faithfully executed, the Military Reconstruction Act would have been unnecessary. *Cong. Globe*, 39 Cong., 2nd Sess. (December 5, 1866), p. 15.

[52] See James G. Blaine, *Twenty Years of Congress* (Norwich, Conn., 1844), I, 377. See also A. C. Cole, "President Lincoln and the Illinois Radical Republicans," *Mississippi Valley Historical Review*, Vol. IV, No. 4 (March, 1918), pp. 417–36.

franchise to Negroes. What united the radical and the moderate wings of the Republicans in Congress was their impatience for Union victories and their determination to crush the rebellion and obtain the unconditional surrender of the South. They differed greatly, however, on means to be used in achieving this objective. Lincoln's refusal to execute Trumbull's confiscation bills and the ease with which he avoided any reprisals, attacks, or censure from Congress does throw doubts on the often repeated theory that sees Lincoln as a martyr suffering from an unreasonable pressure of the radicals. When Horace Greeley wrote in his editorial "The Prayer of Twenty Millions," published in the New York Tribune on August 2, 1862, that twenty million Americans wanted, among other things, the execution of the Confiscation Bill, Lincoln politely but firmly told Greeley that he would be the judge whether and how to execute the law.[53]

In view of the determined opposition of conservative Republicans and of most of the Democrats, the passage of the bill was a tribute to the influence and parliamentary skill of Lyman Trumbull. His three major speeches on the bill were distinguished by legal erudition, debating skill, and a sense of moral mission. He stressed the importance of taking the first step toward the freeing of the slaves, which in Trumbull's views was one of the main objectives of the war. After his speech in the Senate on April 7, the Chicago Tribune published an editorial that contained an excellent appraisal of Trumbull's performance on the Senate rostrum. "The inexorable logic of Judge Trumbull," the Tribune wrote, "never did better service than in his great speech on the Confiscation Bill, in the Senate, on Monday last. Deeply learned [he] . . . weighs testimony like a judge . . . with a moral sense as keen as that of any puritan who ever lived . . . calm, reflective, dispassionate, of eminent blamelessness of personal character and private life. . . ."[54]

[53] Lincoln to Horace Greeley, August 22, 1862, The Living Lincoln, pp. 495–96.
[54] Chicago Tribune, April 9, 1862.

Trumbull became increasingly concerned over the large number of arbitrary arrests of persons in the loyal states suspected of treason to the Union. In the course of a speech that Trumbull delivered in the Senate in the protracted debate on the Confiscation Bill, in April, 1862, he asserted that the President did not have the constitutional power to suspend the writ of habeas corpus and denounced arbitrary arrests as "usurpations of power," which might become "precedents for the destruction of Constitutional liberty." [55]

Trumbull began his fight against arbitrary arrests and the suppression of the freedom of the press by the introduction, on December 12, 1861, of a resolution of inquiry that clearly implied censure of the administration. It stated, "Resolved, that the Secretary of State be directed to inform the Senate whether, in the loyal states of the Union any person or persons have been arrested and imprisoned and are now held in confinement . . . and if so, under what law said arrests have been made . . ." [56] The debate on the resolution lasted all day. The radicals were fuming, and even conservatives like Senators Dixon of Connecticut and Browning of Illinois opposed it as dangerous to the cause of the Union. The arrests, they contended, were necessary to curb treason, and the resolution was an insult to the President. William Pitt Fessenden and John P. Hale supported the resolution, but the vigorous defense of his course was given by Trumbull himself. In his speech he declared that he was for the prosecution of the war with the most stringent measures and with utmost vigor, but "to arrest a man in a peaceable portion of the country and imprison him indefinitely is the very essence of despotism." [57] No one, Trumbull declared, should be thanked (as suggested by Dixon) for assuming "an unconstitutional and

---

[55] *Speech of Honorable Lyman Trumbull of Illinois, Delivered in the Senate of the United States, April 7, 1862*, Congressional Globe Office, Washington, D.C., p. 6.

[56] *Cong. Globe*, 37 Cong., 2nd Sess. (December, 1861), p. 90.

[57] *Ibid.*, p. 91.

unwarranted authority." [58] "What are we coming to when arrests may be made at the whims or the caprice of a cabinet member? Now, Sir, I am for regulating these things by law. That is the object of my inquiry!" [59]

At the conclusion of the debate, a motion to refer the resolution to the Judiciary Committee was adopted by a vote of 25 to 17. Of the Republicans, only Trumbull, Hale and Grimes voted in the negative, but they were joined by all the Democrats.[60] The defeat was softened considerably by the widespread support that Trumbull's fight on arbitrary arrests received in Illinois. General John M. Palmer wrote to him that he was amazed at the insensitivity of the Senate to the attempt to put a restraint on the wave of illegal, arbitrary arrests, which irritated and disturbed the loyal people of the North.[61]

In July the House passed a bill, based largely on Trumbull's original resolution, that directed the Secretaries of State and War to report to the federal judges in the respective districts the names of prisoners suspected of disloyalty. These prisoners were to be subsequently either indicted by grand juries or released. The bill also authorized the President to suspend the writ of habeas corpus in parts of the country where the threat of insurrection existed. The bill was not acted upon before adjournment.

The Democratic victories in the Congressional election in the fall of 1862, in which the Democrats made a big issue of the arbitrary arrests, convinced even some Republican leaders that a curb on the powers of the Secretary of War to imprison po-

[58] Senator Henry Wilson after deploring Trumbull's speech stated that the country applauded the arrests of disloyal men. *Ibid.*, p. 92. Browning said that Trumbull's resolution disturbed the harmony between Congress and the Executive. *Ibid.*, pp. 97–98.

[59] *Ibid.*, p. 91.

[60] Raymond, *op. cit.*, p. 227.

[61] John M. Palmer to Trumbull, January 31, 1862. Similar letters of support were received by Trumbull from J. H. Jordan, December 28, 1861; George Pope, December 31, 1861; W. S. Gilman, December 28, 1861. L. T. Papers. See also Koerner, *Memoirs*, II, 173.

litical suspects was necessary. The pressure on Trumbull was particularly strong in Illinois, where the Democrats defeated Orville H. Browning for the Senate and elected William A. Richardson in his stead. Democratic newspapers and even many Republican leaders were especially critical of the arrest of several prominent Democrats, including Congressman William J. Allen and State Senator William H. Green.[62] Soon after the Thirty-seventh Congress assembled, Trumbull renewed his fight for a law regulating the arrests of political prisoners. He introduced a bill that gave the President full discretionary power to suspend the writ of habeas corpus. The bill upheld Lincoln's action in his Proclamation of September 24 suspending the writ of habeas corpus, but required that lists of all civilians arrested by the military, where the courts were functioning, were to be given to the federal judges within twenty days after their arrest. If not indicted by federal grand juries at their first term, they were to be released. Trumbull, participating in a heated debate in which Democratic Senators Saulsbury of Delaware, Powell of Kentucky, and others attacked the bill, denounced arbitrary arrests as unfortunate and declared that there was a great deal of ill-feeling and unrest on this subject in the country.[63] After a struggle with the House, which wanted a more stringent measure, the bill became a law on March 3, 1863.

Trumbull had an opportunity to demonstrate his political courage and his dedication to the freedom of the press when, on June 1, 1863, General A. E. Burnside suspended the publication of the violently Copperhead paper, the Chicago Times. The general announced that he was suspending the Democratic organ for "repeated expression of disloyal and incendiary statements." [64] The charge was fully substantiated by evidence. It took the full measure of self-restraint to tolerate the vicious at-

---

[62] J. M. Palmer to Trumbull, January 3, 1862, L. T. Papers; Koerner, *Memoirs,* II, 173; *Chicago Times,* June 6, 1862.
[63] *Cong. Globe,* 37 Cong., 3rd Sess. (December 9, 1862), p. 31.
[64] *Illinois State Journal,* June 3, 1863.

tacks on Lincoln and on the war effort of the North that regularly appeared in the *Times*. But to Trumbull the overriding consideration was the fact that a general, by a fiat based on his military power, suppressed a newspaper without due process of law. Trumbull joined Mayor William B. Ogden and Congressman I. N. Arnold in addressing a protest meeting, which was held in the Chicago Circuit Court. The meeting passed a resolution urging the President to revoke the order and Trumbull and Arnold dispatched a telegram asking Lincoln to give serious consideration to the resolution.[65] The *Chicago Tribune* strongly approved the suspension of its hated rival and commended Burnside for striking "at the root of secession evil. . . ."[66] The Republican Clubs of Chicago took the same position.[67] Congressman Arnold, afraid for his chances of re-election, hastily sent another telegram to Lincoln assuring the President that in his joint telegram with Trumbull he did not intend to express an opinion on whether the order of suspension should be abrogated.[68]

Trumbull's position demanding the rescinding of the suppression order brought upon his head a fury of denunciation The *Peoria Daily Transcript* wrote, "Alas, poor Trumbull! We speak of him more in pity and sorrow than in anger." The paper insinuated that Trumbull was motivated in his stand by his jealousy of Lincoln and declared that Trumbull's demand, voiced in his speech at the protest meeting, that suits against subversive papers should be brought in court was "absurd and ridiculous."[69] Lincoln rescinded Burnside's order and later stated that it was the Trumbull-Arnold telegram that "turned the scale

[65] *Illinois State Register,* June 3, 5, 1863.
[66] *Chicago Tribune,* June 2, 1863.
[67] *Chicago Tribune,* June 2, 3, 4, 1863.
[68] Texts of both telegrams in I. N. Arnold Papers, Chicago Historical Society.
[69] *Peoria Daily Transcript*, June 10, 1863.

in favor of revoking the order." [70] Trumbull's action on the *Times* suspension exposed him to many attacks by his opponents. But even when viciously attacked on this issue during his campaign for re-election in 1867, he never "explained" or repudiated the position he had taken.

The Thirty-seventh Congress, which adjourned on July 17, 1862, had an impressive record of accomplishment. In addition to the Confiscation Bill, it had passed the Homestead Act, the Pacific Railroad Bill, the College Land Grant Bill, the Agricultural Bureau Bill, a tariff bill, the Militia Act, an act abolishing slavery in the District of Columbia, a bill establishing schools for Negro children in Washington and Georgetown, and a joint resolution advocating gradual emancipation. Congress also gave Lincoln all he wanted for the raising and maintaining of a rapidly growing Union army. All this constitutes an impressive record of cooperation between Lincoln and the Congress. Although the credit for this cooperation must go to such moderate leaders as Trumbull and Fessenden, chairmen of the Judiciary and the Finance Committees of the Senate respectively, it belongs equally to radical leaders Henry Wilson, John P. Hale, and Charles Sumner, the chairmen of the Armed Services, Naval Affairs, and Foreign Affairs Committees respectively, and to Thaddeus Stevens, chairman of the House Ways and Means Committee. Without the active cooperation of these men the astonishing amount of legislation would not have been passed. The pages of the *Congressional Globe* which report on the sessions of the Thirty-seventh Congress do not bear out the contention, often repeated, that the radicals badgered and abused Lincoln and obstructed his program. On the contrary, the record provides proof that Wilson and Hale had the deepest respect for Lincoln and gave him their faithful and unstinted

---

[70] Lincoln to I. N. Arnold, May 25, 1864. *The Living Lincoln,* p. 605. Judge Davis, who conducted the hearings on the case with Judge Drummond, also sent a telegram to Lincoln urging the revocation, *Diary of Orville Browning,* I, 632.

cooperation and that Sumner, who did not always agree with the President on the ways of dealing with slavery, worked smoothly with him and with Secretary of State Seward in the area of foreign relations. Summer was also a frequent and welcome visitor in the White House, and no matter how much Stevens in private attacked the President, he gave him, in his capacity as chairman of an important House committee, his full cooperation.

11

Father of the
Thirteenth Amendment

IN THE SPRING AND SUMMER OF 1862, TRUMBULL WAS NOT HAPPY with the course of the war. Very few people were. The Union armies had yet to win a decisive victory after suffering a string of defeats. The unwillingness or the inability of General McClellan to go on the offensive was irritating not only to the leaders of Congress, but also to the President. The Chicago postmaster and part owner of the *Chicago Tribune* wrote to Trumbull: "I have made up my mind that McClellan is not preordained to crush the rebellion." General Palmer said virtually the same thing in a letter from his Tennessee headquarters, and Governor Yates of Illinois told Trumbull that he had doubts as to Lincoln's ability to lead the nation to victory. "If I were Lincoln," he said, "I would lead enough of the Potomac army to take Richmond and this though Washington could not be saved—I would march to victory or death." [1] These men, who had been at first friendly to McClellan and had supported his appointment, became disenchanted with him when they saw the "Little

[1] John Locke Scripps to Trumbull, February 1, 1862; John M. Palmer to Trumbull, February 3, 1862; Richard Yates to Trumbull, February 14, 1862, L. T. Papers.

Napoleon" sitting in his headquarters busy writing letters of complaints to the President and to his friends.

It seems wrong to suggest, as some writers have done, that the "Jacobins" were out to get McClellan because he was a Democrat. All that Trumbull and Lincoln wanted was to see General McClellan fulfill the high hopes they had for him when he took over the command of the Army of the Potomac. A careful reading of the long succession of Lincoln's letters to McClellan provides a basis for the assumption that Lincoln would have fired McClellan without being prodded by the radicals. These letters, written in the early weeks of October, prove that the President had decided to give McClellan one more chance and, if he found him wanting, to remove him. On October 13 Lincoln wrote to McClellan: "Are you not over-cautious when you assume that you cannot do what the enemy is constantly doing?" [2] A few days later the President sent his general a note that was so sarcastic and insulting that there is ground to wonder why McClellan did not take the hint and submit his resignation. Replying to a complaint from McClellan that his horses were tired, Lincoln said, "I have read your dispatch about sore-tongue and fatigued horses. Will you pardon me for asking what the horses of your army have done since the battle of Antietam that fatigues anything?" [3] On October 27 the President sharply asked, "Is it your purpose not to go into action again till the men now being drafted in the States are incorporated in the old regiments?" [4] A week later, Lincoln relieved McClellan of the command of the Army of the Potomac. The correspondence between Lincoln and McClellan does not suggest that the general was removed to please Wade, Sumner, or Trumbull. He was removed because his Commander-in-Chief became convinced that he was not the man for the job. The *Chicago Tribune*, which had originally supported McClellan,

---

[2] Lincoln to McClellan, October 13, 1862, Raymond, *op. cit.,* p. 319.

[3] Lincoln to McClellan, October 25, 1862, Raymond *op. cit.,* p. 321.

[4] Lincoln to McClellan, October 27, 1864, Raymond, *op. cit.,* p. 322.

wrote what still remains an accurate and fair epitaph on his career: "History will say of him, that he was weighed in the balance against duties that have rarely if ever fallen to the lot of a military leader and that he has been found wanting." [5]

The anger and the frustration of Republicans in Congress over the bad fortunes of the Union armies needed a scapegoat, and General Burnside's defeat at Fredericksburg brought about a sense of frustration and despair. The ire of the Republican leaders was concentrated not on Lincoln, but on his Secretary of State, Seward. The legend, which had no basis in fact, that the New York statesman was the "Gray Eminence" of the administration still persisted. Seward was accused of pressing for a policy of appeasement of the South and of frustrating Lincoln's moves to emancipate the slaves. The Republican senators were in an uproar and Trumbull, who never forgave Seward for his readiness, in 1858, to support Douglas for the Senate, joined in the chorus of anger and protest. There was strong sentiment in Illinois for the ouster of Seward from the Cabinet. Republican leaders from Springfield sent a petition to Lincoln expressing the country's "non-confidence in your Cabinet as at present constituted." [6] A Republican politician wrote, "For God's sake, let Congress pass a resolution asking the Prest. to make Butler Secty. of War, Banks of Navy and Fessenden Secty. of State," and another said that the Northwest Republicans were "amazed to see pro-slavery Blair and Bates and envious, ambitious Seward retained as chief advisors in the Cabinet." [7] Governor Yates was worried that Union defeats had increased the danger of secession in southern Illinois. "Secession," he wrote, "is stronger there than you have any idea. Its advocates are numerous and powerful and respectable." [8] Trumbull believed that unless the

[5] *Chicago Tribune,* March 12, 1862.

[6] Text of the petition in the William Butler Collection, Chicago Historical Society.

[7] Grant Goodrich to Trumbull, January 31, 1867, and T. Maple to Trumbull, December 28, 1862, L.T. Papers.

[8] Richard Yates to Trumbull, February 14, 1862, L. T. Papers.

Union army won some decisive victories, England and France might intervene and force a truce.[9] The fiery Herndon demanded to know "What is Lincoln doing? Does he suppose that he can crush-squelch out this huge rebellion by pop guns filled with rose water?"[10] and Chandler wrote to Trumbull, "Your president is unstable as water, if he has as I suspect been bullied by those traitor generals. . . . For God and Country's sake, send someone to stay with the President who will control and hold him."[11]

Pressed and badgered on all sides, Trumbull concluded that some action had to be taken. On Tuesday, December 16, he demanded at a caucus of Republican senators that the Senate take decisive action to save the nation from a disastrous defeat.[12] The caucus passed a resolution demanding changes in the Cabinet and sent a delegation to the White House composed of seven senators to demand from Lincoln Seward's dismissal. The delegation of seven senators included such moderates and conservatives as Trumbull, Fessenden, Grimes, Collamer, and Harris. Senator Collamer, of Vermont, was elected chairman of the delegation, which met with Lincoln twice, first with the President alone and the second time with Lincoln and his Cabinet. Lincoln skillfully exploited Salmon P. Chase's refusal to press publicly his charges against Seward, which he often expounded to the members of the deputation privately, and the senatorial intervention came to naught.

The intervention by the group of senators, including Trumbull, to force the President's hand on the choice of his Cabinet was contrary to established tradition and thus has been roundly and deservedly condemned by historians. But it was not a sinister

[9] Trumbull to Richard Yates, February 6, 1862, Uriah Reavis Collection, Chicago Historical Society.

[10] William H. Herndon to Trumbull, November 20, 1862, L. T. Papers.

[11] Zachariah Chandler to Trumbull, September 5, 1862, L. T. Papers.

[12] The proceedings of the caucus based on account in *Life and Public Services of William Pitt Fessenden,* by his son Francis Fessenden (Boston, 1907), II, 231–36.

plot of a "Jacobin Cabal." The majority of the delegation, men like Collamer, Trumbull, Fessenden, and Grimes, had a deep respect for the Constitution and believed in the principle of separation of power. Theirs was a misguided act of exasperated patriots in an hour of a dire crisis that confronted the nation. It is doubtful that these senators "confused the American system with the British and tried to establish the doctrine of parliamentary supremacy and the responsibility of the executive to Congress." [13] But they did receive from Lincoln a masterful lesson in the basic constitutional tenet that Congress declares war but that the President conducts it as the chief executive and Commander-in-Chief and that Congress cannot be permitted to dictate the composition of the Cabinet. David Donald pointed out that the harsh criticism of the attempt to have Seward removed should be tempered by the fact that the administration was under fire by "nearly everybody—in Washington and in the North." He stated: "The famous senatorial caucus of December 1862 which sought to eliminate Seward from the administration, has often been treated as a Radical effort to take the reins from Lincoln's hands. In fact, however, that caucus was attended by all but two Republican members of the Senate, and Radicals and Conservatives joined in unanimously adopting the resolution." [14]

The moderate and radical Republicans were not united on most social or economic programs. There were among them high tariff men and free traders; some were concerned about land speculation and wasteful bounties of land grants to railroads, others were not—but they were united in wanting a tough war on the South. They were also increasingly in favor of employment of Negro troops to help the army and the Northern war effort. Trumbull was delighted when Lincoln, using the

[13] Williams, *op. cit.,* p. 213.
[14] David Donald, *Lincoln Reconsidered* (New York, 1956), pp. 112–13. See also Richard Hofstadter, *The American Political Tradition* (New York, 1957), p. 127.

Confiscation Act, authorized the employment of Negroes as laborers and then ordered the formation of Negro regiments.[15]

As senator from Illinois, where the pressure for the emancipation of slaves was particularly strong, Trumbull received many letters and petitions urging the freeing of the slaves. But he refused to press Lincoln on the matter. Unlike the radicals, Trumbull appreciated Lincoln's overriding concern to keep the border states and the bayonets of their sons on the Union side. He supported the joint resolution of Congress, which was approved by Lincoln, calling for the support of the United States for any state wishing to abolish slavery.[16] When on July 12, 1862, in a message to Congress, Lincoln recommended the passage of a bill that provided for payment of compensation to the states for freeing the slaves, Trumbull gave the move his full support. On January 29, 1863, Trumbull moved for the postponement by the Senate of all other legislation in order to take up a bill to give Missouri $20,000,000 to be used for the freeing of its slaves in thirteen years.[17] He rejected the arguments of Sumner and Wilson, who said that the Missouri slaves ought to go free without compensation, and he reminded them that Congress in a resolution adopted in April accepted the principle of compensated emancipation. "I would be glad," Trumbull stated, "if the shackles could fall from every slave, not only in Missouri but throughout the United States and the world; but Sir, I cannot accomplish it . . . I am not prepared to say that because we cannot have immediate emancipation, therefore we will do nothing for gradual emancipation." [18] When Sumner moved to strike the word "gradual" from the bill, Trumbull joined the moderate Republicans and the Democrats in defeating the motion 27 to 11. [19]

In Illinois the reaction to Lincoln's Emancipation Proclama-

[15] Trumbull to Norman G. Flagg, December 18, 1862, Jayne Papers.
[16] Raymond, op. cit., p. 231.
[17] Cong. Globe, 37 Cong., 3rd Sess. (January 29, 1863), p. 586.
[18] Ibid., p. 593.
[19] Ibid., p. 901.

tion was largely favorable. The *Chicago Tribune*, which had pressed hard for the proclamation, was elated.[20] On January 1, 1863, the day when the proclamation became effective, the paper stated that "The New Year is begun under brighter and better auspices when the Proclamation shall call to the aid of the government 400,000 eager freedmen, to be henceforth men, no more slaves." [21] The *Alton Telegraph* declared that "the document is everywhere received with the greatest enthusiasm." [22]

There was a strong feeling among the Republican leaders in Illinois that the proclamation would improve the chances for a Republican victory in the fall elections.[23] Governor Yates, exasperated by the growing strength of the Democrats in his state, telegraphed Lincoln that loyal Negroes must be recruited to the Union army. Lincoln answered him, "Dick, hold still and see the salvation of God." There were, of course, exceptions to this chorus of approval. Orville H. Browning denounced the emancipation of slaves and the *Chicago Times* was convinced that the proclamation would unnecessarily prolong the war.[24]

Lyman Trumbull generally approved of the Emancipation Proclamation, although he was not enthusiastic about it. His restraint was caused by his doubts as to whether or not the President, in his capacity as Commander-in-Chief, had the constitutional authority to free the slaves even if the jurisdiction of the proclamation was limited to the territory of the United States under the rule of the Confederacy. To resolve these doubts, he determined to support a resolution as an amendment to the Constitution abolishing slavery forever. The idea did not originate with Trumbull, but the resolution was adopted only after he, as chairman of the Judiciary Committee, reworded and sponsored its adoption by the Senate. The first resolution for the

[20] On July 4 the *Tribune* published an editorial entitled "Let My People Go."
[21] *Chicago Tribune*, January 1, 1863.
[22] *Alton Telegraph*, January 3, 1863.
[23] D. L. Phillips to Trumbull, March 22, 1862, L. T. Papers. See also Cole, "President Lincoln and the Illinois Radical Republicans," *op. cit.,* p. 426.
[24] *Diary of Orville Browning*, I, 578; *Chicago Times*, September 23, 24, 1862.

amendment was offered in the House by Representative James F. Wilson of Iowa on December 14, 1863. A few weeks later, on January 13, 1864, Senator John B. Henderson of Missouri offered a similar resolution in the Senate. Henderson's resolution was referred to the Judiciary Committee. On February 15, at the request of Trumbull, Congressman I. N. Arnold of Illinois introduced the following resolution in the House: "Resolved, that the Constitution shall be so amended as to abolish slavery in the United States wherever it now exists, and to prohibit its existence in every part thereof forever." [25] The resolution was adopted by a vote of 78 to 62, far short of the needed two-thirds majority.

Undaunted by this initial defeat, Trumbull introduced to the Senate a reworded resolution intended to constitute Amendment XIII in the Constitution. Its wording followed closely the phraseology of the 1787 Northwest Ordinance, which was familiar to the nation. By using the new wording, Trumbull hoped to increase the chances for the adoption of the resolution, which read: "Neither slavery nor involuntary servitude except as punishent for crime whereof the party shall have been duly convicted shall exist within the United States or any place subject to their jurisdiction. Congress shall have power to enforce this article by appropriate legislation." [26]

In a major speech in support of his resolution, Trumbull told the Senate that a large number of slaves could have been emancipated if the Confiscation Bill of July, 1861, had been enforced. "So far as I am advised," he said, "not a single slave has been set at liberty under it." [27] Trumbull also expressed his regret that for a long time Lincoln had delayed the employment of Negro troops, as authorized in the Confiscation Bill. He declared that slavery was the main cause of the secession and recalled that, "If these Halls have resounded from our earliest

[25] *Cong. Globe,* 38 Cong., 1st Sess. (February 15, 1864), p. 659–660.
[26] *Ibid.,* p. 1313.
[27] *Ibid.,* p. 1.

recollections with strifes and contests of sections, ending sometimes in blood, *it was slavery which almost always occasioned
them.*" [28]

Trumbull pointed out that the Emancipation Proclamation
of January 1, 1863, pertained only to slaves in the territory under
the rule of the Confederacy and that many people doubted
whether the President had a constitutional right to issue the
proclamation. Slavery still existed in Delaware, Maryland, Kentucky, Tennessee, and Missouri, and in parts of Louisiana and
Virginia. Trumbull contended that Congress did not have the
right to abolish slavery in the states by passing a law to that
effect. "Only slavery prohibited by an amendment to the Constitution," he stated, "will make sure that no state or Congress
could ever restore slavery." [29] He agreed with the radicals, like
Charles Sumner, that it would have been much more convenient
to abolish slavery by a law of Congress, but he said that "it is
not because a measure would be convenient that Congress has
authority to adopt it." [30]

Trumbull's insistence on a constitutional amendment and his
opposition to the stand taken by Sumner, Wade, Howard, and
other radicals that an act of Congress would suffice, exposed him
to harsh attacks from the radical wing. The most bitter attack
came from Senator Morton S. Wilkinson of Minnesota, who
accused Trumbull of timidity and of throwing legal roadblocks
in the path of those who wished to abolish slavery. Expressing
the sentiments of Sumner, Wade, and others, Wilkinson stated
that Trumbull could not be relied upon as an ally of radicalism.
He said, ". . . there are a few others around me in this floor who
have, from the beginning, steadily and consistently acted upon
the same principle. The eloquent Senator from Massachusetts
[Mr. Sumner], the just and uncompromising Senator from Ohio
[Mr. Wade], the honorable members from Iowa [Messrs. Harlan

28 *Ibid.* (Italics mine.)
29 *Ibid.,* p. 1314.
30 *Ibid.*

and Grimes] and from Michigan [Messrs. Chandler and Howard] have never for one moment hesitated or faltered in their determination to destroy slavery. . . . While others, more timid, have been from the beginning rolling constitutional logs in the way of our armies, these honorable Senators have been clearing the way for the rapid and triumphant march of our forces." [31] The moderates were put on notice that they could not claim membership in the militant group of Republicans unless they agreed to follow the leadership of Sumner, Wade, Chandler, and Howard.

Seeing that they had no chance of getting the Senate to pass a bill outlawing slavery, the radicals voted for Trumbull's resolution, which passed the Senate on April 8, 1864, by a vote of 38 to 6. Even Senator Reverdy Johnson of Maryland, an influential Democrat, voted for the measure.[32] Finally, on February 1, 1865, after one more unsuccessful attempt, the House passed the resolution by the needed two-thirds majority. The Thirteenth Amendment became part of the Constitution when it had been ratified by three-fourths of the states, on December 18, 1865. Lincoln gave the resolution his full support. He approved the inclusion of a declaration in favor of the amendment in the 1864 Republican platform [33] and urged Congress to pass it in his Annual Message to Congress of December 6, 1869. Faced with the possibility of the defeat of the measure in the House, Lincoln applied all the pressure he could to assure its passage.[34]

Lincoln's Proclamation of Amnesty and Restoration or Reconstruction (he did not want to make an issue of which term was to be used) of December 8, 1863, declared that a minimum of ten percent of the voters who had voted in the 1860 election in any of the seceded states could re-establish a state government

[31] *Ibid.* (March 21, 1864), p. 314.
[32] *Ibid.* (April 8, 1964), p. 1490.
[33] Lincoln's Letter to the President of the Baltimore Convention, June 9, 1864, in *The Living Lincoln*, p. 607.
[34] Luthin, *op. cit.*, pp. 571-74.

that would be recognized by the Federal government. The qualifications of voters were to be those that were in force in the states before secession. With the exception of the officials of the Confederacy and officers of the Confederate Army above the rank of colonel, all others were granted full pardon and amnesty, provided that they took an oath of loyalty to the Union. The President emphasized that the restoration of the South could not be accomplished by the Executive alone, because, as he stated, "whether members sent to Congress from any State shall be admitted to seats, constitutionally rests exclusively with the respective Houses, and not to any extent with the Executive." [35] In addition, Lincoln wisely pointed out that he had no intention of insisting that his plan was the only one that would be acceptable to him. He, in fact, invited Congress to suggest other plans by stating that "while the mode presented is the best the Executive can suggest with his present impressions, it must not be understood that no other possible mode would be acceptable." [36] It has been suggested that by the end of 1863, "The Radicals had a design for the New South already worked out. . . . The Jacobins believed that Lincoln was not the man to handle the process of reconstruction. They feared that his kindly nature and conservative temperament would lead him to contrive a policy which would bring back the seceded states with the slavocracy unscathed and unpunished and the former slaves still mere hewers of wood for the ruling class." [37] Whatever the private thoughts of the radicals might have been, the fact is that in public statements their reaction to Lincoln's plan was overwhelmingly positive. Greeley wrote that the plan had given him general satisfaction. The New York Evening Post found nothing to criticize in the plan, and the Chicago Tribune, which often expressed its demand for a complete social revolution in the South, gave its general support to Lincoln's proclamation but

[35] Raymond, op. cit., p. 459.
[36] Ibid.
[37] Williams, op. cit., pp. 294-95.

expressed its satisfaction that the President was ready to consider other plans of reconstruction.[38] What was more important, Charles Sumner and Zachary Chandler, as Nicolay and Hay later remembered, were delighted with Lincoln's plan.[39] The only critical comments came from the Democrats.[40]

Historians have generally agreed that Lincoln's plan was mild and conservative. It has often been suggested that unlike the radicals, Lincoln did not particularly care about the Republican domination of the reconstructed state governments or about Negro suffrage. There is, however, evidence to support a contrary opinion. In a letter to Andrew Johnson, the military governor of Tennessee, dated September 11, 1863, Lincoln instructed him to form a government composed of trusted Union men and to exclude all others from it. He said, ". . . . the reinauguration must not be such as to give control of the state and its representation in Congress to the enemies of the Union, driving its friends there into political exile. . . . Let the reconstruction be the work of such men *only* as can be trusted for the Union. Exclude all others, and trust that your government so organized will be recognized here as being the one of the republican forms to be guaranteed to the State." [41] The letter would seem to indicate that Lincoln, with all of his magnanimity, had no intention of allowing ex-rebels to seize the reconstituted state governments and that he would not have favored the admission to Congress of former members of the Confederate Cabinet and of former Confederate generals.

As to Negro suffrage, very few senators, including Trumbull, advocated it in 1863. In the Senate only Sumner and Gratz

[38] *New York Tribune,* December 11, 1863; *New York Evening Post,* December 10, 1863; *Chicago Tribune,* December 11, 1863. The *New York Times* endorsed the plan on December 11, 1863.

[39] John G. Nicolay and John Hay, *op. cit.,* IX, 109.

[40] See an excellent résumé of the reaction of Republicans and Democrats to Lincoln's plan in William B. Hesseltine, *Lincoln's Plan of Reconstruction* (Tuscaloosa, Ala., 1960), pp. 95–98.

[41] Henry Steele Commager, *Documents of American History* (New York, 1949), II, 429. (Italics mine.)

Brown of Missouri spoke for Negro suffrage as part of any scheme of the reconstruction of the South.[42] But Abraham Lincoln did believe that Negroes who fought with the Union and who had some education should be given the right to vote. In a letter to General James W. Wadsworth, Lincoln wrote: "How to better the condition of the colored race has long been a study which attracted my serious and careful attention. I cannot see, if universal amnesty is granted, how, under the circumstances, I can avoid exacting in return, universal or at least partial suffrage on the basis of intelligence and military service." [43] In a letter to James C. Conkling, Lincoln asked, "Why should they (the Negroes) do anything for us, if we do nothing for them?" [44]

The best prospect for success of Lincoln's plan for reconstruction was in Louisiana, where General Nathaniel F. Banks set the election for state officers for February 22. In the election, about 5,000 voters chose Michael Hahn as governor. The new governor took office on March 4, 1864, and the new constitution adopted by the constitutional convention, including a clause abolishing slavery, was ratified by a vote of the people in which 6,836 votes were cast for ratification and 1,566 against it.[45] In spite of the small number of voters and in spite of the fact that the proposals for Negro suffrage that were sponsored by Louisiana radicals were rejected by the convention, Lincoln was generally satisfied with the way reconstruction proceeded in that state. He wrote General Banks that the state should elect senators and congressmen, but cautioned him that "if Louisiana shall send members to Congress, their admission to seats will depend, as you know, upon the respective Houses, and not upon the President." [46]

[42] See speech of Senator James R. Doolittle in the Senate of February 16, 1867, *Cong. Globe,* 39 Cong., 2nd Sess., p. 1444.
[43] Lincoln to General James W. Wadsworth (undated but written in January of 1864), published in *Chicago Tribune,* September 27, 1865.
[44] Lincoln to James C. Conkling, August 26, 1863, *The Living Lincoln,* p. 577.
[45] Raymond, *op. cit.,* p. 489.
[46] *Ibid.,* p. 490.

Louisiana did elect two senators who presented themselves for admission in Washington. Their credentials were referred to the Judiciary Committee. Trumbull, as chairman of the committee, went to the White House and pledged to the President his full cooperation. A few days later, he presented to the Senate a resolution on behalf of his committee, recognizing the government of Governor Hahn and admitting the Louisiana senators. The resolution met with a determined opposition from Sumner, who launched into a filibuster arguing that an ex-rebel state that refused to grant suffrage to Negroes was not deserving of readmission to the Union. He was supported by Senators Wade and Henderson. Several Democratic senators, including Senator Powell of Kentucky, joined the radicals in attacking Lincoln for allowing General Banks to determine who could and could not vote in Louisiana. Senator Henderson wondered whether Lincoln really supposed that he could govern the ex-rebel states through generals and provost marshals. Sumner declared that the Republicans needed the Negro votes as much as they once needed their bullets. Trumbull's position of advocating admission of Louisiana was supported by Senator Doolittle, who stated that the vote of that state was needed for the Thirteenth Amendment.[47] Since there were only seven working days left until the adjournment and much business still had to be transacted, Trumbull, in the face of Sumner's filibuster, had no choice but to withdraw the resolution, and the Louisiana senators were not admitted.

The failure of the reconstruction in Louisiana came after similar failures in Arkansas and Florida. In the meantime, the mood of Congress had changed from support for Lincoln's plan to outright opposition, and by the passage of the Wade-Davis bill Congress showed its determination to take the reconstruction of the South out of the exclusive jurisdiction of the Presi-

[47] *Cong. Globe,* 38 Cong., 2nd Sess., pp. 1001–11, 1120–29.

dent.[48] The reasons for the defeat of Lincoln's plan, or more accurately, plans, for reconstruction were many and complex. Professor William B. Hesseltine wrote that Lincoln's plan was "defeated in succession by the quarrels among Unionists he had hoped to unite, by the failure of the Confederates to respond to offers of amnesty [and] by Radical insistence on programs that contemplated social reform and economic penetration of the South and even by the revolt of his cabinet. . . ." [49]

Lincoln devoted his last public speech, delivered to a crowd celebrating the Union victory on April 11, almost exclusively to the question of reconstruction. He reiterated that he was not committed to his plan as the only inflexible scheme for reconstructing the South. "No exclusive and inflexible plan," he said, "can safely be prescribed as to details and collaterals." [50] He envisaged the possibility of devising different plans for different states and emphasized that Congress had the exclusive right to determine if and when Congressmen from the South would be admitted. He declared that he considered the question of whether or not the ex-rebel states were in or out of the Union irrelevant and impractical. While Lincoln admitted many imperfections in the reconstruction of Louisiana, he went on to suggest that these imperfections might be gradually eliminated after the admission of the state.

Trumbull was cautious and reserved on Lincoln's renomination in 1864. He resented the fact that Lincoln virtually ignored his two Confiscation bills and was convinced that the President had not prosecuted the war with the necessary efficiency and vigor. "There is a distrust and a fear," he wrote to a friend, "that he [Lincoln] is too undecided and inefficient to put down the rebellion. You need not be surprised if a reaction sets in before the nomination in favor of some man supposed to possess

[48] In speaking in support of his bill, Senator Wade stated that reconstruction must be a *joint* undertaking of the President and of the Congress, *Cong. Globe,* 38 Cong., 1st Sess. (July 2, 1864), p. 3450.

[49] Hesseltine, *Lincoln's Plan of Reconstruction,* p. 139.

[50] Commager, *op. cit.,* p. 450.

more energy." [51] Doubts as to the wisdom of renominating Lincoln were widespread and were not limited to the radical Republican leaders in Congress. Republican papers such as the *Missouri Democrat* and the *Chicago Telegraph* advocated the nomination of Frémont.[52] Henry Raymond, chairman of the National Republican Committee, reported to the President that Elihu B. Washburne, Simon Cameron, and Oliver P. Morton had stated that should Lincoln be renominated, he would lose Illinois, Pennsylvania, and Indiana.[53] Senator Samuel C. Pomeroy of Kansas circulated a letter urging nomination of Secretary Chase.[54]

On the other hand the support for Lincoln, especially in Illinois, was very strong. The *Chicago Tribune*, always in "Old Abe's" corner, gave him unflinching support. An editorial on November 1, 1863, stated: "Abraham Lincoln is making his way nearer and nearer to the peoples' hearts. He is this day the most popular man in the United States, not alone among the Radicals with whom we labor, but among the classes who are pleased to call themselves Conservatives—among soldiers and officers as well as among civilians, among men of the East as well as the West." [55] General John M. Palmer wrote to Trumbull that "Lincoln is popular with the army, and will, as far as the soldiers can vote, beat anything the Copperheads can start. No civilian or mere book-making general can get votes in the army against him.[56] Governor Yates was quite outspoken in warning Trumbull to drop his opposition to Lincoln's nomination. "As you are Senator from *Illinois*," he wrote, "the state of Mr. Lincoln, please be cautious as to your course till I see you. I have such a strong regard for you personally that I do not wish either ene-

[51] Trumbull to H. G. McPike, February 6, 1864, L. T. Papers.

[52] Clipped in the *Chicago Times*, March 28, May 3, 1864.

[53] Nicolay and Hay, *op. cit.*, IX, 218–19. See also Gershom Martin to Trumbull, September 3, 1864, L. T. Papers.

[54] J. G. Randall and David Donald, *The Civil War and Reconstruction* (Boston, 1961), p. 465.

[55] *Chicago Tribune*, November 1, 1863. See also strong editorials supporting Lincoln, December 17, 1863, June 9, 1864.

[56] John M. Palmer to Trumbull, January 24, 1864, L. T. Papers.

mies or friends on our side, who would like to supplant you, to get any undue advantage over you." [57] Yates wrote this letter of warning after the receipt of a letter from a Republican state leader who told him that Trumbull talked too much against Lincoln and was "ausgespielt" (politically bankrupt) and might well lose his election to the Senate.[58] Another warning reached Trumbull from his close political ally and friend Norman B. Judd, who wrote to him from Berlin: "When I last saw you your conviction was that L. would be reelected. I tell you combinations can't prevent it. Events possibly may. But until some event occurs, is it wise or prudent to give an impression of hostility for no earthly good?" [59]

Trumbull took his friends' advice and ceased opposing Lincoln's renomination. He scrupulously stayed away from any involvement with the Cleveland convention called by radical Republican insurgents. In October, he was campaigning for Lincoln's election, addressing scores of meetings in Illinois and in other states.[60] Trumbull's opposition to Lincoln did not signify personal animosity. He did not believe that Lincoln could win the election in the face of Union defeats, the uproar over arbitrary arrests and the charges of the inefficient conduct of the war. Lincoln himself believed that he would be defeated, and his belief was shared by Greeley, Chase, Sumner, Stevens, Wade, Judge Davis, Chandler, Browning, Washburne, Grimes, Cameron, and Weed. David Donald wrote that "opposition to Lincoln's renomination in 1864 [cannot] be correctly equated with Radicalism. It is true that many Radical anti-slavery men were discouraged and hopeless about Lincoln's prospects, but so was Conservative Thurlow Weed, who declared in August: "Mr. Lincoln's reelection is an impossibility.'" [61]

[57] Governor Richard Yates to Trumbull, February 26, 1864, L. T. Papers.
[58] George N. Rutherford to Richard Yates, February 26, 1864, Richard Yates Papers, Illinois State Historical Society, Springfield, Ill.
[59] Norman B. Judd to Trumbull, January (no day), 1864, L. T. Papers.
[60] Koerner, Memoirs, II, 434–35.
[61] Donald, op. cit., p. 114.

12

The Conservative Radical
and Reconstruction

TRUMBULL WAS DEEPLY SHOCKED AND CHAGRINED BY LINCOLN'S assassination. While their relations during Lincoln's Presidency were proper but cool, their mutual respect was deep and abiding. Trumbull's sense of devotion to the principles of law and order were outraged by the brutal assassination, and he must have recoiled when told that Ben Wade exclaimed during a visit to the White House, "Johnson, we have faith in you. By the gods, there will be no trouble now in running the government."[1] But he, like the Republicans in Congress and the Republican press throughout the North, had a great deal of sympathy for Andrew Johnson who, in his address upon his inauguration as President, said with appropriate humility, "I feel incompetent to perform duties so important and responsible as those which have been so unexpectedly thrown upon me."[2] Trumbull wrote a letter to Johnson in which he assured him of his "cordial and hearty support." He assured the President of his

[1] George W. Julian, *Political Recollections, 1840–1872* (Chicago, 1884), p. 257. See also *Life of Zachariah Chandler,* by the *Detroit Post and Tribune* (Detroit, 1880), pp. 280–82.

[2] Inaugural Address of Andrew Johnson, text in *A Compilation of the Messages and Papers of the Presidents* (Washington, D.C., 1897), VIII, 3503.

readiness to assist him in his efforts to bring the former rebel states back into the Union." [3]

On May 29, 1865, President Johnson issued his Proclamation of Restoration and added a special message appointing William W. Holden as provisional governor of North Carolina. The proclamation provided for the speedy organization of the government of that state. Johnson's plan of restoration for the South granted pardon and amnesty to all persons who participated in the rebellion, directly or indirectly, with the exception of high civil, diplomatic, and military officers of the Confederacy. Expressing his life-long antagonism against the rich, Johnson arbitrarily denied the right to automatic amnesty to all those whose taxable property exceeded $20,000. The plan also declared the President's readiness to pardon those in the exempted classes and Johnson promised that "such clemency will be liberally extended." [4]

While Johnson's plan for the restoration of the South generally followed Lincoln's ten percent proclamation, there were two significant differences. Johnson, unlike Lincoln, failed to stress that the plan was neither final nor exclusive of other plans that might be suggested by Congress, and he failed to emphasize, as did his predecessor, that the admission of Southern senators and representatives to Congress was to remain the exclusive prerogative of both houses of Congress. Johnson rather naively assumed that, in the long run, he, a Democrat and a Southerner, who was thrust into the Presidency by the assassination of his predecessor, would be allowed by Congress to push through the complete restoration of ex-rebel states into the Union without consultation with Congressional leaders. It became obvious that Johnson was rushing his plans toward realization before the reconvening of Congress.

However, the initial reaction in Congress and in the Repub-

[3] Lyman Trumbull to Andrew Johnson, April 20, 1865. Copy of the letter in L. T. Family Papers.
[4] *A Compilation of the Messages and Papers of the Presidents*, VIII, 3510.

lican press in the North was tentatively favorable. Almost everybody seemed to be willing to give the President's plan a chance. Some had doubts whether the President's plan, which he pushed with vigor in the South would really work, but even they were willing to wait and see.[5] There was a feeling of disappointment that Johnson's plan made no provision for even a partial Negro suffrage, but the dissatisfaction on this point was subdued. Greeley's New York Tribune stated that while it did not fully agree with Johnson's view that the question of franchise belonged to the jurisdiction of the states, it respected his position on the matter.[6] Johnson's supporters included Senators Trumbull, Fessenden, Grimes, Sherman, and Doolittle; Congressmen John Bingham, Rutherford B. Hayes of Ohio, and James G. Blaine of Maine; Governor Oliver P. Morton of Indiana among the Republicans; and among the Democrats, the Blair family and such outspoken Democratic papers as the Chicago Times and the Detroit Free Press.

What happened between June and November of 1865 to cause this feeling of sympathy for the new President to change into open hostility? First there was the speed with which Johnson pushed his plan of restoration, consulting much more often with delegations from the Southern states than with the leaders of his own party in Congress. Then there was Johnson's indiscriminate and wholesale granting of pardons to high officials and leaders of the Confederacy, which made a mockery of his own proclamation of May 29, in which he had promised to exclude the ex-rebel leaders from control of the new state governments. Even more damaging to the smooth functioning of the machinery of reconstruction was the fact that the leaders of the South-

[5] See an excellent discussion of the reaction of the Republicans and of the North to Johnson's proclamation in Eric L. McKitrick, Andrew Johnson and Reconstruction (Chicago, 1960), pp. 76–79. See also Robert Selph Henry, The Story of Reconstruction (New York, 1951), pp. 46–57.

[6] New York Tribune, June 2, 1865. The New York Times of June 21, 1865, wrote, "It is an open question whether the Government should or should not attempt to secure suffrage to the Southern blacks."

ern states, encouraged by Johnson's sympathetic attitude, failed to act with prudence and restraint. Gustave Koerner, who was also, at first, sympathetic to Johnson, wrote in his Memoirs that "the President had carried out this plan without a shadow of justification by law. Yet it is possible that the people and the Congress . . . might have overlooked these irregularities and sanctioned the experiment, if the South had behaved with the least discretion and prudence." [7]

The new state governments were dominated by the old crowd of planters, generals, and secessionist fire-eaters. The "Black Codes," which the Southern legislatures had passed, ostensibly to provide a measure of social control over the four million freedmen, were generally looked upon in the North as a brazen attempt by the beaten South to return the Negroes to peonage. It was indeed galling to Northern Republicans that the newly elected senator from Georgia was a former vice-president of the Confederacy, the new governor of South Carolina a former Senator in the Confederate Senate. Republicans in Congress were enraged when they heard that Alabama elected a Confederate major general to Congress and Mississippi rejected the Thirteenth Amendment.

Trumbull's correspondence provides clues to the reasons for the gradual change from support for Johnson's reconstruction scheme to serious doubts about its workability. He received a large number of letters from Louisiana, where several former Republican leaders from Illinois held Federal appointments. Other communications came from R. King Cutler, a white Unionist from Louisiana and close friend of Trumbull, who was elected United States Senator. In the summer of 1865 Cutler wrote to Trumbull that Governor Wells had betrayed the loyal Unionists in the state and had placed all power in the hands "of those Scoundrels who carried the State so swiftly into the late rebellion." [8] He pleaded with Trumbull to prevent the Sen-

[7] Koerner, Memoirs, II, 458.
[8] R. King Cutler to Trumbull, August 29, 1865, L. T. Papers.

ate from admitting Louisiana to the Union. After a state election in November, Senator Cutler reported to Trumbull that "the Election here resulted in favor of the Rebels. . . . Unless Congress does something for these loyal people, they will leave the State. . . . Rebels reign Supreme here." [9] Several other correspondents from Louisiana informed Trumbull that ex-Confederate officials were holding important posts and that "nothing has been gained by the struggle through which we have passed." [10]

George T. Brown, formerly of Alton, for whom Trumbull obtained the job of Senate's sergeant-at-arms, informed him that several senators had visited Johnson to discuss the disturbing news from the South. While the President, according to Brown, was able to reassure the senators, "his Southern policy is far from giving satisfaction and many look upon the present movement in the South with absolute dread." [11] A few days later, Brown had even more alarming news for Trumbull. He told him that there was "an evident inclination North and Northwest to break with Johnson." [12] Former Vice-President Hannibal Hamlin reported from Boston that the people of New England looked on the developments in the South with deep anxiety.[13]

Trumbull, while concerned by the reports from the South and by the growing unrest among the Republicans in the North, continued his support of Johnson and his policies. In a letter to his brother-in-law, he complained that some Republican leaders condemned the policies pursued by Johnson while they approved the same policies when advocated by Lincoln. "The President," he wrote, "wishes no issue with Congress and if our friends would be reasonable we would all get along harmoniously." [14] The harmonious cooperation between the President

[9] R. King Cutler to Trumbull, December 6, 1865, L. T. Papers.

[10] Charles H. Fox to Trumbull, September 26, 1865; J. C. Holbrook to Trumbull, December 5, 1865, L. T. Papers.

[11] George T. Brown to Trumbull, September 8, 1865, L. T. Papers.

[12] George T. Brown to Trumbull, September 25, 1865, L. T. Papers.

[13] Hannibal Hamlin to Trumbull, December 7, 1865, L. T. Papers.

[14] Trumbull to Dr. William Jayne, December 24, 1865, Jayne Papers.

and Congress for which Trumbull hoped, and which he assumed was also desired by Johnson, would come about, he wrote, if the reconstructed state governments in the South would "treat the negroes fairly" and "secure the rights of persons and property to the freedmen." The Southern states, Trumbull predicted, would be admitted to Congress if the South secured to the Negro "all his civil rights and this is all that will be required of them." [15] Trumbull obviously was no "Jacobin." The moderate Republicans in Congress were, at the opening of the Thirty-ninth Congress, ready to support Johnson's policies of reconstruction provided that the South and the President would, in good faith, guarantee and secure the civil rights of Negroes and of Unionists in the ex-Confederate states. They did not have a harsh Congressional plan of reconstruction but were gradually pushed into embracing one. Their cooperation with the radical minority resulted from the intransigence of the South and from Johnson's support of white supremacy and his unwillingness to compromise with Congress.

The Thirty-ninth Congress was not dominated by the radical wing of the Republican party as it is often suggested. The leadership of the party in Congress belonged to the moderate Republicans, led by Lyman Trumbull and William Pitt Fessenden of Maine. On crucial votes, when they had determined to oppose extreme measures passed by the more radical House or submitted by the radicals in the Senate, Trumbull and Fessenden were usually able to muster a majority by getting the support of the three Johnson Republicans, Senators Doolittle of Wisconsin, Dixon of Connecticut, and Cowan of Pennsylvania, and of most of the Democrats. It was this moderate Republican-Democratic coalition that ruled the Thirty-ninth Congress. The refusal of the Southern states to make concessions on the question of Negro rights and security, and Johnson's stubborn adherence to the strictest construction of the Constitution and his

[15] *Cong. Globe,* 39 Cong., 1st Sess. (December 12, 1865), p. 24.

inability to engage in a give and take bargaining with the moderate Republican leadership pushed Congress inexorably into adopting ever harsher reconstruction measures.

The first clash between the moderates and the radicals came on the resolution that was submitted by the House to create a Joint Committee of Fifteen to inquire into the condition of the ex-Confederate states and report whether or not they should be admitted to Congress. The House resolution contained the provision that "until such a report shall have been made, and finally acted by Congress, no member shall be received into either House from any of the so-called confederate states." [16] Trumbull and Fessenden stated that the House resolution went too far and that the last section should be stricken. Trumbull told the Senate that he did not see any necessity for a joint committee of inquiry and would have preferred that the matter be referred to his Judiciary Committee. He declared, however, that if the last section was stricken, he would vote for the bill because he was convinced that harmony and cooperation must exist between the Senate, the House, and the President. "All the friends of the Union, all men who desire to see harmony and good feeling restored between all parts of the Union," Trumbull said, "must desire harmonious action between the different branches of Congress and all the departments of the Government." [17] The Senate, under Trumbull's and Fessenden's pressure, and in spite of the vigorous opposition of the radicals, adopted the House resolution without the last clause forbidding either House to admit Southern Congressmen until the report was submitted. [18] Even after the passage of the bill, Trumbull was still unhappy over the establishment of the committee, and wrote to Dr. Jayne: "I do not expect much from the Committee of the two Houses—it had better never been

[16] *Ibid.*, p. 24.
[17] *Ibid.*, p. 29.
[18] *Ibid.*, p. 30. The resolution went to the conference and since the House members were adamant in insisting on the retention of the last section, the Senate reluctantly agreed to accept the House version.

created in my opinion, though I voted for it after the House had asked for a Joint Committee." [19] The committee had a majority of moderates, including Senators Fessenden, Grimes, Harris, and Reverdy Johnson and Congressmen Washburne, Bingham, Boutwell, and Henry Grider.[20] William Pitt Fessenden was the chairman of the committee, and he, not Thaddeus Stevens, who was a member, usually dominated its proceedings.[21] Charles Sumner was refused a seat on the joint committee because of his "ultra views." [22]

Paradoxically, on one crucial issue before the committee, Fessenden voted as a radical and Stevens as a conservative. On January 20, 1866, the joint committee had before it two propositions for a constitutional amendment. The one introduced by Fessenden read: "Representatives and direct taxes shall be apportioned among the several States within this Union, according to the respective numbers of citizens of the United States in each State; and all provisions in the Constitution or laws of any State, whereby any distinction is made in political or civil rights or privileges, on account of race, creed or color, shall be inoperative and void." Stevens' motion did not contain a direct prohibition of voting discrimination but provided for the proportionate reduction in the states' representation in Congress. By a vote of 11 to 3, the joint committee adopted Stevens' proposal.[23]

[19] Trumbull to Dr. William Jayne, January 11, 1866, Jayne Papers.

[20] Claude G. Bowers called the Joint Committee "The Committee of Public Safety." *The Tragic Era* (Cambridge, Mass., 1929), p. 91. For later views see J. G. Randall and David Donald, *op. cit.* p. 576; and McKitrick, *op. cit.,* pp. 275–77.

[21] A reading of the proceedings of the sessions of the Joint Committee on Reconstruction reveals that on most crucial votes the committee was split, and the votes usually stood 8 to 7 or 6 to 8. Stevens' amendment to the Constitution, which he submitted on April 21, 1866, and which forbade discrimination by any state by reason of race, color, or previous condition of servitude, was rejected by a vote of 7 to 5. Benjamin B. Kendrick, *Journal of the Joint Committee of Fifteen on Reconstruction* (New York, 1914), pp. 55, 59, 61, 83.

[22] Letter of William Pitt Fessenden to Elizabeth Warriner, December 24, 1865, quoted in Kendrick, *op. cit.,* p. 175.

[23] Kendrick, *op. cit.,* pp. 50–51.

Lyman Trumbull watched the growing estrangement between President Johnson and the Republicans in Congress with puzzlement and disapproval. He had expected Johnson to work well with Congress on reconstruction in the South and was still ready to give him his full support. But the President's actions had him puzzled. "What Johnson means," he wrote to his wife, "nobody can tell . . . The President is daily separating farther and farther from Congress and getting closer and closer to the democrats. I very much fear we will be unable to agree by a two-thirds vote to any plan of reconstruction, and if such should be the result, there would be great danger of the government falling into the hands of the Democrats and unconstructed rebels." [24] In May, 1866, Trumbull was far from embracing Sumner's or Steven's views on reconstruction.

Trumbull's position of support for Johnson brought a negative reaction from the anti-slavery elements in Illinois. A German leader wrote asking that Trumbull affirm or deny rumors "circulated throughout the German Press that L. Trumbull once of the Staars [sic] of Liberty has left our Banner and become a Conservative, not to say a Johnsonite or as many say a 'Copperhead.' " [25] Jesse W. Fell, an influential Republican leader, reminded Trumbull that the North had a moral obligation "to adopt measures for the safety and elevation of the African race. Their present nominal freedom is nothing but a mockery." [26] The most disturbing was the news that reached Trumbull from the South. His correspondents reported that ex-rebels were assuming full control of the reconstituted governments and were persecuting and oppressing blacks and Union men. "They are," wrote one correspondent from New Orleans, "drunk with power, ruling and abusing every loyal man white and black." [27] A Union army officer wrote from Mississippi:

[24] Lyman Trumbull to Julia Jayne Trumbull, May 8, May 15, 1866, L. T. Family Papers.
[25] D. H. Schroder to Trumbull, December 23, 1865, L. T. Papers.
[26] Jesse W. Fell to Trumbull, December 26, 1865, L. T. Papers.
[27] R. King Cutler to Trumbull, August 29, 1865, L. T. Papers.

"To the great mass of the Southern people the Government of the U. S. means only the hated embodiment of *Yankeeism*." He also informed Trumbull that the "Black Codes" were intended "under the guise of vagrant laws to restore all of slavery but its name." [28]

Trumbull decided that something had to be done to secure the rights of freedmen in the South, and on December 19 gave notice to the Senate that he intended to introduce "An act to establish a Bureau for the Relief of Freedmen and Refugees." Trumbull told the Senate that the bill would constitute an enforcement clause of the Thirteenth Amendment, since it aimed to make sure that Negroes were free in fact and that their freedom was protected by law.[29] Senator Wilson of Massachusetts, supported by Sumner, thought that Trumbull's bill did not go far enough and proposed a sweeping measure that declared "inequality of civil rights and immunities among the inhabitants of said [ex-rebel] states . . . null and void." The radicals demanded that Wilson's bill be acted upon on the floor of the Senate without reference to a committee. The move met strong opposition from Trumbull, Fessenden, and other moderates who argued that a bill of such importance should not be railroaded without careful deliberation. The radicals were beaten by the votes of moderate Republicans and of Democrats, and Wilson's bill was referred to the Judiciary Committee.[30]

The Freedmen's Bureau Bill was introduced by Trumbull on January 5. It extended the existence of the Freedmen's Bureau indefinitely and provided that the bureau would care for and protect the civil rights of the freedmen. The bureau was also directed to work out a new relationship between the employers and the freed Negroes. The bill voided the "Black Codes" and gave the bureau powers to provide military and judicial protection to freedmen in cases when their civil rights were violated.

[28] C. E. Lippincott to Trumbull, August 29, 1865, L. T. Papers.
[29] *Cong. Globe*, 39 Cong., 1st Sess. (December 19, 1865), p. 77.
[30] *Ibid.*, (December 13, 1865), p. 39.

Trumbull considered his bill a basically humanitarian measure. He had no intention of extending to the Negroes any other rights beyond their protection as persons and as free men. When Senator John B. Henderson of Missouri prophetically stated that only the right of franchise would guarantee the Negro rights in the South,[31] Trumbull sarcastically remarked: . . . "the zeal of my friend from Missouri seems to have run away with him. . . . It [suffrage for Negroes] is the most sovereign remedy that I have heard since the days of Townsend's Sasparilla. (Laughter.)"[32]

Trumbull and other Republican moderates in Congress were convinced that Johnson would sign the Freedmen's Bureau Bill. Answering an attack on the bill by the Democratic senator Thomas Hendricks of Indiana, Trumbull stressed that he had said "nothing in these bills about the political rights of the Negro." The bill was "designed to aid these helpless, ignorant, and unprotected people until they can provide for and take care of themselves.[33] Senator Fessenden attempted to reassure President Johnson of the desire of the Republicans in Congress to work with him in harmony. He castigated the insinuations of the Democrats that a break was about to occur between the Republicans and the President and declared: "Sir, there is no collision. . . . Why? Because the President has done nothing that his friends complain of, and his friends in Congress have done nothing that he can complain of."[34] Even Ben Wade said, "There is no great difference in principle between what he [Johnson] has done and what I want him to do. He is right as far as he has gone."[35] Similar sentiments were expressed in the House by Representative John Bingham of Ohio.[36]

[31] Henderson concluded his speech with the words: "Give them the ballot, Mr. President, and then they are protected." Cong. Globe, 39 Cong., 1st Sess. (February 8, 1865); p. 745.
[32] Ibid., p. 746.
[33] Ibid. (January 19, 1866), p. 319.
[34] Ibid., p. 366.
[35] Ibid. (January 18, 1866), p. 296.
[36] Ibid. Cong. Globe, 39 Cong., 1st Sess. (January 9, 1866), p. 158.

In spite of these reassurances and expectations, Johnson vetoed the Freedmen's Bureau Bill because, in his opinion, it violated the Constitution by giving judicial powers to military officers. He also considered it too expensive and felt that it legislated on matters of concern to the South while the Southern states had no representation in Congress. The moderates in Congress were bitterly disappointed by Johnson's veto. They had hoped that the bill, practical and humanitarian in nature, would alleviate the conditions in the South and make any sweeping reconstruction measures pressed by the radicals unnecessary. Their ground was cut from under them by the President. Trumbull expressed his views on the veto in a speech delivered in the Senate on February 20, 1866. It was an effective and eloquent performance. Trumbull expressed his surprise and regret at the veto, which was especially shocking to him because he had assumed that "in advocating it [the Freedmen's Bureau Bill] . . . I was acting in harmony with the views of the President." He stated: "The President believes it unconstitutional; I believe it constitutional. He believes that it will involve great expense; I believe it will save expenses. He believes that the freedman will be protected without it. I believe he will by tyrannized over, abused and virtually re-enslaved without some legislation by the nation for his protection." [37] Addressing himself to the basic issue of reconstruction and echoing Lincoln's views, Trumbull stated that the debate on the legal position of the ex-Confederate states was largely irrelevant. He had no objection to Johnson's plan to restore the government to the ex-rebel states, but argued that Congress had the right and the duty to decide whether the state governments thus constituted were legitimate.[38] He still did not wish to see a break with the President. "I regret exceedingly," he said, "the antagonism which his message presents to the expressed views of Congress." [39] Trumbull con-

[37] *Ibid.* (February 20, 1866), p. 936.
[38] *Ibid.*, p. 942.
[39] *Ibid.*, p. 943.

cluded his address by an appeal to the Senate to override the President's veto. The vote fell short of the two-thirds majority, but on a later date the veto was overridden by both the Senate and the House.

Simultaneously with the Freedmen's Bureau Bill, Trumbull introduced the Civil Rights Bill, which conferred citizenship upon "all persons born in the United States." The bill also confirmed the right of all citizens of every race and color to own and sell personal property and to the equal protection of laws. The jurisdiction for the protection of the civil and personal rights of freedmen was vested in the Federal courts. Trumbull met several times with the President to discuss with him the provisions of the measure and to assure his support for the bill. An abstract of the Civil Rights Bill, in Trumbull's handwriting, has been found among the Johnson Papers.[40] Since the President voiced no objections, Trumbull assumed that he would not veto the bill. In his speech in support of the bill, Trumbull asserted that Congress was competent to declare the Negroes citizens, because they could not be free under the Thirteenth Amendment without the rights of citizenship.[41] He stressed that the bill "does not propose to regulate the political rights of individuals; it has nothing to do with the right of suffrage or any other political right; but it is simply intended to carry out a constitutional provision guaranty to every person of every color the same civil rights." [42] The Senate passed the bill by a vote of 33 to 12 and the House by a vote of 111 to 38.

It was generally assumed in the North that Johnson would sign the Civil Rights Bill. This expectation was not shaken even by the intemperate speech of Johnson to the crowd of serenaders who gathered on the lawn of the White House on Washing-

[40] See John H. and LaWanda Cox, "Andrew Johnson and His Ghost Writer: An Analysis of the Freedmen's Bureau and Civil Rights Veto Messages," *The Mississippi Valley Historical Review*, Vol. XLVIII, No. 3 (December, 1961), pp. 462–63.

[41] *Cong. Globe*, 39 Cong., 1st Sess. (January 29, 1866), p. 475.
[42] *Ibid.*, p. 599.

ton's birthday. Unmindful of the dignity of his office and of the danger of inciting a mob against a branch of government, the President denounced Congress for its refusal to admit the Southern states and pinned the label of traitor on Stevens, Sumner, and Wendell Phillips.[43] Answering this assault, the moderate Senator John Sherman of Ohio took the floor of the Senate to assure Johnson, once again, that the Republicans in Congress wanted to work with him on the issue of reconstruction in a spirit of harmony. "No word from me," he said, "shall drive him [Johnson] into political fellowship with those who, when he was one of the moral heroes of this war, denounced him, spit on him, and despitefully used him." [44] In a speech at Bridgeport, Connecticut, on March 17, Sherman expressed his conviction that "Andrew Johnson never will throw away the power we have given him." [45] The New York Herald, which supported Johnson, endorsed the Civil Rights Bill and expressed its conviction that the "President will cheerfully approve [it]." [46] The Chicago Tribune wrote that Johnson's stand on the Civil Rights Bill would decide the issue of Johnson's "unmistakable identification with one or the other of the existing parties . . . dodging of issues will no longer be practicable." [47]

Johnson, however, vetoed the Civil Rights Bill. He based the veto on his belief that Negroes were not ready for citizenship and that the bill discriminated against whites in favor of blacks for whom it accorded the special protection of Federal laws and Federal courts. The consequences of the veto were disastrous and far-reaching. Trumbull, Fessenden, Sherman, Grimes, and other moderates who up to now had been able to stem the pressure for universal Negro suffrage and for unilateral Congressional reconstruction were pushed into the arms of the radicals.

[43] Randall and Donald, op. cit., p. 578.
[44] John Sherman's Recollections of Forty Years, An Autobiography (New York, 1895), p. 368.
[45] Ibid., p. 369.
[46] New York Herald, March 17, 1866.
[47] Chicago Tribune, January 27, 1866.

William A. Dunning, in a comment on Johnson's election campaign in the fall of 1866, wrote: "The alienation by the president of this essentially thoughtful and conservative element of the northern voters was as inexcusable as the alienation of those moderate men in Congress whom he had repelled by his narrow and obstinate policy in respect to the Freedmen's Bureau and Civil Rights Bills." [48]

The reaction of the people in Illinois to Johnson's vetoes was considerably more extreme than that of Trumbull. There were protest rallies throughout Illinois at which Trumbull was hailed and Johnson denounced. The mass meeting in Chicago was addressed by Lieutenant Governor "Deacon" Bross and the rally in Springfield by Governor Richard J. Oglesby. [49] The *Chicago Tribune* wrote that the President's veto provided "conclusive proof to doubting souls of Johnson's recreancy to the great cause for which our people laid down their lives and property." [50] Horace White wrote to Trumbull expressing his appreciation for his speech on Johnson's veto of the Freedmen's Bureau Bill. He told him that he had managed "to strike a blow which [would] both uplift the country and redound to your fame." [51] Gustave Koerner informed Trumbull that he opposed the admission of the representatives of the South to Congress unless the ex-rebel states give "some guarantees for the future." [52] Norman B. Judd assured his friend in Washington that the people of the North were determined that something be done to assure the status and safety of the freedmen in the South." [53] In addition to these letters from leading Republicans, the Trumbull Papers contain scores of letters from humble folk in Illinois denouncing Johnson. [54]

[48] William A. Dunning, *Reconstruction, Political and Economic, 1865–1877* (New York, 1907), p. 82.
[49] *Chicago Tribune*, February 26, 27, 1866.
[50] *Chicago Tribune*, February 1, 1866.
[51] Horace White to Trumbull, February 21, 1866, L. T. Papers.
[52] Gustave Koerner to Trumbull, February 9, 1866, L. T. Papers.
[53] Norman B. Judd to Trumbull, January 11, 1866, L. T. Papers.
[54] Jason Marsh to Trumbull, January 7, 1866, and Henry Asbury to Trumbull,

On April 4, 1866, Trumbull took the floor of the Senate to attack the President's veto. This time his tone was sharp and his expectations for peace between the President and Congress dim, *but he was still hopeful.* He told the senators that the bill had been framed in consultation with Johnson, with whom he had had "frequent interviews," and to whom he had submitted the full text of the measure for his opinion. While Trumbull refused to divulge to the Senate the content of his personal conversations with the President, he assured his colleagues and the country that "the controversy which exists between him and the Congress in reference to this measure is of his [Johnson's] own making." [55] When it became known that Johnson would veto the Freedmen's Bureau Bill, new efforts were made, Trumbull related, to ascertain the President's position on the Civil Rights Bill. "He never indicated," said Trumbull, "to me nor, as far as I know, to any of his friends, the least objection to any of the provisions of the bill. . . ." [56] Trumbull still expressed a hope that the breach between the President and Congress could be healed. Trumbull's speech was widely praised in Illinois and by the press in the North. *The Nation* thought that the speech had "exceptional cogency and power," [57] and the *Springfield* (Mass.) *Republican* wrote that Trumbull discussed the issues with courage and coolness and was able to promote both "the welfare of the country and the interests of Republican politics." [58]

Trumbull's hopes for reconciliation between Johnson and Congress were rapidly fading. "I have no faith in his good intentions," he wrote in May to Julia. "How could I have after he

---

February 11, 1866, L. T. Papers. Horace White assured Trumbull that "Illinois is united almost without an exception among Republicans in antagonism to the President's policy." March 7, 1866. E. M. Beardsley wrote, "You have the approval and admiration of all Republicans." March 8, 1866, L. T. Papers.

[55] *Cong. Globe,* 39 Cong. 1st Sess., p. 1756.

[56] *Ibid.*

[57] *The Nation,* April 12, 1866.

[58] *Springfield Republican,* April 14, 1866.

so deceived me about the Civil Rights Bill and the Freedmen's Bureau Bill." [59] Two months later Trumbull was ready for an out-and-out confrontation with the President. He told his brother-in-law: "We have got to fight Johnson because he will fight us." [60] The rejection by the South of the Fourteenth Amendment and the Memphis anti-Negro riots were a contributing factor, but more decisive was President Johnson's policy of dismissing Federal officials who supported Congress on reconstruction. As early as December, 1865, Trumbull began to receive warnings from Federal appointees in Illinois that Johnson intended to dismiss all who were opposed to his policy.[61] Since most of these officials had gotten their jobs through Trumbull's influence and had constituted his political machine in the unruly Illinois politics, Trumbull could not ignore this threat. He was due for re-election in 1867, and the removal of Federal officials who were also leaders of Republican county organizations would have greatly imperiled his chances for victory. Trumbull felt personally threatened by the impending removal of many of his friends and supporters who held Federal jobs as postmasters, U.S. marshals, pension agents, and revenue collectors.[62]

Johnson's purge of Federal officials in Illinois started late in April, and Trumbull's mail was filled with letters of protest and pleas for help from his friends who lost well-paying jobs.[63] The prediction of Jonas Hoard, postmaster of Chicago, who told Trumbull that he had heard that Johnson had decided "to make a clean sweep of all federal officials in this city" proved to be

[59] Lyman Trumbull to Julia Jayne Trmbull, May 29, 1866, L. T. Family Papers.

[60] Lyman Trumbull to Dr. William Jayne, July 2, 1866, Jayne Papers.

[61] C. D. Hay to Trumbull, December 5, 1855, L. T. Papers.

[62] The Trumbull Collection in the Illinois State Historical Society contains over 160 letters pertaining to patronage problems in the years 1865–67.

[63] A. P. Bartlett to Trumbull, April 20, 1866; John Olney to Trumbull, April 19, 1866; H. S. Thomas to Trumbull, May 19, 1866; Peter Smith to Trumbull, June 7, 1866; Walt Talcott to Trumbull, June 2, 1866; James Y. Cory to Trumbull, June 6, 1866, L. T. Papers.

correct. Within a few weeks, Trumbull was faced with a destruction of his political organization in Illinois, which he had laboriously built in the course of ten years and which he had conscientiously cultivated from Washington.

Trumbull reluctantly decided to fight Johnson and thus join, at least for the time being, the company of the radicals. Dr. Charles Ray testified as late as April, 1866, that "Trumbull has no desire to quarrel with the President. I know that his instincts and aspirations are for a Democratic policy and that he has been very unwillingly forced into antagonism to Mr. Johnson. . . ." [64] In order to stop Johnson from the wholesale firing of Federal officials, Trumbull introduced an amendment to an appropriation bill that would have held up the payment of salaries of all officials whose appointments required Senate confirmation and who were appointed by Johnson during the recess of Congress. Speaking for his motion, Trumbull cited a case of an official in Illinois who was fired because he had attended a meeting that passed a resolution supporting Congress in its controversy with Johnson.[65] Trumbull's amendment, which many considered unconstitutional, was voted down 23 to 16. Even Fessenden and Sherman voted against it.[66]

Trumbull was disappointed with the rejection of the amendment and blamed a few "misguided" Republican senators for the defeat. The Senate's action he thought, would encourage Johnson in his policy of wholesale removals.[67] A few weeks later, Trumbull was told that two high Federal officials in Illinois, whose appointments he had recommended, had been removed. He concluded that "this action on the part of the President shows we are to have no peace with him.[68]

Pushed into an alliance with the radicals, Trumbull made no secret of the fact that he supported their demand for universal

[64] Quoted in Howard K. Beale, *The Critical Year* (New York, 1930), p. 111.
[65] *Cong. Globe,* 39 Cong., 1st Sess., p. 2420.
[66] *Ibid.,* p. 2559.
[67] Lyman Trumbull to Julia Jayne Trumbull, May 8, 1866, L. T. Family Papers.
[68] Lyman Trumbull to Julia Jayne Trumbull, June 25, 1866, L. T. Family Papers.

Negro suffrage with great reluctance. He believed, as did Lincoln, that the right of suffrage should be extended gradually, beginning with Negroes who had served in the Union forces and those who had some education. Basically he had moved very little from the position he took in 1858 when he had told the Senate: "In the great controversy which we have had upon the slavery question I have never contended for giving the Negro equal privileges with the white man. That is a doctrine I do not advocate." [69]

Trumbull voted for the Fourteenth Amendment but did not speak in its support. He joined Fessenden and other moderates in defeating Sumner's resolution, which would have put the amendment, as Sumner said, "in a positive language, forbidding discrimination in voting on account of color or race." [70] Sumner's resolution was beaten by the combined votes of moderate Republicans and the Democrats. Trumbull did not participate in the long debate on giving Negroes the right of franchise in the District of Columbia. He voted for the bill when the final vote came, but he did not speak in the debate on the measure.

President Johnson's extremism on the racial question made, once again, the position of the moderate elements in Congress very difficult. Johnson sided with those in Congress who advocated the principle of white supremacy. In his third annual message to Congress he said that the white man had proven his capacity for government, but "if anything can be proved by known facts, if all reasoning upon evidence is not abandoned, it must be acknowledged that in the progress of nations, Negroes have shown less capacity for government than any other race of people. No independent government of any form has ever been successful in their hands. On the contrary, wherever they have been left to their own devices they have shown a constant tendency to relapse into barbarism." [71]

[69] *Cong. Globe*, 35 Cong., 1st Sess. (May 5, 1858), p. 1858.
[70] *Cong. Globe*, 39 Cong., 1st Sess. (February 7, 1866), p. 702.
[71] *A Compilation of the Messages and Papers of the Presidents*, VIII, 3763.

Trumbull's interest in reconstruction extended only to his determination to keep the former Confederate leaders from controlling the new state governments. He also wished to assure the civil and personal rights and safety of the white Unionists and Negroes in the South. With these two conditions fulfilled, he would have been ready to vote for the admission of the ex-Confederate states into Congress.

In a letter to a former pupil of his from Georgia, Trumbull wrote, ". . . the Union men demand that the slave population be protected in their rights of person and property and that the men who encouraged the rebellion, its leaders, shall be excluded from political power. Is this too much to ask?" [72] In a speech in the Senate, in which he spelled out his views on reconstruction, Trumbull made no reference to Negro suffrage and stated that while, in his view, Congress had the obligation, under the Constitution, to control the readmission of the South, he was ready to support Johnson's plan, provided that the President would have been successful in getting loyal Unionists to run the new governments. "But, sir," he stated, "the people of this country are not willing that the rebellious states shall continue to be ruled over by rebels and Union men be persecuted for their loyalty." [73] His reports from the South, Trumbull declared, indicated that there was no loyalty to the Union and that the loyal people were oppressed.

The New Orleans massacre of Negroes, the rejection of the Fourteenth Amendment by the Southern states, the support given by Johnson to the abortive attempt to organize a National Union Party, and his bitter and undignified attacks on Congress during his "swing around the circle" tour, spurred Trumbull into

---

In his veto of the bill which gave Negroes suffrage in the District of Columbia, Johnson argued that Negroes, just freed from slavery, "cannot be expected to comprehend the duties and responsibilities which pertain to suffrage." *Cong. Globe,* 39 Cong., 2nd Sess. (January 7, 1867), p. 304.

[72] Trumbull to Mrs. F. C. Gary (from Morgan, Georgia), May 17, 1866, L. T. Papers.

[73] *Cong. Globe,* 39 Cong., 2nd Sess. (December 17, 1866), p. 160.

strenuous campaigning for the Republican ticket in the crucial Congressional election of November of 1866. Trumbull's standing with Illinois Republicans was never higher. In July, 1866, he spoke to a huge rally in Chicago's Opera House that was organized in his honor.[74] Trumbull's intensive campaigning in Illinois was motivated not only by his opposition to Johnson, but also by his determination to maintain a Republican majority in the Illinois Legislature to assure his re-election to the Senate in 1867.[75]

While the Republican victory in the November election greatly strengthened the radical Republican position in Congress, there is little evidence to substantiate the statement that "Thaddeus Stevens and Charles Sumner now saw the triumph of their doctrines which had long been treated with contumely and ridicule." [76] While it is true that in the House, Stevens, exploiting the rules of the House that allowed the suspension of debate, dominated the proceedings the situation was greatly different in the Senate, where Charles Sumner, far from being a dominating factor, continued to find himself in a minority. The Senate, which met for its second session of the Thirty-ninth Congress on December 4, 1866, was again dominated not by Sumner or Wade or Chandler, but by moderate Republicans led by Trumbull and Fessenden. There is also ample evidence to cast doubt on another oft-repeated assertion that "under the existing conditions there was left to the moderates only the function of a drag on the reckless and revolutionary policy to which the radicals gave an irresistible impulse." [77] Trumbull and Fessenden, forced by Johnson's stubborn inflexibility, by his refusal to support measures to assure the safety and the rights of the Unionists and the Negroes, and by the excesses

[74] Fehrenbacher, *The Chicago Giant,* p. 204.

[75] Trumbull to E. B. Washburne, September 24, 1866, Elihu B. Washburne Papers, Library of Congress; F. H. Pieper to Trumbull, November 9, 1866; Michael Piggott to Trumbull, November 2, L. T. Papers.

[76] Dunning, *op. cit.,* p. 86.

[77] *Ibid.,* p. 88.

of the Ku Klux Klan, had accepted the position of the radicals on the necessity for Congressional Reconstruction, but they opposed the excessive measures proposed by the radicals. If, even at that later date, Johnson had expressed his readiness to accept a sensible compromise, there is reason to believe that the moderates, in coalition with the Democrats, would have been able to prevent the imposition of a harsh military rule upon the South.

The tug of war between the moderates and the radicals began in the Senate on the first day of the new session. Zachariah Chandler pressed for the immediate adoption of his bill to take away from Johnson the power to grant pardons, which had been given to Lincoln in the Second Confiscation Bill. Trumbull opposed the bill on the ground that no legislation of importance was to be put to a vote on the floor of the Senate without careful deliberation and a report by an appropriate committee. "I think," he said, "we had better act deliberately and understandingly and not under excitement." [78] In spite of the powerful support that Chandler's move received from Sumner, Wade, Wilson, and other radicals, Trumbull and Fessenden, with the support of the Democrats, defeated the move in a tie vote of 21 to 21.[79] The second, and more important, test of strength came when the Senate moved to the consideration of the Reconstruction Act passed by the House of Representatives. Immediately after the opening of the debate, Trumbull took the floor to denounce the House version of the bill, which limited itself to putting the South under military rule in five districts but failed to provide for the steps and the machinery under which readmission to the Union would take place. Trumbull accused the radicals of wanting to delay the admission of the South by insisting on more and more conditions. "Now, sir," he stated, "if you ever mean that these rebel States shall be organized, peace and harmony and good will be restored in this country, will you afford no means to do it? *What more do you ask? What else*

[78] *Cong. Globe*, 39 Cong., 2nd Sess., p. 9.
[79] *Ibid.*

would you have? Can anybody think of anything else to require of these people except to put their governments in loyal hands, adopt the constitutional amendment [Fourteenth], adopt universal suffrage, and keep rebels out of power? *What more I ask can be required of them.*" [80] Serving notice on the radicals that he had not joined their ranks, he added, "It matters not to me whether a man is a good Radical or not in the execution of the duties of his office." [81] Sumner supported the House version of the bill and proposed to add to it a provision that would have assured a homestead for all freed Negroes.[82] Trumbull, with the powerful support of John Sherman, was able to muster a majority for the Senate version of the bill, which provided steps for the readmission of Southern states. On February 20, the House accepted the bill as passed by the Senate.[83]

The Senate passed the First Reconstruction Act by a vote of 35 to 7, and even Reverdy Johnson, the Democrat of Maryland, voted for it.[84] Reverdy Johnson, who enjoyed bipartisan respect in the Senate, said that he voted for the measure in the conviction and the hope that it would restore peace and harmony to the country.[85] Trumbull, a dedicated supporter of the principle of civilian control over the military, supported the bill with reluctance. He felt, however, that the behavior of the Southern leaders gave him no choice. "It is the last thing," he wrote to his brother-in-law, "to put the rebel states under military rule but the People there behave so badly, there seems to be no other way of protecting loyal men." [86]

On March 11, 1867, Charles Sumner proposed a number of resolutions constituting "*further* guarantees required in the reconstruction of the rebel states." [87] The resolutions declared the

[80] *Ibid.*, p. 1561. (Italics mine.)
[81] *Ibid.*, p. 1562.
[82] *Ibid.*, p. 1563.
[83] *Ibid.* (February 20, 1867), p. 1625.
[84] *Ibid.*, p. 1645.
[85] *Ibid.* (March 2, 1867), p. 1953.
[86] Trumbull to Dr. William Jayne, February 17, 1867, Jayne Papers.
[87] *Cong. Globe,* 40 Cong., 1st Sess. (March 11, 1867), p. 49.

existing state governments in the South illegal and provided for the establishment of an integrated public school system in the ex-rebel states. Another resolution provided that every freedman, head of a family, would be given a free homestead.[88] Sumner's resolutions met with the determined opposition of Trumbull, Fessenden, Grimes, and Sherman. The moderate Republicans were joined in their assault on Sumner by the Democratic Senator Reverdy Johnson and the pro-Johnson Republican James Dixon of Connecticut. The motion to table Sumner's resolution won by a vote of 36 to 10, with only the radical wing voting against tabling. When, on the next day, Sumner again moved for the consideration of his resolution, Trumbull and Fessenden proposed to go on to other business. They had no difficulty in getting the Senate to agree. On March 14 Trumbull introduced the Second Supplementary Reconstruction Bill, which set the date of September 1, 1867, as the final day of voter registration, provided for a loyalty oath and set up boards of registration to compile voters' lists.[89] The radicals, led by Charles Drake of Missouri and Sumner, attacked the bill as weak and made repeated attempts to add conditions to the admission of the Southern states to the Union. Their amendments aimed at enlarging the list of disfranchised whites and added a harsh condition that the new state constitutions were to be ratified by a majority of all qualified voters on the lists of registration and not by a majority of voters who cast their ballots, as provided in the bill. Irked by Trumbull's refusal to support his and Sumner's amendments, Senator Drake assailed Trumbull as a "Conservative Radical."[90] Trumbull answered that he did not care about the labels that were pinned on him— he was only interested in having the bill passed as it was submitted by the Judiciary Committee. He told the Senate that his bill excluded from franchise only a small number of ex-rebel

[88] Ibid.
[89] Ibid. (March 14, 1867), p. 94.
[90] Ibid., p. 100.

leaders and that his sole aim was to assure the speedy admission of loyal governments in the South to Congress.[91] Finally, after a bitter debate, Sumner's amendment, providing for the ratification of state constitutions by a majority of all registered voters, was defeated by a vote of 25 to 20.[92] Once again an extreme radical measure was beaten by the moderate Republican-Democratic coalition.

Even more significant and crucial was the struggle between the radicals and the moderate Republicans that came at the end of the first session of the Fortieth Congress. The radicals demanded that Congress remain in continuous session to make sure that Johnson would execute the Reconstruction Acts. "If we abandon our posts," Sumner warned, "if we leave this Government in the hands of an Executive who sympathizes with the policy and views of our enemies . . . I for one do not know what the result may be." [93] Trumbull, who considered the radical motion unconstitutional, moved a resolution that Congress adjourn on Tuesday, March 26, and reconvene at the next regular session on "the first Monday of December, 1867." [94] His resolution was supported by Fessenden, who in a masterful speech argued that to keep Congress in session would violate the principle of separation of powers.[95] Trumbull followed his colleague and friend to the platform and stated that he did not share the fears of the radicals that the President would either fail to execute or sabotage the laws passed by Congress. "It is his [Johnson's] province," he said, "to convene Congress on extraordinary occasions. Congress has no authority to vest it in anybody else." [96] The resolution to adjourn Congress to its regular session was adopted by the Senate by a majority of moderate Republicans and Democrats. The vote was 29 to 16.[97]

[91] Ibid., p. 110.

[92] Cong. Globe, 40 Congs., 1st Sess., p. 147.

[93] Ibid. (March 23, 1867), p. 308.

[94] Ibid., p. 303.

[95] Ibid. (March 26, 1867), p. 354.

[96] Ibid., p. 357.

[97] Ibid., p. 308. In the face of stubborn opposition of the House to adjournment, the Senate finally agreed to a special session of Congress on July 3. Cong.

In March, 1868, Trumbull became involved in a legal case before the Supreme Court that allowed his enemies to question his integrity. The case began in November, 1867, when W. H. McCardle, an editor in Vicksburg, Mississippi, attacked, in his newspaper, the local military commander as a despot. He was arrested and imprisoned for the publication of libelous and inflammatory material and was charged with interfering with the execution of the Reconstruction Acts. McCardle appealed to the Supreme Court for a writ of habeas corpus. After long delays the Supreme Court finally set the hearing for March, amidst indications that an attempt would be made in Congress to pass a law prohibiting the Supreme Court from dealing with cases pertaining to the execution of the Reconstruction Acts. When Henry Stanbery, the attorney general, refused to appear in the case, General Grant, then Acting Secretary of War, requested Trumbull to present the government's case. Trumbull accepted the job and on March 4 made his argument. He argued that the Court had no jurisdiction in the case, because a law passed by Congress on February 5, 1867, exempted persons held by the military authorities and charged with "any military offense" from the jurisdiction of the Supreme Court. Apparently Republican leaders in Congress, including Trumbull, believed that the legal case against the writ of habeas corpus for McCardle was a thin one, because they decided to pass a new law that would specifically deny the Supreme Court jurisdiction in habeas corpus cases stemming from the execution of the Reconstruction Acts. The bill, which was railroaded through the House and Senate in one day, was adopted on March 13, 1868.[98] Trumbull, in spite of his involvement in the case, voted for the bill. The Supreme Court at its next term declared that it had no jurisdiction and dismissed McCardle's petition. For his services in the case, Trumbull submitted to the War Department a bill for $10,000, which the government paid out in several install-

---

Globe, 40 Cong., 1st Sess. (March 28, 1867), p. 408. The Senate, however, refused to keep Congress in a continuous session.

[98] King, op. cit., p. 264; and White, op. cit., p. 329.

ments. In 1880, when Trumbull ran for governor of Illinois on the Democratic ticket, the State Republican Committee published a leaflet attacking Trumbull for extracting from the government an exorbitant fee in the McCardle case. The leaflet also charged that Trumbull's compensation violated the United States Statutes, which forbid an "officer of any branch of public service . . . [to] receive any additional pay." [99] Trumbull answered the charges by stating that General Grant and the government did not consider his fee excessive and cited precedents to prove that government officials were in the past compensated for special services by the government.

[99] The leaflet is in the Trumbull Collection in the Chicago Historical Society.

13

One of the Recusant Senators

WHEN THE MANAGERS OF THE HOUSE OF REPRESENTATIVES, LED BY the feeble but determined Thaddeus Stevens, appeared on March 13, 1868, before the Senate to present the articles of impeachment against Andrew Johnson, it was generally believed that a two-thirds majority of the Senate would convict the President. Leading Union papers throughout the country expressed their confidence that Republican senators, with the exception of the three Johnson-Republicans, Senators Dixon of Connecticut, Doolittle of Wisconsin, and Daniel S. Norton of Minnesota, would vote solidly for conviction.

Among the most vigorous supporters of the impeachment was the Chicago Tribune, edited by a veteran abolitionist and one of the founders of the National Free-Kansas Committee, Horace White.[1] The Chicago Tribune had been a powerful and influential newspaper during the Civil War. It had been ably edited in succession by Dr. Charles Ray, Joseph Medill, and Horace White. In addition, it had one of the most modern presses in the country and, in 1865, about 50,000 subscribers in the North-

---

[1] Text of White's testimony before the Senate's Select Committee of Inquiry on John Brown's raid, Horace White Papers, Illinois State Historical Library, Springfield, Ill.

west.[2] The editors and the owners of the *Tribune*, John Locke Scripps and William Bross (known as the "Deacon"), were active and powerful in the turbulent politics of Chicago and Illinois. They were proud that their paper had been the first in the country to "bring Lincoln before the country" during the Lincoln-Douglas debates and the first to propose him for the Presidency.[3] Ray, as the paper's editor, had given strong support to Lincoln's nomination and campaign. The *Tribune* had opposed any compromise with the South and consistently advocated, during the entire period of the Civil War, the most vigorous prosecution of the war and the unconditional surrender of the Confederacy.[4] The *Chicago Tribune* had been an early advocate of Negro emancipation and of the use of Negro troops.[5] While occasionally mildly critical of the administration, the paper had never wavered in its support of Abraham Lincoln even when the fortunes of the Union were at their lowest point. When, at the end of 1863, prominent leaders of the Republican party and even the Central State Republican Committee of Illinois declared that Lincoln had no chance to be re-elected, the *Tribune* had written, "All the world knows that we are for Old Abe. We have been for him all the while. . . . We are for him still."[6] Reacting to the efforts to ditch Lincoln in favor of Salmon P. Chase, Joseph Medill had written in the *Tribune*, "I presume it is true, that Mr. Chase's friends are waiting for his nomination, but it is all lost labor."[7]

The outspoken editorials of the *Tribune* were widely reprinted in other Republican journals throughout the country and especially in Illinois. These small-town weeklies and biweeklies often voiced their admiration for and gratitude to the *Tribune* as "the ablest, most sterling paper in the West."[8]

[2] Kingsley, *op. cit.*, I, 154.
[3] William Bross to Trumbull, February 13, 1861, L. T. Papers.
[4] Strevey, *op. cit.*, p. 40.
[5] *Chicago Tribune*, July 22, December 2, 3, 1861, January 12, July 4, 1862.
[6] *Ibid.*, October 16, 1863.
[7] Kinsley, *op. cit.*, p. 70.
[8] *Rockland Republican*, December 8, 1864; and *Jacksonville* (Ill.) *Journal*, December 14, 1864.

The *Tribune* had mourned Lincoln deeply and sincerely, and while willing at first to give Andrew Johnson a chance to prove his allegiance to the Republican party, it had become quickly disillusioned with him after his proclamation on the reconstruction of North Carolina. It had advocated a plan of reconstruction of the South that directly conflicted with Johnson's ideas and purposes. The *Tribune* adopted Thaddeus Stevens' concept of the Southern states as "conquered provinces" and called for the complete overthrow of the "Southern slavocracy." "We have from the first," said a *Tribune* editorial, ". . . branded the war as a war of aristocracy, against democracy, of slave holders against working men, of oligarchs against the people. . . . Let us have such a peace as shall open up the South forever for free labor." [9] Johnson's vetoes of the Freedmen's Bureau Bill and of the Civil Rights Act had incurred the wrath of the *Tribune*.

When the second and successful attempt was made in the House of Representatives to impeach Johnson, the *Tribune* gave the move its full support. "There are timid people," it wrote, "who think the impeachment of a President a matter of such serious moment that they doubt whether the country can long survive such a fearful precedent . . . this is all nonsense . . . the impeachment of Johnson . . . is the most hopeful sign of the times. . . ." [10] The paper exercised no restraint when attacking Andrew Johnson as the President and as an individual. It told its readers that he was a habitual drunkard and an opium user, and that he was guilty of associating with lewd pardon brokers and degenerates. The *Tribune*, nevertheless, made it clear that it considered him sane and liable to stand trial.[11] These virulent attacks on Johnson and calls for his conviction continued through March and April of 1868.

[9] *Chicago Tribune*, April 1, 1865.
[10] *Ibid.*, February 28, 1868.
[11] *Ibid.*, March 14, 1868. On March 31 of that year, an editorial stated, "We believe he [Johnson] deserves to be impeached by the House, tried by the Senate, convicted and removed from office for treason, bribery and other high crimes and misdemeanors. . . ."

The first hint that Horace White was beginning to have some second thoughts on the desirability of Johnson's removal from office came on April 21. An editorial quoted an article from *Iron Age* stating that manufacturers expected a higher tariff bill to be passed during the brief administration of Senator Benjamin Wade of Ohio, who as President pro tempore of the Senate would become President once Johnson was convicted on the impeachment charges. The editorial went on to say: ". . . there is no need of concealing from the public the fact that one of the chief obstacles to the impeachment of Andrew Johnson is the belief which many Senators entertain that Mr. Wade would seize the occasion of his *ad interim* Presidency to crowd upon Congress a bill to plunder the public anew under the miserable pretense of protecting the home industry." But the editorial still expressed support for Johnson's conviction. "We see no reason," the paper concluded, "why any Senator should hesitate on that ground to convict Andrew Johnson of the high crimes and misdemeanors of which he has been guilty." [12] A few days later, the *Tribune* appealed to the senators to act "without partisan bias or inducement, without fear or favor, reward or hope of reward." Cautiously, White injected the thought that the impeachment trial might not be completely legal. "In so far as the trial is legal it involves the rights of an individual which must be protected." Finally, the Delphic editorial condemned the "ill-advised pressure of some newspapers on the Senators." "We trust," it concluded, "Senators will be too wary and independent either to accept the virtual bribe to yield to the implied threats or on the other hand to vote on the wrong side because the right side is burdened with unwise friends." [13]

Having implanted the seeds of doubt, Horace White decided to await public reaction. Consequently, no editorial comment on the impeachment appeared until May 6. On that day the *Tribune* published a lead editorial entitled, "The Probable

[12] *Chicago Tribune,* April 21, 1868.
[13] *Ibid.,* April 25, 1868. (Italics mine.)

Failure of Impeachment." The editorial was rather ambiguous, reflecting, no doubt, the fact that White had still not made up his mind whether his dislike and mistrust of Ben Wade and his opposition to high tariffs should outweigh his hatred of Johnson and his reconstruction policies. "The unwelcome intelligence comes from Washington," said the editorial, "that Johnson may not be convicted and removed." This editorial, carefully preparing its readers, listed several reasons for the probable acquittal of Johnson: First, ". . . two or three Republican Senators of ability and high standing oppose conviction . . ." (Senator William Pitt Fessenden of Maine was mentioned in this connection, but Senator Trumbull was not), and second, the fear that Wade as a President would push through Congress a high tariff bill. The *Tribune* added its own view that the "Wade ring would surely plunder the people," but that "while Johnson is President they cannot pass their insatiable demand by a two thirds majority over his veto."

In addition to the tariff issue, White used another reason for opposing Wade's ascendancy to the Presidency. The *Tribune* declared its conviction that the devious and resourceful Wade would, as President, be in a position to force the Republican National Convention, which was scheduled to meet several days after the impeachment vote, to nominate him for President and thus "fasten himself and his peculiar followers upon the Republican party and the country." With all this, White still did not dare to oppose Johnson's conviction. The editorial concluded with these words: "*Still, we shall hope for the conviction of the wretched apostate*, notwithstanding the alleged defection of Fessenden and others." [14]

There was widespread interest and speculation as to how Senators William Pitt Fessenden and Lyman Trumbull would vote in the hour of decision. It was clear that the stand taken by these highly respected and influential senators might sway

[14] *Ibid.*, May 6. 1868. (Italics mine.)

enough votes of their fellow Republicans to prevent the conviction. Fessenden, smarting under a vicious attack made upon him by Senator Zachariah Chandler of Michigan, in which he was bitingly and repeatedly referred to as the "Conservative Senator from Maine," served notice on his Republican colleagues that he would be an impartial judge of Johnson's guilt or innocence and impartially keep "his mind as free as he could from prejudice and passion." [15] In spite of his attempt to be objective about Johnson's guilt there is no doubt that Fessenden disliked and distrusted Ben Wade.[16]

Lyman Trumbull gave no hint about how he intended to vote on Johnson's conviction. Like most Republican leaders, Trumbull had had no reservations about Johnson's succession to the Presidency. Even after Johnson put into effect his reconstruction plans for the South without the advice or cooperation of Congress, Trumbull had felt that congressmen and senators should give the President's plan a chance. When Johnson vetoed his Freedmen's Bureau Bill and his Civil Rights Act, Trumbull had been bitterly disappointed. He had denounced the vetoes but refrained from personal attacks on Johnson.[17] Even when the break between Johnson and Congress became irreparable, Trumbull's treatment of the President had remained dignified and restrained. After the passage of the Military Reconstruction Act, of March 2, 1867, Trumbull had told the Senate, "Personally, of the Executive I do not indulge in remarks. I believe I have never been guilty of making any personal attacks on the Executive." [18] Trumbull was, however, deeply angered by Johnson's policy of removing officials in

[15] *Cong. Globe*, 40 Cong., 1st Sess. (July 20, 1867), p. 752.

[16] During the debate on the tariff, Fessenden spoke with bitter sarcasm about Senator Wade. "He is in the habit of telling us," he told the Senate, "that his motives are perfectly pure; that he always acts exactly according to his views of right, and that he is very certain he is right on all occasions. . . . I concede now and hereafter all that he claims for himself of perfect purity and perfect knowledge. . . ." *Cong. Globe*, 39 Cong., 2nd Sess. (January 24, 1867), p. 707. For another acrimonious and revealing exchange between Fessenden and Wade, see *Cong. Globe*, 39 Cong., 2nd Sess. (January 25, 1867), pp. 792–95.

[17] *Cong. Globe*, 39 Cong., 1st Sess. (February 20, 1866), pp. 942–43, 950–57.

[18] *Cong. Globe*, 40 Cong., 1st Sess. (March 26, 1867), p. 357.

Illinois and elsewhere as a punishment for opposition to what he called "my policy." In a Senate speech urging a tougher Tenure of Office Act, Trumbull said: "We go to the country and say we have passed a bill upon principle, that public policy requires that the officers of the Government should be independent and not hold their office at the will, the whim and the caprice of the appointing power. . . ." [19]

There is contradictory evidence on Trumbull's attitude toward Johnson's impeachment when it was debated in the House of Representatives. In October, 1866, Trumbull said at a mass meeting in Chicago, "It is my conviction that the said Johnson ought to be immediately impeached and removed." [20] But a few months later, he called those in Congress who pressed for impeachment "excited demagogues" and expressed a hope that Congress would act "coolly and deliberately" on the issue. [21] Keeping in mind Lyman Trumbull's cool and unemotional approach to political affairs, his well-deserved reputation as an excellent lawyer and his devotion to the principle of separation of power among the three branches of the United States Government, there is reason to believe that he would weigh the legal issues involved in the impeachment with great care and deliberation. [22] His record in the Senate suggested that Trumbull's vote for the removal of the President from office was very much in doubt. [23]

On the other hand, Trumbull was reasonably ambitious and

[19] Cong. Globe, 39 Cong., 2nd Sess. (February 2, 1867), p. 967.

[20] Chicago Republican, May 14, 1868.

[21] Trumbull to Dr. William Jayne, December 7, 1866, Jayne Papers.

[22] In a speech on a bill limiting the powers of the Supreme Court, Trumbull said, "No person in this Chamber or elsewhere recognizes more fully than I do the necessity of a division of the powers of the Government. . . . It is the division of the powers of government among different departments . . . that constitutes the safety of the liberties of the people." Cong. Globe, 41 Cong., 2nd Sess. (December 16, 1869), Part I, p. 167.

[23] On March 26, 1867, Trumbull had a revealing exchange on the floor of the Senate with Senator Richard Yates, who complained that Johnson's vetoes might "prevent reconstruction." Trumbull answered: "It may prevent reconstruction by the veto of the bill, but it is a perfect right belonging to the Executive. It is no cause for impeachment if he vetoes a bill. It is his right." Cong. Globe, 40 Cong., 1st Sess. (March 26, 1867), p. 359.

too good a politician to ignore the overwhelming sentiment for Johnson's conviction among the Republicans in Illinois. The Republican leaders, foes and friends of Trumbull alike, Representative John A. Logan, Senator Richard Yates, Governor Richard J. Oglesby, General John M. Palmer, Shelby M. Cullom, J. Y. Scammon, Dr. William Jayne; and the Republican press led by the *Chicago Tribune*, the *Chicago Republican* and the *Illinois State Journal*; all strongly advocated Johnson's removal from office. Even the moderate and usually pro-Johnson *Springfield Republican* acknowledged that "Popular will was for conviction." [24]

Trumbull had good reasons to pay careful attention to the position taken by the *Chicago Tribune*. Its owners and editors had supported his political aspirations from the very inception of his career,[25] and the *Tribune* gave extensive publicity to his speeches in the Senate.[26] He certainly did not wish to antagonize the *Tribune*. Had he done so, Horace White could have considered him an ingrate. His re-election to the Senate for a six-year term, in January, 1867, was made possible in large measure by the staunch support he had received from White and his paper.

Brooding over the impeachment of Johnson, whom he hated with the passion of an old abolitionist, Horace White was confident that Trumbull would, out of gratitude, consider his stand for conviction. It is doubtful, however, that he expected that the senator would obediently follow the *Tribune's* dictates. Trumbull, high-principled, proud, and aloof, was not a man to be dictated to. As a matter of fact, White's letters to Trumbull reveal that the aggressive editor took every precaution not to

---

[24] *Springfield Republican*, May 26, 1868. On February 20, 1868, the Chicago City Council passed an impeachment resolution. Kinsley, *op. cit.*, II, 75.

[25] The *Tribune* approved of Trumbull's election to the Senate in 1855 and in 1856 the *Tribune* mentioned Trumbull as an excellent choice for the Republican Presidential nomination. *Chicago Tribune*, June 17, 1856.

[26] When on one occasion Trumbull neglected to send a reprint of one of his speeches, the editor wrote to ask him for it. Horace White to Trumbull, July 13, 1806, L. T. Papers.

give Trumbull the impression that he was attemping to tell him what to say or how to vote. White carefully limited himself to complimenting Trumbull and occasionally offered suggestions.[27]

But as the day of the Senate's vote on impeachment drew closer, the tariff issue loomed ever larger in Horace White's agile mind. He was a strong free-trader and after taking over the control of the paper, on April 14, 1865, from the protectionist Joseph Medwill, he gradually reversed the *Tribune's* long-standing high tariff position. The *Chicago Tribune* had come out in support of a high tariff in the early days of the Republican party. In January, 1860, Dr. Ray, then the editor of the *Chicago Press and Tribune*, had written a series of articles on the proposed Republican platform. He had strongly advocated a protective tariff plank.[28] The *Tribune* had praised Lincoln as a "good tariff man" and supported the 1861 Morrill Tariff Act.[29] Two weeks after the new tariff bill went into effect, the *Tribune* had written that it "already is demonstrating its excellent revenue qualities and is silencing its slanderers." [30]

Considering protection an evil, White had the *Tribune* launch a full-fledged attack on senators of both parties who in January, 1866, had supported a new and higher tariff bill in Congress. He denounced the bill as "a financial monstrosity" and castigated Wade, Sumner, Chandler, Butler, and Stevens for their support of the tariff measure. "They propose," White wrote, "to give the American manufacturer a bounty of five percent per pound for exporting . . . to be paid by you and me. . . . Have we killed King Cotton and set up King Sheeting." [31] Charles Ray, who had left the *Tribune* and became a strong free-trader, also exhorted Trumbull to oppose the tariff bill lest Illinois become "consumed by the good of New England and

[27] Horace White to Trumbull, February 21, March 7, 1866, L. T. Papers.
[28] Jay Monaghan, *The Man Who Elected Lincoln* (Indianapolis, 1956).
[29] *Chicago Tribune*, March 29, May 6, 1860.
[30] *Ibid.*, April 15, 1861.
[31] Horace White to Elihu Washburne, January 30, 1866, Washburne Papers, Library of Congress.

Pensylvania." [32] Significantly, opposition to protection had considerable bipartisan support. The Chicago Times, the organ of
Illinois Democracy, which seldom if ever agreed with anything
that the Tribune stood for, charged that the tariff bill was "a
scheme for plundering the people." [33] The Free Trade League,
organized in Chicago in January, 1866, under the presidency of
Dr. Ray, had a bipartisan Executive Committee.[34] To counter-
act the activities of the league, Chicago manufacturers organized the American Industrial Union to propagate protection.
Joseph Medill became its president.[35]

On the issue of protection, White would accept no compromise. When David A. Wells, Special Commissioner of the
Revenue, prepared a compromise tariff bill, the Tribune continued its opposition. Ben Wade, a leading supporter of the
higher tariff, was the special target of White's attacks. The
animosity toward Wade may be explained by the special effectiveness of his arguments for protection. He placed the empha-
sis not on the need to protect domestic industries, but on the
protection of the jobs and wages of American workers.[36] This
was an effective argument, and Horace White acutely sensed
the danger that the tariff bill might pass (it passed the House
with the support of "Long John" Wentworth of Chicago) and
split the Republican party before the crucial Congressional election, which was to decide the issues between President Johnson and Congress. In desperation, White wrote to Trumbull
suggesting that he use his influence to kill the bill by parliamentary delays. "Would it not be well," he wrote, "to get that fatal
tariff bill postponed, smothered or in some way put out of sight
when it comes to the Senate?" [37] Trumbull was glad to oblige
and with the help of other moderates prevented the bill from

---

[32] Dr. Charles Ray to Trumbull, February 2, 1866, L. T. Papers.
[33] Chicago Times, June 29, 1866.
[34] Chicago Tribune, January 5, 17, 1866.
[35] Ibid., February 22, 1866.
[36] Cong. Globe, 39 Cong., 2nd Sess. (January 28, 1867), p. 795.
[37] White to Trumbull, July 5, 1866, L. T. Papers.

coming to a vote in spite of the desperate pressure from Wade and Sumner.

Trumbull's readiness to cooperate with White stemmed in part from his desire to prevent a split in the party, but most of all from the fact that he had no strong conviction on the tariff issue. He spoke rarely when the bill was debated, perfectly content to leave the fight against Wade's more extreme protectionist amendments to his friend Fessenden, who was the acknowledged expert on financial matters in the Senate.

On May 6 the *Tribune* bluntly put the blame for the probable acquittal of Johnson on Wade's "insatiable lobby." It told its readers that Wade had declared to a reporter of the *Cincinnati Gazette* that he was determined when President to have Congress pass "an adequate tariff." [38] The *Chicago Times*, eager to exploit the growing dissension in the Republican ranks, asked, "Why these bitter attacks upon Wade in the special organ of Grant? . . . Tariff and free trade are at the bottom of the business. . . ." [39] On the same day, White charged that Peter Cooper, the New York industrialist, told an audience in New York that he favored Johnson's removal so that Wade as President would "protect American industry." [40]

Those who suspected that the *Tribune* was about to execute a sensational about-face on Johnson's impeachment found additional confirmation in the proceedings of the Illinois State Republican Convention which met in Peoria on May 6. White successfully used all of his power and influence to prevent the convention from adopting a resolution endorsing Johnson's impeachment and instructing Senators Trumbull and Yates to vote accordingly. [41] On May 7 the *Tribune* undertook to prepare its readers for Trumbull's vote for acquittal. "Mr. Trumbull," it wrote, "resembles Mr. Fessenden. . . . He too has a conservative

[38] *Chicago Tribune*, May 6, 1868.
[39] *Chicago Times*, May 11, 1868.
[40] *Chicago Tribune*, May 11, 1868.
[41] *Chicago Evening Journal*, May 12, 1868.

turn of mind and a natural dislike of measures like this [the impeachment] . . . . [He] has been exceedingly discreet. . . . But it may be noted as a significant circumstance that his wife is a warm impeacher." [42]

It was apparent that there were forces in the *Tribune's* hierarchy that were fighting against the switch. White was bitterly opposed by the protectionist Medill. On May 7 the paper had actually succeeded in speaking from both sides of its editorial mouth. It assured its readers that the Republican party would survive Johnson's acquittal, but added that to "acquit Andrew Johnson is to impeach the Senate, to insult and degrade the House and to betray the people. . . . No matter what personal antipathy Senators may feel for the man who will become Johnson's sucessor, no matter about the plots and schemes of the high tariff lobby, the Senate has a solemn duty to perform and that is to punish a willful and malicious violation of the law." [43]

A few days later, however, all doubts vanished and the *Tribune* came out boldly for Johnson's acquittal. It stated that Wade as President would not have the interests of the people at heart and that Johnson would be harmless if allowed to serve out his term. The paper in the same issue excused the Republican senators who were expected to vote against conviction. "They know," the editorial stated, "that they jeopardize their popularity *for the time being* by resisting political prejudices but they are sworn to act with a single eye to the question whether Johnson is guilty or not guilty." [44] The *Tribune's* Washington correspondent reported that he had talked to Trumbull and become convinced that he had decided to vote in the negative. He added that the Illinois congressmen and Senator Yates refrained from attempts to influence Trumbull's vote

[42] *Chicago Tribune,* May 7, 1868. Julia Trumbull was the sister of Dr. William Jayne of Springfield, Illinois. In contrast, the *New York World* wrote on May 6, "Mr. Trumbull is spoken of on both sides as a 'slippery person.' That appears to be the chief reason why he is expected to vote for acquittal."

[43] *Chicago Tribune,* May 7, 1868.

[44] *Chicago Tribune,* May 11, 1868. (Italics mine.)

because they knew that "no outside pressure would avail . . . so Judge Trumbull was not labored with that time." [45] On May 12 the paper stated editorially that Johnson's "legal guilt was not made out according to the satisfaction of a majority of the Senate. *Far better his acquittal than his conviction upon grounds that might be condemned by the next generation.*" [46]

The reaction of Republican leaders in Illinois and the Republican press against the *Tribune's* sudden switch was bitter and violent. The *Chicago Evening Journal* said the *Tribune* "had encouraged Republican Senators to unite their votes with those of the copperheads. . . ." [47] The *Chicago Republican* asked: "Is the *Tribune* drifting to the Democratic Party? After predicting the acquittal of Andrew Johnson, it proceeds to lay the whole blame on the shoulders of Ben Wade." The *Republican* charged that the *Tribune's* objective was to prevent Wade from becoming Grant's running mate.[48] The *Illinois State Journal* asked: "What has so suddenly weakened the backbone of the *Tribune* in reference to this great and momentous question? What new light has dawned upon the sheet, that, whereas, five days ago it declared that a verdict of acquittal by the Senate would be 'self-stultification' and . . . 'self condemnation,' now discovers that the Senators will only be performing a conscientious duty. . . ." [49] The condemnation of the *Tribune* was not limited to Illinois. Its stand was deplored by the *St. Louis Democrat,* the *Toledo Blade,* the *Detroit Post,* the *Cleveland Leader,* and others.[50]

In Washington Lyman Trumbull faithfully listened to the testimony, often holding his young son Henry on his knee. Once his mind was made up he announced his vote against con-

[45] *Ibid.,* May 11, 1868.
[46] *Ibid.,* May 12, 1868. (Italics mine.)
[47] *Chicago Evening Journal,* May 12, 1868.
[48] *Chicago Republican,* May 12, 1868. The charge was true since the *Tribune* wanted Schuyler Colfax of Indiana as vice-president.
[49] *Illinois State Journal,* May 14, 1868.
[50] *St. Louis Democrat,* May 13, *Toledo Blade,* May 14, *Detroit Post,* May 13, *Cleveland Leader,* May 14, 1868.

viction. In a closely reasoned legal opinion Trumbull declared that the evidence was not sufficient to convict Johnson of high crimes and misdemeanors as charged in article eleven of the impeachment. Taking into account Trumbull's integrity and courage, his long training and experience as a judge and a lawyer, and his devotion to the principle of separation of powers, it cannot be argued that had it not been for the *Tribune's* dramatic switch on Johnson's impeachment, he would have voted for conviction and thus brought about Johnson's removal. What can be argued, however, is that the *Tribune's* stand for acquittal made it immeasurably easier for him to reach his decision, because it considerably minimized the political risk involved and softened the effectiveness of the barrage of denunciation that immediately descended upon his head.

Illinois Congressmen were furious with Trumbull. "The swearing of Washburne, Logan, Ingersoll and Farnsworth," wrote a Washington correspondent, "was said to be absolutely shocking." Trumbull's colleague, Senator Yates, who voted for conviction, prevented the Illinois Congressional delegation from sending Trumbull a letter requesting his resignation. Washburne stated that he "now prefers Yates drunk than Trumbull sober." [51] The *Chicago Republican* wrote that should Trumbull come to Chicago, "thousands of his fellow townsmen, who would, a few weeks ago, have taken him cordially by the hand, would now consider such touch contamination. . . ." [52] The powerful Grant Clubs of Chicago held a mass rally at which a former Trumbull supporter and prominent Republican leader and banker, J. Y. Scammon, violently denounced the *Tribune* and Trumbull. A resolution declared, "Senator Lyman Trumbull is not worthy to occupy the place to which he was elevated." [53] Some papers even suggested that Trumbull had been bribed.[54]

[51] *Chicago Times,* May 16, 1868.
[52] *Chicago Republican,* May 17, 1868.
[53] *Chicago Tribune,* May 13, 1868.
[54] *Philadelphia Bulletin,* May 13, *Toledo Blade,* May 13, 1868. Horace Greeley wrote, "We are assured that his democratic son had quietly made bets through

The *Tribune* defended Trumbull's right as a lawyer to vote his legal convictions and rejected the contention that the Republican party would suffer because of Johnson's acquittal. "Those who demand," it wrote, 'that Trumbull should vote for conviction whether he believed Johnson guilty or not, ought rather to thank God that they have a senator who has the high courage and manliness to go through the Red sea of obloquy and odium for conscience sake." [55] White courageously maintained that Trumbull, by his action, brought "glory to Illinois by his statesmanship and wisdom." [56] The *Tribune* acknowledged that "a small portion of our readers are vexed with us. . ." but it assured the public that the storm would pass and that the Republican party had nothing to fear from Johnson's remaining a few months more in office, while Wade's Presidency would have split the party and jeopardized the fate of the reconstruction. White took the responsibility of advising Trumbull in a private letter to vote his conviction and ignore the pressure. In the letter, which was published in the *Tribune*, White wrote: "If I were a member of the Court, I would vote my honest convictions, if a thunderbolt were prepared to strike me dead for it." [57]

Trumbull, unlike Ross of Kansas, did not suffer political martyrdom for his vote, and his subsequent leaving of the Senate and of the Republican party was not related to the impeachment trial.[58] Protected by the long and powerful arm of the *Chicago Tribune*, he was soon able to regain his leadership and standing in the Republican party in Illinois.

The *Tribune's* position quite rapidly influenced other Republican organs in the state to moderate their stand. The *Illinois State Journal*, while regretting Trumbull's vote, repudiated its

---

third parties by which he expects to win $5,000 by his father's resistance to impeachment." *New York Tribune,* May 14, 1867.

[55] *Chicago Tribune,* May 15, 1868.
[56] *Ibid.,* May 17, 1868.
[57] *Ibid.*
[58] See Ralph J. Roske, "The Seven Martyrs?" *American Historical Review,* Vol. XLVII, No. 4 (March, 1961).

own Washington correspondent who had insinuated that Trumbull was bribed and that "being a good hater, his dislike of Stanton and Wade . . . instigated his course on impeachment." The *Journal* editorially rejected the accusation of bribery and added: "We cannot believe that Judge Trumbull is the man to be approached by anybody in the manner in which it is suggested." [59]

His vote for acquittal did not lose for Trumbull the support and friendship of the Republican leaders of Illinois. He retained the friendship and support of Palmer, Koerner, Cullom, Cook, Yates, and of the lesser-known but influential downstate leaders, D. L. Phillips, Joseph Gillespie, and Dr. William Jayne. When his Senate term expired in 1873, it was not the Republican party that abandoned Trumbull—it was Trumbull who a long while back had, in disgust with the Grant administration, decided to break with the party.[60]

[59] *Illinois State Journal,* May 19, 1868.

[60] Lyman Trumbull informed General James Harrison Wilson on January 4, 1876, "I became satisfied in 1872 that the Republican organization became a body corrupt . . . its power must be broken." James H. Wilson, MSS Library of Congress.

14

Years of Disillusionment

TRUMBULL CONSISTENTLY REFUSED TO ANSWER NEWSPAPER AT-
tacks and denunciations in connection with his vote to acquit
Johnson, and he never apologized for his decision. He preferred to
stand by the legal opinion he filed with the Senate, in which he
gave the reasons for his vote. When public opinion swung to the
approval of acquittal, Trumbull continued to refrain from men-
tioning the stand he had taken. He held no grudge against those
who had castigated and attacked him. He refused, however, to
forgive his friend and political associate of many years, Norman
B. Judd, for insinuating in his speech at the Republican Convention in Chicago on May 20, 1868, that Trumbull was bribed
to vote for acquittal. In 1869, when Judd was re-elected to Congress, he met Trumbull in the Capitol rotunda and extended his
hand to him, "but Mr. Trumbull took no notice of him and
the friendship was never renewed." [1]

Trumbull's position of leadership in the Senate remained unimpaired. He was still the chairman of the powerful Judiciary
Committee and a member of the select "club" of senators who
usually direct the affairs of that exclusive body. When Congress
reconvened in December of 1868, Trumbull served on the Inner

[1] Mary Trumbull to Horace White, July 26, 1907, Horace White Papers, Illinois State Historical Society Library, Springfield, Ill.

Policy Committee, which decided upon the offices and the committee chairmanships. If there was still some bitterness over the impeachment trial it was clearly receding. "There is a little of the venom of impeachment left," Trumbull wrote to his brother-in-law, "which creeps up occasionally." [2] Trumbull's relations with his colleague Senator Yates, who strongly supported Johnson's removal, remained friendly. Trumbull used his decisive influence to retain Yates as chairman of the Committee on Territories in spite of strong demands for his removal by several senators who claimed that the junior senator from Illinois was absent from the Senate a great deal because of his addiction to alcohol.[3]

But it was, nevertheless, increasingly clear that the impeachment trial and the record of Grant's administration had caused Trumbull to commence an agonizing reappraisal of his views and attitudes toward reconstruction. He ceased to be convinced that Congressional Reconstruction, based on the use of Federal troops, would work against the massive resistance of the white population of the South. Deeply committed to the constitutional principle of checks and balances, he began to fret over continued Federal invasion of states' rights. The first straw in the wind of change was Trumbull's opposition to the harsh and punitive measures discussed in Congress when the Georgia Legislature expelled its Negro senators and representatives. He disagreed with the report of his own committee, which recommended that Georgia senators not be admitted until the expulsion measure was rescinded.[4] He agreed with his friend John M. Palmer who, in his inaugural address as governor of Illinois, stated, "Now that the war is ended, and all proper objects attained, the public welfare demands a recurrence to the true principles that underlie our system of government, and one of the best established and most distinctly recognized of those

---

[2] Trumbull to Dr. William Jayne, December 19, 1868, Jayne Papers.
[3] Ibid.
[4] Cong. Globe, 41 Cong., 2nd Sess. (December, 1869), p. 232.

is that the federal government is one of enumerated and limited powers." [5]

The death of his wife Julia, which came after a long, lingering illness on August 16, 1868, was a heavy blow to Trumbull. She was only forty-five years old. Their marriage had been a very happy one and they gave each other the full measure of love and devotion. Only a little over a year before her death, Julia wrote to her husband: "Because I am calm in my exterior and rarely express myself strongly, does not mean that I have less warmth, or am not stirred with the same feelings that move other women. I yield to no woman in true womanly devotion to a kind, loving, generous husband." [6] Trumbull fully reciprocated his wife's feelings. In a revealing letter to Julia he succinctly described his life. "The first fifteen years I was watched over by the kindest and best of mothers, the next fifteen I was a wanderer and for the most part deprived of the beautiful female influence, the last fifteen I have had the companionship and affection of the best and loveliest whom it was my good fortune to know." [7]

Julia was deeply religious and attended her Presbyterian church in Washington and in Springfield regularly. She often chided her husband, whose religious convictions were not as deep as hers. Trumbull usually attended church on Sundays, but when alone in Washington he often went to Methodist or Unitarian services. Julia, as her pastor said in the funeral oration, "trusted in Christ as her Savior." When told by her doctor that there were no prospects for her recovery, she said, "I am in the hands of the Lord. He knows what is best. He always does what is best." [8]

Mild and composed, Julia was unusually outspoken in her support of the Union and her condemnation of the Confederacy. When Jefferson Davis was captured by Union troops, she advo-

---

[5] Palmer, *Personal Recollections*, p. 287.
[6] Julia Jayne Trumbull to Lyman Trumbull, July 8, 1867, L. T. Family Papers.
[7] Lyman Trumbull to Julia Jayne Trumbull, October 20, 1858, L. T. Family Papers.
[8] Funeral Oration by Rev. Frederick Howard Wines, L. T. Family Papers.

cated that the President of the Confederacy be tried and hanged.[9] Julia was in favor of harsh reconstruction measures and favored the conviction of President Johnson on the impeachment charges. In the last two years of her life, Julia Trumbull was president and manager of the Soldiers' and Sailors' Orphan's Home in Washington, which she founded.

Trumbull was left to care for two young sons, Perry and Henry. Eventually, he found life in the big house unbearable and moved with his sons to an apartment on 13th Street just north of F.[10] While he was still conscientious about his attendance and work in the Senate, his heart was clearly not in it. He paid frequent visits to his own family in Connecticut,[11] and his relations with his late wife's family, the Jaynes of Springfield, Illinois, remained close and affectionate. Dr. William Jayne remained his political eyes and ears in the state's capital, and in exchange for his favors Trumbull got for Jayne a well-paid job as Pension Agent.[12] To occupy his time and to shore up his finances, Trumbull greatly increased his law practice before the Supreme Court. "I am busy arguing cases in the Supreme Court," he wrote to Jayne, "of which I have several to argue this winter." [13]

Trumbull did not participate in the long Senate debates of February, 1869, on the adoption of the joint resolution providing for universal suffrage, which later became the Fifteenth Amendment. This was the first time that Trumbull did not take the floor to express his views on a major piece of reconstruction legislation. His silence is understandable, because he had never advocated universal Negro suffrage, being convinced that the suffrage privilege should be extended to Negroes gradually as

[9] Julia Jayne Trumbull to Lyman Trumbull, May 17, 1865, L. T. Family Papers.
[10] Trumbull to Dr. William Jayne, November 18, 1870, Jayne Papers.
[11] Trumbull to Dr. William Jayne, August 5, 1870, Jayne Papers.
[12] Letter of Appointment of Dr. Jayne, in Jayne Papers, dated April 21, 1869.
[13] Trumbull to Dr. Jayne, November 18, 1870, January 8, 1871, Jayne Papers. See also Storrs and Wilson to Trumbull, March 17, 1870, and Trumbull to Isaac G. Wilson, March 19, 1870, L. T. Papers.

their level of education increased. In his advocacy of the Civil Rights Bill Trumbull had taken special pains to emphasize that the bill "does not propose to regulate the political rights of individuals; it has nothing to do with the right of suffrage, or any other political right. . . ." [14] There were obvious signs that with the exception of the remaining radical senators like Sumner of Massachusetts, Morton of Indiana, Howard and Chandler of Michigan, Yates of Illinois, Drake of Missouri, and Wade of Ohio, there was not much enthusiasm for the passing of the resolution. On occasion many senators were absent, and even repeated quorum calls were of no avail. [15]

Trumbull voted against an amendment to the resolution that would have positively affirmed the right of Negroes to franchise. He also opposed an amendment by Senator Henry Wilson of Massachusetts that would have prohibited the denial or abridgement of voting to any citizen, not only because of race, but also because of "nativity, property, education, or creed." [16] He supported, however, an amendment introduced by Senator Vickers of Maryland that provided that the right of franchise was not to be denied to those who participated in the rebellion. The amendment was not adopted, but Trumbull made clear that he wished the disabilities on some Southern whites imposed in the Fourteenth Amendment removed. [17] Trumbull revealed his reservations about the amendment during one of his infrequent interventions in the debate. Taking the floor for a brief statement, Trumbull said, on February 9: "After all, there has been a great confounding of terms, it seems to me, in this debate—of which I have taken no part, and I do not propose to take any now—by supposing that citizenship had anything to do with voting in this country. Citizenship and the right of suf-

[14] *Cong. Globe*, 39 Cong., 1st Sess., p. 599.
[15] *Cong. Globe*, 40 Cong., 3rd Sess., pp. 909, 985.
[16] *Ibid.*, p. 1012. In a brief remark on Wilson's amendment, Trumbull stated that its adoption would abolish "the constitutions of perhaps all, certainly of half, the States of the Union." *Ibid.*, p. 1036.
[17] *Ibid.*, p. 911.

frage were never synonymous terms, they do not necessarily go together at all." [18]

On the final vote, however, Trumbull voted for the amendment. There was undoubtedly a good reason for his affirmative vote. His negative vote cast' against a nearly unanimous stand of Republican senators might have forced him to break with the party. In February of 1869 Lyman Trumbull was not ready for such a decisive step.

This was one of the last major pieces of positive reconstruction legislation. The inefficiency, graft, and corruption in Washington turned the attention of many Republican senators and representatives toward reform. "After the Fifteenth Amendment was passed," writes C. Vann Woodward, "the North rapidly lost interest in the Negro voters. They were pushed out of the limelight by other interests, beset by prejudice and neglected by politicians . . . Reformers and Mugwumps of the North identified corruption with the radical wing of the Republican party, lost interest in the Negro allies of the radicals, and looked upon them as a means of perpetuating corrupt government all over the nation as well as in the South." [19] Trumbull, no longer convinced that the ascendency of the Republican party in Congress was of paramount importance, influenced the Judiciary Committee to propose a bill removing all legal and political disabilities from several hundred white leaders of the South. Trumbull testified that the list of those whose rights were restored was drawn up without regard to party affiliation of the persons affected. Attacked by several radical senators, Trumbull hastened to reassure the Senate that he was opposed to a general amnesty. "We are not prepared at this time," he said, "to pass a general bill relieving disabilities from all persons. . . . We may do so in the future time; but I trust it will be a long time before the disabilities will be removed from the leaders of the wicked rebellion. . . . I trust the dis-

[18] *Ibid.*, p. 1030.
[19] C. Vann Woodward, *The Burden of Southern History* (Baton Rouge, 1960), pp. 105–06.

abilities will never be removed from the Davises and Masons and Slidells and Benjamins and others. I shall not be prepared to vote for any bill that will remove disabilities from that class of persons." [20] When, some time later, Congress did pass the general amnesty bill, Trumbull insisted on the exemption of about three hundred leaders of the rebellion.

This was the extent of Trumbull's participation in the third session of the Fortieth Congress—quite a restrained and inactive role for a senator who had been a legislative leader for fourteen years. Trumbull's correspondence reveals that in addition to his increased practice before the Supreme Court, he devoted a considerable amount of time to his duties as legal counsel of the Illinois Central Railroad, for which he received an annual retainer of $2,500 per year.[21] It is a commentary on the public ethics of the time that this man of unimpeachable integrity saw nothing wrong in serving as a salaried official of one of the big railroads while holding the office of a United States senator. Trumbull did not consider his connection with the railroad interests sufficient cause to refrain from speaking on and voting on pending railroad legislation.[22] Similarly, John M. Palmer, who had a reputation of high standards of personal honesty, decided when elected governor of Illinois, in 1868, to continue as a salaried trustee of the Illinois Central Railroad. J. Y. Scammon, president of the Marine Bank of Chicago, dispelled his doubts about the matter by assuring him that there was no more impropriety involved than if he, Scammon, a trustee of the University of Chicago, were elected governor.[23]

[20] *Cong. Globe,* 40 Cong., 3rd Sess., p. 1258. One of the most effective pleas for the removal of "all disabilities from the people of Mississippi" was made on the floor of the Senate by the Negro senator from Mississippi, Hiram Revels. Senator Revels was praised for his stand in an editorial in the *New York Journal of Commerce.* The editorial was reprinted in the *Chicago Tribune,* May 23, 1870.

[21] Letters from Illinois Central Railroad to Trumbull, November 8, 1871, L. T. Papers.

[22] *Cong. Globe,* 40 Cong., 3rd Sess., p. 85.

[23] J. Y. Scammon to Palmer, November 16, 1868, Palmer Papers, Illinois State Historical Library, Springfield, Ill. Scammon refers to a small college in Chicago, not to the present University of Chicago, which was founded in 1890.

Trumbull, while not wealthy, was financially well off. He owned small land properties in Springfield and Versailles, Illinois, in Afton, Iowa, and in Morgan County, Missouri, and was major stockholder and director of the Cook County National Bank of Chicago.[24] This increased prosperity did not, however, make Trumbull insensitive to the needs of the mass of poor people. On the contrary, he exhibited a keen concern for the welfare of the underprivileged, the workers and the farmers, an interest that was to become stronger with the passage of years. When the Senate debated, early in 1871, a new tariff bill, Trumbull, otherwise not very vehement on the tariff issue, battled the Pennsylvania senators, demanding the repeal of duty on coal. He denounced the coal monopoly and urged the Senate "not to make the poor people of this country pay two prices for coal that keeps them from freezing." [25]

Rather lonely and growing increasingly unhappy with the Grant administration and with reconstruction, and annoyed by the "all is well" attitude of the leaders of the Republican party, Trumbull decided to get away from Washington for a long trip to the West. He left immediately after the session of Congress, which ended in April. Before leaving he rented his house and left his old Illinois associate George T. Brown to look after his interests and properties in the capital. Trumbull's letters to Brown from Utah, Montana, and California told how greatly he enjoyed the trip.[26] It was good to get away from Washington and see the growing Western frontiers of the country. Trumbull's trip refreshed him and restored his health, but also gave him an opportunity to make important political contacts that were to prove to be valuable in the 1872 cam-

[24] Trumbull to Dr. William Jayne, December 24, 1865, Jayne Papers; Trumbull to Strover and Neilson, September 6, 1870, James McDill to Trumbull, January 19, 1872, and D. D. Spencer to Trumbull, November 1, 1871, Map of Trumbull property in Morgan County in the Trumbull Collection, Illinois State Historical Society, Springfield, Ill.

[25] *Cong. Globe*, 41 Cong., 3rd Sess. (March 3, 1871), p. 2006.

[26] George T. Brown to Trumbull, May 19, 1869, August 23, 1869, L. T. Papers.

[27] James Fergus (Helena, Montana) to Trumbull, August 28, 1869, L. T. Papers.

paign.[27] In September, 1869, Trumbull returned to Chicago, where he had settled in 1863. Here he decided to stay, since the hopes that Alton would become an important railroad, shipping, and industrial center had not been realized, and the city was suffering a severe economic depression.[28]

His trip to the West apparently confirmed Trumbull's increasingly critical attitude toward the Republican party and its national and state machines. He decided not to participate in the canvass for the Congressional and state elections in Illinois. His friend, Judge Ebenezer Peck, to whom he communicated his decision, agreed with him. "I am inclined to think . . . ," wrote Peck from Washington, "that besides in Chicago, the Republicans need cleansing. The fault is in the nominations which enable the worst and least scrupulous men in the party to control it." [29]

In a curt answer to the Republican Campaign Committee of Illinois, which invited him to "address the Republicans of Chicago," Trumbull stated that "engagements both of a public and private character will not admit of my entering actively into the canvass this fall. . . ." [30] Trumbull obviously had no desire to help in the election to Congress of Norman B. Judd, his erstwhile friend, and of General John A. Logan, who had bitterly fought his re-election to the Senate in 1867. Both men, however, won the election without difficulty, as did Trumbull's friends Burton C. Cook, John F. Farnsworth, and Shelby M. Cullom.

When the Forty-first Congress reconvened on December 6, 1869, the Republican leaders decided to renew efforts to curb the powers of the Supreme Court in order to prevent its interference with reconstruction, which was rapidly losing support in the North and was meeting with the massive resistance of the

---

[28] George T. Brown to Trumbull, September 22, 1869, L. T. Papers.

[29] Ebenezer Peck to Trumbull, October 8, 1869, L. T. Papers.

[30] J. P. Root to Trumbull, October 8, 1869; Trumbull to Root, October 9, 1869, L. T. Papers.

white population of the South. The small and diminishing group of radicals introduced two bills to prohibit the Supreme Court from declaring any act of Congress unconstitutional and to prevent it from taking any action in proceedings for a writ of habeas corpus.[31] Trumbull quickly overcame the objections of Drake and Sumner, who introduced the bills and had the proposals referred to his Judiciary Committee. On December 16 he reported a bill prepared by his committee that stated that "under the Constitution, the judicial power of the United States does not embrace political questions." [32] The bill further provided that since the Reconstruction Act of March 2, 1867, and the supplementary acts were political, they were not subject to review by the Supreme Court. It specifically enjoined the Court from any rulings on habeas corpus proceedings stemming from the execution of the Reconstruction Acts. Trumbull compounded the bad judgment he had displayed in the McCardle case and supported the bill. Speaking in support of the bill, Trumbull tried to explain his position. "I do not join," he said, "in the hue and cry which is raised in some quarters against the Supreme Court of the United States. . . . It is the division of the powers of government among different departments and then again between the States and Federal Government that constitutes the safety of liberties of the people. . . . I assent to the authority of the court to decide a law unconstitutional and void as applied to a particular case when a private right is involved. But, sir, . . . the Supreme Court had never claimed authority to decide political questions." [33]

When Congress turned to the consideration of the application of several of the ex-rebel states for admission, Trumbull devoted himself to obtaining their unconditional admission. For this effort he incurred the bitter opposition and often the enmity of the radical group of Republican senators.

---

[31] *Cong. Globe,* 41 Cong., 2nd Sess. (December 6, 1869), pp. 2–3.
[32] *Ibid.,* p. 167.
[33] *Ibid.* (December 16, 1869), pp. 167–69.

The debate on the admission of Virginia revealed that Trumbull had decided to oppose all further postponements and conditions to the admission of the Southern states. When Sumner proposed to postpone consideration of the bill, Trumbull voted with the Democrats to beat down the motion. He stated: "Now, it does seem to me, Mr. President, that there is an attempt in the Senate to devise some means by which to prevent the restoration of Virginia to her relations in the Union. Why is this, when is it to stop? *When is this question of reconstruction to end? . . . Mr. President this country is tired of this question.*" [34] This statement accurately reflected the state of mind of a basically conservative senator who had given his consent to the extreme reconstruction measures, against his better legal judgment, because of a sense of outrage at the rebels and a deeply felt moral obligation to protect the white Unionists and the freedmen in the South. It was now clear that he became disappointed with the consequences of that legislation.

The radical wrath against Trumbull exploded when he expressed his opposition to Senator Drake's amendment, which provided for the automatic exclusion of Virginia's Congressional delegation in case the legislature of that state should at any time in the future repeal its ratification of the Fifteenth Amendment.[35] Drake took the floor and stated that Trumbull's opposition did not surprise him. "I think," he continued, "it has been very apparent from the beginning of the work of Reconstruction until this time that the Senator from Illinois has had a great aversion to anything in those laws that had a grip in it." [36] Trumbull did not find it necessary to defend his record. He acknowledged that the laws he had piloted through the Senate were not perfect and sarcastically concluded: "If the Senator from Missouri had been here at that time . . . shedding the light of his knowledge . . . there would, of course, never

---

[34] *Ibid.* (January 13, 1870), p. 418. (Italics mine.)
[35] *Cong. Globe*, 41 Cong., 2nd Sess., p. 352.
[36] *Ibid.*, p. 353.

have been any occasion for any amendment of the Reconstruction Acts. . . ." [37] In supporting the admission of the Southern states, Trumbull reflected the emerging Northern state of mind on the issue of reconstruction which, in a short time, spelled the doom of the Republican governments in the South. In blunt words he told the Senate: "The people of Illinois . . . are anxious to see all the Southern states restored . . . anxious to see the material interests of the South developed, anxious to see peace and prosperity prevail. We have opened trade with them." Illinois businessmen, Trumbull concluded, wished to see the "old avenues of trade re-established." [38]

Trumbull voted against Drake's amendment, which was defeated by a vote of 44 to 11.[39] Only the radical wing voted for it. Another amendment that was adopted provided for a strong loyalty oath for the Virginia legislators. This amendment passed by a vote of 45 to 13, with almost all of the Republicans voting for it, while Trumbull joined the Democratic senators in opposition.[40] The senior Illinois senator was clearly defying party allegiance and regularity.

As the debate progressed, Trumbull became annoyed by Sumner's insistence that he was speaking on behalf of the loyal people of the South. He had suffered patiently from what he considered to be Sumner's destructive tactics when the latter opposed as inadequate the Trumbull-sponsored Thirteenth Amendment, the Freedmen's Bureau Bill, and the Civil Rights Bill. This time his patience gave way and he attacked the Massachusetts senator with an unusual sharpness. "Who inaugurated him," he asked, "as the leader of the loyal people in this country? Upon what sort of food has he fed that he comes here and talks about the loyal people of the country? Has he any higher claims to patriotism or to loyalty or to devotion to the country than anybody else?" [41]

[37] *Ibid.*, p. 352.
[38] *Ibid.*, p. 419.
[39] *Ibid.*, p. 416.
[40] *Ibid.*, p. 463.
[41] *Ibid.* (January 13, 1870), p. 421.

In his counterattack, Sumner supported Drake's charge that the Illinois senator was never a convinced member of the radical group of senators. "I know too well," Sumner said, "that the loyal people of the South, including the millions of the colored race, find little support in the Senator from Illinois . . . his course, we know, on the great subject of Reconstruction, from the early beginning to this date, has been wayward, eccentric, running off from the line of just safety and protection. . . . How often has he shown his tenderness for the remains of the rebellion and refused to join in trampling it out." [42] While Trumbull could allow himself to brush off the attack made against him by Senator Drake with a biting remark, he could not dispose of Sumner with the same ease. Trumbull reminded his colleagues that he had actively worked for and voted for all reconstruction bills. He added: ". . . and I have had charge in the Senate of the passage of nearly every one of them." Turning on Sumner, Trumbull said: "His impracticable, unreasonable, unconstitutional, and ineffectual measures would never have accomplished the object. I do not say that the Senator from Massachusetts is not the sincere friend of freedom; and especially of the colored man. I think he is, but I think his zeal outruns his judgment." [43]

Trumbull reminded the Senate that all of the reconstruction measures, except the First Reconstruction Act, which was considered by a separate committee, originated in the Committee on the Judiciary of which he was the chairman. "And yet," he said, "there rises here a Senator who charges me with having been opposed to the Reconstruction measures." Concluding Trumbull stated that he was willing to stand on his record "on the subject of Reconstruction and on the subject of freedom." [44]

Sumner in a bitter rebuttal hit at a sensitive point in Trumbull's record—his reluctance to vote for Negro suffrage. Sumner accused Trumbull of advocating, in 1865, the admission of

[42] *Ibid.*
[43] *Ibid.*, p. 423.
[44] *Ibid.*, p. 424.

Louisiana without insisting on Negro suffrage. He asked Trumbull to affirm or deny the fact that when Negro suffrage was first proposed in the Senate, it encountered his "vehement opposition." [45] When the controversy reached the peak of intensity, Senator Yates stepped in and assured the two battling senators that both of them were considered "very clever Republicans." [46]

The issue of the admission of Georgia sharpened the cleavage between Trumbull and the Republican party leaders. The attempt to prolong, by illegal legislation, the life of a corrupt state government in Georgia, just because it was Republican, was repugnant to Trumbull. He was shocked by the support given to Georgia's Governor Bullock by Senators Morton, Chandler, and Howard, even after the public disclosure that Bullock and his henchmen had given a $3,500 bribe to D. C. Forney, publisher of the Washington Chronicle. The bribe was given in exchange for editorial support.[47] On December 6, 1869, President Grant reported in his message to Congress that Georgia had, in violation of its ratified Constitution, "unseated the colored members of the legislature and admitted to seats some members who are disqualified by the third clause of the Fourteenth Amendment to the Constitution." [48] The reaction in Congress to this illegal and defiant act was swift and bitter. On December 17 the Senate passed, by an overwhelming vote of 45 to 9, an amendment to the bill for the admission of Georgia, which called on the Legislature of Georgia to ratify the Fifteenth Amendment as a condition precedent to its admission. Trumbull, who was not too much exercised over the expulsion of the Negro members, considered this amendment an "ultra measure." [49]

Later in December Congress passed a comprehensive bill

[45] Ibid., p. 422.
[46] Ibid., p. 423.
[47] Chicago Tribune, May 23, 1870.
[48] Cong. Globe, 41 Cong., 2nd Sess., p. 4.
[49] Trumbull to Dr. William Jayne, December 19, 1869, Jayne Papers.

for the "Reconstruction of the State of Georgia," [50] which converted Georgia into a separate military district. The admission of Georgia was made conditional upon the readmission of the Negro members, the taking of a loyalty oath by all legislators under the Fourteenth Amendment, and the ratification of the Fifteenth Amendment. All of these measures were put into effect by Major General Alfred H. Terry, who was appointed military commander of the Georgia Department. Republican leaders in the House, led by Representative Benjamin F. Butler, pressed for the admission of Georgia with a proviso that would have kept the Legislature in power two years beyond the legal expiration of its tenure in November, 1870. Representative John Bingham of Ohio was able to get a majority in the House for his amendment, which provided for new elections in Georgia as provided in the State Constitution.

The amended bill faced rough going in the Senate. Morton, Howard, Sumner, Wilson, and Chandler fought to have the Senate reject the Bingham amendment, but Trumbull was determined that this flagrant violation of the Constitution should be prevented. His speech on April 19, 1870, revealed Trumbull's break with the philosophy and practice of Congressional reconstruction. He adopted the traditional "states' rights" position. He told the Senate: *"So far as the Constitution goes, so far as the Reconstruction Acts go, it was perfectly competent for the people of Georgia to exclude colored men from office."* [51] He cast doubt on the veracity of the stories on the Ku Klux Klan atrocities in Georgia. Even more significant was the expression of his conviction that Republican Reconstruction could not be made to work in view of the united opposition of the white population. Reconstruction in the South was not succeeding, he argued, when a Republican regime supported by state and Federal armed forces was unable to assure the peace and safety of

[50] *Cong. Globe*, 41 Cong., 2nd Sess., p. 232.
[51] *Cong Globe*, 41 Cong., 2nd Sess., Appendix, p. 288. (Italics mine.)

all its citizens.[52] Trumbull was ready to leave the maintenance of law and order to the states, and if the price was to be the loss of political rights by the Negro population, he was ready to pay it. He said: "It is the duty of the States to preserve the peace within their own borders. Let the law abiding people of the South learn to rely on themselves." [53]

Addressing himself directly to the Negroes in the South, Trumbull appealed to them, for the sake of their own future, to resist Bullock's efforts to perpetuate himself in power. Hinting that Federal intervention in their behalf would soon cease, Trumbull warned the Negroes that "another Legislature in Georgia . . . once in power may seek to . . . exercise power in violation of your rights if you now set the example." [54] Trumbull recalled that he had never been in favor of universal franchise for the Negroes but had advocated gradual enfranchisement. Negroes, he charged, have misused the franchise by allowing themselves to be manipulated by scheming and corrupt politicians. Negro leaders and their friends should, instead, concentrate on organizing the Negroes "into labor organizations, teach them sobriety, industry and the importance of having a home that they may call their own." [55]

But Trumbull was not ready, as yet, to break with the Republican party. He tried to soften the impact of his speech by adding an eloquent tribute to the party for its record on the abolition of slavery and pro-Negro legislation. He concluded with an attack on the Democratic party. "When the history of this country shall be written it will appear that a race was emancipated and freedom established in spite of the votes of the Democratic Party." [56] Trumbull's farewell address to Reconstruction was greeted with approval in many quarters. The Nation stated that "The South ought now to be dropped by

[52] *Ibid.*, p. 290.
[53] *Ibid.*
[54] *Cong. Globe*, 41 Cong., 2nd Sess., Appendix, p. 293.
[55] *Ibid.*, p. 294.
[56] *Ibid.*, p. 294.

Congress. All that paper and words can do for it had been done. . . . Some men in Congress, notably Messrs. Trumbull and Schurz, or the Senate have urged all these considerations with force and clearness. . . ." [57] The *Springfield* (Mass.) *Republican* urged Grant to restore peace and harmony with the South.[58] Most important for Trumbull was the support he received from the *Chicago Tribune*. The *Tribune's* Washington correspondent perceptively analyzed the rift within the Republicans in the Senate. He saw "two sets of Republicans, one which may be called the *Obdurates*, composed of Howard, Sumner, Drake, Morton, Nye, Thayer, Yates, Chandler, Cameron and Brownlow; and another set which we may call the *Juridicals*, led by the Judiciary Committee, and embracing nearly all the carpetbaggers and everybody who is tired of demagoguery and misgovernment. . . ." The correspondent continued: "The two irreconcilable wings are led, probably, by Howard and Trumbull. It is an unequal contest, all the brains being on one side and all the passion and bluster on the other." [59] The pro-Grant Republican leaders in Illinois made an attempt to punish the *Tribune* for its support of Trumbull and its lack of enthusiasm for reconstruction, but the *Tribune* had "too much power to be be read out of the party." [60]

The ease with which General Logan was elected Senator to succeed Richard Yates on January 17, 1871, was distressing to Trumbull.[61] It showed clearly that the pro-Grant Republicans were in full control of the Republican party organization in Illinois. Trumbull poured his heart out to his brother-in-law: "I am disgusted at what I hear from Illinois of the *bragging, blowing,* and *bluster* of Logan's friend." [62] He was later to find,

[57] *The Nation,* April 28, 1870.
[58] *Springfield* (Mass.) *Republican,* April 23, 1870.
[59] *Chicago Tribune,* October 17, 1870.
[60] Trumbull to Dr. William Jayne, November 18, 1870, Jayne Papers.
[61] In the Republican caucus Logan received 98 votes, Oglesby, 23, and Trumbull's friend Koerner, 8. Church, *op. cit.,* p. 109.
[62] Trumbull to Dr. William Jayne, January 8, 1871, Jayne Papers.

LYMAN TRUMBULL

to his great surprise, that he worked in greater political agreement with Logan than he ever did with Yates.[63] But in the summer and winter of 1870, Trumbull was a lonely man, not only in his apartment in Washington, but also in the Senate of the United States.

[63] Trumbull to Dr. William Jayne, April 9, 1871, Jayne Papers.

15

The Making of the Reformer

AMONG THE SMALL GROUP OF PUBLIC FIGURES WHO GAVE THEIR support and leadership to the first civil reform movement, Lyman Trumbull was one of the most prominent. The movement began immediately after the Civil War and ended in failure ten years later. However, the failure was only temporary, and the early push for the reorganization of the inadequate, inefficient, and often corrupt governmental machine prepared the ground for a genuine reform. The appointment of approximately 100,000 government officials was largely in the hands of congressmen and senators whose recommendations, if they belonged to the party in power, were practically binding on the Cabinet members and even on the President. Appointments were given to friends and relatives, but most of all to political associates, in order to build a political machine in the home state or district so that re-election would be assured.

Trumbull, when elected to the Senate in 1855, and Lincoln in 1860 both faced a particularly difficult patronage problem. The elected Republican officials had no choice but to build a strong network of state and county Republican organizations, and patronage was the only sure way to accomplish this aim. Over half of Trumbull's mail between December, 1860, and April, 1861, consisted of applications or recommendations for

Federal jobs, from postmaster of Chicago to mail-route agent in Center Point, Illinois.[1]

In January and February of 1861 Trumbull received one hundred sixty-two requests for jobs.[2] Some of these letters were not requests but demands. One correspondent told Trumbull that he gave someone fifty dollars because the person told him that "he had some claims on you and would secure it [the job] for me." [3] Another wanted to become postmaster so that "the voice of at least two-thirds of the Republicans of Chicago may be heard in the matter." [4] Seldom, if ever, did Trumbull's correspondents bother to mention their qualifications for the jobs they wanted. The brazen and often shocking method of asking for or demanding jobs was not limited to the lowly and uneducated. Even when Joseph Medill of the *Chicago Tribune* asked for the appointment of his partner, John Locke Scripps, as Chicago's postmaster, he did not hesitate to explain that "If Mr. Scripps has it, the country postmasters of the Northwest would work to extend our circulation." [5]

Reluctantly but patiently, Trumbull went about the patronage business, because he had no other choice. County conventions nominated state senators and representatives who, when elected, usually went to Springfield pledged to vote for a candidate for the U.S. Senate. In order to assure his re-election, Trumbull was compelled to recruit key Republican leaders in most Illinois counties. These men remained indebted to him and owed him their political allegiance—they kept faith with him as he did with them. This group included Burton C. Cook of LaSalle County, George T. Brown and Joseph Gillespie of Edwardsville, Dr. George T. Allen of Alton, D. L. Phillips of

---

[1] Ebenezer Peck to Trumbull, February 25, 1861; A. J. Swam to Trumbull; February 24, 1861; Alexander Moore to Trumbull, February 16, 1861, L. T. Letters.

[2] Most of the patronage mail is in the L. T. Letters.

[3] Miller Husky to Trumbull, L. T. Letters.

[4] A. Jonas to Trumbull, March 16, 1861, L. T. Letters.

[5] Joseph Medill to Trumbull, March 4, 1861, L. T. Papers.

Springfield, Ebenezer Peck of Chicago, and many others. His most intimate political lieutenant was his brother-in-law, Dr. William Jayne of Springfield, who often served in the Illinois Legislature. Accepting patronage as a fact of contemporary political life, Trumbull always managed to keep Dr. Jayne on the public payroll. During the Civil War, he got Jayne appointed governor of the Dakota Territory,[6] and in 1869, after failing to get for him a consular job in Russia, Trumbull succeeded in having Grant appoint his brother-in-law a pension agent, a post which carried a relatively large salary and demanded little work.[7] With the notable exception of the Cabinet post for Norman B. Judd, which Lincoln refused to give him, and Lincoln's delay in giving John M. Palmer of Illinois a general's commission, Trumbull had no reason to complain about his success as a patronage dispenser. Lincoln testified that an Illinois congressman, William Kellogg, "has had more favors than any other Illinois member, not excepting, I think, Judge Trumbull." [8]

As years went by, Trumbull became alarmed at the operations of the political patronage system, its inefficiency and corruption, and the abuses that became particularly apparent during the Grant administration. His own mail reflected the corrupting influence of the spoils system. Disregarding his own excellent reputation for propriety, honesty, and integrity, his friends did not hesitate to deluge him with requests for jobs that amounted to blatant robbing of the public treasury. Dr. C. H. Ray wrote to urge Trumbull to have him appointed a tax appraiser in Chicago, because he simply needed an additional job. General John McClernand asked to have his son, a West Point graduate, assigned to the staff of General Sheridan, who was being sent to observe the war between France and Prussia, so that he could

---

[6] Certificate of appointment signed by Secretary of State William Seward, in Jayne Papers.

[7] Letter of recommendation from Trumbull to Grant, March 9, 1869, L. T. Papers.

[8] Thomas, *op. cit.*, p. 252.

see Europe.[9] An old friend and political associate, H. G. McPike of Alton, bluntly asked Trumbull to get him a job as a "special agent" of the Treasury Department, because he planned to take a trip to California. He added, "I want something that will pay my expenses, I do not care for more. Will you do me the favor to solicit this for me?" [10]

The movement for a civil service reform was started in the House by Representatives Thomas A. Jenckes of Rhode Island and William H. Armstrong of Pennsylvania.[11] Jenckes introduced the first civil service reform bill on December 20, 1865. The bill provided for competitive examinations for all but a few Federal civil servants and for the establishment of a board of three civil service commissioners.[12] On Thaddeus Stevens' motion, the Jenckes bill was tabled, because the Republicans were eager to pass the Tenure of Office Bill in its stead.[13] In July, 1868, Jenckes attempted to revive his bill but failed to get a two-thirds majority to support him.[14]

On December 7, 1869, Lyman Trumbull announced his support for the reform bill submitted by Senator Carl Schurz, which embodied the main features of the Jenckes measure. He then introduced a bill of his own, which in effect supplemented the Jenckes and Schurz bills. The bill prohibited members of Congress to solicit jobs from the President and from the Cabinet. The measure provided that any member of Congress who should, unsolicited, recommend an appointment to a Federal office would be guilty of misdemeanor and fined $1,000. The President was prohibited from lawfully appointing anyone so

[9] Dr. C. H. Ray to Trumbull, August 18, 1870; General John A. McClernand to Trumbull, July 19, 1870, L. T. Papers.

[10] H. G. McPike to Trumbull, August 2, September 21, 1869, L. T. Papers.

[11] See an excellent monograph on Jenckes and the early civil service reform movement in Ari Hoogenboom, "Thomas A. Jenckes and Civil Service Reform," *The Mississippi Valley Historical Review,* Vol. XLVII, No. 4 (March, 1961), pp. 636–38.

[12] *Cong. Globe,* 39 Cong., 1st Sess. (December 20, 1865), p. 98.

[13] Hoogenboom, *op. cit.,* p. 642.

[14] *Cong. Globe,* 40 Cong., 2nd Sess. (July 13, 1868), p. 4003.

recommended.[15] Appointments, Trumbull said, are "dictated and controlled in a vast majority of cases by influence unknown to the Constitution." [16]

Trumbull confessed that he too had to engage in distasteful patronage practices, because a senator who refused to solicit jobs was "subject to the imputation of being neglectful of [his] friends." [17] His bill, if adopted, Trumbull concluded, would allow Congressmen to devote more time to their legislative duties. After a brief debate, the bill was removed from the agenda by a resolution to send it to a committee.

On June 30, 1870, Representative Armstrong, having consulted with the reform group that included Trumbull, Jenckes, Schurz, and Sumner, introduced a joint resolution that authorized the President to establish rules and regulations governing the appointment of civil servants. These regulations included steps to ascertain the candidate's "age, health, character, knowledge and ability for the branch of service into which he seeks to enter." The bill also provided for the appointment of commissioners to execute its provisions.[18] Representative Armstrong had also consulted Grant and had received his approval for the resolution,[19] but in spite of this endorsement, Armstrong was not able to get the resolution adopted in the House. A short time before the adjournment of the session, Trumbull ingeniously moved the adoption of the Armstrong resolution as a rider to the civil appropriation bill. Senator Williams of Oregon moved to table the amendment, but the motion lost by one vote, 26 to 25. The amendment was then adopted by a vote of 32 to 24.[20] When the House, a few hours later, debated the civil appropriation bill, Representative John A. Logan of Illi-

---

[15] *Cong. Globe,* 41 Cong., 2nd Sess. (December 7, 1869), 17–18.
[16] *Ibid.,* p. 17.
[17] *Ibid.,* p. 18.
[18] Bill discussed on the basis of the text printed in the *Cong. Globe,* 41 Cong., 3rd Sess. (March 3, 1871), p. 1997.
[19] Hoogenboom, *op. cit.,* p. 656.
[20] *Cong. Globe,* 41 Cong., 3rd Sess. (March 3, 1871), p. 1993.

nois denounced Trumbull's rider as "the most obnoxious bill of this character which has come before this House." [21] But since the House was in a hurry to adjourn, the bill, with the Senate's amendment, was approved by a vote of 90 to 20.[22] This was the first civil service reform bill in the history of the country, and the major credit for its adoption belongs to Trumbull.

When the Senate reconvened in December, 1871, Trumbull pressed for a thorough investigation of abuses and corruption and for civil service reform. To attain these objectives he introduced a motion to form a Joint Select Committee on Retrenchment to include four senators and seven representatives. The motion gave the committee sweeping powers to investigate the expenditures of all branches of government, to examine accountability of the monies spent, and to inquire whether any funds had been expended illegally. The committee was also to report on what offices could be abolished, to recommend laws to revamp the civil service so as to provide for competitive examinations to be given by "proper boards," and to make recommendations for "withdrawing the public service from being used as an instrument of political or party patronage." [23] A few days later Trumbull delivered an impassioned plea for cleaning up corruption and for civil service reform. He told the Senate that he was convinced that since Grant in his message to Congress of December 4 referred to "numerous defalcations and convictions of dishonest servants," the President would welcome a thorough inquiry by the Joint Congressional Committee. As a matter of fact, said Trumbull, Grant specifically asked Congress to aid him in having the defrauders punished. He specifically pointed to the abuses and corruption uncovered in the operations of the New York Custom House and urged a rigorous inquiry as

[21] *Ibid.*, p. 1935.
[22] *Ibid.*, p. 1936.
[23] *Cong. Globe*, 42 Cong., 2nd Sess. (December 7, 1871), p. 42.

to "whether money is expended for partisan purposes, for selfish purposes of a faction in the party." [24]

Trumbull received a great deal of mail from leaders and plain folk in Illinois hailing his position on the need for a drastic civil service reform. A Republican leader from Bloomington, Illinois, where Trumbull was not very popular, wrote him that the Bloomington Pantagraph had published the entire text of Trumbull's Senate speech. A constituent from a small hamlet expressed his conviction that only reform could save the Republican party, and a Chicago businessman wrote: "You and Carl Schurz are held in highest estimation by the educated classes and property owners." A farmer from Carbon Cliff, Illinois, simply said, "Thank God, you are in the United States Senate." [25]

In a speech defending the platform of the Missouri liberal Republicans, delivered on February 23, 1872, Trumbull angered Republican leaders by a blunt charge that Federal patronage was treated by them "mainly as party spoils." [26] Senator Morton counter-attacked by accusing Trumbull of doing his share in enjoying the spoils of his high office by recommending many of his friends for Federal appointments. Before answering the charge, Trumbull decided to find out how many recommendations for jobs he had made during the Grant administration. He wrote to all Cabinet members requesting a list of his recommendations for jobs. The replies indicated that Trumbull had recommended and gotten about one hundred Federal jobs for his constituents and friends. [27] Among those who had benefited were four of his downstate Illinois most faithful county leaders: Dr. Jayne, who had been appointed pension agent, Dr. George T. Allen, who had become governor of Wyoming, George T.

[24] Ibid., p. 52.

[25] A. Gridley to Trumbull, December 13, 1871; Joseph Whitmire, to Trumbull, December 15, 1871; George H. Chambers to Trumbull, December 15, 1871; William S. Thomas to Trumbull, December 18, 1871, L. T. Papers.

[26] Cong. Globe, 42 Cong., 2nd Sess., Appendix, p. 84.

[27] Cong. Globe, 42 Cong., 2nd Sess., Appendix, p. 1174.

Brown, who had been appointed a member of the Mexican Treaty Claims Commission, and George Edward Kitchell, who had been appointed U.S. marshal of southern Illinois. Trumbull's papers include a compilation of the replies he received, to be used undoubtedly in a reply to Morton. Recognizing that Morton's charge was basically true, he did not bring the question to the Senate floor.[28]

The relations between Sumner and Trumbull were not friendly, but Trumbull came to his adversary's aid when President Grant decided to oust the Massachusetts senator from his post as chairman of the Senate's Foreign Relations Committee. Trumbull did not take part in the heated debates on the ratification of the treaty proposed by Grant calling for the annexation of Santo Domingo. In a remark to his colleagues he said that he sat for a month without making any speeches because he considered the debate senseless since there was no bill before the Senate on the question.[29] However, when Grant, with the aid of Senators Morton, and Chandler, decided to punish Sumner for his opposition to the Santo Domingo Treaty, Lyman Trumbull did speak out against this unjust and unprecendented action. Horace White later related that he went to Washington and, after consultation with Trumbull, visited Senator Howe of Wisconsin, chairman of the Republican caucus, and pleaded with him "past midnight" not to drop Sumner, but to no avail.[30]

Trumbull defended Sumner, in spite of their long and often bitter political differences, purely as a matter of principle. The flagrant interference of the President in the internal matter of the organization of the Senate was contrary to his life-long devotion to the principle of the separation of powers. The dictatorial manner in which Morton and Chandler imposed their will on the Republican caucus that took the ouster decision con-

---

[28] Departments of Justice, Treasury, War, and Interior to Trumbull, February 28, 1872; Attorney General and Postmaster General to Trumbull, February 29, 1872; and the Department of State to Trumbull, March 1, 1872, L. T. Papers.

[29] Cong. Globe, 42 Cong., 1st Sess. (April 1, 1871), p. 472.

[30] White, op. cit., pp. 346–47.

firmed his disillusionment and distrust of his own party. "I am not," Trumbull stated, "a special friend of the Senator from Massachusetts. He and I, during our long course of service here, have had occasion to differ, and differ, I am sorry to say, unpleasantly. But sir, that will not prevent me from trying to do justice to the Senator from Massachusetts." [31] Trumbull suggested that the party could hardly afford any more division and bitterness in its ranks, but his pleas were not heeded. The majority approved the report of the caucus, and Sumner was removed.

Trumbull's relations with the Republican party leaders were severely tested in March, 1871, when the radicals proposed in Congress to curb the Ku Klux Klan terror in the South. He deplored the beatings, the lynchings and the massacres of Negroes, but he was moving to a view that the continuous imposition of Federal armed force on the Southern states was undermining orderly constitutional processes and violated the principle of states' rights. He was also convinced that the Republican governments in the South were corrupt and inefficient and that opposition to them of the overwhelming majority of the white population would soon sweep them out of existence. In view of this prospect, the sooner the Negroes made peace and came to terms with the Redeemers the better it would be for their own safety. "The moment political power," he asserted, "is likely to pass from the hands of the carpetbaggers and scalawags in the South, as everybody knows it must after a short time, a hue and cry is set up so as to enable them to retain power." [32]

The Ku Klux Klan Bill, which was introduced in the Senate with the backing of the Grant administration, authorized the suspension of the writ of habeas corpus in sections of the South where the Redemptionist terror reigned and where the state authorities were unable to suppress the violence. It also gave the President the right to send Federal army and navy units to the

[31] *Cong. Globe,* 42 Cong., 1st Sess. (March 10, 1871), p. 49.
[32] Trumbull to Dr. William Jayne, March 24, 1871, Jayne Papers.

South to suppress insurrection and terror.[33] Contemplating his
vote on the measure, Trumbull at first hesitated. "I am in
doubt," he wrote to his brother-in-law, "whether to vote for
the Ku Klux Bill or not. It is a great humbug got up by Butler,
Morton for political purposes to enable them to carry the
South." [34] Trumbull was too well informed to have really believed
that the Ku Klux Bill was "humbug." The Klan's record of
beatings, maimings, and lynchings was no humbug, but a stark
horrible reality. Professor Randall wrote that, "Whatever
credit the Klan may have had as a champion of the Southern
white was marred by the irresponsible and unscrupulous methods
which it used. . . . In the case of an organization whose methods
were in fact criminal it was a serious thing to have its deeds
masked by a false front of patriotism, with its members claiming
popular applause as protectors of society." [35] A Southern editor
and historian put it this way: "Most of the white South resisted
the Radicals with any weapon and with any means at hand. . . .
Southern white man was almost always the aggressor." [36]

Violence was used because "many so-called conservatives . . .
plainly and simply . . . thought it was sinful to give so-called
Africans the right to share in governments framed by a clearly
superior Anglo-Saxon race." [37] In his study on the Negro militia
in the South, Professor Singletary, after an examination of the
generally accepted story of pillage, rape, and killings committed
by Negro soldiers, concludes, "For even had the [Negro] militia
refrained from committing a single act antagonistic to the
whites, in all probability they would still have been destroyed.
The very fact that the Negro wore a uniform and thereby en-

[33] Walter L. Fleming, *Documentary History of Reconstruction*, 2 vols. (Cleveland, 1907), II, 123–28.
[34] Trumbull to Dr. William Jayne, April 9, 1871, Jayne Papers.
[35] J. G. Randall, *The Civil War and Reconstruction*, pp. 855–57.
[36] Hodding Carter, *The Angry Scar* (Garden City, N.Y., 1959), p. 199.
[37] Bernard A. Weisberger, "The Dark and Bloody Ground of Reconstruction Historiography," *The Journal of Southern History*, XXV (November, 1959), pp. 437–38.

joyed certain rights was an affront to most Southern States." [38]

When the Judiciary Committee passed the bill, Trumbull refused to present it to the Senate, and Senator George F. Edmunds of Vermont took charge of the bill. By April 11, the day the bill was presented, Trumbull had resolved his doubts and decided to oppose it on constitutional grounds. He told the Senate that the bill under consideration violated a basic principle that "the Government of the United States was formed for national and general purposes and not for the protection of the individual in his personal rights of person and property." [39] Trumbull argued that the Civil Rights Act merely guaranteed for Negroes the same rights that the whites had, while the Ku Klux Klan Bill was specifically intended for the protection of Negroes. [40]

Trumbull further argued that the expression "privileges and immunities" in the Constitution applied only to civil rights and not to political rights, and that the states might, if they so chose, abridge the latter for any class of its citizens. [41] The Federal government, he maintained, had the right to use its power only to protect the authority and interests of the United States. "But, sir," he continued, "I am not willing to undertake to enter the States for the purpose of punishing individual offenses against another. We, in my judgement, have no authority to do that . . . individual rights are safest, as a general rule, when left to the protection of the locality." [42] His speech was frequently interrupted by Senators Edmunds, Howe, and Wilson, who pointed out that in 1866 and in 1867 Trumbull had expressed different views on the same subject. [43]

[38] Otis A. Singletary, *Negro Militia and Reconstruction* (Austin, Texas, 1957), p. 152.

[39] *Cong. Globe*, 42 Cong., 1st Sess. (April 11, 1871), p. 575.

[40] *Ibid.*, p. 575.

[41] *Ibid.*, p. 576.

[42] *Ibid.*, p. 578.

[43] The *Chicago Tribune*, always sympathetic, praised Trumbull for "replying with utmost equanimity and readiness to the many interruptions of the other Senators." April 20, 1871.

Reconciliation with the South became Trumbull's primary objective. "It is amnesty that I want," he told the Senate in a speech advocating the repeal of disabilities, "I want to see the peace of the country restored." [44] In pressing for the removal of political disabilities from the white Southerners he was well aware that the amnesty and the return of the Southern governments to the Democratic rule would mean the disfranchisement of the Negroes. In order to end the corruption and to attain peace and harmony, which would bring increased trade and economic cooperation between the North and the South, he was willing to pay this price. The Fourteenth Amendment, he reiterated, did not pertain to political or social rights—only to the rights of citizens as individuals.

Trumbull opposed Sumner's effort to attach to the amnesty bill a civil rights amendment that would have outlawed racial discrimination. "I vote no," Trumbull said, "without regard to the merit of the particular amendment . . . as I am against them all." [45] In the vote on the bill, with Sumner's amendment, Trumbull voted with the Democrats. The vote was 33 to 19 for the bill, not enough to pass because as a proposed constitutional amendment it needed a two-thirds majority.

"I became satisfied in 1872," wrote Trumbull a few years later, "that the Republican organization had become a body corrupt and that the people were being plundered in almost all branches of the public service." [46] Trumbull was not ready to leave the party although he felt that some of its leaders were forcing him to do so.[47] "I have not committed myself," Trumbull wrote to a friend, "to any independent movement." [48] However, he admitted that it was becoming for him ever harder to stay in a

[44] *Cong. Globe,* 42 Cong., 2nd Sess (February 8, 1872), p. 901.
[45] *Ibid.,* p. 896.
[46] Trumbull to James H. Wilson, January 4, 1876, General James H. Wilson MSS, Library of Congress.
[47] Trumbull to W. G. Flagg, January 10, 1872, L. T. Papers.
[48] *Ibid.*

party whose leaders "hate and despise you." [49] Evidence was quickly piling up that the Republican leaders were determined to oppose any genuine investigation of corruption "in fear that its exposure would injure the party." [50]

The long-delayed encounter between Trumbull and the leaders of the Republican party came on the Senate floor on February 23, 1872. The offensive was launched, surprisingly, by Trumbull, who began his elaborate and well-prepared speech with an attack on Senator Oliver P. Morton. "Chief among those," he stated, "who would subordinate the public welfare to party stands the Senator from Indiana." [51] During the many years that Trumbull had been in the Senate, he had carefully avoided such personal attacks. As a rule he spoke about issues and not about persons. It now became obvious that Trumbull had made his decision to throw his lot with the insurgent reform group of Republicans, acting within the framework of the party. He castigated Morton and several other pro-Grant senators who had blocked or vitiated the work of the select investigation committees appointed by Congress. "And so, sir," he continued, "when the country is reeking with corruption, and an investigation is proposed to ascertain whether it exists among government officials, we are met with the cry of 'party'! 'party'!" [52] In speaking about reconstruction, Trumbull confessed that the disfranchisement of the whites in the South was a tragic mistake, because it brought to power "corrupt and dishonest persons." Consequently, "the people of some of these States have been plundered by their State governments without example in the history of this country." [53] Trumbull, who had often spoken of his hatred and contempt for the rebels, now asserted that the rule of the ex-confederates in the South would have been

[49] *Ibid.*
[50] Trumbull to Hiram R. Enoch, February 29, 1872, L. T. Papers.
[51] *Cong. Globe,* 42 Cong., 2nd Sess., Appendix, p. 82.
[52] *Ibid.*, p. 83.
[53] *Ibid.*, p. 85.

preferable, because "whatever may be said of their guilt as rebels, [they] were neither robbers nor thieves." [54]

Morton answered Trumbull with a hard-hitting speech. He wondered why Trumbull, who had spoken so eloquently about the corruption of the reconstruction government had "very little to say in regard to the murders, whippings, exiles and burnings that have taken place in the South for the last four years." [55] He charged that Trumbull had for two years resisted the passage of any bill that would have protected the Southern Negroes from the Ku Klux Klan terror. Morton took Trumbull to task for defeating Sumner's civil rights amendment to the amnesty bill by voting with the Democrats. Since a change of two votes would have given the bill a two-thirds majority, Morton held the Illinois senator personally responsible for its defeat. Commenting on Trumbull's castigation of interference by congressmen in Federal appointments, Morton charged that Trumbull was not averse to making full use of the spoils system. His inquiries proved, said Morton, that Trumbull got from the Grant administration jobs for 103 of his friends.[56]

As for partisanship, Morton pointed out that until recently Trumbull had been as partisan as any Republican senator. Morton suggested that Trumbull's quarrel with the Republican party had its origin in his aspirations for the Presidential nomination, which he hoped to get either from the Democrats or "at the hands of a new party, yet to be organized." [57] Acknowledging Trumbull's power, Morton concluded by saying that he still wished for Trumbull to remain a Republican but, he said, "I have not been so blind that . . . I could not see where he was drifting." [58]

[54] *Cong. Globe*, 42 Cong., 2nd Sess., Appendix, p. 82.
[55] *Ibid.*, p. 1180.
[56] *Ibid.*, p. 1181.
[57] *Ibid.*
[58] *Ibid.*, p. 1182.

16

The Reluctant Candidate

NO ONE IN WASHINGTON COULD HAVE BEEN MORE PLEASED THAN was Lyman Trumbull to hear the news in the summer of 1870 that 250 liberals, under the leadership of Carl Schurz and Gratz Brown, had bolted the regular Missouri Republican State Convention. Trumbull was in full agreement with the platform of the Missouri Liberal Republicans, which included amnesty for the South, the withdrawal of Federal troops from the Southern states, civil service reform, and the curbing of monopolies. He was also in sympathy, although without very strong convictions in the matter, with the free trade movement, which sought an alliance with the Liberal Republicans and which had its base in New England and in New York, under the leadership of E. L. Godkin and William Cullen Bryant of New York, Edward Atkinson of Massachusetts, and David A. Wells of Connecticut. Horace White, the editor of the *Chicago Tribune* and an old-time free-trader, had close ties to this group. In spite of White's urgings, Trumbull, who had lacked strong convictions on the tariff issue, made no overtures to the free-trade Eastern leaders. He felt that any strong free-trade pronouncement would antagonize the protectionists led by Horace Greeley.[1]

[1] Horace White to Trumbull, January 31, 1872, L. T. Papers.

The subsequent election of the Liberal Republican slate of candidates, headed by Brown, who was elected governor of Missouri, pleased Trumbull very much. His disillusionment with reconstruction, his disgust with the corruption and abuses of the Grant administration, and his constant feuding with the leaders of the Republican party had caused him to reassess his political affiliations and future. He did not contemplate leaving the Republican party, to which he had a strong allegiance and through which he gained power and prominence in national affairs. He was also inordinately proud of the record of the Republican party in saving the Union, in defeating the attempt to extend slavery into the territories, and in abolishing Negro slavery. He was still bitter about the record of the Democrats during the Civil War and during Reconstruction. The Democratic party was still, in his eyes, the party of Copperheads that had for years aided and abetted the hateful rebels and that had done all it could to perpetuate slavery. He also repeatedly told his correspondents that the " democrats are so demoralized that they cannot rally as a party." [2] Thus, in fact, Trumbull was in the awkward position of being nominally a Republican, but unwilling to return to the Democratic fold. This was an uncomfortable position for an active, reasonably ambitious politician and a United States senator whose term in the Senate was to expire in 1873. The emergence of the Liberal Republican movement in Missouri, whose leaders announced their intention to convert it into a national movement, provided a solution to his personal dilemma.

Reflecting popular opinion, Trumbull did not blame Grant personally for the corruption in his government. He estimated that about one fourth of all the government revenues were being stolen, but he tended to absolve the President of blame. The guilty ones were, he was convinced, Grant's associates and the determined group of Republican senators led by Morton, Conkling, and Chandler, who insisted on blocking any move

[2] Trumbull to A. Grimshaw, February 29, 1872, L. T. Papers.

for effective investigation and the elimination of abuses. In an interview with a reporter of the *New York Times*, in December, 1871, Trumbull stated that "Grant is in the main, a conservative man. He has made mistakes. But I cannot say they justify his removal." [3] He assured the reporter that his personal relations with the President were "very friendly" and that it was disagreeable to him to see his name mentioned as a possible candidate for President in 1872. "I believe," he continued, "that the defeat of General Grant would involve a reaction in the South whose consequences would be even worse than the present state of affairs." [4] To a direct question of the reporter as to whether he would allow his name to be put forward as Grant's opponent as a "conservative candidate," Trumbull answered in the negative. He was satisfied in his Senate post, and while he was daily striving to accomplish reforms within and through his party, he did not believe that "a revolution of parties would be salutary." [5] Trumbull was conciliatory, but the pro-Grant leaders in Congress were not. When they finally agreed to the establishment of a Select Investigating Committee, they severely limited its scope of activity and its authority and added insult to injury by failing to include Trumbull, who had proposed the investigation, as a member of the committee.[6] Charles Sumner, whose reform sympathies brought him into closer relations with Trumbull, protested this arbitrary action.

Early in 1871 Trumbull began to receive letters from many parts of the country urging him to run for the Presidential nomination at the Republican National Convention as an alternate choice to General Grant. Significantly, the first letters came from the Far West, testifying to the impression and the

---

[3] *New York Times,* December 6, 1871.

[4] *Ibid.*

[5] *Ibid.* Much later Trumbull still attempted to picture Grant as the innocent victim of his crooked associates. "I think," he wrote, "much better of him [Grant] than of his surroundings." Trumbull to W. G. Flagg, January 10, 1872, L. T. Papers.

[6] White, *op. cit.,* p. 367.

contacts Trumbull made on his long trip to Montana, Utah, and California in the summer of 1869. A San Francisco Republican leader wrote to Trumbull that "there is a strong current moving here in favor of Trumbull and Hancock for our next President on a conservative national platform embracing Civil Service Reform, Revenue Tariff, and the subordination of the military to the civil power." [7] Joseph T. Brown, mayor of St. Louis and president of the Pacific Railroad of Missouri, suggested to Trumbull that he should realize that he had no future in the regular Republican organization and suggested that he declare himself as a liberal or independent candidate for the highest office in the country.[8] Several of the correspondents assured him that he would have the support of the Democrats. Wilbur F. Storey, the influential editor of the Democratic *Chicago Times*, stated that he was ready to support Trumbull as a second choice, after the Supreme Court justice David Davis.[9] Some reports indicated that the anti-Grant sentiment was growing in Illinois, especially in the traditionally Democratic southern part of the state.[10] An important Republican newspaper, the *Rockford Journal*, indicated that it was ready to support a Republican insurgent movement. Trumbull was warned, however, that he must declare himself soon as a candidate and must build an organization in Illinois, because Judge Davis' supporters were very active. He was repeatedly assured that he had many warm friends and supporters in the Republican and Democratic ranks. Gradually, the pro-Trumbull movement was gaining strength and its leaders urged the Illinois senator to give them a sign of encouragement.[11]

[7] O. P. Fitzgerald to Trumbull, January 4, 1871, L. T. Papers. (Italics mine.) It is of interest to note that Trumbull was acceptable for the Presidency by some as a *conservative* and by others as a *liberal* candidate. To both groups the terms meant the same—a man advocating reform.

[8] Joseph T. Brown to Trumbull, December 12, 1871, L. T. Papers.

[9] W. T. B. Jackson to Trumbull, December 29, 1871, L. T. Papers.

[10] D. W. Wood to Trumbull, December 12, 1871, L. T. Papers.

[11] W. B. Fyfe, Henry L. Boltwood to Trumbull, December 1, December 19, 1871, L. T. Papers.

Trumbull's candidacy also attracted some notice in the East. The *Springfield* (Mass.) *Republican* listed him among six men who could get its support for the Presidency.[12] The *New York Sun* came out with Trumbull's name on the masthead as its candidate for President.[13] In the fall and winter of 1871, Trumbull held several meetings in New York with political leaders and publishers of varying shades of political opinion. They differed on many questions, but were united in their determination to defeat Grant and Grantism. Among those attending their meetings were August Belmont, William Dorsheimer, Charleton Lewis, Whitelaw Reid, Henry Watterson, and Horace Greeley. The agenda included some weighty questions. There were some who felt that the Liberal Republicans should remain an integral part of the Republican party and should not attempt to nominate their own candidates for the 1872 elections; others counseled a complete break with the party and the establishment of a third party.

Trumbull's reaction to the many expressions of support he received, and to the pressure put on him to declare himself as a candidate for the Presidency, was cautious. He informed a relative that "Some persons are writing me on the subject, but I do not think it best for me to do anything about it." He added that while Horace White of the *Chicago Tribune* and Charleton Lewis of the *New York Evening Post* were for him, he believed that the "old impeachment radical element" would be strong enough to defeat him in any national convention.[14] Mayor Brown of St. Louis was told that his talk of Trumbull as a candidate was not only not helpful, but it actually "impairs the influence I might otherwise have in uncovering abuses and bringing about those reforms which I have advocated for some years." [15] Trumbull assured his correspondent that he was happy

[12] *Springfield* (Mass.) *Republican,* November 17, 1871.
[13] C. D. Hay to Trumbull, January 3, 1872, L. T. Papers.
[14] Trumbull to Dr. William Jayne, March 24, 1871, Jayne Papers.
[15] Trumbull to Joseph Brown, December 25, 1871, L. T. Papers.

as a Senator and that his highest ambition was to introduce into public life standards of purity and morality.[16] He ignored requests from important Republican leaders in several states urging him to work for his nomination or at least to permit them to announce that he would accept the nomination.[17] And yet there was a hint of a well-concealed desire for the nomination in the fact that Trumbull sent to his friends hundreds of copies of the *New York Sun*, which carried his name as its candidate for the Presidential nomination.

The exchange of correspondence between Trumbull and the venerable and respected Republican leader from Salem, Illinois, Judge Silas Bryan (father of William Jennings Bryan) supports the contention of Trumbull's critics, who have maintained that his lack of warmth and of the popular touch kept him from the White House. Bryan wrote Trumbull a warm letter of support. He told him that he had come to believe in him as a "Providential Man" in the nation's history and expressed the belief that Trumbull would be elected the next President on a "moderate Republican" ticket. Bryan volunteered to write a number of articles "on the Providential Man for the next Presidency." In his answer, Trumbull, after a rather perfunctory expression of thanks, coldly repeated his contention that he was only interested in cleaning out corruption and that any talk about his possible nomination merely hampered his efforts in that direction.[18] Silas Bryan never repeated his offer to promote Trumbull's name for the Presidency.

The Liberal Republicans in Missouri, greatly encouraged by the widespread sympathy for their victory in the state's elections, gave the impetus for a national reform movement. The Missouri State Liberal Republican Convention met in Jefferson City on January 24, 1872, and passed a platform that called for

[16] *Ibid.*

[17] A. Bainbridge, C. D. Hay, and Levi North, S. S. Prime to Trumbull, January 4 and 3, 16 and 18, 1872, L. T. Papers.

[18] Silas Bryan to Trumbull, December 19, 1872; Trumbull to Silas Bryan, December 25, 1872, L. T. Papers.

reconciliation with the South, a general amnesty, the removal of disabilities from Southern whites, a reduction of the tariff, state autonomy, and civil service reform. It also called for a mass national convention of Liberal Republicans to meet in Cincinnati on the first Monday in May, 1872. Trumbull ignored earnest pleas from several prominent men in Missouri who were ready to work to have the Missouri convention pledged to him and not to Governor Gratz Brown.[19] He still was not sure whether to break his remaining ties with the Republican party or whether to concentrate on working for reform within its ranks. "I have not committed myself," he confided to Dr. Jayne, "to any independent movement. I do not intend to be driven out of the Republican party, although some men would be glad to drive me out." [20] Trumbull conceded that many faithful Republicans were of the opinion that the only way to clean up the Washington mess was to run "an Independent Republican who would probably get most of the Democratic vote and be elected." [21] He did not concur in this appraisal of the political situation, but he vigorously defended the Missouri Liberal platform from attacks of the pro-Grant Republican leaders. Answering a charge by Senator Morton that the liberal platform contradicted established policies and commitments of the Republican party, Trumbull read to the Senate the planks of the platform and argued that they embodied the true historical aims and principles of the party.[22]

This clearly defined public position of Trumbull on the nature of the Liberal Republican movement was not as unequivocal in his private views expressed to his friends and supporters. After a great deal of soul-searching, Trumbull made up his mind on several cardinal points and evolved an approach to the Cincinnati convention. He was determined to do all in his power

[19] Robert L. Lindsay to Trumbull, January 19, 1872, L. T. Papers.
[20] Trumbull to Dr. William Jayne, January 10, 1872, Jayne Papers.
[21] Ibid.
[22] Cong. Globe, 42 Cong., 2nd Sess. (February 23, 1879), Appendix, pp. 84–85.

to make the Cincinnati convention an impressive and representative meeting. This was to be, for the time being, the main
objective, and therefore all talk about the nomination of candidates, including his own nomination, was to be pushed into the
background. Trumbull became convinced that in view of the
efforts of Grant's leaders in Congress to block any meaningful
investigation of corruption, reforms could be accomplished only
by rescuing "the Republican Party . . . from the hands of those
who are using it for mere selfish and partisan purposes." [23] The
support given to the Cincinnati convention by Senators Schurz,
Tipton, Fenton, and Robinson, and with some reservations by
Sumner, lessened to some extent the degree of Trumbull's
political isolation in the Senate.[24]

The Democrats, Trumbull reasoned, were demoralized and
"cannot rally as a party." [25] Their objective was to beat Grant,
and since they could beat him only with the help of a Republican split, Trumbull was sure, as early as February, 1872, that
the Democratic national convention would not nominate its
own candidates and would support any reform candidate chosen
in Cincinnati.[26] Since he was convinced that the Democrats had
no freedom to chart their own course in 1872, he was determined to keep them away from the Cincinnati convention and
prevent the leaders of the new movement from making any
deals or bargains with them. There were several other reasons
for Trumbull's insistence on this point. He knew that because
of his record on reconstruction legislation he would not be the
first choice of the Democrats. They preferred Judge Davis, who
had opposed the Emancipation Proclamation and most of the

[23] Trumbull to A. M. Grimshaw, February 29, 1872, L. T. Papers.

[24] These senators held many consultations in Washington to chart their course.
George Julian, *op. cit.,* p. 333. Also Carl Schurz to Trumbull, January 21, 1872,
L. T. Papers.

[25] *Ibid.*

[26] Trumbull to Hiram R. Enoch, February 29, 1872, L. T. Papers. Trumbull was
assured by a correspondent who toured many big cities in the East that any Liberal
Republican nominee would get "the almost universal support of the Democracy,"
J. H. Caldwell to Trumbull, January 27, 1872, L. T. Papers. Also D. H. Danolds
to Trumbull, January 29, 1872, L. T. Papers.

reconstruction measures and had issued the celebrated opinion in the Milligan case.[27] Furthermore, the Democratic party was still considered by the mass of Republican voters as the party of treason, and any alliance with it would mean a loss of many votes for the reform candidate. However undecided and ambivalent he was about his own nomination, Trumbull knew that if the Democrats were allowed to come, in substantial number, to Cincinnati, they would veto his nomination by a threat of withdrawal of their support from the Liberal Republican ticket.

Trumbull insisted that the Cincinnati meeting should include only "loyal republicans" getting together for the *sole* purpose of consulting on how to achieve needed reforms.[28] He was, for a long time, strongly opposed to having the Cincinnati convention nominate candidates for the Presidency, apparently hoping that an impressive show of Liberal Republican strength would cause the leaders of the party to ditch Grant and put forth a candidate acceptable to the reformers. While he did not exclude the possibility that the Cincinnati meeting might make the nominations, he pleaded time and time again that this matter should be left to the future.[29] He argued that the Democrats must not be allowed to influence the Cincinnati platform or its choices if and when the convention spontaneously should decide to make them. The *Chicago Tribune*, reflecting, as usual, his views, asserted editorially that, "The Cincinnati Convention is a Republican movement and when it ceases to be that, it will fail altogether. It was begun by Republicans and, unless it be managed and governed by Republicans exclusively to the end, it will fail in its purpose." [30]

Trumbull wanted to postpone the question of nominations

[27] In January, 1863, Judge Davis visited Lincoln in the White House and told him that the Emancipation Proclamation had made the suppression of the rebellion and the victory of the Union impossible. King, *op. cit.,* p. 208.

[28] *Ibid.* To another correspondent, Trumbull wrote: "Nobody else, certainly no Democrats, should go there," Trumbull to Thomas Conway, Trumbull Letters, Chicago Historical Society.

[29] Trumbull to Caldwell, Trumbull Letters, Chicago Historical Society.

[30] *Chicago Tribune,* May 1, 1872.

because of his conviction that any impression that the Cincinnati convention was managed by the usual maneuverings of politicians would be fatal to the image of a pure and idealistic reform movement he had been striving to create. "A reform movement cannot succeed," Trumbull wrote White, "which starts under auspices of trading politicians." [31] Trumbull did not underestimate the sagacity and political resourcefulness of Morton and Chandler, who were to manage Grant's campaign. He did not want to give them an opportunity to charge that the Liberal Republican movement was "a mere tail to a democratic kite," [32] and that the exalted reform movement was managed by ambitious politicians whose opposition to Grant, the savior of the Union, was based not on ideological grounds but on a thirst for power. "The best Republicans in the land," he asserted, "if understood to have been brought forward by the Democrats will get very few Republican votes." [33] While he believed that a reform Republican candidate could win, Trumbull was not underestimating Grant's popularity with the masses of the people. His private samplings of public opinion showed that while the reformers had the support of the better-informed and better-educated people, the "common people [were] . . . generally for Grant." [34]

It soon became clear that his attempt to prevent any discussion or planning for nominations at the convention was bound to fail. Practical politicians in the Liberal Republican camp argued that the Cincinnati convention would neither attract the desired attendance nor generate interest without an advance notice that nominations for President and Vice-President would be made. There was little popular appeal in a consultative assembly on reform as envisioned by Trumbull, and the zealous

[31] Trumbull to Horace White, April 24, 1872, L. T. Papers.

[32] Trumbull to Horace White, April 6, 1872, White Papers, Illinois State Historical Library, Springfield, Ill.

[33] Trumbull to R. Brinkerhoff, March 20, 1872, L. T. Papers.

[34] W. C. Flagg to Trumbull, January 25, 1877, L. T. Papers.

supporters of the new movement were more eager to discuss candidates than reforms. "As it became manifest that the Cincinnati Convention," Gustave Koerner reminisced later, "would be very numerously attended by a very many prominent Republicans, some of whom were among the founders of the Republican Party, the idea of making no nominations was soon given up." [35]

[35] Koerner, *Memoirs*, II, 538.

17

The Battle for Illinois

EARLY SIGNS OF AN IMPENDING BITTER FIGHT FOR THE NOMINATION in Cincinnati came from Trumbull's home state. The struggle was precipitated by Judge David Davis' acceptance of the Presidential nomination offered him by the National Labor Union. This was indeed a strange affair. It was the first national political convention attended by labor leaders from seventeen states, and it met on February 15 in Columbus, Ohio. The convention passed a relatively radical platform, which included several planks that were later adopted by the Populists. The platform declared that both major political parties had betrayed the best interests of the American people and that a few capitalists controlled the economy of the country.[1] The politically naive labor leaders, who had been told that the Liberal Republicans and the Democrats would endorse their candidate, nominated Judge Davis as their candidate for President.

It was clear that the conservative millionaire Davis, who had made most of his money on real estate transactions, could not find much agreement with the Columbus platform. The Judge, "very nervous," [2] nevertheless accepted the nomination in a

[1] Text of platform apparently sent to Trumbull and signed by A. M. Puett from Indiana and A. Campbell from Illinois, in L. T. Papers.

[2] Mrs. David Davis to David Davis, March 3, 1872, David Davis Papers, Chicago Historical Society.

314

telegram that was considered very clever by newspapers friendly to him. "The chief magistracy of the republic," he wired, "should neither be sought nor declined by an American citizen."[3]

Davis and his managers, Leonard Swett and Jesse H. Fell, constituted, in the main, the same "team" that had put over, by relentless bargaining and deals, Lincoln's nomination at the 1860 Chicago convention. Judge Davis wanted to become President and to get off the Supreme Court. He wanted to restore harmony and peace with the South and to eliminate from public life the Republican radicals, whom he hated with all the strength of a former Marylander whose family owned slaves. Davis was a formidable candidate in Illinois. During the years of his service as a circuit judge, he had made many friends, "for besides being a good judge, he was a most affable gentleman."[4] He was particularly popular in and around Bloomington. Many Republicans gratefully remembered that Davis had been devoted to Lincoln, for whose nomination in 1860 he was, in a large measure, responsible.

The feud between the "Davis Clique" and the "Tribune Clique" headed by Trumbull was of long standing. Davis never forgave Trumbull for defeating Lincoln for the Senate seat in 1855. The feud between Davis and Trumbull continued all through Reconstruction. It was particularly bitter in Chicago, where Trumbull supported Norman B. Judd for leadership in the Republican party, while Davis supported "Long John" Wentworth, his close ally and a sworn enemy of Lyman Trumbull. Things had not changed in 1872. Political friendships and hatreds were usually durable in the hectic politics in Illinois, and in April, 1872, John Wentworth, who also was a million-

---

[3] *Chicago Times*, February 23, 1872. "It was indeed by many considered a huge joke," wrote Koerner, "for the labor party to select a millionaire as their standard bearer, who, from what was known of his politics, must have considered most of the principles enumerated . . . on that platform downright heresies. . . ." Koerner, *Memoirs*, II, 541.

[4] Koerner, *Memoirs*, II, 539.

aire, traveled extensively in the East on behalf of Davis' candidacy.[5] Trumbull's supporters who gave battle to the Davis forces were also his old friends and political allies. The support of the Chicago Tribune and of Horace White, its editor, was, of course, of great importance. It was, however, balanced by the enthusiastic endorsement received by David Davis from the Chicago Times.[6]

Illinois was considered an important key state in the 1872 campaign, and the struggle between the Davis and Trumbull factions was quite intense. One fact did emerge very quickly. While Judge Davis, as an announced candidate, skillfully directed his campaign in Illinois, Trumbull, who, as late as the middle of April, only two weeks before the convention, still doubted the desirability of making nominations in Cincinnati,[7] refused to do anything to further his own candidacy.

From the very outset of the contest, Trumbull and his allies thought that the Democratic embrace of Judge Davis would prove to be a kiss of death. "Outside of Illinois," wrote Trumbull, "I do not know of any republicans who are sustaining Davis, but the Democrats are fast making him their candidate. Will not this prevent our taking him up if we should want to? As a democratic candidate we could not give him much Republican support."[8] Thus Trumbull's strategy was to eliminate Davis by branding him a "Democratic candidate." The strategy of Davis' managers was to checkmate the Trumbull movement by convincing the liberal voters that Trumbull could not get the support of the Democrats. "T. cannot get their [the Democrats'] support," asserted Leonard Swett, "and when the time comes the movement can be checkmated there."[9]

[5] John Wentworth to David Davis, April 16, 18, 1872, Davis Papers, Chicago Historical Society Library.

[6] Chicago Times, April 9, 1972.

[7] Trumbull to Jesse W. Fell, April 11, 1872, L. T. Papers.

[8] Trumbull to Horace White, March 6, 1872, Horace White Papers, Illinois State Historical Library, Springfield, Ill.

[9] Leonard Swett to David Davis, February 25, 1872, David Davis Papers, Chicago Historical Society Library.

The Davis campaign had a distinct advantage, not only because it had an active and declared candidate, but also because it was managed by two professional politicians, Leonard Swett and Jesse W. Fell, who displayed a single-minded devotion to Davis. On the other hand, Horace White, who represented Trumbull's interests in Illinois and was looked upon as his spokesman, was never convinced that he had, in Trumbull, a candidate who had a chance of winning the nomination. In the Illinois politics, with its intense rivalries, where people were accustomed to ruthless methods of political warfare, this was a fatal handicap.[10]

Davis' managers lost no time in spreading rumors, especially in Springfield, which was Trumbull's stronghold, that Trumbull would not be a candidate.[11] They persisted in their plans to have leading Illinois Democrats go to Cincinnati and assure the delegates that "Judge Trumbull cannot secure the democratic votes and that his nomination would re-elect Grant." [12] Since both Davis and Fell were wealthy men, and since there were no elections for the delegates, Davis' supporters were enticed to go to Cincinnati by the distribution of free railroad tickets and assurances that their hotel bills would be paid. Swett and Fell decided to run special trains of their followers to the convention. "It must be arranged," wrote Swett to Fell, "that a train with a low rate of fare, if not entirely free, should start from Bloomington with a view of taking a large delegation from McLean, Tazewell, Livingston, Logan, Dewitt, Champaigne, Ford, Iroquois, and Vermillion." [13] Trumbull was warned that "Davis and Fell—both being rich men—may get a crowd of 'strong' fellows to go to Cincinnati to follow for Davis." [14]

[10] White, *op. cit.*, p. 379.
[11] Gustave Koerner to Trumbull, April 5, 1872, L. T. Papers.
[12] General A. Gridley to David Davis, April 15, 1872, David Davis Papers, Chicago Historical Society.
[13] Leonard Swett to Jesse W. Fell, April 1, 1872, David Davis Papers, Chicago Historical Society. Koerner wrote: "Free passage was given to anyone who would go." Koerner, *Memoirs*, II, 544.
[14] Jesse K. Dubois to Trumbull, April 20, 1872, L. T. Papers.

And yet, in spite of the efforts of Davis' supporters, the trend was running in Trumbull's favor. Swett acknowledged that "there is a strong Trumbull feeling at Springfield, Alton and Belleville—I suppose fifty people will go from Springfield to Cincinnati in his interest, and if we don't look out, after all we will be oversloughed [sic] by numbers." [15] With the approval of Trumbull and Davis, White and Swett collaborated on the issuance of a "call" for the Cincinnati convention, which was to be signed by prominent Republican leaders in the state. Since it was a general appeal to Republicans to support and attend the convention, Trumbull felt no compunctions in actively soliciting signatures to the call.[16] It was issued on April 18 and was signed by about forty Republican leaders. If judged by the preferences of its signers, it represented a clear victory for Trumbull. Only two signers, Fell and Swett, were Davis supporters; the others were predominantly Trumbull allies and friends.[17] An Illinois friend rubbed salt into his wounds when he wrote to Judge Davis: "Did it strike you as a little funny that in your own State, of 250,000 inhabitants, there could only be found two (2) of your friends to sign the Call." [18] John Wentworth mournfully asserted "everybody in Springfield seems to be against us . . . in our own State Trumbull may be put first. We are to be swamped in Illinois by numbers. Hundreds opposed to us in Illinois are to come to Cincinnati." [19]

There were good reasons for "Long John's" concern. Trumbull was gaining some ground and he was repeatedly assured by his friends that he would be nominated.[20] A former chairman

[15] *Ibid.*

[16] White to Trumbull, March 17, 1872; Horace S. Leland to Trumbull, April 9, 1872; telegrams from Trumbull to A. Babcoci and D. L. Phillips, urging them to sign the appeal, in L. T. Papers.

[17] O. M. Hatch to Trumbull, April 11, 1872, L. T. Papers.

[18] S. B. Brown to David Davis, April 15, 1872, David Davis Papers, Chicago Historical Society.

[19] John Wentworth to Davis, April 16, 1872, David Davis Papers, Chicago Historical Society.

[20] Jesse K. Dubois to Trumbull, April 10, 1872, L. T. Papers.

of the Republican party in Kankakee County assured him that his county was determined to support his nomination.[21] Many letters endorsing him came from doctors, lawyers, school board members, and editors from many parts of the state.[22]

The campaign waged by Davis and his lieutenants to have the Democrats torpedo Trumbull's nomination encountered great difficulties. Three influential Illinois Democrats, former Senator William R. Morrison; General John McClernand, former Illinois representative; and E. L. Merritt, the editor of the influential *Illinois State Register*, endorsed Trumbull's nomination. Merritt wrote to Trumbull: "The people, especially of Illinois, who propose the overthrow of the Grant government desire you. . . ."[23] Other prominent Democrats who came out for Trumbull included General S. Singleton and Charles Lanphier, a prominent Springfield Democratic leader and businessman. Many other prominent Democrats gave their support to Judge Davis.

The Trumbull camp was successful in receiving the endorsements of Gustave Koerner and John M. Palmer. Koerner, former lieutenant governor of the state and an acknowledged leader of the Germans in Illinois, at first hesitated to oppose Grant, because the Republican party, and especially its radical wing, had been very popular with the German immigrants all through the Civil War and reconstruction. But gradually many German voters became disgusted with the corruption of Grant's regime and threw their support to Trumbull and to the Liberal Republicans.[24]

Even more important was the support that Trumbull received

[21] D. C. Taylor to Trumbull, March 27, 1872, L. T. Papers.

[22] Dr. Edward G. Newhall and Charles Baldwin to Trumbull, March 26, 1872, L. T. Papers. Hiram R. Enoch, editor of the *Rockford* (Ill.) *Journal* wrote to pledge support. Hiram R. Enoch to Trumbull, February 7, 1872, L. T. Papers.

[23] E. L. Merritt to Trumbull, February 26, 1872, L. T. Papers. Merritt in an interview said that he supported Trumbull because he was an honest man and a former Democrat and because he believed that "he can overcome the great majority against us in Illinois." *Chicago Tribune,* May 2, 1872.

[24] Gustave Koerner to Trumbull, February 19, 1872, L. T. Papers.

from the governor of Illinois, John M. Palmer. Palmer had a distinguished record as a Union general and was a popular and effective governor. He had a reputation for honesty and integrity and was an excellent speaker with a great deal of appeal. Palmer's relationship with Grant and the leadership of the Republican party became severely strained when he, as governor of Illinois, denounced Grant's sending of Federal troops to prevent looting during the Great Chicago Fire.[25] His unhappy experience with the intervention of Federal troops caused Governor Palmer to oppose, with ever increasing vigor, the presence of Federal forces in the South, and he urged their withdrawal in order to restore the harmony and unity of the country.

Palmer's hesitant position on the Cincinnati convention resulted from his belief that the Liberal Republicans of Illinois could, like their counterparts in Missouri, defeat the regular Republicans in the state convention and that he could then get the nomination for governor.[26] Trumbull decided to make an effort to get his influential friend off the fence. Palmer's support was essential, he felt, if Illinois was to have a large delegation and an important voice in Cincinnati. On April 8 Trumbull sent Palmer a carefully written letter in which he explained his stand on the current political situation. The Grant administration, he stated, was run for the benefit of "selfish unscrupulous men who, in the name of party, manage to keep themselves in power." He did not think that reform could be accomplished through the regular Republican or Democratic organizations. The only hope was in the Cincinnati meeting, which, if it must, should nominate only "known and tried Republicans." As for himself, Trumbull said that he "had no desire for the nomination," but wanted the convention to choose a candidate who could carry Illinois "whether it was somebody else or myself."

[25] John H. Bryant, I. N. Morris, D. L. Phillips, Norman C. Warner to John M. Palmer, November 20, 1871, November 22, 1871, November 15, 1871, November 11, 1871, John M. Palmer Papers, Illinois State Historical Society Library, Springfield, Ill.

[26] Horace White to Trumbull, March 9, 1872, L. T. Papers.

Trumbull concluded his letter by urging Palmer to drop his hesitation, to "take hold of it in earnest [and] see that men went to Cincinnati from all over the State." [27] In his reply, Palmer told his friend that if Trumbull should become the Cincinnati nominee he would support him.[28]

Trumbull was convinced that "whoever can carry Illinois can be elected." [29] There is evidence to suggest that Trumbull could have beaten the Davis forces and then come to Cincinnati with a delegation committed to him as a favorite son. Instead, Trumbull's delegates came to the convention without advance planning and without much encouragement from their candidate. As a consequence, they were a bewildered, helpless lot in Cincinnati.

Trumbull, a skillful and experienced politician, stubbornly ignored the warnings and pleas of many of his Illinois friends and associates who urged him to declare his candidacy and assume active leadership of his campaign. He paid no heed to the warnings that his campaign in Illinois was floundering, especially in view of the determined maneuverings of the Davis men. He was told that Illinois would go to Davis by default unless he intervened directly. "The time is short," wrote one supporter, "and action must be taken by those who are competent to say how it should be done." [30] Koerner pleaded with Trumbull: "Could you send me a telegram informing me that you will be a candidate and accept if nominated? There is no time to lose." [31] Jesse K. Dubois argued that since the Davis men were spreading rumors that he would not be a candidate, Trumbull was duty-bound to correct the misrepresentation. This experienced politician predicted that if Trumbull declared himself as a candidate and then got the nomination, he would carry Illinois by a margin of about 50,000 votes against Grant.[32] The Democratic leader

[27] Trumbull to John M. Palmer, April 8, 1872, L. T. Papers.
[28] John M. Palmer to Trumbull, April 13, 1872, L. T. Papers.
[29] Trumbull to Palmer, April 8, 1872, L. T. Papers.
[30] L. Dubois to Trumbull, April 18, 1872, L. T. Papers.
[31] Gustave Koerner to Trumbull, April 5, 1872, L. T. Papers.
[32] Jesse K. Dubois to Trumbull, April 21, 1872, L. T. Papers.

General John A. McClernand, who on his own initiative toured several Midwestern states on behalf of Trumbull, pointedly wrote that he hoped "that your concern for your success will be equal to the zeal of your friends." [33] Horace White told Trumbull that Illinois Republicans were reticent about going to Cincinnati because of Trumbull's passive attitude. "It will not answer to us," he added, "to stand in the background any longer." [34] Trumbull was unmoved by these pleadings. Three weeks before the opening of the Cincinnati gathering he still reiterated: "My own position is this in regard to candidates. I would have the friends of the liberal movement keep that question for the present in the background. . . ." [35]

The speech that Trumbull delivered to a large New York audience at Cooper Union, and which attracted considerable national attention, could have done for Trumbull what a similar occasion did for Abraham Lincoln a dozen years before. To be sure, he lacked the personal magnetism, the humor, and the leadership qualities of Lincoln, but his speech must be considered one of Trumbull's best oratorical efforts. It contained a detailed indictment of the corruption and abuses of the Grant administration and a harsh indictment of the record of reconstruction. Trumbull charged that the Southern states had fallen ino the hands of "inexperienced and . . . corrupt adventurers who were plundering and oppressing the people.[36]

Trumbull pleaded for a general amnesty and civil service reform. Foreseeing the conditions of the 1877 "Bargain," he listed several "dead issues" that he thought the country and its leaders should cease to discuss. Among them were slavery, equal rights, pensions for war widows and orphans, and the

---

[33] John A. McClernand to Trumbull, April 24, 1872, L. T. Papers.
[34] Horace White to Trumbull, April 3, 1872, L. T. Papers.
[35] Trumbull to John M. Palmer, April 8, 1872, L. T. Papers.
[36] *Speech of Hon. Lyman Trumbull of Illinois, Delivered at the Cooper Institute, New York* (Pamphlet), F. & J. Rives and Geo. A. Bailey Printers (Washington, D.C., 1872).

Confederate debt. "All these questions have been settled," Trumbull asserted.[37]

Trumbull received many letters of commendation on his speech.[38] *The Nation* praised it as being "a strong, clear but unadorned statement of charges brought by the promoters of the new movement against the administration." [39] But since Trumbull was not an announced candidate, the effect of the speech was limited.

The indications of support that Trumbull received from other states in the Union were impressive. Discounting the inevitable exaggerations of those who wrote to Trumbull about the political situation in their respective states, the picture was quite encouraging. Trumbull had strong support in California, where he was assured by leading Republicans that he could carry the state by a large majority.[40] Former Senator Edmund G. Ross in Kansas pledged to Trumbull the support of his newspaper and assured him of the solid support of the Liberal Republicans and the Democrats in Kansas.[41] The Republican leader in Boston and in Massachusetts, Edward Atkinson, pleaded with Trumbull "to give the word publicly" and promised substantial support in New England.[42] In spite of the fact that the New England Liberal Republicans felt obliged to support Adams, Trumbull's following there was strong and enthusiastic. His followers were especially numerous in his native state of Connecticut, where the Trumbull name carried an aura of eminence and distinction. Trumbull's relations with David A. Wells, the acknowledged leader of the Connecticut Republican insurgents, were close and friendly. He was endorsed as a native son by the

[37] *Ibid.*, p. 7.

[38] Walter Scates, R. G. Murphy, John H. Swearingen, E. J. Avery, George W. Wright, and A. M. Pruett to Trumbull, April 15, 16, 1872, L. T. Papers.

[39] *The Nation,* April 18, 1872.

[40] F. R. Payne to Trumbull, February 10, 1872. Payne asserted: "You can carry California by a larger majority what [*sic*] Gov. Booth did last fall." See also Thomas Gray to Trumbull, April 7, 1872, L. T. Papers.

[41] E. G. Ross to Trumbull, February 21, 1872, L. T. Papers.

[42] Edward Atkinson to Trumbull, March 13, 1872, L. T. Papers.

Litchfield Journal and received many individual letters of support.[43] James R. Doolittle, the former senator and now an influential Democratic leader, made a tour of Connecticut, where he addressed Democratic mass rallies in New Haven and Hartford. He reported to Trumbull that Connecticut Democrats would vote either for Judge Davis or for him as the Cincinnati nominee. Either man, Doolittle asserted, would get 3,000,000 Democratic votes. Doolittle pleaded with his friend, with whom he later formed a law partnership in Chicago, to drop his passivity and fight for his nomination.[44] John Wentworth, a seasoned and shrewd political observer, concluded, after a tour of the Eastern states, that the Cincinnati nomination would be decided by the Illinois delegation. If Illinois should hold out for Trumbull, he said, the nomination would go to him, because the New England states would then abandon Adams.[45]

Trumbull had strong support in Missouri, as was later clearly shown by the votes of the Missouri delegates in Cincinnati.[46] Similar support came from places in the South, where Trumbull's opposition to the Ku Klux Klan Bill and his advocacy of a general amnesty were very popular.[47] McClernand's and Merritt's tour of Indiana on behalf of Trumbull's nomination apparently met with considerable success. When the Indiana delegation met in caucus in Cincinnati on May 2, it cast eleven

[43] John Cotton Smith, John Danforth, L. F. S. Foster to Trumbull, February 22, March 18, April 15, 1872, L. T. Papers.

[44] James R. Doolittle to Trumbull, March 18 and March 22, 1872, L. T. Papers. Doolittle, in spite of his friendship for Trumbull, became irked with his indifference and passivity and threw his support to Davis. He wrote to his wife from Cincinnati, where he arrived on April 28, that Trumbull was "selfish" for not throwing his support to Davis. James R. Doolittle to Mrs. Doolittle, April 28, 1872, James R. Doolittle Papers, State Historical Society of Wisconsin, Madison, Wis.

[45] John Wentworth to David Davis, April 16, 1872, David Davis Papers, Chicago Historical Society.

[46] John D. Strong and T. J. Howell to Trumbull, March 19, 1872, L. T. Papers.

[47] George T. Bartlett, W. W. H. Lawrence to Trumbull, March 14, March 22, 1872, L. T. Papers. See also Trumbull to J. A. Caldwell, March 9, 1872, L. T. Papers.

votes for Trumbull, nine for Adams, six for Davis and two for Palmer.[48]

The reluctant candidate attracted wide editorial support among influential newspapers. These included the *Chicago Tribune*, the *Illinois State Journal*, the *New York Evening Post*, the *New York Sun*, the *Cincinnati Enquirer*, the *Milwaukee News*, the *Maryland Journal*, the *Rockford* (Ill.) *Journal* and many others.[49] The *Springfield* (Mass.) *Republican* and the *Cincinnati Commercial* endorsed Trumbull for the vice-presidency on a ticket with Adams. The *Springfield Republican* wrote on the eve of the convention: The ticket should be indeed double-headed. And it should be Charles Francis Adams and Lyman Trumbull." [50] Murat Halstead wrote in the same vein in his *Cincinnati Commercial*.[51] The ever faithful *Chicago Tribune* unequivocally urged the Cincinnati convention to nominate "the name, everywhere honored and trusted, of Lyman Trumbull of Illinois." [52]

Trumbull finally clarified his stand on the nomination in a letter to Horace White of April 24. The letter, even at that late date, was still ambiguous and clearly reflected Trumbull's ambivalent feelings about running for the Presidency. Trumbull disposed of his candidacy in one paragraph: "I do not think I ought to be nominated unless there is a decided feeling among those assembled and are outside of rings and bargains, that I would be stronger than anyone else. Unless this is the feeling, I think it would not be wise to present my name at all." [53] The rest of the long letter pertained to Trumbull's advice that the

---

[48] *Cincinnati Commercial*, March 3, 1872.

[49] Charleton Lewis (*New York Evening Post*), February 26, 1872; George H. Paul (*Milwaukee News*), April 19, 1872; William H. Ruby (*Maryland Journal*), April 19, 1872, to Trumbull, L. T. Papers.

[50] *Springfield* (Mass.) *Republican*, April 25, 1872.

[51] *Cincinnati Commercial*, April 26, 1872.

[52] *Chicago Tribune*, April 26, 1872.

[53] Trumbull to Horace White, April 24, 1872, L. T. Papers.

Cincinnati convenion should avoid taking any strong stand on the tariff issue.[54]

That Trumbull did have a clear conception of the crucial role of the Illinois delegation is indicated in his letter to Koerner, to whom he wrote three days after his last pre-convention communication to White. He was convinced, he said, that the nominee would come from Illinois, unless the competing factions there would cancel out each other's strength. He added: "I do not desire to be nominated as the result of any combination or arrangements between rival interests, nor unless there is a general feeling not manufactured for the occasion, on my behalf." [55]

[54] White to Trumbull, May 4, 1872, L. T. Papers.
[55] Quoted in Koerner, *Memoirs*, II, 543.

18

The Defeat

THE CINCINNATI CONVENTION WAS AN IMPRESSIVE AND ENTHUSI-
astic gathering. Although composed of diverse elements and
groups, which differed on many issues and policies, it was
united on the need for reform and on beating Grant. The
delegates were, on the whole, better educated and more idealistic and enthusiastic than the usual run of delegates to national
conventions. This was at once its strength and its weakness.
It was as a strength because the convention attracted a devoted
following and raised important issues, but its weakness lay in its
amateur approach to the rough and tumble of American politics.
The leaders of the reform movement were also unable to trans-
late their lofty ideas into a campaign language understandable to
the masses of the voters. An eyewitness related that "the streets
of Cincinnati had never beheld a more orderly, single-minded
public spirited crowd." [1] The Davis supporters, led by Swett
and Wentworth, did everything to generate enthusiasm for
Davis. They paraded incessantly, carrying placards and pictures
of their candidate, and shouted themselves hoarse for Judge
Davis.[2] These shenanigans, which were acceptable techniques in
the regular party conventions, did not sit well with the sober,

[1] White, *op. cit.*, p. 380.
[2] Koerner, *Memoirs*, II, 548.

high-principled leaders of the Liberal Republican movement. Murat Halstead told the Davis men, in an editorial, that they were wasting their time. "The Cincinnati Convention," he wrote, "will not be composed of a small lot of fellows whose railroad and hotel expenses can be paid by an ambitious candidate or two, as was the case with the squad that nominated Davis and Parker at Columbus. Mr. Davis may as well subside." [3] Halstead, whose excellently edited newspaper was snapped up every morning by the delegates, eager to get the latest news on the nominations, also refuted the rumors, spread by Davis' supporters, that Trumbull and Adams would not be acceptable to the Democrats. He told his readers that the Democrats would have no choice but to endorse the reform platform and support either Adams or Trumbull. [4]

The Democrats, in spite of Trumbull's wishes and desires, did come to Cincinnati in large numbers, but were more onlookers than participants. [5] They, in the main, favored Davis and opposed Adams and Trumbull. While their opposition to Trumbull was based on his record on Reconstruction legislation and his repeated denunciation of the Democrats as "traitors," [6] their antagonism to Adams was based on personal considerations. Five prominent Democratic Congressmen interviewed in Washington by a correspondent of the *Cincinnati Commercial* called Adams "cold and stiff," "a hater of the Irish," "more of an Englishman than an American," and "an unsympathetic New Englander." [7] Many delegates were also angered by Adams' letter to David A. Wells, in which he stated his position on the nomination. As Adams' biographer put it, the letter "could

[3] *Cincinnati Commercial,* April 22, 1872. The *Chicago Tribune* expressed similar views on May 1, 1872.

[4] *Cincinnati Commercial,* April 25, 1872.

[5] Koerner, *Memoirs,* II, 548.

[6] Trumbull used that expression in his Cooper Union speech and, in spite of White's request, refused to publicly withdraw the charge. Horace White to Trumbull, April 25, 1872, L. T. Papers.

[7] *Cincinnati Commercial,* April 30, 1872.

hardly have been more chilling." [8] But it was more than chilling; it was downright condescending, and it included a reference to the reform movement as "that crowd," which insulted the sensibilities of many delegates. Adams stated that he did not want the nomination and could only be "induced to consider it" if he received an "unequivocal call" without any bargains or commitments. Otherwise, he asked Wells to "draw [him] out of that crowd." [9]

Resenting Democratic pressure, the powerful group of editors decided to kill the Davis candidacy in one bold stroke. On the evening before the day the convention was to be opened, four editors of powerful newspapers that supported the Cincinnati movement met and formed a "Quadrilateral," so named after the four impregnable fortresses in the Italian Alps, to "guide" the decisions of the convention on the nominations. The four included Murat Halstead of the *Cincinnati Commercial*, Horace White of the *Chicago Tribune*, Samuel Bowles of the *Springfield* (Mass.) *Republican*, and Henry Watterson of the *Louisville Courier-Journal*. A day later Whitelow Reid of the *New York Tribune* was also admitted to the group. At a meeting held in a sitting room between Schurz's and Watterson's bedrooms in the St. Nicholas Hotel, they decided to announce to the delegates and to the nation, in identical editorials that were to appear the next day, that they were opposed to Judge Davis and would not support him if he were nominated.[10] This action killed any prospect for Davis' nomination and left Trumbull, Adams, Governor Gratz Brown, and Greeley as serious contenders. Governor Brown was the favorite son nominee of the Missouri delegation, and Adams had strong support mainly from

[8] Martin B. Duberman, *Charles Francis Adams, 1807–1886* (Cambridge, 1961), p. 359.
[9] Text in *Cincinnati Commercial*, April 25, 1872.
[10] Joseph Frazier Wall, *Henry Watterson: Reconstructed Rebel* (New York, 1956), p. 104. See also Henry Watterson, *Marse Henry* (New York, 1919).

the New England delegation led by David A. Wells, Edward Atkinson, and Samuel Bowles.[11]

A participant in the Quadrilateral meeting testified that Greeley"'s nomination was not treated seriously at the editors' meeting, but the New York delegation was committed to him. However, Greeley's popularity among the rank and file delegates, especially those from the Midwest, where his newspaper and his editorials had been widely read from the early days of the Civil War, has been generally underestimated.[12] Brown's candidacy was seriously handicapped by the bitter hostility to him of the senior Missouri Senator Carl Schurz, who was the undisputed leader of the German voters in Missouri, Illinois, and Iowa. Schurz himself made no secret of the fact that he favored Trumbull.

In this rather confused situation, the Illinois delegation, if united, could have played an important role. Horace White, the acknowledged leader of the Trumbull forces, was handicapped by Trumbull's injunction against any bargains or agreements with other delegations.[13] He therefore devoted most of his time to the Quadrilateral and to his arduous tasks as chairman of the Committee on Resolutions. This left the task of masterminding Trumbull's campaign to Gustave Koerner who, while he supported Trumbull, actually preferred Governor Palmer.[14] Dr. William Jayne, Trumbull's brother-in-law, had neitheir the stature nor the influence needed for this difficult task.

The first step for the divided and unhappy Illinois delegation was to decide for whom to cast its forty-two votes. The delegation met in Greenwood Hall. Fell and Swett influenced the delegation to agree to cast half of its votes for Davis, one-quarter for Trumbull, and one-quarter for Palmer. Leonard

[11] *Cincinnati Commercial,* April 28, 1872.

[12] The *Cincinnati Commercial* editorialized on the day the convention opened: "It did not, last night, seem wholly improbable that Mr. Greeley himself might be the man." May 1, 1872.

[13] Horace White to Trumbull, May 4, 1872, L. T. Papers.

[14] Koerner, *Memoirs,* II, 545.

Swett, a few days later, wrote Judge Davis: "We divided the delegation because they had the organization [of the convention] and if we had not done it—that organization . . . would have rejected us altogether." [15]

The convention opened on May 1, under circumstances seemingly auspicious for Trumbull. The temporary chairman, William Grosvenor, in his opening remarks stated that the convention was a reform movement within the Republican party, and Carl Schurz, the permanent chairman, urged the convention to select a convinced reformer and a gentleman of unimpeachable integrity. It was clear that only Trumbull and Adams were acceptable to him.[16]

When the voting began, on May 3, Adams received 205 votes, Greeley 147, Trumbull, 110, Brown 95, Davis 92½, Curtin 62 and Chase 2½. After the first vote was announced, Governor Gratz Brown of Missouri, who arrived the day before in Cincinnati with Senator Francis Blair, Jr., asked for the floor and released the Missouri delegation. He then appealed to the convention to nominate Horace Greeley. It was rumored that Gratz Brown had made a deal with Greeley in exchange for the second spot on the ticket, but it was later proven that Greeley had no part in these negotiations.[17] One must agree with Horace White's judgment that writers have made too much of the "Gratz Brown trick." [18] The net effect of Brown's move was rather limited. It actually added more strength to Trumbull than to Greeley since the Missouri delegation, after the release, voted 16 for Trumbull, 10 for Greeley, and 4 for Adams. Once again it became clear that a decisive, united stand of the Illinois delegation could have stopped Greeley and given the

[15] Leonard Swett to David Davis, May 4, 1872, David Davis Letters, Chicago Historical Society.

[16] *Cincinnati Commercial*, May 1, 1872.

[17] *Springfield* (Mass.) *Republican*, May 8, 1872.

[18] Horace White's correspondence to the *Chicago Tribune*, May 3, 1872. See also Earle Dudley Ross, *The Liberal Republican Movement* (New York, 1919), pp. 97–100.

nomination to Lyman Trumbull or to Charles Francis Adams. Murat Halstead desperately appealed to the Trumbull and Adams men to unite.[19] The Maine delegation circulated a printed ticket that read: "The Ticket to Win, For President Charles Francis Adams, for Vice President Lyman Trumbull." [20] But even now that the Davis candidacy had been eliminated, there were no prospects for uniting the Illinois delegation for Trumbull. "Before she [the Illinois delegation] could settle her differences," wrote Samuel Bowles, "and come to strengthen Adam's column, the fire [for Greeley] was kindled." [21] Why was it impossible for the Illinois delegation to unite? Because the leaders of the Davis faction, and particularly Leonard Swett, were determined to see to it that anyone else *but Trumbull* should receive the nomination. Swett was convinced that Trumbull had encouraged Judge Davis to run and then had betrayed him as he allegedly betrayed Lincoln in 1855. "If he [Trumbull] had been nominated the rule of virtue would have been reversed," Swett reported to Davis, "and the world would have been taught that meanness was the sure road to success." [22] In justice "to the memory of Lincoln" and in justice to the laws of fairness, Swett and his associates felt that they had the duty "to see to it that he [Trumbull] was not nominated." [23] In their determination to act as spoilers they also stubbornly refused to agree to a unanimous vote of the Illinois delegation either for Adams or for Greeley. The final caucus took place before the sixth ballot was to be taken. Since Greeley and Adams made gains on the fifth ballot, it was clear that the sixth ballot would be decisive. Koerner, now convinced that Trumbull had no

[19] *Cincinnati Commercial,* May 3, 1872.

[20] *Ibid.*

[21] *Springfield* (Mass.) *Republican,* May 3, 1872. Horace White also believed that the Brown-Blair gambit was not a result of a deal with Greeley, but was an attempt to diminish Schurz's influence in Missouri. White, *op. cit.,* p. 385.

[22] Leonard Swett to David Davis, May 4, 1872, Davis Papers, Chicago Historical Society.

[23] *Ibid.*

chance to be nominated, urged the delegation to support Adams, but his appeal was rejected by the Davis men.[24]

The caucus voted to cast 27 votes for Adams and 14 votes for Greeley. Ironically, but as a fitting climax to its inept record at the convention, when the Illinois delegation entered the hall, Greeley had already clinched the nomination and the traditional bandwagon was rolling. Thus, this hapless delegation, which could have, if united, nominated Trumbull or Adams on the third or fourth ballot, found itself ignored in the crucial moments of the convention.

Many theories have been advanced to explain Greeley's victory. These included the intervention of Brown and Blair,[25] Greeley's personal popularity with the delegates and in the country,[26] the inexplicable underestimation of Greeley's strength, and the strong support that Greeley received from the Southern delegation. There is undoubtedly a great deal of truth in all these explanations, but Trumbull's and Adams' reluctance to conduct an active campaign and declare early their candidacy was of decisive help to Greeley. Here were two candidates and two delegates largely representing the same principles and often the same supporters. Had they reached an understanding they could have determined the outcome of the convention. But such an understanding needed the *active* guidance of Trumbull and Adams, and neither of them was willing to drop his air of aloofness toward the nomination turmoil in Cincinnati.

There is evidence to suggest that the New England delegations gave serious consideration to the casting of their votes for Trumbull, on the third or fourth ballot, but that Horace White

[24] Koerner, *Memoirs,* II, 555.

[25] Horace White discounted this theory by claiming that Brown's announcement "had not the least effect upon the convention." Horace White to Trumbull, May 4, 1872, L. T. Papers.

[26] Neither Trumbull nor White underestimated Greeley's strength. Trumbull wrote to William Cullen Bryant that Greeley had "a good deal of strength among the people." Trumbull to William Cullen Bryant, May 19, 1872, L. T. Papers. White was sure that "the nomination of Mr. Greeley was accomplished by the people." *Chicago Tribune,* May 4, 1872.

refused to give them the go-ahead signal. D. A. Wells, the most influential leader in the New England contingent, wrote to Trumbull after the convention: "Atkinson and myself were only awaiting his [White's] word to change our New England votes from Adams to yourself *but the opportunity was never afforded to us*." [27] F. W. Bird, a prominent leader of the Massachusetts delegation, advised Sumner that the entire Massachusetts delegation was willing to switch to Trumbull, but it received no encouragement from the Trumbull men.[28] White himself admitted to Trumbull that "Mass. and Conn. were at heart for you." [29]

Trumbull received the news of Greeley's nomination with calm and dignity. A reporter who brought the news from Cincinnati to the Senate Chamber noted that "Trumbull was the most undisturbed of all those on the floor. His equanimity astonished his friends as well as the numerous strangers in the galleries, who watched closely for indications of excitement on his parchment-like face. . . ." [30] When pressed by the reporter to assess Greeley's chances, he answered with a statement that proved to be, in the following months, wise and prophetic. "If the country," he said, "can stand the first outburst of mirth the nomination will call forth, it may prove a strong ticket." [31] There is reason to wonder whether Trumbull's admirable self-possession was not made easier by a sense of relief. His quite untypical indecisiveness and procrastination in handling his nomination suggest that his feelings about the nomination were ambivalent. Trumbull hated campaigning and addressing large crowds, and the thought of having to campaign for the Presidency undoubtedly filled him with dread.[32] His dislike of petty

[27] D. A. Wells to Trumbull, May 8, 1872, L. T. Papers. (Italics mine.)

[28] F. W. Bird to Charles Sumner, May 7, 1872, Sumner Papers, Houghton.

[29] White to Trumbull, May 4, 1872, L. T. Papers.

[30] *Chicago Tribune*, May 5, 1872. Gustave Koerner blamed Trumbull's defeat in Cincinnati on "Davis' intrigues." Gustave Koerner to Trumbull, May 24, 1872, L. T. Papers.

[31] *Chicago Tribune*, May 5, 1872. *Ibid.*

[32] Koerner, *Memoirs*, II, 435.

political bargaining and political deals was also deep-seated, but probably the most important was his conviction that his vote to acquit Andrew Johnson would be exploited to the hilt by the managers of the Grant campaign to alienate the Republicans. He also feared that his support of the Reconstruction Acts and his attempts to limit the jurisdiction of the Supreme Court would be used to frighten the Democratic voters.

Trumbull fully redeemed the pledge he had made to support the nominees chosen in Cincinnati. He promptly sent a telegram of congratulations and support to Greeley, who graciously replied that Trumbull's message meant more to him than any of others he had received.[33] In answer to William Cullen Bryant, who appealed to him not to support Greeley because his administration would be "shamefully corrupt," Trumbull replied, "I wish I could see something better than to support Mr. Greeley but I do not . . . Greeley's nomination is a bombshell which seems likely to blow up both parties. This will be an immense gain." [34]

Even if his sense of integrity and his life-long determination to follow his commitments had not been as strong as they were, Trumbull, in fact, had little choice but to come out for Greeley, because Greeley's nomination had considerable support in Illinois. It was promptly endorsed by the *Chicago Tribune*,[35] the *Illinois State Register*, the *Chicago Times*, and by Governor Palmer.[36]

Trumbull's disappointed supporters met in Cincinnati after the debacle and decided to urge Trumbull to run for governor of Illinois and "thereby [save] the presidential ticket and the legislature." [37] Trumbull promptly rejected the offer and sug-

[33] Greeley's telegram in L. T. Papers.

[34] William C. Bryant to Trumbull, Trumbull to Bryant, May 20, May 14, 1872, L. T. Papers. Trumbull took the same position at an anti-Grant meeting, called by Bryant in New York on June 20, 1872. White, *op. cit.*, pp. 391–92.

[35] *Chicago Tribune*, May 4, 1872.

[36] *Illinois State Register*, May 4, 1872.

[37] John A. McClernand and Charles Lanphier to Trumbull, May 3, 1872. Also Gustave Koerner to Trumbull, May 24, 1872, L. T. Papers.

gested Koerner instead.[38] After holding separate conventions in Springfield, the Illinois Liberal Republicans and the Democrats agreed on a fusion ticket for all state offices. Both conventions, which met concurrently at Springfield, were addressed by Lyman Trumbull, and both endorsed the Cincinnati platform.[39] The selection of the slate for state officers was assigned to special committees appointed by both conventions. When Trumbull got word that the committees were planning to recommend him for governor, he personally appeared before each committee requesting that his name not be put forward. He told them that should the Liberal Republican-Democratic ticket win in Illinois and get a majority in the state legislature, he would prefer to be elected for another term to the Senate.[40] Some of his supporters pleaded with him that his name might greatly strengthen the state ticket and that he could resign his governorship after the election and go to the Senate, but Trumbull demurred, saying that that would be an act of political dishonesty.[41]

Gustave Koerner, with Trumbull's and Palmer's support, was nominated for governor at a climactic joint session of both conventions. While the cheering, enthusiastic conventioners met inside the State House, many thousands of supporters gathered outside. General James Shields was the main speaker in the convention hall, and the outside crowds were addressed by Lyman Trumbull. Ex-Senator James R. Doolittle of Wisconsin and Carl Schurz were also brought in to address the multitudes of Liberal Republicans and Democrats who rejoiced, after many

[38] Horace White to Trumbull, May 13, 1872, L. T. Papers; and White to Dr. William Jayne, May 14, 1872, Jayne Papers.

[39] Church, op. cit., p. 113.

[40] Koerner, Memoirs, II, 561.

[41] Ibid. It is of interest to note that Richard J. Oglesby, the Republican candidate for governor, did just that. He was elected, but promptly resigned and was elected United States senator.

years of relentless political strife and bitterness, in the spirit of harmony and brotherhood.[42]

In spite of his intense dislike for election campaigns and speech-making, Trumbull was an enthusiastic and untiring campaigner in 1872. He spoke to large crowds in New York, Maine, Pennsylvania, Ohio, Michigan, Indiana, and of course Illinois. Greeley's decisive defeat, while expected, was a disappointment to Trumbull. Grant proved to be correct when he predicted the defeat of the Liberal Republicans. He reasoned that the split had "harmonized the party by getting out of it the 'sore heads' and knaves who made all the trouble because they could not controll [sic]." [43] Unencumbered by the idealism of the reformers, Morton and Chandler were successful in reviving the "bloody shirt" campaign of 1866 and raised the cry of a sell-out to the Democrats.[44] All this, plus Grant's personal popularity, the lack of mass interest in reforms, and the aversion of the American people to third parties, made the defeat of Greeley a certainty. Greeley was able to win only Georgia, Kentucky, Maryland, Missouri, Tennessee, and Texas. The victory of the regular Republicans in Illinois was no less decisive. Richard Oglesby received a 40,690 plurality over Koerner and was elected governor, and the state gave Grant a 56,465 majority. On January 20, 1872, the Illinois Legislature elected Oglesby, who had resigned as governor, to the United States Senate over Trumbull by a vote of 84 to 62.[45]

Trumbull's career in the Senate of the United States, which

[42] Daniel Cameron (Secretary, Illinois State Central Democratic Committee) to James R. Doolittle, June 24, 1872, James R. Doolittle Papers, State Historical Society of Wisconsin, Madison, Wis.

[43] Ozias M. Hatch to Lyman Trumbull, August 17, 1872, L. T. Family Papers, Illinois State Historical Library, Springfield, Ill. U. S. Grant to E. B. Washburne, May 26, 1872, Elihu B. Washburne Papers, Library of Congress

[44] On March 24, 1871, Trumbull wrote to Dr. Jayne: "Morton wants to conduct the next Presidential campaign on old issues of the war." Trumbull to Dr. William Jayne, Jayne Papers.

[45] Lusk, op. cit., p. 229; Church, op. cit., p. 117.

he entered in 1855, was ended, but he had no regrets.[46] The political situation had changed radically, most of his old associates were no longer in the Senate, and he no longer wished to belong to the Republican party. In a few months, together with Palmer and Koerner, he officially returned to the Democratic fold. Because of his attacks on the Democratic party and its record of the last twenty years, there were some who looked upon Trumbull's identification with the Democrats as an act of expediency.[47] This distrust might, in some measure, account for the fact that Trumbull was never again able to get into office on a Democratic ticket.

[46] Lyman Trumbull to General James H. Wilson, January 4, 1876, James H. Wilson Papers, Library of Congress.

[47] Church, *op. cit.*, p. 118.

19

The "Grand Old
Man of America"

GREELEY'S DEFEAT AND GRANT'S OVERWHELMING ELECTION TO A
second term, in spite of the record of corruption of his first administration, strengthened Trumbull's determination to retire, at
least for a time, from active politics. His opposition to Grant,
his break with the policy of Congressional reconstruction, and his
attacks on corruption and abuses in the government made his
position in the Republican party untenable. While he officially
returned to the Democratic party, his relations with the Democrats were not much better. The Democratic leaders in the nation and in Illinois did not forget his break with the party in
1854, his castigation of the Democrats during the Civil War,
and his authorship of most of the Reconstruction measures.
Trumbull, on the other hand, thought that the Democratic
party was still demoralized by the abuse and contempt heaped
upon it during the war and during the Reconstruction period.
The Democrats, he maintained, had no clear program for fighting corruption and for civil service reform.

This political isolation, Trumbull later testified, convinced
him, as early as 1872, of his uselessness in the Senate. Because

he felt that his service in the Senate could no longer be effective, Trumbull was not unduly concerned with the anticipated defeat in his bid for re-election to the Senate.[1]

Trumbull's defeat for re-election to the Senate came on January 21, 1873, when the Illinois Legislature elected Governor Richard J. Oglesby to Trumbull's seat. The end of Lyman Trumbull's career came quietly, without much drama. The outcome of the vote was a foregone conclusion, because Trumbull and his friends did almost no campaigning and offered only token resistance. Oglesby's victory was overwhelming with the Senate voting 33 for Oglesby and 16 for Trumbull, and the House, 84 for Oglesby and 62 for Trumbull.[2]

Packing his belongings for an intended return to Chicago, Trumbull had good reason to look with satisfaction on his eighteen years as a United States senator. These were turbulent, but exciting, years during which Trumbull emerged as one of the most powerful men in the Senate. His home life in Washing with Julia and the three sons had been happy and rewarding.

Upon his return to Chicago, Trumbull resumed his law practice. He lived in a spacious home at 4008 Lake Avenue, which he purchased in 1863. His law firm became one of the most respected law offices in Chicago. The firm did a great deal of corporate law and Trumbull continued his practice before the United States Supreme Court. Perry Trumbull joined his father's firm after his graduation from Yale College.

Trumbull, or "Judge Trumbull" as he became known till the end of his life in deference to his service on the Illinois State Supreme Court from 1848 to 1853, was active in the Chicago Bar Association and served as president of the Illinois Bar Association. After his strenuous years in Washington, which were devoted almost exclusively to his difficult tasks as a legislator and to the many demands of his Illinois con-

[1] Lyman Trumbull to General James H. Wilson, January 4, 1876, James H. Wilson Papers, Library of Congress.
[2] Church, *op. cit.*, p. 119.

stituents, Trumbull had every intention of getting more enjoyment out of life. He was sixty years old but of a rugged constitution and enjoyed good health. Circumstances, however, forced him to become entirely engrossed in his law work. Providing for his three sons proved to be a heavy burden. Walter, his oldest son, made several unsuccessful attempts to establish himself in business in Chicago and in Old Mission, Michigan, but each venture, although liberally subsidized by his father, ended in failure. Perry studied law and Henry was a sickly teenager who needed constant and expensive care.[3]

His divorce from politics in the years following his return to Chicago was complete. For three years he did not attend a political meeting and refused to express himself on political matters. When a "Gentleman of great influence and prominence" wrote to him suggesting the organization of a third party, with Trumbull as its leader, he refused, stating that the time was not yet ripe for such a step.[4]

Trumbull emerged again on the political scene during the long dispute over the outcome of the Presidential election in 1876. He was convinced that the election was won by Samuel J. Tilden and that the canvassing boards in Florida, Louisiana, and South Carolina were ready, by a dishonest count of ballots, to give the electoral votes of those states to the Republican nominee, Rutherford B. Hayes. Trumbull was chosen by Abram S. Hewitt, chairman of the National Democratic Committee, to serve on a commission of "visiting statesmen" to supervise a fair count of ballots in Louisiana. The other Democratic members included John M. Palmer and William R. Morrison of Illinois, A. G. Curtiss and William Bigler of Pennsylvania, Joseph R. Doolittle of Wisconsin, and Henry Watterson of Kentucky. The Republican members of the com-

---

[3] Lyman Trumbull to Mary Ingraham, September 13, 1877, L. T. Family Papers.
[4] Lyman Trumbull to General James H. Wilson, January 4, 1876, James H. Wilson Papers, Library of Congress.

mission, appointed by President Grant, included John W. Sherman and James A. Garfield of Ohio, and Eugene Hale of Maine. Palmer was elected chairman of the Democratic contingent and Sherman headed the Republican commissioners. The bipartisan commitee found itself completely deadlocked, with the Democrats claiming the state for Tilden and the Republicans asserting that a fair count of ballots showed that the state voted for Hayes. Before leaving Louisiana, the Democratic visitors issued an *Address to the People*, which claimed that Tilden had received a majority of votes and charged that the Republicans had stolen the state for the Republican nominee.[5]

When on January 29, 1877, Congress created an Electoral Commission, which consisted of five senators, five representatives, and five judges of the Supreme Court, to inquire into the disputed election and render a decision, Trumbull was appointed as one of the attorneys to present the case on behalf of Tilden. He appeared before the Electoral Commission on February 14, and argued, on the basis of the evidence that he had collected in Louisiana, that the vote in that state showed a majority of between six and nine thousand votes for Tilden and that the canvassing board of Louisiana had had no evidence from any of the election boards in the parishes of riots, violence, or intimidation that would justify the voiding of the vote. He denounced the Louisiana state government as corrupt and charged that it was kept in power by brute military power. Trumbull's efforts were in vain, because the Electoral Commission, by a vote of 8 to 7, decided the election in favor of Hayes.[6]

The life as a widower in a large house began to weigh heavily on Trumbull. He was lonely and craved feminine

[5] Palmer, *Personal Recollections*, p. 429.
[6] Ernest Ludlow Bogart and Charles Manfred Thomas, *The Industrial State, 1879–1893*, in *The Centennial History of Illinois*, Vol. IV (Chicago, 1922), p. 122.

company and affection. At sixty-four he looked much younger than his years and enjoyed perfect health. A contemporary wrote: "Judge Trumbull is now about sixty-two or sixty-three years of age, but does not look to be more than fifty. He has always been a very temperate man, and having had a good constitution, is therefore very well preserved." [7]

On one of his many trips to his sister, Sarah, in Connecticut, Trumbull became a frequent visitor at the home of Mrs. John D. Ingraham and her daughter, Mary, who lived at Saybrook, Connecticut. Mrs. Ingraham, a descendant of a distinguished Connecticut family, was Trumbull's first cousin. In the summer of 1877 Trumbull and Mary Ingraham, an attractive woman of thirty-two, decided to get married. Trumbull, aware of the age difference, was frank in explaining his financial circumstances and responsibilities. He made it clear in his letter to Mary that he wanted more than just a companion for his older age. "Perhaps I crave too much," he wrote, "more than I deserve, I am sure, but I do want to feel that one in whom my life is bound up feels for me something more than respect or admiration even." [8] At sixty-four, Trumbull regretted that in his youth and adulthood he had been too busy to enjoy the "gaieties and pleasures" of life. He told Mary that he had "mistakenly, as I now think, sacrificed too many of life's real enjoyments to the cares and anxiety of business." [9]

Trumbull carefully explained to Mary that after the respect and acclaim that he had enjoyed in public life, he was now a private citizen. However, he added, unlike many others, his becoming an "ordinary individual," had not soured him or made him a bitter person. He wanted his future wife to know that he was out of public life and "in all human probability shall never enter it again." [10] Another letter explained fully

[7] Linder, op. cit., p. 168.
[8] Lyman Trumbull to Mary Ingraham, September 7, 1877, L. T. Family Papers.
[9] Ibid.
[10] Lyman Trumbull to Mary Ingraham, September 23, 1877, L. T. Family Papers.

Mary Ingraham Trumbull.

his financial circumstances. "My circumstances are moderate," Trumbull wrote, "My income has depended all my life chiefly on my salary. . . . I have not laid up a fortune but I am not in debt." He explained that he would have had more if his sons could have taken care of themselves "which to this time none of them have been able to do." [11]

The marriage took place on Saturday, November 3, 1877, at the bride's home in Saybrook. The ceremoney was performed by Reverend Jesse Heald, rector of the local Grace Church. [12] Trumbull's sons Walter, Perry, and Henry expressed their delight that their father should have acquired a loving companion. Perry wrote: "I know better than I can tell you . . . how much disposed I am to love anyone who makes you happier." [13] Mary Ingraham proved herself to be a kind stepmother who lavished her love and attention on Trumbull's sons, especially on Henry. [14] Mrs. Ingraham, who was a widow, was delighted with the marriage and treated Lyman with deference and affection. [15]

The newly-wed couple moved into the Lake Avenue house where, on August 21, 1878, a daughter Mae was born. Trumbull, who loved children, was a kind and devoted father. Mary was a thoughtful and loving wife. She was very much in love with her husband, whom she found to be, in spite of his often forbidding manner, a kind and devoted husband. [16] When separated from Trumbull, she wrote him warm letters. "I hope my husband," she wrote "is comfortably housed tonight, I miss him so much when he is away." [17] Lyman and Mary were

[11] Lyman Trumbull to Mary Ingraham, September 18, 1877, L. T. Family Papers.
[12] Mrs. Mary I. Trumbull to Horace White, September 18, 1907, Horace White Papers, Illinois State Historical Library, Springfield, Ill.
[13] Perry Trumbull to Lyman Trumbull, November 9, 1877 and Walter Trumbull to Lyman Trumbull, November 10, 1877, L. T. Family Papers.
[14] Diary of Mary Ingraham Trumbull, L. T. Family Papers.
[15] Mrs. John Ingraham to Mary I. Trumbull, March 21, 1880, L. T. Family Papers.
[16] Diary of Mary Ingraham Trumbull, entries dated January 3, January 7, February 6, 1884, L. T. Family Papers.
[17] Mary I. Trumbull to Lyman Trumbull, January 2, 1882, L. T. Family Papers.

desolate when on August, 1884, the six-year-old Mae fell ill of scarlet fever and passed away.

Trumbull's last attempt to win public office came in 1880 when he ran on the Democratic ticket for governor of Illinois. He did not want to run, but gave in to the pressure of party leaders. The platform adopted by the Democratic state convention advocated a thorough reform of the civil service and a "constitutional currency of gold and silver and of paper convertible into coin." Other planks expressed opposition to high protective tariffs and demanded better laws relating to the collection of wages by working people. Trumbull's opponent was the popular and able Governor Shelby M. Collum who ran for re-election.

The Democratic candidate for governor did not conduct a vigorous campaign, but his trips and visits to factories gave him an opportunity to become acquainted with the conditions of the laboring people in Illinois. The alleviation of the working conditions in factories and sweatshops and the legal protection of the rights of labor became objectives for which he was to fight until the end of his life. The Republicans had a distinct advantage in the campaign, because they stressed the prosperous economic conditions that succeeded the bleak years of the late seventies. Collum's fine record as governor was also used to good advantage. Republican leaders defended the protective tariff as necessary for continued prosperity and charged that the Democrats lacked a clear economic program for the state and for the country. For the first time in his political career, Lyman Trumbull ran without the support of the *Chicago Tribune*. On the contrary, the *Tribune's* editorials excoriated him daily as a renegade Republican.[18] Collum defeated Trumbull by a decisive majority.

Trumbull's interest in legislation to curb monopolies and in the rights of the underprivileged and the needy were undoubtedly stimulated by his friendships with William Jennings

18 *Chicago Tribune*, September 7, 14, 21, 1880.

Bryan and Clarence Darrow. He befriended Bryan, who became a law clerk in his office and a frequent visitor in his home. Alma Trumbull and Bryan's young daughter Ruth were playmates.[19] Darrow, who had his law office in the same building on Monroe Street, where Trumbull's firm was located, greatly admired the old judge. When Darrow undertook to carry the case of Eugene V. Debs, the Socialist labor leader, to the Supreme Court and appeal his conviction for violating a federal court injunction in the Pullman strike, Trumbull volunteered his services in the case.[20] Trumbull, who supported the railroad workers in their strike and who condemned the sending of Federal troops to Chicago, argued, together with Darrow, Deb's petition for a writ of habeas corpus before the Supreme Court. The Court did not grant the petition.

The eighty-year-old Trumbull continued the struggle for the rights of labor against the excessive power of wealth. In his opening address, as president of the Congress on Jurisprudence and Law Reform by the Illinois Bar Association, Trumbull declared that legislation must cease to protect the wealthy and the propertied. He urged legislatures and lawyers to protect the interests of the mass of humanity. Trumbull urged that a limit be put on vast fortunes that are transmitted from generation to generation without the inheritors meriting the wealth by their skill, labor, or contribution to society.[21]

Once again a deep personal tragedy intruded on Trumbull's happy life. In the spring of 1894 the beautiful eleven-year-old Alma died suddenly. Lyman Trumbull, who had in the past borne personal losses with calmness, was this time inconsolable. He wrote to deeply-stricken Mary, who fled their Chicago home to find a haven refuge in Saybrook: "The dear little girl. How I miss her, and how little I expected that she would precede

[19] William Jennings Bryan to Lyman Trumbull, February 8, 1886, L. T. Family Papers.
[20] Clarence Darrow, *The Story of my Life* (New York, 1932), p. 67.
[21] *Chicago Legal News*, August 12, 1893.

Lyman Trumbull and his daughter Alma in Chicago.

me. Who will go next? We think Henry." [22] Mary Trumbull mourned her lovely little daughter long and deeply. For months she refused to attend church or to celebrate holidays. Informing Trumbull that she would not celebrate Thanksgiving, she added: I do not think I shall ever take pleasure in them [holidays] again." Before 1894 was over, Henry, who had suffered for a number of years from tuberculosis, passed away. A few months later, Walter died, leaving only Perry as the sole survivor of Trumbull's eight children.

Contemplating the inability or unwillingness of both the Democratic and Republican parties to deal forthrightly and effectively with rights of labor, civil reform, and with the control of trusts and monopolies, Trumbull was increasingly attracted to the program of the Populists. At eighty-one he had no political ambitions and no desire to re-enter politics, but had decided to raise his voice in the cause of the laboring man and warn the nation against the abuses of large corporations.

In late September, 1894, Trumbull accepted an invitation to address a mass election rally sponsored by the People's Party. The meeting was held on Saturday, October 6, in Chicago's Central Music Hall. The immense hall was packed by 3,000 Populists who gave Trumbull, "a recent convert to the People's Party," a long, standing ovation.[24] Clarence Darrow, the chairman of the meeting, introduced Trumbull. In his introduction, Darrow pointed out that the main speaker of the evening had not been consistent in his party allegiance, but was as steadfast as a rock in his determination to "remove the cause of discontent and suffering among the laboring masses and bring them into harmonious relations with their employers." [25]

Trumbull chose to speak on the "Cause and Suggestion for

[22] Lyman Trumbull to Mary I. Trumbull, October 28, 1894, L. T. Family Papers.
[23] Mary I. Trumbull to Lyman Trumbull, November 14, 1894, L. T. Family Papers.
[24] Chicago Tribune, October 7, 1894.
[25] Ibid.

the Cure of Labor Troubles." He declared that the basic causes
of the economic unrest were inadequate pay for labor and the
wealth and luxury of the "pampered few." He decried the constant amassing of wealth and property by one percent of the
population and castigated the greed of big New York and
Chicago corporations and oil and coal syndicates. Big Business,
he said, was indifferent to the fact that one hundred thousand
people were unemployed. The corporations were not wealthy
by their own efforts but were being helped by the government,
which catered to monopolies and business while ignoring the
laboring masses. "For many generations," Trumbull stated,
"laws have been framed for the protection of property rather
than to protect the rights of man." [26]

Trumbull proposed that Congress and the state legislatures
pass strict laws to control corporations and syndicates and
adopt legislation to assure fair pay for employees and force
profit-sharing in most industries. He urged the assembly to
work for the election of representatives of labor to Congress.
"A devoted majority of law makers," he said, "devoted to the
people's interest will soon find a way to protect them against
the oppression of the money power." [27] Federal courts, Trumbull declared, undoubtedly referring to the Pullman strike,
should cease issuing injunctions in labor disputes. Trumbull
concluded his address with an appeal for the support of
Negroes for the Populist cause. He proudly recalled that he was
the author of the first Civil Rights Bill in the history of the
nation. Raising his hand, Trumbull exclaimed, "It is a law
written by this right hand of mine." [28]

As Trumbull sat down, the audience went wild with enthu-
thusiasm and when he rose to leave the hall, Henry Demarest
Lloyd, who was on the platform, asked the audience to cheer
the "Grand Old Man of America." The assembled rose and

26 *Ibid.*
27 *Ibid.*
28 *Chicago Tribune,* October 7, 1894.

cheered Trumbull as he walked down the aisle. For a man of eighty-one, this was a remarkable performance.

Trumbull received many letters of congratulations and thanks for his address. The letters came from all parts of the country. The most touching was this brief letter from Clarence Darrow. He wrote: "My dear Judge Trumbull, If you could give me one of your photographs . . . I would prize it very highly. If you can spare one, I will call for it either at your house or office." [29]

The leaders of the People's Party had assumed that Trumbull would help in the election campaign and speak on behalf of the Populist candidates for state and national offices. They deluged him with requests to speak at election meetings. The requests came from Illinois, Wisconsin, Indiana, and Missouri.[30] Trumbull refused all invitations in almost identical letters. In one such letter to the chairman of the People's Party in Indiana, he wrote: "You will have to excuse me from speaking in Indianapolis. I am not actively engaged in politics. It was only in behalf of the rights of man that I was induced at all." [31] In another he said: "My address at Music Hall was chiefly devoted to the Labor question." [32] In spite of his sympathy for the Populist program, Trumbull had no intention of campaigning for the Populist candidates.

In December of the same year, Populist leaders in Chicago requested Trumbull to prepare a declaration of principles, which was to be presented by them at the People's Party Convention, scheduled to take place in St. Louis on December 28. The platform, as written by Trumbull, was presented at the St. Louis convention by Henry Demarest Lloyd and was adopted without any changes. The text was published by the *Chicago Times* and reads in part as follows:

[29] Clarence Darrow to Lyman Trumbull, October 10, 1894, L. T. Family Papers.
[30] James E. Lincoln, A. L. Maxwell, George Merrick, Richard Ely to Lyman Trumbull, October 10, October 13, October 14, October 15, L. T. Family Papers.
[31] Lyman Trumbull to N. T. Butts, October 12, 1894, L. T. Family Papers.
[32] Lyman Trumbull to L. Berrier, October 10, 1894, L. T. Family Papers.

Resolved, that human brotherhood and equality of rights are cardinal principles of true democracy.

Resolved, that forgetting all past differences, we unite in the common purpose to rescue the government from the control of monopolies and concentrated wealth, to limit their powers of perpetuation by curtailing their privileges. . . .

We endorse the resolution adopted by the National Republican Convention in 1860, which was incorporated by President Lincoln in his inaugural address as follows:

That the maintenance inviolate of the rights of a state to order and control its own domestic institutions according to its own judgement exclusively is essential to that balance of power on which the endurance of our political fabric depends, and we denounce the lawless invasion by armed forces of the soil of any state or territory, no matter under what pretext, as among the greatest of crimes.

Resolved, that to check the rapid absorption of the wealth of the country and its perpetuation in a few hands, we demand the enactment of laws limiting the amount of property to be acquired by devise or inheritance.

Resolved, that we inscribe as our banner, "Down with monopolies and millionaire control! Up with the rights of man and the masses! And under this banner we march to the polls and to victory." [33]

Trumbull was not allowed to enjoy the praise and limelight that shone upon him after his speech at Music Hall. He still grieved for his sons, Walter and Perry, and his daughters, Mae and Alma. Fortunately, Perry, his wife, their three children, whom Trumbull pampered and adored, and his loving and devoted wife Mary remained to console him in the twilight of his life. He continued his law practice and his regular hours in his law office.

In the spring of 1896 Trumbull became ill, but seemed to have recovered rapidly. After receiving a telegram on April 10, 1896, that his long-time political ally and friend, Gustave Koerner, died in Belleville, Trumbull decided against the advice of his

[33] *Chicago Times,* December 27, 1894.

doctors to attend the funeral and deliver the funeral oration. Mary, who had also advised him not to attend the funeral, went with him. Trumbull was also accompanied by his brother John and his wife. After the funeral, at which Trumbull eulogized his friend, he became seriously ill. A Belleville physician went with Trumbull to Chicago and in St. Louis Dr. William Jayne boarded the train to take care of his friend and former brother-in-law.[34] In Chicago, Trumbull was taken by ambulance to the hospital, where doctors performed an operation on what proved to be cancer of the prostate.

In May Trumbull recovered sufficiently from his operation to take short walks and go for rides with his wife. He wrote to his sister that he was "improving rapidly." [35] He was, however, aware that complete recovery was impossible and was ready to accept the inevitable.[36] Trumbull received an invitation to speak at graduation exercises at his alma mater, the Bacon Academy, Colchester, Connecticut. He told his wife that he would want to go, because he was eager to see his old school, and because he also wanted to visit his sister Sarah, who had just celebrated her seventy-sixth birthday, and Mrs. Trumbull's mother, at Saybrook.[37] On June 15, however, Trumbull's condition worsened, and he passed away on the morning of June 25, 1896.

The father of the Thirteenth Amendment, of the first civil rights bill, and of the first civil service bill in the history of the nation had gone to eternal rest amidst the deep grief of his loving family and the widespread mourning in the community. In its obituary, the Chicago Tribune said: "Judge Trumbull hated war and loved his country . . . he was firm and true."

[34] Lyman Trumbull to Sarah Trumbull, May 3, 11, 1896, L. T. Family Papers.
[35] Lyman Trumbull to Sarah Trumbull, May 23, 1896, L. T. Family Papers.
[36] Lyman Trumbull to John Trumbull, May 15, 1896, L. T. Family Papers.
[37] Mary Ingraham Trumbull to Horace White, September 26, 1912, Horace White Papers, Illinois State Historical Library, Springfield, Ill.

Selected Bibliography

PAPERS AND MANUSCRIPT COLLECTIONS

Isaac N. Arnold Collection, Chicago Historical Society, Chicago, Ill.
Mason Brayman Papers, Chicago Historical Society, Chicago, Ill.
William Butler Collection, Chicago Historical Society, Chicago, Ill.
Zachariah Chandler Papers, Library of Congress, Washington, D.C.
Salmon P. Chase Papers, Library of Congress, Washington, D.C.
David Davis Papers, Chicago Historical Society, Chicago, Ill.
James R. Doolittle Papers, State Historical Society of Wisconsin, Madison, Wis.
Stephen A. Douglas Papers, University of Chicago, Chicago, Ill.
Jesse W. Fell Papers, Illinois State Historical Library, Springfield, Ill.
William Pitt Fessenden Papers, Library of Congress, Washington, D.C.
Joseph Gillespie Papers, Chicago Historical Society, Chicago, Ill.
Joseph Gillespie Papers, Illinois State Historical Library, Springfield, Ill.
Ozias M. Hatch Papers, Illinois State Historical Library, Springfield, Ill.
William H. Herndon Papers, Illinois State Historical Library, Springfield, Ill.
Herndon-Weik Papers, Library of Congress, Washington, D.C.
Dr. William Jayne Papers, Illinois State Historical Library, Springfield, Ill.
Andrew Johnson Papers, Library of Congress, Washington, D.C.
Gustave Koerner Papers, Illinois State Historical Library, Springfield, Ill.
Charles H. Lanphier Papers, Illinois State Historical Library, Springfield, Ill.

Lincoln Collection, Illinois State Historical Library, Springfield, Ill.
Robert Todd Lincoln Collection, Library of Congress, Washington, D.C.
John A. Logan Papers, Library of Congress, Washington, D.C.
John A. McClernand Papers, Library of Congress, Washington, D.C.
William R. Morrison Papers, Illinois State Historical Library, Springfield, Ill.
John M. Palmer Papers, Illinois State Historical Library, Springfield, Ill.
Benjamin M. Prentiss Collection, Chicago Historical Society, Chicago, Ill.
Uriah Reavis Collection, Chicago Historical Society, Chicago, Ill.
Carl Schurz Papers, Library of Congress, Washington, D.C.
William Henry Seward Papers, University of Rochester, Rochester, N. Y.
John Sherman Papers, Library of Congress, Washington, D.C.
Charles Sumner Papers, Houghton Library, Harvard University, Cambridge, Mass.
Lyman Trumbull Collection, Chicago Historical Society, Chicago, Ill.
Lyman Trumbull Letters, Illinois State Historical Library, Springfield, Ill.
Lyman Trumbull Papers, Library of Congress, Washington, D.C.
Lyman Trumbull Family Papers, Illinois State Historical Library, Springfield, Ill.
E. B. Washburne Papers, Library of Congress, Washington, D.C.
Henry Watterson Papers, Library of Congress, Washington, D.C.
Thurlow Weed Papers, University of Rochester, Rochester, N. Y.
Gideon Welles Papers, Library of Congress, Washington, D.C.
Horace White Papers, Illinois State Historical Library, Springfield, Ill.
General James M. Wilson Papers, Library of Congress, Washington, D.C.
Richard Yates Papers, Illinois State Historical Library, Springfield, Ill.

Abbreviations are used for the following collections when cited in the footnotes:

Dr. William Jayne Papers,   Jayne Papers
Illinois State Historical
Library, Springfield, Ill.

Robert Todd Lincoln Collection,   R. T. L. Collection
Library of Congress, Washington,
D.C.

Lyman Trumbull Letters, Illinois   L. T. Letters
State Historical Library, Spring-
field, Ill.

Lyman Trumbull Papers, Library   L. T. Papers
of Congress, Washington, D.C.

Lyman Trumbull Family Papers,   L. T. Family Papers
Illinois State Historical Library,
Springfield, Ill.

PRINTED SOURCE COLLECTIONS AND OFFICIAL REPORTS AND DOCUMENTS

"A Collection of Letters from Lyman Trumbull to John M. Palmer, 1854–1858," George T. Palmer, ed. *Journal of the Illinois State Historical Society.* Sprinfield, Ill., April-July, 1923.

A Compilation of the Messages and Papers of the Presidents, Vol. VIII. Washington, D.C., 1897.

The Congressional Globe, 34, 35, 36, 37, 38, 40, 41, and 42 Congresses.

Documentary History of Reconstruction, Walter L. Fleming, ed. 2 vols. Cleveland, 1907.

Documents of American History, Henry Steele Commager, ed. New York, 1949.

House Journal of Illinois Legislature, 1840–1841. Springfield, Ill., 1841.

Illinois Constitutions, Emil Joseph Verlie, ed. Collections of the Illinois State Historical Library, Vols. XII and XIII. Springfield, Ill., 1919.

Journal of the House of Representatives of the State of Illinois, 1836–1837. Springfield, Ill., 1837.

Journal of the Joint Committee of Fifteen on Reconstruction, Benjamin B. Kendrick, ed. New York, 1914.

Journal of the Senate of the State of Illinois. Springfield, Ill., 1837.

Laws of the State of Illinois, 1849–1869. Springfield, Ill., 1849–1869.

"Letters of Trumbull to James R. Doolittle of Wisconsin," *Journal of the Illinois State Historical Society*, Vol. II. Springfield, Ill., 1909–1910.

Lincoln, Abraham. *The Collected Works of Abraham Lincoln*, Roy P. Basler, ed., 8 vols. New Brunswick, N.J., 1953–1955.

Lincoln, Abraham. *Complete Works of Abraham Lincoln*, John G. Nicolay and John Hay, eds. 2nd ed. New York, 1905.

———. *The Lincoln Reader*. New York, 1954.

———. *The Living Lincoln*, Paul M. Angle and Earl Schenck Miers, eds. New Brunswick, N.J., 1955.

"A Lincoln Correspondence," *Century Magazine*, February, 1909.

The Lincoln-Douglas Debates of 1858, Edwin Erle Sparks, ed. Springfield, Ill., 1908.

Proceedings of the First Three Republican National Conventions of 1856, 1860, 1864, C. W. Johnson, ed. Minneapolis, 1893.

Raymond, Henry J. *The Life and Public Services of Abraham Lincoln, Together with His State Papers*, New York, 1865.

Reconstruction Speeches, Congressional Globe Office. Washington, D.C., 1876.

Report of the Joint Committee on Reconstruction. Washington, D.C., 1866.

Reports Made to the Senate and House of Representatives of the State of Illinois, 1842–43 and 1844–45. Springfield, Ill.

Speech of Honorable Lyman Trumbull of Illinois, Delivered in the Senate of the United States, Congressional Globe Office. Washington, D.C., April 7, 1862.

DIARIES AND AUTOBIOGRAPHIES

Bates, Edward. *The Diary of Edward Bates*, Howard K. Beale, ed. Washington, D.C., 1933.

Bates Diary. *Annual Report, American Historical Association, 1930,* Vol. IV. Washington, D.C., 1933.

Blaine, James G. *Twenty Years of Congress.* Norwich, Conn., 1884–86.

Browning, Orville Hickman. *The Diary of Orville Hickman Browning,* Theodore Pease and James G. Randall, eds. 2 vols. Illinois Historical Collections, Springfield, Ill., 1925.

Collum, Shelby M. *Fifty Years of Public Service.* Chicago, 1911.

Darrow, Clarence. *The Story of My Life.* New York, 1932.

Diary of a Public Man. Chicago, 1945.

Greeley, Horace. *Recollections of a Busy Life.* New York, 1869.

Inside Lincoln's Cabinet: The Civil War Diaries of Salmon P. Chase, David Donald, ed. New York, 1954.

John Sherman's Recollections of Forty Years in the House, Senate, and Cabinet: An Autobiography, 2 vols. Chicago and New York, 1895.

Julian, George W. *Political Recollections, 1840–1872.* Chicago, 1884.

Koerner, Gustave. *Memoirs of Gustave Koerner, 1809–1896,* 2 vols. Cedar Rapids, Iowa, 1909.

Lincoln and the Civil War in the Diaries and Letters of John Hay, Tyler Dennett, ed. New York, 1939.

Linder, General Usher F. *Reminiscences of the Early Bench and Bar of Illinois.* Chicago, 1879.

Palmer, John M. *The Bench and Bar of Illinois, Historical and Reminiscent,* 2 vols. Chicago, 1899.

———. *Personal Recollections: The Story of an Earnest Life.* Cincinnati, 1901.

Pierce, Edward L. *Memoirs and Letters of Charles Sumner,* 4 vols. Boston, 1877–94.

Reynolds, John. *My Own Times, Embracing Also the History of My Life.* Belleville, Ill., 1855.

Schurz, Carl. *The Reminiscences of Carl Schurz,* 3 vols. New York, 1907–08.

———. *The Autobiography of Carl Schurz.* An abridgement in one volume. New York, 1961.

Seward, Frederick W. *Reminiscences of a War Time Statesman and Diplomat, 1830–1915.* New York, 1916.

Sumner, Charles. *The Works of Charles Sumner,* 15 vols. Boston, 1870–83.

Watterson, Henry. *Marse Henry*. New York, 1919.

Weed, Thurlow. *Memoirs of Thurlow Weed*, Thurlow Weed Barnes, ed. Boston, 1884.

Welles, Gideon. *Diary of Gideon Welles, Secretary of the Navy under Lincoln and Johnson*, John T. Morse, ed. 3 vols. Boston, 1911.

NEWSPAPERS AND MAGAZINES

Alton Courier
Alton Telegraph
Alton Telegraph and Democratic Review
Alton Weekly Journal
Aurora Beacon
Belleville Advocate
Belleville Democrat
Bureau County Republican (Princeton, Ill.)
Cairo Gazette
Carbondale Times
Chicago Daily Democrat
Chicago Daily Journal
Chicago Democratic Press
Chicago Evening Post
Chicago Legal News
Chicago Press and Tribune
Chicago Republican
Chicago Times
Chicago Tribune
Cincinnati Commercial
Cincinnati Enquirer
Cleveland Leader
Detroit Post
Golconda Weekly Herald
Illinois Staats Zeitung
Illinois State Journal
Illinois State Register

Jacksonville (Ill.) Journal
Joliet Signal
Jonesboro Gazette
Louisville Courier-Journal
Marion Intelligencer
Missouri Republican
The Nation
New York Evening Post
New York Herald
New York Times
New York Tribune
New York World
Ottawa Free Trader
Peoria Daily Transcript
Philadelphia Bulletin
Philadelphia North American
Quincy Herald
Rock River Democrat
Rockford Forum
Rockland Republican
St. Louis Democrat
Sangamo Journal
Springfield (Mass.) Republican
Toledo Blade
Western Citizen

ARTICLES AND MONOGRAPHS

Baxter, Maurice G. "Orville H. Browning, Lincoln's Colleague and Critic," Journal of the Illinois State Historical Society, Vol. XVI, No. 5 (Springfield, Ill., 1955).

Buckingham, J. H. "Illinois as Lincoln Knew It," Harry E. Pratt, ed., Papers in Illinois History and Transactions for the Year 1937, Illinois State Historical Society (Springfield, Ill., 1938).

Cochran, Thomas C. "Did the Civil War Retard Industrialization?" Mississippi Valley Historical Review, Vol. XLVIII, No. 2 (September, 1961).

Cohen, Stanley. "Northeastern Business and Radical Reconstruction: A Re-examination," *Mississippi Valley Historical Review*, Vol. XLVI (June, 1959).

Cole, Arthur C. "Lincoln and the Presidential Election of 1864," *Transactions of the Illinois State Historical Society* (Springfield, Ill., 1917).

———. "President Lincoln and the Illinois Radical Republicans," *Mississippi Valley Historical Review*, Vol. IV, No. 4 (March, 1918).

Cox, John H., and LaWanda Cox. "Andrew Johnson and His Ghost Writers: An Analysis of the Freedmen's Bureau and Civil Rights Veto Messages," *Mississippi Valley Historical Review*, Vol. XLVIII, No. 3 (December, 1961).

Davis, McCann. "The Senator from Illinois—Some Famous Political Combats," *Transactions of the Illinois State Historical Society for the Year 1909* (Springfield, Ill., 1910).

Ellis, Lewis Ethan. "A History of the Chicago Delegation in Congress, 1843–1845," *Transactions of the Illinois State Historical Society for the Year 1930* (Springfield, Ill., 1930).

Fehrenbacher, D. E. "Lincoln, Douglas, and the 'Freeport Question,'" *American Historical Review*, Vol. LXVI, No. 3 (April, 1961).

Hand, Hon. John P. "Negro Slavery in Illinois," *Transactions of the Illinois State Historical Society for the Year 1910* (Springfield, Ill., 1912).

Harris, Newton D. "Negro Servitude in Illinois," *Transactions of the Illinois State Historical Society*, No. 11, 1906.

Hoogenbloom, Ari. "Thomas A. Jenckes and Civil Service Reform," *Mississippi Valley Historical Review*, Vol. XLVII, No. 4 (March, 1961).

Krug, Mark M. "On Rewriting the Story of Reconstruction in the United States History Textbooks," *Journal of Negro History*, Vol. XLVI (July, 1961).

———. "The Republican Party and the Emancipation Proclamation," *Journal of Negro History*, Vol. XLVIII (April, 1963).

Luthin, Richard H. "Salmon P. Chase's Political Career before the Civil War," *Mississippi Valley Historical Review*, Vol. LXXIX, No. 4 (March, 1943).

Roske, Ralph J. "The Seven Martyrs?" *American Historical Review*, Vol. XLVII, No. 4 (March, 1961).

Selby, Paul. "Genesis of the Republican Party in Illinois," *Transactions of the Illinois State Historical Society for the Year 1906* (Springfield, Ill., 1906).

Snyder, John F., M. D. "Forgotten Statesmen of Illinois: Hon. Richard M. Young," *Transactions of the Illinois State Historical Society for the Year 1906* (Springfield, Ill., 1906).

Stoller, Mildred C. "The Democratic Element in the Republican Party in Illinois, 1856–1860," *Papers in Illinois History* (Springfield, Ill., 1944).

Strevey, Tracy E. "Joseph Medill and the *Chicago Tribune* in the Nomination and Election of Lincoln," *Papers in Illinois History* (Springfield, Ill., 1939).

Weisberger, Bernard A. "The Dark and Bloody Ground of Reconstruction Historiography," *Journal of Southern History*, Vol. XXV (November, 1959).

Wesley, Charles. "Lincoln's Plans for Colonizing the Emancipated Negroes," *Journal of Negro History*, Vol. IV (January, 1919).

White, Horace. "Abraham Lincoln in 1854," *Transactions of the Illinois State Historical Society for the Year 1908* (Springfield, Ill., 1909).

Woodburn, James A. "Attitude of Thaddeus Stevens Toward the Conduct of the Civil War," *American Historical Review*, Vol. II (April, 1907).

Wright, Esmond. "Lincoln Before His Election," *History Today*, Vol. X, No. 11 (November, 1960).

BOOKS

Agar, Herbert. *The Price of Union.* Boston, 1950.

Anderson, Frank M. *The Mystery of "A Public Man."* Minneapolis, 1948.

Angle, Paul M. *One Hundred Years of Law.* Springfield, Ill., 1928.

———. *"Here I Have Lived": A History of Lincoln's Springfield, 1821–1865.* Springfield Ill., 1935.

Baringer, William E. *A House Dividing: Lincoln as President Elect.* Springfield, Ill., 1945.

Beale, Howard K. *The Critical Year.* New York, 1930.

Beveridge, Albert J. *Abraham Lincoln, 1809–1858.* Boston, 1928.

Bogart, Ernest Ludlow, and Charles Manfred Thomson. The Industrial State, 1879–1893, in The Centennial History of Illinois, Vol. IV. Chicago, 1922.

Carter, Hodding. The Angry Scar. Garden City, N. Y., 1959.

Church. Charles A. History of the Republican Party in Illinois, 1854–1912. Rockford, Ill., 1912.

Clemenceau, Georges. American Reconstruction, 1865–1880, and the Impeachment of President Johnson, Ferdinand Baldensperger, ed. New York, 1928.

Cole, Arthur C. The Era of the Civil War, 1848–1870, in The Centennial History of Illinois, Vol. III. Springfield, Illinois, 1919.

Craven, Avery. The Coming of the Civil War. New York, 1950.

Created Equal: The Complete Lincoln-Douglas Debates of 1858, Paul M. Angle, ed. Chicago, 1958.

Davidson, Alexander, and Bernard Stuvé. A Complete History of Illinois From 1673–1873. Springfield, Ill., 1876.

Davis, Jefferson. The Rise and Fall of the Confederate Government. New York, 1961. (Collier Books, paperback edition).

DeWitt, David M. The Impeachment and Trial of Andrew Johnson. New York, 1903.

Dickens, Charles. American Notes, 2 vols. London, 1922.

Dixon, Susan Bullett. The True History of the Missouri Compromise and Its Repeal by Mrs. Archibald Dixon. Cincinnati, 1899.

Donald, David. Charles Sumner and the Coming of the Civil War. New York, 1960.

———. Lincoln Reconsidered. New York, 1956.

Duberman, Martin B. Charles Francis Adams, 1807–1886. Cambridge, Mass., 1961.

Dunning, William A. Reconstruction, Political and Economic, 1865–1877. New York, 1907.

———. Essays on the Civil War and Reconstruction. New York, 1897.

Fehrenbacher, Donald E. Chicago Giant: A Biography of "Long John" Wentworth. Madison, Wis., 1957.

Fessenden, Francis. Life and Public Services of William Pitt Fessenden, 2 vols. Boston, 1907.

Ford, Thomas. A History of Illinois, Milo Milton Quaife, ed., 2 vols. Chicago, 1946.

Foulke, William Dudley. Life of Oliver Morton. Indianapolis, 1894.

Franklin, John Hope. *Reconstruction After the Civil War*. Chicago, 1961.

Fuess, Claude M. *Carl Schurz—Reformer, 1829–1906*. New York, 1932.

Grippen, Lee F. *Simon Cameron*. Oxford, Ohio, 1942.

Gunderson, Robert Gray. *The Log Cabin Campaign*. Lexington, Ky., 1957.

Hamlin, Charles E. *The Life and Times of Hannibal Hamlin*. Cambridge, Mass., 1890.

Harris, Newton D. *History of Negro Slavery in Illinois and of the Slavery Agitation in that State*. Chicago, 1906.

Harris, Wilmer C. *The Public Life of Zachariah Chandler, 1851–1875*. Lansing, Mich., 1917.

Hart, Albert Bushnell. *Salmon P. Chase*. Boston, 1899.

Hendrick, Burton J. *Lincoln's War Cabinet*. Boston, 1946.

Henry, Robert Selph. *The Story of Reconstruction*. New York, 1951.

Herndon, William H., and Jesse W. Weik. *Herndon's Lincoln: The True Story of a Great Life*, 3 vols., with an introduction by Horace White. New York, 1938.

Herndon's Life of Lincoln, Paul M. Angle, ed. New York, 1961.

Hesseltine, William B. *Lincoln's Plan of Reconstruction*, in *Confederate Centennial Studies*, Vol. XIII. Tuscaloosa, Ala., 1960.

———. *Lincoln and the War Governors*. New York, 1955.

Hofstadter, Richard. *The American Political Tradition*. New York, 1957.

Jaffa, Harry V. *Crisis of the House Divided: An Interpretation of the Issues in the Lincoln-Douglas Debates*. Garden City, N. Y., 1959.

Johnson, Allen. *Stephen A. Douglas: A Study in American Politics*. New York, 1909.

King, Willard L. *Lincoln's Manager, David Davis*. Cambridge, Mass., 1960.

Kinsley, Philip. *The Chicago Tribune: Its First Hundred Years*, 3 vols. New York, 1943.

Kirkland, Joseph. *The Story of Chicago*. Chicago, 1892.

Klement, Frank L. *The Copperheads in the Middle West*. Chicago, 1960.

Leech, Margaret. *Reveille in Washington, 1860–1865*. New York, 1941.

Life of Zachiariah Chandler, by the *Detroit Post and Tribune.* Detroit, 1880.

Logan, John A. *The Great Conspiracy: Its Origin and History.* New York, 1886.

Lusk, D. W. *Eighty Years of Illinois.* Springfield, Ill., 1889.

———. *Politics and Politicians: A Succinct History of the Politics of Illinois from 1856–1884.* Springfield, Ill., 1884.

Luthin, Reinhard. *The Real Abraham Lincoln.* Englewood Cliffs, N. J., 1960.

Lynch, John R. *The Facts of Reconstruction.* New York, 1913.

McKitrick, Eric. *Andrew Johnson and Reconstruction.* Chicago, 1960.

Milton, George Fort. *Abraham Lincoln and the Fifth Column.* New York, 1942.

———. *The Eve of Conflict: Stephen A. Douglas and the Needless War.* Boston, 1934.

Monaghan, Jay. *The Man Who Elected Lincoln.* Indianapolis, 1956.

Moses, John. *Illinois: Historical and Statistical,* 2 vols. Chicago, 1895.

Nevins, Allan. *The Emergence of Lincoln,* 2 vols. New York, 1950.

———. *Ordeal of the Union,* 2 vols. New York, 1947.

———. *The War for the Union,* 2 vols. New York, 1959, 1960.

Nye, Russell B. *Midwestern Progressive Politics.* Ann Arbor, Mich., 1959.

Pease, Theodore C. *The Frontier State, 1818–1848,* in *The Centennial History of Illinois,* Vol. II. Chicago, 1922.

Pierce, Bessie Louise. *A History of Chicago,* Vol. II. New York, 1940.

Quarles, Benjamin. *Frederick Douglass.* Washington, D.C., 1948.

Randall, J. G. *The Civil War and Reconstruction.* Boston, 1937.

———. *Lincoln the President, Springfield to Gettysburg,* 4 vols. New York, 1945.

Randall, J. G., and David Donald. *The Civil War and Reconstruction,* 2nd ed. Boston, 1961.

Randall, Ruth Painter. *Mary Lincoln.* New York, 1953.

Robertson, Arthur H. "The Political Career of Lyman Trumbull," M. A. dissertation, University of Chicago, 1910.

Roland, Charles P. *The Confederacy.* Chicago, 1960.

Ross, Earle Dudley. *The Liberal Republican Movement.* New York, 1919.

Rourke, Constance M. *Trumpets of Jubilee.* New York, 1927.

Sandburg, Carl. *Abraham Lincoln: The Prairie Years,* 2 vols. New York, 1939.

———. *Abraham Lincoln: The War Years,* 4 vols. New York, 1939.

Simkins, Francis B., and Robert H. Woody. *Reconstruction of South Carolina.* Chapel Hill, N. C., 1932.

Singletary, Otis A. *Negro Militia and Reconstruction.* Austin, Texas, 1957.

Smith, George W. *History of Illinois and Her People.* Chicago, 1927.

The Southerner as American, Charles Greer Sellers, Jr., ed. Chapel Hill, N. C., 1960.

Stryker, Lloyd Paul. *Andrew Johnson: A Study in Courage.* New York, 1929.

Thomas, Benjamin P. *Abraham Lincoln.* New York, 1952.

———. *Lincoln, 1847–1853, Doing the Day by Day Activities . . .* Springfield, Ill., 1936.

———. *Stanton, The Life and Times of Lincoln's Secretary of War* (with Harold M. Hyman), New York, 1962.

Upton, George P., and Elias Colbert. *Biographical Sketches of the Leading Men of Illinois.* Chicago, 1868.

Wall, Joseph Frazier. *Henry Watterson: Reconstructed Rebel.* New York, 1956.

White, Horace. *The Life of Lyman Trumbull.* Boston, 1913.

Williams, T. Harry. *Lincoln and the Radicals.* Madison, Wis., 1960.

Whitney, Henry Clay. *Life on the Circuit with Lincoln.* Caldwell, Idaho, 1940.

Woodward, C. Vann. *The Burden of Southern History.* Baton Rouge, La., 1960.

Index